Principles of Multimedia Database Systems

The Morgan Kaufmann Series in Data Management Systems

Series Editor, Jim Gray

Principles of
MULTIMEDIA
DATABASE SYSTEMS

V. S. Subrahmanian

Morgan Kaufmann Publishers, Inc.
San Francisco, California

Sponsoring Editor Diane D. Cerra
Production Manager Yonie Overton
Senior Production Editor Julie Pabst
Editorial Assistant Antonia Richmond
Copyeditor Ken DellaPenta
Text Design Windfall Software
Illustration Illustrious Interactive
Color Insert Preparation Side by Side Studios
Composition Ed Sznyter
Proofreader Jeff Van Bueren
Cover Design Ross Carron Design
Indexer Ted Laux
Printer Courier Corporation

Figure credits: Figure 5.6(a) ©1997 Bill and Carol Lofton; Figure 5.6(b) courtesy of Cincinnati Zoo and Botanical Garden ©Ron Austing; Figure 5.6(c) and (d) courtesy Steve Hogan.

Cover Credit: Microfiche image ©1997 PhotoDisc, Inc.

Morgan Kaufmann Publishers, Inc.
Editorial and Sales Office
340 Pine Street, Sixth Floor
San Francisco, CA 94104-3205
USA
Telephone 415 / 392-2665
Facsimile 415 / 982-2665
Email mkp@mkp.com
Web site www.mkp.com
Order toll free 800 / 745-7323

Library of Congress Cataloging-in-Publication Data

Subrahmanian, V. S.
      Principles of multimedia database systems / V. S. Subrahmanian.
          p. cm.
      Includes bibliographical references and index.
      ISBN 1-55860-466-9
      1. Database management. 2. Multimedia systems. I. Title.
QA76.575.S825 1998
025.04—dc21
                                                  97-44810
                                                     CIP

To *Amma, Appa, Sherry,* and *Suja*

Contents

5   Image Databases   99

9 Multimedia Databases 227

PART III   Physical Storage and Retrieval   265

10 Retrieving Multimedia Data from Disks 267

11   Retrieving Multimedia Data from CD-ROMs   295

12   Retrieving Multimedia Data from Tapes   311

A   Term Projects   397

Preface

Over the last several years, there has been an increasing awareness in the computer science community that there will be more and more nontextual data to process in the future. Examples of such new data types include image data, audio data, video data, and document data. Handling these new multimedia data types brings new challenges to traditionally established areas of computer science. For example, database management systems need to reassess existing data-handling paradigms to accommodate these new forms of data, as well as the new types of operations that processing such data requires. Network systems need to reassess the need for flexible, dynamic bandwidth allocation policies to accommodate the significant new requirement of continuous delivery of multimedia data. Operating systems and storage/resource management programs again need to accommodate the need for allocating resources to facilitate continuous retrieval of data by multiple, concurrent clients.

Human-computer interaction research needs to take into account the need for interfaces to handle interactive media objects in an intelligent fashion. Artificial intelligence research, especially computer vision and audio analysis methods, are needed to handle the automatic identification of features/objects of interest in media data.

Three basic fundamental premises underly the writing of this book. First, creating multimedia databases requires a mix of techniques from many disparate fields in computer science. Computer vision alone does not allow us to create large usable multimedia archives because it lacks scalable and accurate query and delivery capabilities. Likewise, network management techniques alone cannot handle the querying of multimedia data because they are only concerned with network scheduling, traffic shaping, and reliable retrieval issues. In general, each of the above five fields (database management systems, network systems, operating systems, human-computer interaction, and artificial intelligence) plays a critical role in the creation, querying, and delivery of multimedia data. The primary aim of this book is to present a synthetic view of end-to-end design of a multimedia database management systems.

Unfortunately, when teaching a course in multimedia database systems a few years ago, I found that no such synthetic, comprehensive treatment of multimedia databases exists in the literature. Excellent collections of papers on multimedia databases do exist [203, 150], as do excellent books on specific aspects of multimedia, such as image databases [60, 107, 80]. But, in general, there is no single comprehensive book that attempts to cover the broad range of material required to successfully build state-of-the-art, high-performance multimedia data systems. This book is a first attempt to fulfill this need.

The second premise behind this book is that multimedia databases are currently tied closely to technology: basic principles that can adapt over time with changes in hardware technology are likely to be of longer-term value to students, while technological insights into the current state of the art are likely to hold maximal value for practitioners. This book is primarily intended as a textbook for students, but it has obvious value to industry practitioners as well. Students who graduate with degrees in computer science usually go on to long careers in the field. In a rapidly changing field such as computer science, hardware advances occur every day. For instance, 10 years ago, CD-ROM jukeboxes were barely visible on the storage horizon. Today, they are proliferating rapidly. It is our contention that the long-term needs of multimedia practitioners are best served by teaching students the basic theoretical principles upon which the design and analysis of multimedia systems is based. To date, there is no book that does this in a way that teaches students how to build multimedia databases to support efficient querying, storage, retrieval, and delivery of distributed media data. This book provides a first step in this direction.

At the same time, we recognize that there are short-term goals that must also be served. A student or practitioner interested in the commercial multimedia market should certainly be aware of products and practices in the commercial sector. This knowledge is an important requirement for innovative on-the-job performance. This book also addresses products and practices in the commercial sector (future editions of this book will contain revisions of this material).

The third premise of this book is that multimedia databases are of interest to both graduate and undergraduate students. During my last course on multimedia databases, I was struck by the fact that the number of undergraduates who wished to register for the class was almost as large as the number of graduate students. Accordingly, this book attempts to address the need of both graduate students interested in multimedia databases as well as undergraduates (at the senior level) who have had exposure to a variety of basic computer science courses such as discrete mathematics, data structures, and a few programming courses.

How to Use This Book

This book may be used as a textbook for a one-semester course (approximately 42 hours), at either the graduate or the undergraduate level. The book is divided broadly into four basic parts: Part I covers, very briefly, the basic ideas underlying relational and object-oriented databases. Part II describes how media content may be organized. This part contains several chapters, each devoted to a different kind of media type; a final chapter covers how to construct multimedia databases that use a mix of media types. Part III covers storage management techniques for disks, CD-ROMs, and tapes. Part IV covers techniques for the creation and delivery of multimedia presentations.

Most chapters in this book have a few exercises, as well as one project that should take about two weeks to complete. These exercises may be used by instructors who want to assign several different programming assignments during the semester so that students are forced to write programs covering different aspects of multimedia databases. In addition, Appendix A contains some term projects that may be assigned, with interim deadlines. Should an instructor choose to assign a term project to the class, we recommend not assigning other programming projects to avoid placing an undue burden on the student.

For a Graduate Course

At the graduate level, we recommend skipping Part I entirely because most graduate students are likely to be familiar with both relational and object-oriented databases. A 14-week graduate course could follow this plan:

Week	Chapter/sections	Remarks
1	Chapters 1–3	Brief introduction. What is a multimedia database?
2	Sections 4.1–4.3	One lecture each on k-d trees and point quadtrees (explain why these are useful for images)
3	Sections 4.4–4.6	One lecture each on MX-quadtrees and R-trees
4	Chapter 5	One lecture on Sections 5.1–5.4; rest in second lecture
5	Chapter 6	One lecture of Sections 6.1–6.5; one lecture on Sections 6.4–6.5
6	Chapter 7	One lecture on Sections 7.1, 7.2.1; one lecture on Sections 7.2.2–7.2.3, 7.3, 7.4
7	Chapter 8 + midterm exam	One lecture on Chapter 8
8	Sections 9.1–9.4	One lecture on Sections 9.1–9.2; one on Sections 9.3–9.4
9	Sections 9.5–9.6, 10.1	One lecture on Sections 9.5–9.6; one on Section 10.1
10	Sections 10.2–10.4	One lecture on Sections 10.2–10.3; one on Section 10.4
11	Chapter 11	Use plenty of examples contained in overheads
12	Chapter 12	Use plenty of examples contained in overheads
13	Chapter 13	One lecture on Sections 13.1–13.2; one on Sections 13.3–13.4
14	Chapter 14	One lecture on Sections 14.1–14.4; one on Section 14.5

Should your semester be a bit longer than this, it is easy to fill in an extra week with the contents of Chapter 15, supplemented with relevant reading material specified in that chapter.

For an Undergraduate Course

There are two distinctions between an undergraduate course and a graduate course. First, the undergraduate course assumes only a rudimentary knowledge of databases. Second, undergraduate courses are usually taught more slowly than graduate courses. A 14-week undergraduate course could follow this plan:

Week	Chapter/sections	Remarks
1	Chapters 1–2	Half a lecture on Chapter 1, rest on Chapter 2
2	Chapter 3	One lecture on Sections 3.1–3.3; one on Sections 3.4–3.5
3	Sections 4.1–4.3	One lecture on k-d trees; one on point quadtrees
4	Sections 4.4–4.6	One lecture on MX-quadtrees; one on R-trees
5	Sections 5.1–5.6, 5.8	Skip Section 5.7
6	Chapter 6	Use lots of examples; drop mathematical details in Section 6.3.1
7	Chapter 7	one lecture on Sections 7.1, 7.2.1, one lecture on Sections 7.2.3, 7.3
8	Sections 9.1–9.4	One lecture on Sections 9.1–9.2; one on Sections 9.3–9.4
9	Sections 9.1–9.4	Review and midterm exam
10	Sections 9.5–9.6	One lecture on Section 9.5; one on Section 9.6
11	Sections 10.1–10.4	Explain Section 10.4 by example
12	Sections 11.1–11.3	One lecture on CD-ROMs; skim mathematics
	Sections 12.1–12.2	One lecture on tapes; skim mathematics
13	Chapter 13	One lecture on Sections 13.1–13.2; one on Sections 13.3–13.5
14	Chapter 14	One lecture on Sections 14.1–14.4; one on Section 14.5

This syllabus is geared toward maximizing the breadth of the undergraduate course content, but it does sacrifice some depth. For instance, most lectures for an undergraduate course will skip some, but not all, of the mathematical models and details.

For an Industrial Project

For industry practitioners who are interested in creating some type of multimedia database product or application, this book may be used in conjunction with the following steps:

1. Identify the types of data you will need to access in the application you are building. Split this data into two types—*media* data (such as images, documents, audio, and video) and *traditional* data (such as relational data, object-oriented data, etc.).

2. Split the media data into types (audio, video, etc.). If some software already exists at your company to access/process one or more of these types, you will *probably* want to use the hybrid representation of data described in Chapter 9. For media types for which software is not available, read the appropriate chapter in Part II of this book. In addition, read Chapter 9.

3. Read Chapter 9 to see if you can use the hybrid representation of data described there to integrate your traditional, possibly legacy, data sources with media sources.

4. Identify the different types of storage mechanisms (tape, CD-ROMs, disks) that are available to you for storage needs. Depending on which of these is available for your application, read the appropriate chapters in Part III of this book. Split your data into parts that are frequently accessed, moderately frequently accessed, and infrequently accessed, and place those bodies of data on disks, CD-ROMs, and tapes, respectively. For applications requiring a lot of browsing/interaction, read Part III of this book to determine the advantages/disadvantages of using these different storage media.

Teaching Aids

A comprehensive set of overhead transparencies is available to instructors wishing to teach this course. The slides are packaged in two sets—one for an undergraduate course and one for a graduate course. The slides may be downloaded from the password-restricted Web site listed below. Slides may only be downloaded by instructors using this book as a course textbook. To determine if you qualify, send email to *textbooks@mkp.com*.

Solutions Manual

Solutions to all exercises (not projects) listed in this book are available in Word format. Instructors using this book as a textbook for a course may download these materials from the Web site listed below. Solutions manuals may only be downloaded by instructors using this book as a course textbook. To determine if you qualify, send email to *textbooks@mkp.com*.

Web Site

Information pertinent to this book will be maintained at *http://www.mkp.com/books_catalog/1-55860-466-9.asp.*

In particular, any errors discovered in this book will be posted at this site. This site will also contain links to the author's Web site for the book, which will be periodically augmented with examples of completed projects, new projects, new exercises, and new reading material. Password-based access to teaching materials (lecture overhead slides and solutions manuals) will also be available from this site.

Errors and Suggestions

We welcome comments from readers pointing out errors and making suggestions that would improve future editions of the book. Please send such remarks by email to *Subrahmanian@mkp.com.*

Acknowledgments

First, I would like to thank Chitta Baral, Karen Watterson, Stefano Ceri, and Tamer Ozsu for working with me over the past six months on revising and improving the manuscript. Without their numerous emails and extensive comments, and painstakingly careful readthroughs, this book would not have been possible. I am particularly grateful to Karen Watterson for a very detailed set of pointers to industry sources.

I would also like to thank the initial set of reviewers of the book proposal. In addition to the above, these reviewers included Loretta Moore, Bill Grosky, Mike Wirth, and Harry Wechsler. Their comments on the initial proposal caused substantial changes in both the coverage and the presentation. I am grateful to K. Selcuk Candan, B. Prabhakaran, and Alex Chan for their useful comments on parts of the book.

For many years of useful discussions that have shaped many of the ideas described in this book, I am grateful to Sibel Adali, Raymond Ng, George Pick,

Eenjun Hwang, and Sherry Marcus. I also profited greatly from my discussions with Larry Davis, Christos Faloutsos, Leana Golubchik, and Hanan Samet on image databases, similarity-based retrieval, and storage servers. Special thanks to Leana for sending me useful bibliographies on tertiary storage.

Robert Ross played an invaluable role in shaping this book. I am grateful to him for his meticulous reading of the entire manuscript, finding numerous errors, and generally for honestly critiquing the book's contents. He also prepared an excellent solutions manual for the book.

This book would not have been possible without the encouragement and dedication of Diane Cerra and Antonia Richmond of Morgan Kaufmann Publishers, who helped me at every step in innumerable ways. Carol Zielke's assistance with decoding all the complex files I sent around was also very valuable. I'd also like to thank Ken DellaPenta for his meticulous copyediting of the manuscript and Julie Pabst for her smooth and timely coordination of the production process.

I am grateful to the General Library of the University of Texas at Austin and UT-Online, whose public domain maps from the Perry-Castañeda Library Map Collection are used for illustration purposes in Chapter 4.

PART I

PRELIMINARIES

1 Introduction

CHAPTER

Ever since their inception, computers have largely been thought of as *symbolic* processing devices—devices that take *symbols* from a specified legal alphabet as input and produce another set of symbols as output. This has been the model around which the standard computing environments based on Turing machines have worked.

In recent years, however, there has been a tremendous need for the ability to *query* and *process* vast quantities of data that are not always easy to describe with mere symbols. Some examples of such data include the following:

- *Image data:* A surgical trainee in Miami may wish, for instance, to practice a particular surgical procedure on a virtual patient having certain physiological symptoms. In order to find a patient with the desired symptoms, the trainee may wish to query a large, distributed image database containing X rays or MRIs of patients with such symptoms. Sometimes, the symptom may be easily described through textual means. In other cases, however, it may be far easier for the trainee to graphically render the kind of pattern he is looking for in the patient's X rays. In either case, a database of images must be maintained that can be queried based on vastly different criteria—textual inputs at one extreme or image matching at the other.

- *Video data:* In a slightly different context, an individual interested in obtaining videotaped lectures on a particular technical topic (e.g., PR-quadtrees) may wish to query a video library housing a collection of technical videotapes. For example, the University of Maryland offers courses, using a satellite link, to various sites across the nation. In the future, the videotapes created in this way may be electronically accessible, making available to students course materials ranging over many years, many topics, and many different instructors. This particular student's query may involve accessing a large number of videotapes pertaining to PR-quadtrees. For example, Subrahmanian, teaching Data Structures in Fall 1993, may have covered PR-quadtrees in the latter part of lecture 21 and the whole of lecture 22. In this case, the student may wish to access just this relevant part—especially if he is being charged by the bit!

- *Audio data:* A history student studying ancient Egypt may wish to access some of the early radio interviews by famous Egyptologists (e.g., William Flinders Petrie) detailing their early finds at various Egyptian sites. Perhaps an aspect of his research pertains to an old question that was debated many years ago by Petrie and Gardiner. In this case, he may wish to access these old audiotapes based on the content of these tapes (i.e., relevant aspects of Egyptology). Similarly, a police investigation attempting to track somebody making a bomb threat may wish to obtain a voice match by matching the audio signals in the call (in which the bomb threat was made) against a known database containing the speech patterns of various known terrorists.

- *Document data:* A *text* database has traditionally consisted of a large corpus of text, consisting of words, sentences, paragraphs, chapters, and so on. A *document* database differs in the sense that documents include not just raw textual information, but they contain both structure and embedded images. For instance, document data may be created, indexed, and retrieved using standard markup languages such as HTML or SGML. In such cases, the structure of the document may be exploited in indexing the data. Alternatively, suppose we consider a book (e.g., this book). The book contains not only textual material, but pictures as well. Some of these pictures may be line drawings, while yet others may be photographs. For instance, a user looking for a picture of the Mughal emperor Akbar may not find the picture within an image database. However, if he has an electronic digital library available to him for electronic accesses, then he may be able to find the desired picture by perusing "relevant" books on Indian history. Thus, document data comprises an important medium within which information may be electronically stored.

- *Handwritten data:* Many of us take notes on small pieces of paper that then mysteriously get wrinkled, washed with the laundry, or obliterated in other ways. Some of these notes are unimportant, while others need to be carefully preserved. Recent trends both in the marketplace as well as in academia suggest that electronic note taking (e.g., using a device such as the Apple Newton) will become more and more prevalent in the future. Users will use electronic devices to take (and store) notes. Although many notes can be transcribed into ASCII text using handwriting analysis techniques, most such data cannot be because, in addition to words, notes often contain doodles, block diagrams, and so on. A user who takes electronic notes may wish at some point in the future to issue a query like "Find all notes I made during January 1994 pertaining to John Smith." Such queries can be greatly facilitated by efficiently indexing the existing collection of notes on their content.

The types of data listed above form a mere fragment of the vast array of data representations that arise naturally in a variety of applications. For instance, were we to consider image data alone, we would find ourselves confronted with numerous formats (e.g., raster, bitmap, GIF, TIFF, PCX, etc.), all of which depict images when viewed through the appropriate graphical rendering devices (e.g., JPEG viewers or through XV for Sparc users). The same situation applies to the other types of data described.

Informally speaking, a *multimedia database management system* (MMDBMS) is a framework that manages different types of data potentially represented in a wide diversity of formats on a wide array of media sources. In order to work successfully, an MMDBMS must have the following abilities:

- It must have the ability to uniformly query data (media data, textual data) represented in different formats. For instance, an MMDBMS should have the ability to query and seamlessly integrate data contained in different relational databases (e.g., PARADOX and DBASE) that may possibly use different schemes, as well as to query flat file data and data stored in an object-oriented DBMS or a spatial DBMS, as well as arbitrary legacy data sources. Processing such queries is further complicated by the fact that eliciting the *content* of media data is often a challenging problem and is highly dependent on the media type and storage format. Finally, queries may span multiple media types, and the MMDBMS must be able to merge results from different data sources and media types.

- Similarly, it must also have the ability to query data represented in diverse media. For instance, an MMDBMS must be able to query not only pictorial image databases, but also audio and relational databases, and merge their results together.

- The MMDBMS must have the ability to retrieve media objects from a local storage device in a smooth, jitter-free (i.e., continuous) manner. Because media objects (e.g., video) often occupy tremendous amounts of space, running into tens of gigabytes even for a single, highly compressed video, we need to take into account that such data may be stored on secondary (disk) and tertiary (e.g., CD-ROM, tape) storage devices, or a mix of storage devices that exhibit different performance characteristics. Retrieval of the data so as to guarantee a smooth, continuous presentation while making efficient use of system resources is a formidable scheduling problem.

- The MMDBMS must have the ability to take the answer generated by a query (the notion of "answer to a query" may be a mathematical structure of some sort) and develop a presentation of that answer in terms of audiovisual media. Though the actual form and content of such presentations may vary from one application to another, the user must have the ability to specify the *structure* of the form and content of the answer presentation he would like to obtain from the system.

- Finally, once the system has authored a presentation along the lines described above, it must still have the ability to deliver this presentation in a way that satisfies various quality of service requirements. For example, if the MMDBMS has decided that an audio stream and a video stream must be concurrently presented, then the MMDBMS must be able to ensure that this presentation does not suffer from phenomena such as jitter and hiccups. Even more importantly, the MMDBMS must take into account that the data being delivered to the relevant output devices (e.g., audio speakers and console) may reside at distributed networked nodes. Thus, factors such as buffer availability and bandwidth need to be taken into account when delivering the presentation to the user. Furthermore, quality of service requirements dictate that various performance characteristics be optimized subject to the above restrictions.

As in all areas of human endeavor, the creation and management of multimedia archives must leverage from previous advances, both in academia and the commercial sector. It is our contention throughout this book that the database technology developed over the last 40 years forms the appropriate foundation upon which MMDBMSs must be built. Today, query languages, indexing techniques, retrieval algorithms, and update methods have been developed for a variety of relational, object-oriented, spatial, temporal, and other databases. Each of these languages extends previous languages and algorithms to handle new and important types of data or reasoning paradigms. In this respect, multimedia data is no different. It is a new and emerging data/reasoning paradigm that must fit into the existing body of academic research work and commercial practice, leveraging maximally from existing techniques (without reinventing a wheel), while forging new directions. Thus, for instance, a query language for image data should take into account the over 30 years of research into database query languages rather than starting from scratch. The same applies to other forms of media data, as well as other research topics (indexing, retrieval, updates, transactions, etc).

1.1 Plan of the Book

The primary aim of this book is to present a unified view of multimedia databases that addresses all the points listed above. In order to do so, we will start out by presenting a "Sample Multimedia Scenario." The scenario is reasonably broad and denotes a sample interaction that an end user may have with the MMDBMS. The scenario will include a wide variety of media data, as well as more "classical" data (such as relational data, object-oriented data, etc.). Furthermore, many of the queries expressed by the user will reflect different kinds of interactions that the user may reasonably have with the system. This example will provide a running thread throughout the rest of this book. We will revisit the Sample Multimedia Scenario in each and every chapter in order to illustrate the technical concepts described in that chapter. Of course, where appropriate, each chapter will have its own specific examples as well.

This book is divided into four basic parts. Part I consists of preliminaries that you may or may not already know. Chapter 2 presents the basic notations and terminology of relational databases. The main idea is to introduce you, very quickly, to the basic terminology that you will need to get through the rest of the book. Chapter 3 discusses the principles underlying object-oriented databases.

Part II focuses on how to logically represent the content of media data and to organize/manipulate this content using sophisticated indexing structures. Chapter 4 discusses certain types of specialized data structures that will be of use in multimedia systems. In particular, this chapter includes information on spatial data structures such as quadtrees and k-d trees. Chapter 5 discusses various kinds of image databases. Chapter 6 studies purely textual databases (no embedded images) and shows how we may efficiently index these databases so as to facilitate easy retrieval. Chapter 7 extends the static image domain to handle video data and defines indexing structures and query paradigms for video databases. Chapter 8 presents techniques for content-based indexing and retrieval of audio data. In Chapter 9, we develop a formal theoretical model of multimedia databases that encompasses all the preceding types of media data discussed individually before. This chapter provides a unifying framework within which the individual indexing structures for the above media may be integrated and queried.

Part III deals with storage and retrieval of media data. The query languages (and their implementations) described in Part II dealt with identifying the media objects or subobjects that the user wished to retrieve, but did not say how the media objects were *physically* retrieved from the storage device on which it was located. This section focuses on physical retrieval of media objects from different kinds of storage devices. Chapter 10 describes different properties of disk-based systems and shows how multimedia data may be stored and retrieved from disks in an efficient way. Chapter 11 describes how CD-ROMs may be used to store continuous media data and includes a description of how a multimedia database system may retrieve data from CD-ROM jukeboxes. Chapter 12 does the same for tapes.

Part IV deals with the creation and delivery of multimedia presentations across the network in such a way that the available resources are utilized in an "optimal" (to be defined) fashion. Chapter 13 describes the properties of existing multimedia authoring systems and describes how the answer to a query posed to an MMDBMS may be viewed as a request to develop a multimedia presentation based on that query. In Chapter 14, we will show how to ensure that presentations generated in Chapter 13 may be delivered so as to satisfy (whenever possible) the desired performance criteria. Chapter 15 presents some exciting new directions in multimedia-related research. The appendix contains a list of term projects suitable either for individual projects or group projects.

1.2   Sample Multimedia Scenario

Consider a police investigation of a large-scale drug operation. In order to carry out this investigation successfully, the police use a large number of electronic devices that conduct (hopefully legal) surveillance of the suspected members of the drug ring. Such an investigation may use the following devices to gather data:

1. The police may have *video surveillance cameras* that record the activities taking place at various locations. For example, each of these surveillance cameras may monitor the activities occurring at a given location over a relatively large period of time (e.g., 6 months), generating, for that single location alone, several million video frames. Since this one drug investigation alone may involve potentially 50–100 surveillance cameras located at dif-

ferent sites, the number of video frames that need to be managed increases substantially. Even more importantly, most law enforcement agencies carry out hundreds of such operations at a given point in time, in a variety of areas such as drug investigations, wire fraud investigations, financial crimes, terrorist investigations, espionage investigations, and so on. The amount of video data that thus becomes (at least potentially) available for investigation is staggering.

2. In addition, the police may have legally authorized *telephone wiretaps* in place, collecting audio data involving conversations that a given suspect has participated in. Though the amounts of telephone usage may vary from crime to crime, some crime areas (such as drug rings) typically make heavy use of the phone. This leads, in turn, to a vast array of audio recordings that have been collected over a period of time by the investigators during the course of the investigation. The ability to organize and query this audio data becomes very significant.

3. In addition to all the above, the police may also have a large number of *still photographs* taken by an investigator (say, while following one of the suspects); furthermore, in such large-scale criminal investigations, numerous smaller crimes may have occurred (for instance, a small-time drug pusher may have been photographed selling drugs, or a drug-related murder may have occurred and may have its own associated body of photographic data). This body of photographs, too, must be placed within some kind of digital photographic archive, ready for searches and retrievals when there is a need.

4. The police may also have access to a vast quantity of *documents* that have been seized from places that have been searched by the police in connection with this or other crimes. Which of this vast quantity of documents may be immediately relevant to the crime may not be obvious at the beginning. As the drug investigation continues, it may become apparent that there are more and more connections with existing documentation gleaned in the course of this or other previous/concurrent investigations.

5. In addition to all the above, the police may have access to relatively *structured relational data*. Such data could include, for example, data on bank transactions of some of the suspected criminals. This is particularly important because many drug kingpins use a variety of money-laundering schemes, and "following the money trail" often leads to interesting discoveries. Other data falling within this category could include things as

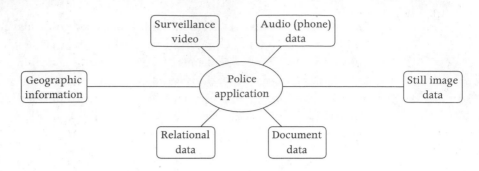

1.1   Data sources used in the Sample Multimedia Scenario

prosaic as phone books in order to determine, for instance, the identity of
the person called by a suspect.

6. The police may also have access to *geographic information systems* (GIS) that
   contain geographic data relevant to the drug investigation being conducted.
   For example, the police may suspect that certain routes are being used to
   ship drugs. In order to test out various hypotheses, they may wish to close
   off one of these routes (perhaps by initiating very rigid checks along this
   route), thus diverting the drug traffic. The pattern of drug flow then may
   provide them with much needed information on the location of the source
   (perhaps). In order to conduct such operations, the police may utilize GIS
   systems to manage this geographic data. These GIS systems may manage
   data including road map data, but may also capture data about the terrain
   in the vicinity of, say, a mountain stronghold (as in Medellín, Colombia).
   Knowledge about the terrain, as well as the types of vehicles possessed by
   the drug runners, may then provide the police with valuable clues as to
   what routes across the terrain are viable options for the criminals.

Figure 1.1 shows a schematic diagram of the different kinds of data and
software packages that are accessed in the Sample Multimedia Scenario. It is
important to note that the above sources of data form just a *small* sample of
the diversity and multiplicity of data that may be available in *one* application.
With the exploding applicability of multimedia data, each single application
area (whether in the travel industry or in the law enforcement arena) may have
a wide array of data sources and media types, and these data sources and media
types may vary dramatically from one application area to another.

Returning to our sample multimedia scenario, we now present a number of sample queries that a user of such a police multimedia system (were it in existence) might wish to use.

Query 1.1 (Image Query) Suppose the user has a photograph in front of him. For instance, this photograph may be a frontal shot of a recently apprehended individual. The police officer may suspect that this person is using an alias. He may then wish to issue the query, "Retrieve all images from the image library in which the person appearing in the currently displayed photograph appears."

This is an interesting query because it can be processed in one of two ways. One possibility is that the user knows that the photograph in front of him contains a picture of "John Doe" (i.e., he knows the name of the person in the photograph); in this case, the query may first be processed using textual information already known about the various images in the image library to retrieve an image that has the associated text annotation. Alternatively, the user may need to apply image-processing techniques to match the face in the given image with the faces appearing in the different photographs in the mugshot library. It is not inconceivable that the second approach will be tried after the first approach fails.

Query 1.2 (Audio Query) Alternatively, the police officer may be listening to an audio surveillance tape. For instance, the tape may contain a conversation between individual A (person under surveillance) and individual B (somebody meeting person A). Depending on the actual content of the conversation, the police officer may wish to search through a voice log database to see if the identity of person B can be ascertained. If such a query succeeds, this may well provide the police with required evidence or may provide leads for further investigation.

This query involves purely audio processing. Speech characteristics are typically stored in a "feature vector" that reflects the values of different parameters that are "important" as far as a given recording is concerned. In order to determine whether a given speech vector (e.g., person B's voice) matches a vector in an audio log database, we need techniques whereby such audio log databases can be indexed in such a way as to facilitate rapid retrieval of "similar" audio sequences (we will define different measures of similarity in Chapter 8).

Query 1.3 (Text Query) On the other hand, the police officer may be browsing an archive of text documents—such text files could include old newspaper archives, police department files on unsolved murder cases, witness statements, and so on. He may now wish to ask the query, "Find all documents (from the corpora of text documents) that deal with the Cali drug cartel's financial transactions with ABC Corp." (which may, for instance, be a suspected front company).

Again, this is a rather interesting query that leads us into the domain of text databases. A simple keyword search through documents is unlikely to find the correct answer—even if an index for searching these text documents already exists. After all, it is rather unlikely that the documents will conveniently mention the words "Cali," "finance," and "ABC Corp." For example, a file that talks of the transfer of funds from Jose Orojuelo's bank account to John Smith's bank account may be the desired file. It may well be the case that Jose Orojuelo is a leader of the Cali cartel and John Smith is a high-placed official in ABC Corp. Text must be indexed not merely on keywords, but also on the semantic content of these keywords. Only by indexing text in such a way is there any hope of answering queries such as this one correctly and succinctly.

Note that this query could be issued by the police officer not just to a text database, but just as easily to a document database or to a database of handwritten information. In all these cases, the police officer would like the query to be processed easily and efficiently, though perhaps using different computational methods.

Query 1.4 (Video Query) Suppose, for instance, the police officer is examining a surveillance video of a particular person being assaulted by an assailant, but the assailant's face is occluded in the segment of video in which the assault occurs. In this case, the police officer may wish to issue the query, "Find all video segments in which the victim of the assault appears." By a visual inspection of some of these segments of video, the police officer may hope to gain some information about the identity of the assailant, especially if the assailant is someone known to the victim. A similar scenario may arise when the activity taking place between the two individuals is a drug transaction.

Notice that in the above case, the police officer is not asking the system to give him frames of video in which the desired activity takes place. Instead, he is asking for segments of video (presumably contiguous) in which the transaction took place. The MMDBMS must have the ability not only to find the video frames in which certain activities occurred, it must also have the ability to synthesize these frames into coherent video segments.

Let's now discuss much more complex queries that the police officer might have. Each of the queries discussed above only accesses a single form of data. Though it has become almost fashionable to think of multimedia data as consisting solely of audiovisual data, we take a much broader view: multimedia data includes not just audio and video data (stored perhaps in multiple formats), but also much broader types of data, such as handwritten data, document data consisting of text and embedded images, relational data, geographic data, terrain maps, three-dimensional polyhedral models, and so on. Complex queries will mix and match data from these different sources; in particular, they will allow the police officers to ask queries that require accessing data residing in multiple packages and on multiple media and that use a diversity of storage techniques.

Query 1.5 (Simple Heterogeneous Query) Let's suppose that the police officer wishes to issue the query, "Find all individuals who have been convicted of attempted murder in North America and who have recently had electronic fund transfers made into their bank accounts from ABC Corp."

On the face of it, this seems like a rather simple query. After all, it only involves processing queries against standard textually represented databases. Unfortunately, as anyone in the law enforcement community knows, answering this query can prove to be a formidable task. First, in order to find out everyone who has had funds transferred electronically into their bank accounts by ABC Corp., it is sufficient to monitor the electronic fund transfer activity of ABC Corp. However, ABC Corp. may have accounts in hundreds of banks worldwide. Rather optimistically, let's assume that the police already have a list of ABC Corp.'s worldwide bank accounts and, furthermore, have obtained legal authority to monitor transactions made from these accounts. However, these banks may be scattered across the world, and most likely, different banks will make reports on suspicious transactions using different formats. Gleaning a list of recipients of funds from ABC Corp. from these reports requires the ability to electronically process diverse report formats. Second, the task remains of identifying which of these recipients of largesse from ABC Corp. have had past convictions for attempted murder, which involves searching the criminal data banks of different nations in North America, all of which are maintained differently. In fact, in the United States alone, different states may maintain their "roster" of criminals in different formats, using flat files in some cases, DBase in some cases, Oracle in others, and Sybase in yet other cases.[1]

---

[1] DBase, Oracle, and Sybase are all commercially available database management systems.

A slightly more complex query involves accessing all the forms of data listed in the above query, but also includes image data as well.

Query 1.6 (Heterogeneous Multimedia Query) Let us suppose that the police officer wishes to issue the query, "Find all individuals who have been photographed with Jose Orojuelo and who have been convicted of attempted murder in North America and who have recently had electronic fund transfers made into their bank accounts from ABC Corp."

In this query, we must not only identify all people who satisfy Query 1.5 above, but also determine whether individuals who satisfy Query 1.5 have been photographed with Jose Orojuelo. This subtask may require access to

- a mugshot database containing the names and pictures of various individuals

- a surveillance photograph database of still images (already described earlier)

- the surveillance video data to see if a meeting between the suspect and Jose Orojuelo was recorded on video

- image-processing algorithms for determining who occurs in which video or still photograph

Overall, this query requires access to diverse types of relational data, to image data, and to a suite of image-processing algorithms.

Query 1.7 (Complex Heterogeneous Multimedia Query) Let us suppose that the police officer wishes to ask the query, "Find all individuals *who have been in contact with Jose Orojuelo* and who been convicted of attempted murder in North America and who have recently had electronic fund transfers made into their bank accounts from ABC Corp."

In this query, the notion of "contact" between a person who satisfies Query 1.5 and Jose Orojuelo may involve a large number of possible modes of contact. For example, one form of contact may be through surveillance images/photographs or video imagery: two people may be considered to be in contact if they have been photographed together. Likewise, two people may be said to be in contact if they have spoken to each other; thus, for instance, if audiotapes reveal that a person spoke to Jose Orojuelo over the phone, then this may be viewed as satisfying the "contact" requirement in the above query. Similarly, the existence of email files (e.g., flat files with mail headers) also reveals yet another form of contact between the concerned individuals. Finally, typed letters or handwritten notes between Jose Orojuelo and a given individual satisfy the "contact" criterion as well. Thus, in order to answer the above query, we need to access a widely varying range of textual data (to answer Query 1.5) including different relational DBMSs, as well as various kinds of image data, video data, audio data, text data, document data, and handwritten data.

In the rest of this book, we will return to this Sample Multimedia Scenario over and over again. In particular, we will show how each and every query listed above may be answered. More importantly, we will identify a core body of multimedia storage and retrieval techniques that apply across a wide variety of application domains. Because the Sample Multimedia Scenario presents just one single application domain, you may wonder, Gee, can the code written for the Sample Multimedia Scenario be reused in a multimedia application for the travel industry?

We will show in the rest of this book that, by following certain simple design principles, a large amount of the code required for most multimedia applications needs to be written only once. In other words, this shared commonality between applications allows us to build, in a domain-independent way, a body of core algorithms. This body of core algorithms then take certain special parameters that do depend upon the application at hand as input. Thus, when building multimedia information systems, certain components of the system can be reused, over and over again, for many applications. We will articulate how these reusable components may be designed, and what form the input parameters to these core components take.

1.3   Other Applications

So that you won't be trapped into believing that the above sample multimedia scenario captures most of the forms of multimedia data and reasoning we are likely to encounter, we will now describe a variety of other examples drawn from widely varying domains.

1.3.1   Educational Multimedia Services

Even today, many universities offer distance learning programs so that individuals who are unable to attend classes because of either geographic or time constraints may take courses. Such courses are typically offered today by mailing them videotapes (in cases where time constraints do not play a role, live broadcasts are often made as well). In the not-too-distant future, computer users will have online access to audio-video-document archives of educational material. For instance, a student using one of these services would access the service provider's host machine and issue a query such as, "Find all lectures on PR-quadtrees that are available in the archive." The archive may contain information in various media (video lectures, mimeographed notes, etc.) on this topic. The solution to this query provided to the user must be a browsable multimedia presentation including, perhaps, small clips of the relevant video. For example, Subrahmanian's lectures in Spring 1993 and Fall 1994 may differ a good deal; additionally, other instructors may have also taught the material involved, and the user should be given brief previews of the options available to him so that he can select the solution that he likes best for further viewing.

1.3.2 The Movie Industry

In the very immediate future, movies-on-demand will be available. Users will be able to select movies from the comfort of their homes and watch them on their home television set. As time goes on, the modes by which users can select the movie that they wish to watch are likely to increase dramatically. As in the case of educational multimedia described above, users may wish to select the movies that they wish to see by a mix of querying/retrieval and browsing. For instance, the user may wish to watch an Alfred Hitchcock movie, but he may not wish to see one of those in which Jimmy Stewart is acting (perhaps he has watched many of those in the past and has become tired of the genre of Stewart movies). A multimedia system supporting such user interactions must have the ability to efficiently retrieve the movies that satisfy the user's requirements; furthermore, the user should have the option of seeing small preview-length segments of the movie, should he so desire. In addition, the user should have the option of seeing critical reviews of the movie—such reviews may help him select the movie he wishes to see.

1.3.3 Expert Advice

Many of us would love to not have to deal with the plumber, or not to have to pay exorbitant prices to an auto mechanic. With the car mechanic, in particular, we are often left with the feeling that we have been ripped off, and we have very little control over even the simplest forms of auto repair. In many cases, these repairs can be made easily and inexpensively if only we had the most elementary knowledge about what to do. Manuals are often useless because they are too voluminous to be of any practical use. An interesting idea is to create automated assistants or agents for different tasks ranging from plumbing repair to car repair.

Take the auto mechanic, for instance. We would like to interact with a program that shows us, on the screen, what we see (or should see) under the hood of the vehicle. Manuals are terse: statements such as "the 16-inch rubber gasket located laterally by the spark plug ignition coil" may convey about as much meaning as an Egyptian hieroglyphic. An automated auto mechanic assistant, however, would bring up an image (retrieved from an electronically stored manual) of the relevant components of the car. The user can easily examine this image (which presumably will have the appropriate component highlighted in some way) and determine which physical part in the car corresponds to the highlighted component in the image. Suppose all that is needed is to replace this gasket with a new gasket. The system would print out a complete technical specification of the gasket (e.g., Gasket RX-764UR) for the user, together with a list (including contact information) of suppliers in his geographic vicinity.

Similar multimedia presentations would greatly enhance the quality of service obtained from repair technicians.

1.3.4 Travel Industry

An area that is ripe for multimedia services is the travel industry. Many individuals planning their annual family vacation make trips to either their travel agent or to their local bookstore in order to identify different possible alternative destinations that fit their budget and satisfy their holiday needs. But you could potentially plan your entire trip from home without ever leaving your desk. A multimedia system implementing an intelligent travel agent would enable the user to articulate his travel needs, and then ask the system to find places that satisfy these travel needs. Subsequently, this system would find destinations that meet the stated criteria and develop, upon request, a multimedia presentation about one or more of these destinations. Thus, for instance, two different users—one with interests in designer fashions and the other with interests in ancient and medieval architectures—may both find Rome to be a target location; however, the multimedia presentation generated by the system in response to the first user's query would perhaps focus on the Via Condotti—Rome's hottest fashion district. In contrast, the user interested in ancient and medieval architectures (as articulated in his query) would receive a presentation describing various architectural sights in Rome such as the Colosseum, the Trevi fountain, the Vatican, and so on. Once the user has, through a combination of querying and browsing, determined where he would like to go, the system should be able to print out for him a proposed itinerary, including full details of his hotel stay, his airplane schedules, and so on. In particular, the system should issue transactions to relevant airline-scheduling systems, making the necessary bookings and transmitting the user's credit card number (obtained during the system's interaction with the user).

1.3.5 Home Shopping

Just as in the case of the travel industry (where travel packages are synthesized and sold to the user using multimedia presentations), we may use the same concept to market consumer products (as well as industrial products) to customers. As in the case of the travel industry, prospective customers can call in or access a relevant service provider who provides online information about products and goods available through the service, together with sale information.

1.4 Conclusions

All the examples listed in this chapter share various common aspects that can be abstracted away to form a core body of data to be represented, and a core body of algorithms to be implemented. These common aspects are largely independent of any specific application.

In the rest of this book, we will first study various specific media types (video, audio, document, text, etc.), and then see what these common aspects are and how we may construct the core body of data and the core body of algorithms. Then, for each specific application, we will describe what new kinds of information need to be added on. The new kinds of data that need to be added on may be far from trivial and may involve devising very complex algorithms. Yet, there will be no need to reinvent the common part alluded to above, thus saving time, effort, and money.

In the next chapter, we will quickly overview the main ideas behind relational database management systems—the most widely used form of database management system around today.

2

A Quick Overview of Relational Databases

What new concepts will you learn in this chapter?
You will learn what a relational database is. You will learn the basic ideas underlying the SQL query language.

What new abstractions are needed to realize these concepts?
You will be introduced to the relational calculus—a declarative paradigm within which a large number of query languages (such as SQL) fall.

What new techniques are needed to implement these abstractions?
You will be introduced to the relational algebra. While the relational calculus is used to express queries declaratively, the relational algebra provides a way of executing them efficiently.

What technological features support these implementation methods?
You will receive a quick overview of existing relational database management systems on both the Unix as well as Windows software platforms.

A *relational database management system* (RDBMS) is a system that manipulates *tables*. Informally speaking, a table consists of *rows* and *columns*. Each row is called a *tuple*. The ith entry in a given tuple is in the ith column of the table.

Perhaps we should illustrate with an example: consider a relational table about employees. Such a table (also called a *relation*) may have the name emp. In addition, it has a *scheme* of the form $(A_1, \ldots, A_n)$, where A_i denotes a set. All entries in the ith column of the relational table emp must be from the set denoted by A_i. For instance, the emp relation may have the scheme

(COMP,SSN,FNAME,LNAME,STREETNUM,STREETNAME,CITY,STATE,ZIP)

where

1. COMP, FNAME, LNAME, STREETNAME, CITY all denote the set of alphanumeric strings,

2. STATE denotes the set of all two-letter strings denoting U.S. states (e.g., MD, VA, etc.)—this represents an enumerated type,

3. SSN denotes the set of nine-digit positive integers,

4. ZIP denotes the set of five-digit positive integers, and

5. STREETNUM denotes the set of positive integers.

An example of such a relation is captured in the table below:

COMP	SSN	FNAME	LNAME	STREET NUM	STREET NAME	CITY	STATE	ZIP
ABC Corp.	992786589	John	Smith	27	Canal St.	Fairfax	VA	22087
ABC Corp.	287456725	Denis	Jones	786	Baker St.	Manassas	VA	22185
ABC Corp.	548923764	Jane	Fox	1224	Cowper Dr.	Bethesda	MD	20984
ABC Corp.	983744470	Lisa	Barnes	17	Edgar Ct.	Rockville	MD	20887
ABC Corp.	189465394	Jill	Davis	26	Canal St.	Fairfax	VA	22087
XYZ Corp.	198473891	Bill	Bosco	11	Lake Dr.	Richmond	VA	23876
XYZ Corp.	837464632	Bill	Dashell	45	Forest St.	Baltimore	MD	24533
XYZ Corp.	193746472	David	Johns	581	Lugar Dr.	Rockville	MD	20845
XYZ Corp.	193284646	Jim	Hatch	2374	Whitman Dr.	Fairfax	VA	22087
XYZ Corp.	193746466	Tina	Budge	198	Wallis St.	Bethesda	MD	20984

2.1 Relational Algebra

In the relational model of data, there are seven basic (as well as other auxiliary) operations that are used to manipulate data. In this section, we will only study the different basic operations in the relational algebra.

2.1.1 Selection

Suppose we wish to find all tuples in a given relation R that satisfy a given condition C. The relational algebra contains a special operator, usually denoted σ, that facilitates this. The notation $\sigma_C(R)$ returns the set of all tuples in relation R that satisfy condition C.

For example, suppose we wish to select all tuples in the emp relation that have ABC Corp. as their COMP field. This can be expressed as the selection

$$\sigma_{\text{COMP=ABC Corp.}}(\text{emp})$$

The answer returned as a result of this algebraic operation is a table itself—the table consisting of the first five rows of the emp relation.

A slightly more complex operation says, "Find all tuples in the emp relation that have ABC Corp. as their COMP field and whose CITY field is Fairfax." In this case, we are looking for all records about employees of ABC Corp. who live in Fairfax." This can be expressed as the selection

$$\sigma_{\text{COMP=ABC Corp. \& CITY=Fairfax}}(\text{emp})$$

Alternatively, this may be expressed as the iterated select

$$\sigma_{\text{COMP=ABC Corp.}}(\sigma_{\text{CITY=Fairfax}}(\text{emp}))$$

Notice that the above formulation first involves selecting all tuples where the CITY field is Fairfax. This leads to an intermediate relation (which is temporary) containing three tuples—those associated with John Smith, Jill Davis, and Jim Hatch. The outer select is now applied to this intermediate relation, finding the tuples in this intermediate relation where the COMP field is ABC Corp.

In general, the selection condition C is a Boolean expression constructed using the predicate symbols $=, <, >, \leq$, and $\geq$. The arguments to these predicates are either constants from the attribute domains or the names of the attribute domains. Thus, for instance, the expressions

```
LNAME = Smith
FNAME = LNAME
ZIP > 59000
```

are all valid selection conditions.

2.1.2   Projection

The operation of selection yields all tuples that satisfy the selection condition. In contrast, the operation of *project*, usually denoted π, simply projects out an entire column. In order to accomplish this, we specify a relation and one or more columns from that relation that we are interested in. The result is a table that is identical to the original relation, except that all columns not explicitly named are eliminated.

As an example, suppose we wish to project out the COMP and CITY fields of the emp relation. This is an operation that may be useful to somebody who is only interested in the cities where the employees of the relevant corporations live, but has no interest whatsoever in the employees themselves. Thus, for instance, the syntactic entity

$$\pi_{COMP,CITY}(emp)$$

specifies the above request. The solution yielded by it is the following table:

COMP	CITY
ABC Corp.	Fairfax
ABC Corp.	Manassas
ABC Corp.	Bethesda
ABC Corp.	Rockville
XYZ Corp.	Richmond
XYZ Corp.	Baltimore
XYZ Corp.	Rockville
XYZ Corp.	Fairfax
XYZ Corp.	Bethesda

It is particularly important for the user to note that the tuple (ABC Corp., Fairfax) could be placed in the result of the projection in two ways—through either the record associated with John Smith or the record associated with Jill Davis. As both these (different) tuples in the original emp relation agree on the fields being projected, we place only one copy of the resulting projected tuple, (ABC Corp., Fairfax), instead of both.

A project and a select may be applied iteratively. For instance, consider a new table called bank having the attributes and values shown in the table below:

FNAME	LNAME	ACCTYPE	TRANS	AMOUNT	DAY	MTH	YR
John	Smith	savings	deposit	8000	5	jan	1993
John	Smith	savings	deposit	9025	17	jan	1993
John	Smith	checking	deposit	5000	24	jan	1993
Denis	Jones	savings	deposit	11500	11	jan	1993
Denis	Jones	checking	withdrawal	8000	4	jan	1993
Denis	Jones	savings	deposit	4500	27	jan	1993
Jane	Fox	checking	deposit	1900	22	jan	1993
Jane	Fox	savings	deposit	987	28	jan	1993
Lisa	Barnes	savings	deposit	16000	5	jan	1993
Lisa	Barnes	checking	deposit	4800	4	jan	1993
Jill	Davis	savings	withdrawal	1400	1	jan	1993
Jill	Davis	checking	deposit	4900	22	jan	1993
Bill	Bosco	savings	deposit	6000	17	jan	1993
Bill	Bosco	checking	deposit	5125	28	jan	1993
Bill	Dashell	savings	deposit	2900	30	jan	1993
David	Johns	checking	deposit	2700	30	jan	1993
David	Johns	checking	deposit	2600	11	jan	1993
David	Johns	savings	deposit	4900	17	jan	1993
Jim	Hatch	checking	deposit	3400	4	jan	1993
Jim	Hatch	checking	deposit	4100	15	jan	1993
Tina	Budge	savings	withdrawal	5800	11	jan	1993
Tina	Budge	savings	withdrawal	7400	14	jan	1993
Tina	Budge	savings	deposit	18000	28	jan	1993

Suppose a police investigator merely wishes to see a list of all deposits (and their dates) of over \$6,000 made by John Smith in 1993. He may obtain this information by asking the query

$$\pi_{\text{TRANS,DAY,MTH,YR}}(\sigma_{\text{FNAME=John \& LNAME=Smith \& AMOUNT} > 6000}(\text{bank}))$$

This query involves first executing a selection operation that produces an intermediate table, and subsequently projecting out the relevant columns from the intermediate table. The final result of this query is

TRANS	DAY	MTH	YR
deposit	5	jan	1993
deposit	17	jan	1993

2.1.3 Cartesian Product

Suppose we have two relations R_1 and R_2 having the schemes $(A_1, \ldots, A_n)$ and $(A'_1, \ldots, A'_m)$. The *Cartesian product* of these two relations, denoted $R_1 \times R_2$, has the scheme $(A_1, \ldots, A_n, A'_1, \ldots, A'_m)$ and consists of all tuples $(t_1, \ldots, t_n, t'_1, \ldots, t'_m)$ such that $(t_1, \ldots, t_n)$ is a tuple in R_1 and $(t'_1, \ldots, t'_m)$ is a tuple in R_2.

Informally speaking, $R_1 \times R_2$ is obtained by picking a tuple from R_1, a tuple from R_2, and concatenating them together. In general, the number of tuples in $R_1 \times R_2$ is at most $card(R_1) \times card(R_2)$ where $card(R)$ denotes the number of tuples in relation R.

For example, consider the two relations $R_1 = \pi_{\text{COMP,CITY}}(\text{emp})$ and R_2 as given below:

COMPANY	EMPLOYEES
ABC Corp.	30000
XYZ Corp.	15000

Then the Cartesian product, $R_1 \times R_2$, of R_1 and R_2 is the relation

COMP	CITY	COMPANY	EMPLOYEES
ABC Corp.	Fairfax	ABC Corp.	30000
ABC Corp.	Manassas	ABC Corp.	30000
ABC Corp.	Bethesda	ABC Corp.	30000
ABC Corp.	Rockville	ABC Corp.	30000
ABC Corp.	Fairfax	XYZ Corp.	15000
ABC Corp.	Manassas	XYZ Corp.	15000
ABC Corp.	Bethesda	XYZ Corp.	15000
ABC Corp.	Rockville	XYZ Corp.	15000
XYZ Corp.	Richmond	ABC Corp.	30000
XYZ Corp.	Baltimore	ABC Corp.	30000
XYZ Corp.	Rockville	ABC Corp.	30000
XYZ Corp.	Fairfax	ABC Corp.	30000
XYZ Corp.	Bethesda	ABC Corp.	30000
XYZ Corp.	Richmond	XYZ Corp.	15000
XYZ Corp.	Baltimore	XYZ Corp.	15000
XYZ Corp.	Rockville	XYZ Corp.	15000
XYZ Corp.	Fairfax	XYZ Corp.	15000
XYZ Corp.	Bethesda	XYZ Corp.	15000

Note that this relation, by itself, may not carry any intuitive meaning as far as the end user is concerned. However, as we shall see later (see Section 2.1.6), the notion of Cartesian product will be key to the development of the important concept of join.

2.1.4 Union

We say that two relations R_1 and R_2 are *union compatible* if they have the same scheme. The union of relations R_1 and R_2 in this case, denoted $R_1 \cup R_2$, has the same scheme as R_1 (and R_2) and contains a tuple t iff t is either in relation R_1 or in relation R_2.

For example, suppose we let relation R_1 be the relation

$$R_1 = \pi_{\text{FNAME,LNAME}}(\text{emp})$$

and suppose R_2 is the relation given by

FNAME	LNAME
Jack	Arnold
John	Smith
Ted	Garroway

Then $R_1 \cup R_2$ contains the following tuples:

FNAME	LNAME
Jack	Arnold
John	Smith
Ted	Garroway
Denis	Jones
Jane	Fox
Lisa	Barnes
Jill	Davis
Bill	Bosco
Bill	Dashell
David	Johns
Jim	Hatch
Tina	Budge

Note that the tuple (John, Smith) appears in both R_1 and R_2, but appears only once in the union.

2.1.5   Difference

We say that two relations R_1 and R_2 are *difference compatible* if they have the same scheme. The difference of two relations, denoted $R_1 - R_2$, has the same scheme as R_1 (and R_2) and contains a tuple t iff t is in R_1 but is not in R_2.

Using the relations R_1 and R_2 described in Section 2.1.4, we will easily see that $R_1 - R_2$ is the relation

FNAME	LNAME
Denis	Jones
Jane	Fox
Lisa	Barnes
Jill	Davis
Bill	Bosco
Bill	Dashell
David	Johns
Jim	Hatch
Tina	Budge

The five operations that we have described thus far—selection, projection, union, Cartesian product, and difference—are the most important basic operations in the relational algebra. However, there are a number of derived operations that may be defined in terms of these, one of which, called *join*, is very important.

2.1.6 Join

A fundamental operation that we execute on relations is the join operation, which is used to integrate information from different tables. While the project and select operations described above only operate on one table at a time, the join operation takes two tables and a Boolean condition, C, as input. Typically, the Boolean condition C links an attribute in the first table with an attribute in the second. For instance, suppose we have a relation called crime of the form shown below:

SSN	FIRST	LAST	CONVICTION	DAY	MONTH	YEAR
992786589	John	Smith	drug	17	may	1990
992786589	John	Smith	assault	5	aug	1986
983744470	Lisa	Barnes	tax fraud	14	june	1987
837464632	Bill	Dashell	drug	27	sep	1990
837464632	Bill	Dashell	theft	11	jul	1986
193284646	Jim	Hatch	mail fraud	21	aug	1984
193284646	Jim	Hatch	drug	14	feb	1989

We may wish to compose together information from different records. For example, a police officer may wish to create a table that has the scheme (FNAME, LNAME, CITY, CONVICTION)—that is, he wants to find all people (and the cities they live in) in the emp relation who have been convicted. To accomplish this, he needs to

1. match social security numbers from the two relations emp and crime to match a person in the emp relation with a person in the crime relation, and

2. then project out the relevant fields (i.e., FNAME, LNAME, CITY, and CONVICTION).

The first operation can be accomplished by the specification

$$\text{emp} \bowtie_{\text{emp.SSN=crime.SSN}} \text{crime}$$

The result of this operation consists of the concatenation of tuples $t_1 \in$ emp and $t_2 \in$ crime such that $t_1.\text{SSN} = t_2.\text{SSN}$.

The following algebraic expression achieves the desired result comprising both operations listed above:

$$\pi_{\text{FNAME,LNAME,CITY,CONVICTION}}(\text{emp} \bowtie_{\text{emp.SSN=crime.SSN}} \text{crime})$$

The result is shown in the table below:

FNAME	LNAME	CITY	CONVICTION
John	Smith	Fairfax	drug
John	Smith	Fairfax	assault
Lisa	Barnes	Rockville	tax fraud
Bill	Dashell	Baltimore	drug
Bill	Dashell	Baltimore	theft
Jim	Hatch	Fairfax	mail fraud
Jim	Hatch	Fairfax	drug

Suppose R_1 and R_2 are two relations whose attribute names are distinct. Then the join operation $R_1 \bowtie_C R_2$ may be defined in terms of the five basic operations as

$$R_1 \bowtie_C R_2 \overset{def}{=} (\sigma_C(R_1 \times R_2))$$

The above definition may be easily modified to capture the notion of join when the two relations share common attribute names.

2.1.7 Intersection

The intersection of two relations R_1 and R_2, denoted by $R_1 \cap R_2$, is defined if R_1 and R_2 are union compatible. It is defined as

$$R_1 \cap R_2 \overset{def}{=} R_1 - (R_1 - R_2)$$

2.2 Relational Calculus

When a user specifies a query in the relational algebra, he specifies a *sequence* of operations to be performed. In other words, he not only specifies what query he wants an answer to, but also specifies precisely how that query is to be computed. For example, in the algebraic query

$$\pi_{\text{FNAME,LNAME,CITY,CONVICTION}}(\text{emp} \bowtie_{\text{emp.SSN=crime.SSN}} \text{crime})$$

discussed in the previous section, the user explicitly says, "First perform the specified join, and then project out the specified columns."

In many cases, however, the user may merely wish to specify his query in a declarative fashion—he wants his query answered, but leaves the system to decide how to answer that query. In other words, the system must synthesize a sequence of algebraic operations that answer the user's query. The *relational calculus* is a logical formalism that is used to articulate such queries. In this section, we will quickly describe a type of relational calculus often referred to elsewhere as the tuple relational calculus.

Suppose $R_1, \ldots, R_k$ is a set of relations, and relation R_i has scheme Sch_i for $1 \leq i \leq n$. The relational calculus consists of logical formulas generated as follows:

1. *Constant symbols:* For each attribute symbol $A \in \bigcup_{i=1}^{k} Sch_i$ and each member $o \in dom(A)$, o is a constant symbol.

2. *Variable symbols:* There exists an infinite set of variable symbols $t_1, \ldots, t_r,$ $\ldots$ ranging over tuples.

3. *Predicate symbols:* $\in$, $=$, $<$, $>$, $\leq$, $\geq$, and $\neq$ are all predicate symbols.

   A *relational calculus atom* is now defined inductively as follows:

1. If t is a tuple variable and R_i is a relation, then $(t \in R_i)$ is an atom. The sole occurrence of t in this atom is said to be *free*. t is said to range over R_i.

2. If t is a tuple variable ranging over relation R_i and A is an attribute in Sch_j, then $t.A$ is said to be a *tuple term*. If $t.A$ is a tuple term, and τ is either a tuple term or a constant symbol, and Θ is any of the comparison operations $=, <, >, \leq, \geq$, or $\neq$, then $(t.A \, \Theta \, \tau)$ and $(\tau \, \Theta \, t.A)$ are atoms. t is said to be free in this atom.

If we return to our example relation bank, and t is a tuple variable ranging over bank, then t.LNAME and t.AMOUNT are both tuple terms. Examples of some relational calculus atoms are the following:

- t.LNAME $=$ Smith

- t.AMOUNT $> 5,200$

A *relational calculus formula* may now be inductively defined as follows:

1. Every relational calculus atom is a relational calculus formula.

2. If F_1 and F_2 are relational calculus formulas, then $(F_1 \, \& \, F_2)$, $(F_1 \lor F_2)$, and $(\neg F_1)$ are all relational calculus formulas. Every variable that is free in F_1 and F_2 is free in these formulas.

3. If t is a free variable in formula F, then $(\forall t \in R)F$ and $(\exists t \in R)F$ are relational calculus formulas in which t is *bound* (not free).

For example, the following expressions are relational calculus expressions:

- $(t \in$ bank$) \, \& \, (t.$LNAME $= \; Smith) \, \& \, (t.$AMOUNT $> 5,200)$. t is free in this formula

- $(t_1 \in$ bank$) \& \, (t_2 \in$ emp$) \, \& \, (t_1.$FNAME $= t_2.$FNAME$) \& \, (t_1.$LNAME $= t_2.$LNAME$) \, \& \, (t_1.$TRANS $= deposit)$.

A *relational calculus query* is an expression of the form

$$\{t \mid F\}$$

where F is a relational calculus formula in which t appears free. Intuitively, a relational calculus query of the above form says, "Find all tuples t such that condition F is true." Examples of some relational calculus queries include the following:

- $\{t \mid (t \in$ bank$) \, \& \, (t.$AMOUNT $> 5,200)\}$. This query says, "Find all tuples in the bank relation where the AMOUNT field of the tuple exceeds \$5,200.

▪ $\{t_1 \mid (\exists t_2)((t_1 \in \text{bank})\, \& \,(t_2 \in \text{emp})\, \& \,(t_1.\text{FNAME} = t_2.\text{FNAME})\, \& $
$(t_1.\text{LNAME} = t_2.\text{LNAME})\, \& \,(t_1.\text{TRANS} = \textit{deposit})\, \& \,(t_2.\text{AMOUNT} > 5,200))\}$.
This query says, "Find all tuples t_1 such that there exists a tuple $t_2 \in \text{emp}$ such that these two tuples have the same FNAME and LNAME fields and such that tuple t_1 reflects a deposit of over \$5,200."

2.2.1 Linking the Relational Calculus and Relational Algebra

The relational calculus is a *declarative query language*. A calculus query of the form $\{t \mid F\}$ says, "Find all tuples t that satisfy condition F." However, this query does not say *how* to go about finding the answer to this query. In contrast, a relational algebra expression provides an explicit sequence (or partial order) of steps that must be executed to compute an answer to an algebraic query.

When confronted with these two query languages, it is natural to ask whether one can express queries that the other cannot. The answer is "yes"—the relational calculus is strictly more expressive than the relational algebra. To see this, note that the query

$$\{t \mid \neg(t \in \text{bank})\}$$

is a perfectly valid (syntactically) relational calculus expression. The answer to this query is the set of all tuples that are not in the relation bank. If, as is reasonable, we assume that the domains of the attributes FNAME and LNAME are all alphabetic strings, and the AMOUNT attribute reflects all positive real numbers, and the YR attribute includes all integers, then the above calculus query has an infinite answer, even though the bank relation is finite. It is easy to verify that all the relational algebra operations return finite relations as long as the relations they are applied to are themselves finite. Thus, the relational algebra cannot express such queries.

Given any relational calculus formula F, we can define a concept called the *space* of F:

1. The space of a relational calculus atom $t \in R$ is the set of all tuples in R.

2. The space of a relational calculus atom $(t.A_i \Theta \tau)$ is the set of all tuples over $dom(A_1) \times \ldots \times dom(A_n)$ that satisfy this condition. Here, $(A_1, \ldots, A_n)$ is the scheme of the relation R over which tuple t ranges. (Note that often the word "attribute" is used to denote the name of an attribute rather than the set denoted by the attribute. The notation $dom(A)$ is used to explicitly refer to the set/domain of an attribute, rather than just the name.)

3. The space of the relational calculus formula $(F_1 \& F_2)$ is the intersection of the spaces of F_1 and F_2.

4. The space of the relational calculus formula $(F_1 \lor F_2)$ is the union of the spaces of F_1 and F_2.

5. The space of the relational calculus formula $\neg F$ involving free variables $t_1, \ldots, t_n$ over relations $R_1, \ldots, R_n$ is the complement of the space of F over the appropriate attribute domains of $R_1, \ldots, R_n$.

6. The space of the relational calculus formulas $(\forall t \in R)F$ and $(\exists t \in R)F$ coincide with the space of F.

A relational calculus query $\{t \mid F\}$ is said to be *safe* if the space of F is finite. The following well-known result tells us that the expressive power of the relational algebra coincides precisely with the expressive power of the safe relational calculus.

Theorem 2.1 Consider the relational algebra and the relational calculus.

1. If A is an expression in the relational algebra, then there exists a safe relational calculus query Q such that the set of answers to A coincides with the set of answers to Q.

2. If Q is a query in the safe relational calculus, then there exists an algebraic expression A such that the set of answers to A coincides with the set of answers to Q.

For further details of safety, see [211].

2.2.2 Structured Query Language (SQL)

In the real world, it is hard for users to write queries in the relational algebra or the relational calculus. For this purpose, Structured Query Language (SQL) was proposed many years ago. To this day, it still remains the most widely used database query language, and numerous voluminous books have been written describing its varied flavors and its varied syntactic constructs. As this chapter is just a very brief introduction to relational databases, we will content ourselves with only expressing very simple relational queries in SQL. The most basic SQL query is of the form

```
SELECT    attr₁, attr₂, . . . , attrₙ
FROM      R₁⟨V₁⟩, R₂⟨V₂⟩, . . . , Rₖ⟨Vₖ⟩
⟨WHERE    F⟩
```

In the above query, $R_1, \ldots, R_k$ are relation names, and $V_1, \ldots, V_k$ are tuple variables that range over the relations $R_1, \ldots, R_k$, respectively. The pointed brackets $\langle V_i \rangle$ indicate that these variables may be absent. Similarly, the WHERE clause is optional. Furthermore, F is any formula.[1] The above SQL query corresponds to the relational calculus query

$$\{t \mid (V_1 \in R_1) \, \& \, \ldots \, \& \, (V_n \in R_n) \, \& \, F\}$$

where t has the scheme $(attr_1, \ldots, attr_n)$, where each $attr_i$ is associated with one of the relations $R_1, \ldots, R_k$. The algebraic version of this query may be expressed as

$$\pi_{attr_1, \ldots, attr_n} \left(\sigma_G \left(R_1 \times \cdots \times R_n \right) \right)$$

where the relations R_i are (for the sake of simplicity) assumed to have attributes with mutually distinct names, and G is obtained from F by replacing all expressions of the form $V_i.attr$ in F with $attr$.

We are now ready to see some simple examples of SQL. Consider the simple query $\pi_{\text{COMP.CITY}}(\text{emp})$ that we had discussed earlier in Section 2.1.2. This query may be expressed in SQL as

```
SELECT   COMP,CITY
FROM     emp
```

This SQL query has an empty WHERE part (which automatically evaluates to "true").

Now consider the slightly more complex query

$$\pi_{\text{TRANS,DAY,MTH,YR}}(\sigma_{\text{FNAME=John \& LNAME=Smith \& AMOUNT>6000}}(\text{bank}))$$

described in Section 2.1.2. This query may be expressed in SQL as

```
SELECT   TRANS,DAY,MTH,YR
FROM     bank
WHERE    FNAME=John & LNAME=Smith & AMOUNT > 6000
```

Finally consider now the *join* query

$$\text{emp} \bowtie_{\text{emp.SSN=crime.SSN}} \text{crime}$$

of Section 2.1.6. This query may be expressed in SQL as

---

[1] The pointed brackets around $\langle$WHERE F$\rangle$ indicate that this portion may be absent from an SQL query.

```
SELECT  FNAME, LNAME
FROM    emp E, crime C
WHERE   E.SSN = C.SSN
```

The above three queries and the discussion in this section provide a very simple and brief overview of SQL. In reality, SQL is substantially more complicated than what we have shown above. However, the simple SELECT-FROM-WHERE form of queries is adequate for the vast majority of operations that most users wish to perform in SQL.

2.3   Selected Commercial Systems

There are now literally hundreds of commercial relational database systems running on a wide variety of hardware platforms. Due to this wide availability, we will not be able to do full justice here to the range of available options, but will merely provide a brief glimpse into the products available.

The four leading vendors of relational database products on the Unix platform are IBM with their DB2 system, Informix, Oracle, and Sybase. Each of these four vendors offers full-fledged systems including efficient transaction processors, crash and recovery management systems, and concurrency control packages. Each also provides techniques that allow users to access multimedia data and third-party software products through their main SQL interface.

On the Windows/PC platform, the most popular relational database implementations are Borland's Paradox system, DBASE, Foxpro, and Microsoft's Access. All these databases adhere to a standard called ODBC ("Open Database Connectivity") that provides an external interface through which these different relational database systems can interoperate.

2.4   Bibliographic Notes

This chapter only provides a quick, informal glimpse of the relational model of data. In reality, the algebra and calculus are much more complicated and involve various operations that have not been discussed in this chapter. However, this chapter does present the basic definitions that you need to know in order to have a working knowledge of the theory and practice of relational databases. For more details on the relational model of data, see any standard textbook in this area (e.g., Korth and Silberschatz [119], Ullman [211], Abiteboul, Hull, and Vianu [2], and Atzeni and De Antonellis [16]).

2.5   Exercises and Projects

1. Consider two relations R and S. Show that the following algebraic relations hold:
   (a) $\sigma_{C_1}(\sigma_{C_2}(R)) = \sigma_{C_2}(\sigma_{C_1}(R))$.
   (b) $\sigma_C(R \cup S) = \sigma_C(R) \cup \sigma_C(S)$, assuming that R, S have the same scheme.
   (c) $\sigma_C(R \times S) = \sigma_C(R) \times \sigma_C(S)$, where C is a selection condition that applies to both R and S.

2. Present an example of a query in the relational calculus that cannot be expressed in the relational algebra. Explain why this is so. Hint: Such a query cannot be safe.

3. Consider two small relations R and S over schemes $(A_1, \ldots, A_m)$ and $(B_1, \ldots, B_n)$, respectively. Show how you would express the following queries using (1) the relational algebra, (2) the relational calculus, and (3) SQL.
   (a) Find all tuples in R such that the A_i attribute is over 25.
   (b) Find all tuples in S such that the B_1 and B_2 attributes are equal.
   (c) Find all tuples in $(R \times S)$ such that the A_i attribute is over 25 and the B_1 and B_2 attributes are equal.
   (d) Find all tuples in the result of the previous computation where the A_1 attribute and the B_3 attribute have the same value.

4. What is the complexity of computing a selection query that accesses a single relation R, having scheme $(A_1, \ldots, A_m)$? State your answer in terms of the number of tuples in R and in terms of m.

5. Suppose you had to compute the join of two relations, $(R \bowtie_{A_i = B_j} S)$. In the worst case, what is the complexity of performing this operation?

3 A Quick Introduction to Object-Oriented Databases

CHAPTER

What new concepts will you learn in this chapter?
You will learn what an object-oriented database is, and what an object-relational database is. You will learn the basics underlying the object definition language (ODL). Finally, you will learn how relational databases may be extended with object-oriented features.

What new abstractions are needed to realize these concepts?
An object hierarchy consists of a formal definition of an object—intuitively, an object encapsulates data accessible through *methods* (segments of code) implemented within the object. External programs access data within an object through these methods. You will learn about abstract data types, as these form the underlying abstraction based on which object techniques may be used in a relational setting.

What new techniques are needed to implement these abstractions?
Objects are implemented using languages such as the object definition language (ODL), as well as method definitions. You will study these techniques. Toward the end, you will study an emerging new paradigm called *object-relational databases*.

What technological features support these implementation methods?
You will receive a quick overview of existing object-oriented database management systems, as well as object-relational systems, on both the Unix and Windows software platforms.

Though the relational model of data has been the best studied and most widely implemented data model, it nevertheless suffers from a number of inadequacies. Some of the drawbacks of the basic relational model include the following:

- Data is organized in the form of relatively "flat" tuples, and there is little scope for tuples with fields that reflect complex data structures.

- The schemes of relations are relatively static, and seamlessly extending them to handle temporary variations in data formats (e.g., through the addition of one or more columns, or the deletion of one or more columns) is not well supported.

- Relationships that might exist between the content of (part of) one table and (part of) another relational table must be explicitly encoded through the use of constructs such as integrity constraints.

Object-oriented programming arose out of a fundamental need in computer science for encapsulation. The basic idea behind object-oriented programming is that the data items being manipulated by an application are "organized" as follows:

1. *Objects*, which are manipulated by the application.

2. *Classes*, which are collections of objects, either implicitly or explicitly specified. Each object may be viewed as a class containing just that one object. In addition to objects, classes also contain associated *methods*, which are algorithms specifying how the objects in that class are to be manipulated.

3. A *hierarchy* that imposes an acyclic graph structure on the set of classes.

What is novel in the above development is that each class may be thought of, conceptually, as an independent entity (collection of programs) that interacts with other classes by *passing messages*. The methods associated with a class may either be *private* (i.e., can be invoked only from within the class) or *public* (i.e., can be invoked both from within the class, as well as by other external classes). Thus, each object provides a uniform method-based interface through which other classes can invoke them.

In the rest of this chapter, we will study the basic theory underlying object-oriented databases, as well as study the techniques used to query such databases.

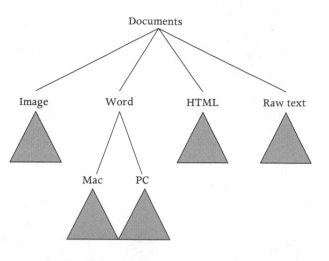

Document hierarchy in Sample Multimedia Scenario

3.1   Objects and Values

Let's return to the Sample Multimedia Scenario described in Section 1.2. Suppose the police inspector has access to a wide variety of document data— some images, some raw text documents, some HTML documents, and some Word documents in two different versions (for PCs and for Macs).

Sample Multimedia Scenario, Revisited Suppose $d_1, \ldots, d_k$ is the set of all documents that the police officer has access to. Each of these documents falls into one of the above classes (some Word documents may be readable on both Macs and PCs and hence may fall into both categories). Figure 3.1 shows a pictorial representation of the files in question.

Museum Example Alternatively, suppose we consider an application involving museums. Each museum may be thought of as an object. Museums may then be grouped into art museums, science museums, natural history museums, and so on. Some museums, such as the Smithsonian, fall into multiple such categories. Figure 3.2 shows a pictorial representation of the organization of these museums.

In addition, each of the objects described above may have *properties*. For instance, a document may have properties such as author, date-created, date-last-modified, keywords, and so on. Similarly, a museum may have

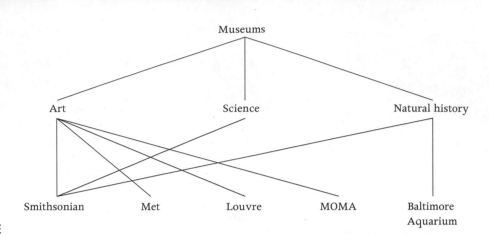

FIGURE

3.2   Hierarchy for museum example

properties such as address, phone, admission-fee, hours, and so on. Each property has an associated domain. For example, the domain associated with the property admission-fee is probably the nonnegative reals; the domain associated with keywords is the set of strings. Based on these intuitions, we are now ready to provide a formal definition of objects and values. Before providing these definitions, we need an *alphabet*.

Definition 3.1 An *object alphabet* consists of the following:

- A set, Oid_Set, of elements called *object-ids*.

- A set, Cid_Set, of elements called *class-ids*.

- A set, Attr_Set, of elements called *attributes*. Associated with each attribute $a \in$ Attr_Set is a set, *dom(a)*, called the *domain* of the attribute.

For example, the set of object-ids may consist of all strings of the form $\{ \flat i \mid i$ is a positive integer$\}$. Similarly, the set of class-ids may consist of all strings of the form $\{ \sharp i \mid i$ is an alphanumeric string$\}$. Examples of attributes could include the following:

- author, whose domain is all alphabetic strings

- date-created, date-last-modified, whose domain consists of all valid (day,mth,year) triples

- admission-fee, whose domain consists of all nonnegative reals having at most two decimal places

Suppose $\Sigma = (\mathtt{Oid\_Set}, \mathtt{Cid\_Set}, \mathtt{Attr\_Set})$ is an object alphabet. Σ generates a space of *values* from which objects (which we are yet to define) are constructed.

Definition 3.2 Suppose $\Sigma = (\mathtt{Oid\_Set}, \mathtt{Cid\_Set}, \mathtt{Attr\_Set})$ is an object alphabet, and $\mathtt{Attr\_Core} \subseteq \mathtt{Attr\_Set}$ is some designated set of attributes. The set of *values* generated by Σ and $\mathtt{Attr\_Core}$, denoted $\mathtt{Values}(\Sigma, \mathtt{Attr\_Core})$, is defined inductively as follows:

1. Every member of $\mathtt{Oid\_Set} \cup \left(\bigcup_{A \in \mathcal{A}} dom(A) \right)$ is a value.

2. $\mathtt{nil}$ is a special value.

3. If $A_1, \ldots, A_n \in \mathtt{Attr\_Ncore}$, and $c_i \in dom(A_i)$ for all $1 \leq i \leq n$, then $[a_1 = c_1; \ldots; a_n = c_n]$ is a value.

4. If $v_1, \ldots, v_m$ are values, then $\langle v_1, \ldots, v_m \rangle$ is a value called a *tuple value*.

5. If $v_1, \ldots, v_m$ are values, then $\{v_1, \ldots, v_m\}$ is a value called a *set value*.

The notation $\mathtt{Values}(\Sigma)$ denotes the space of values generated by the object alphabet Σ.

In the above definition, $\mathtt{Attr\_Core}$ is some set of core attributes. These could include nothing more specific than types that include the reals, integers, strings, Booleans, and doubles. Typically, members within the domain of core attributes should be considered values because they occur more or less ubiquitously. $\mathtt{Attr\_Ncore}$ consists of noncore attributes that may arise in specific data structures.

Sample Multimedia Scenario, Revisited   Let's suppose that we wish to precisely specify the set of values associated with the Sample Multimedia Scenario of Figure 3.1. Here, our object alphabet Σ may be given by the following:

- $\mathtt{Oid\_Set} = \{\flat 1, \flat 2, \flat 3, \flat 4, \flat 5, \flat 6\}$

- $\mathtt{Cid\_Set} = \{\sharp \mathtt{html}, \sharp \mathtt{image}, \sharp \mathtt{rawtext}, \sharp \mathtt{word\_mac}, \sharp \mathtt{word\_pc}\}$

- $\mathtt{Attr\_Set}$ may be given by
  - $\mathtt{Attr\_Core}$: $\{\mathtt{real}, \mathtt{bool}, \mathtt{int}, \mathtt{string}\}$. The domain of these attributes is given in the obvious way.
  - $\mathtt{Attr\_Ncore}$: $\{\mathtt{author}, \mathtt{date\text{-}created}, \mathtt{date\text{-}last\text{-}modified}, \mathtt{related\text{-}docs}\}$. The attribute $\mathtt{related\text{-}docs}$ may have as its domain the set $2^{\mathtt{Oid\_Set}}$ (i.e., the power set of the space of object-ids).

The space of values, Values(Σ), associated with this example includes the following:

- [author = John Smith]

- [author = John Smith; date-created = (15, Jan, 1996)]

- {[author = John Smith;
  author = John Smith; date-created = (15, Jan, 1996)]}

- ⟨[author = John Smith], {[author = Lisa Adams; author = John Smith;
  date-created = (15, Jan, 1996)]}⟩

- [author = Lisa Adams; related-docs = {♭2, ♭3}]

The last item above is interesting because one of the documents (related-docs) has an associated set of object-ids. This example goes to show that a value can include references to object-ids (and hence to objects themselves).

Of course, the above are only a few examples of the members in Values(Σ). In general, due to the inductive nature of the definition, Values(Σ) may contain an infinite number of elements.

Museum Example, Revisited   In this example, our object alphabet Σ = (Oid_Set, Cid_Set, Attr_Set) may consist of the following:

- Oid_Set: This may be the set {♭met, ♭louvre, ♭smithsonian};

- Cid_Set: This may be the set {♯art, ♯history, ♯nature}.

- Attr_Set: This set may include several attributes such as the following:
  1. address: The domain of this attribute may be strings.
  2. director: The domain of this attribute may be strings.
  3. annual_budget: The domain of this attribute may be nonnegative reals.
  4. admission-fee: The domain of this attribute may be nonnegative reals.
  5. special-exhibits: The domain of this attribute may be strings.

Examples of values could include the following:

- [address = "The Mall, Washington DC"; director = Jim Schwartz]

- {[special-exhibits = "Caravaggio paintings"],
  [special-exhibits = "Persian manuscripts"]}

- $\{\langle$ special-exhibits = "Caravaggio paintings",
  director = Jim Schwartz$\rangle$,
  [special-exhibits = "Caravaggio paintings"]$\}$

Now that we know what values are, we are in a position to formally define an object.

Definition 3.3 Given an object alphabet Σ and a core set Attr_Core of attributes, an object o is a pair (id_o, val_o) where $id_o \in$ Oid_Set is called the *identity* of the object, and val_o is called the (property) *value* of o.

Before proceeding any further, let us quickly remark how elegant this definition is. It merely says that an object has an associated identity (which tells us how to refer to the object) and an associated set of properties (with corresponding values). For example, if we have an object whose id is ♭59878 (corresponding to a person like John Smith), and another object whose id is ♭818932 (corresponding to Jill Smith), there is no reason to believe that these two individuals have the same properties. For instance, Jill Smith may have a property called gynecologist, with value Donna Manson, but it seems unlikely that John Smith would have a property called gynecologist. The object-oriented model is powerful in the sense that it allows us to take advantage of the *similarity* between objects (by grouping them into classes, as seen in Section 3.2 below), but also allows them to have their individualized properties. In an object-oriented database (OODB), we may *declare* objects using the syntax

```
declare  oid
values    value
```

Before proceeding any further, we return to our two examples and show some of the objects associated with them.

Suppose we wish to declare some information about a certain document in the Sample Multimedia Scenario. We could declare this as

```
declare ♭2
values  [author=John Smith;
         url = http://www.somewhere.com/index.html;
         date-created= (15, Jan, 1996);
         date-last-modified=(19, Nov, 1996)]
```

The above definition declares that a document with object-id ♭2 exists, and that this document has four attributes—author, url, date-created, and date-last-modified—with the values specified above.

Even two different HTML documents may have different associated sets of attributes. For instance, we may have a slightly different declaration:

```
declare ♭3
values   [author=John Smith;
           url = http://www.somewhereelse.com/index.html;
           { [link = ♭1], [link = ♭2]}]
```

This HTML document that the police investigator in our Sample Multimedia Scenario might be investigating is different from the preceding one in a few significant ways. First, it contains links to two objects (♭2 and ♭1), but it also contains a set of link properties. Furthermore, the attributes date-created and date-last-modified that were associated with the (seemingly similar) document ♭2 are not associated with this document.

Note that this declaration may be equivalently written as

```
declare ♭3
values   [author=John Smith;
           url = http://www.somewhereelse.com/index.html;
           link= {♭1,♭3}]
```

Let us return to the museum example. Suppose we wish to declare the object "Smithsonian Institution." The following is an example of such a declaration:

```
declare ♭smithsonian
values   [address = "The Mall, Washington DC";
           director = "Jim Schwartz";
           special-exhibits = {Caravaggio paintings, Persian manuscripts};
           affiliated-museums = {♭louvre, ♭moma}]
```

Obviously, in reality, the Smithsonian Institution is likely to have several other property values; only a few have been specified above as these are adequate for all pedagogical purposes. Note, in particular, that the last property, affiliated-museums, contains references to the object-ids associated with the Louvre and MOMA (Museum of Modern Art, New York).

3.2   Types and Classes

Almost every computer scientist is familiar with the concept of a *type*. Roughly speaking, a type specifies a "format" for data items. The standard data types include `boolean`, `real`, `double`, `integer`, `char`, and `string`. Complex types are created from elementary types using various standard composition operations. In general, type specifications are inductively defined as follows:

- Each type `Attr_Core` is a type. We assume, without loss of generality, that `Attr_Core` contains the standard data types listed above.

- `Oid_Set` is a type.

- Each member of `Cid_Set` is a type.

- *Record types* have *fields*, each with an associated type. We will use the notation $[f_1 : \tau_1; \ldots; f_n : \tau_n]$ to denote a record type having fields $f_1, \ldots, f_n$ of type $\tau_1, \ldots, \tau_n$, respectively.

- *Set types* are of the form $\{\tau\}$, which denotes a set of data items, each of type τ.

- *List types* are of the form $\langle \tau \rangle$, which denotes a list of data items, each of type τ.

For instance, returning to the Sample Multimedia Scenario, it is easy to see that the following are types.

Suppose we return to the sample declaration in the Museum Example, Revisited. The type associated with the `values` statement here is given by

```
[       author:  string;
        url:  urltype;
        date-created:  datetype;
        date-last-modified:  datetype ]
```

Here, we are assuming that `urltype` and `datetype` are in `Attr_Core`.

Suppose we return to the museum object declared in Example 3.7. This could be viewed as an object having the type

```
[       address:  string;
        director:  string;
        special-exhibits:  { string };
        affiliated-museums:  { Oid_Set } ]
```

The last two components of the above type are of specific interest. The line associated with the field `special-exhibits` says that this field is a set of strings. Likewise, the line associated with the field `affiliated-museums` says that this field is a set of object-ids.

We are now ready to formally define a *class hierarchy*.

Definition 3.4 A *class hierarchy* is a triple, $(G, \leq, \text{types})$, where

1. G is a set of objects and classes,

2. $\leq$ is a partial ordering on G,

3. types is a map that associates a type with each $g \in G$ such that the following condition holds:

$$(\forall g_1, g_2 \in G) \qquad g_1 \leq g_2 \rightarrow \text{types}(g_1) \text{ subtype types}(g_2)$$

The binary subtype relation is defined as follows:

1. $[f_1 : \tau_1; \ldots; f_{n+k} : \tau_{n+k}]$ is a subtype of $[f_1 : \tau_1; \ldots; f_n : \tau_n]$.

2. If τ_1 is a subtype of τ_2, then $\{\tau_1\}$ is a subtype of $\{\tau_2\}$.

3. If τ_1 is a subtype of τ_2, then $\langle \tau_1 \rangle$ is a subtype of $\langle \tau_2 \rangle$.

The above relation is closed under reflexivity and transitivity.

The first condition above basically says that the result of adding new fields $f_{n+1} : \tau_{n+1}, \ldots, f_{n+k} : \tau_{n+k}$ to an existing type $[f_1 : \tau_1, \ldots, f_n : \tau_n]$ results in a subtype of $[f_1 : \tau_1, \ldots, f_n : \tau_n]$. This new subtype has more attributes than $[f_1 : \tau_1, \ldots, f_n : \tau_n]$ but "carries" over all the original properties of $[f_1 : \tau_1, \ldots, f_n : \tau_n]$.

Let us return now to Figure 3.2. This figure represents a simple class hierarchy (the set G consists of the nodes in that figure, while the partial ordering, $\leq$, is defined as $g_1 \leq g_2$ if there is a link between g_1, g_2 and g_2 is "above" g_1 in the figure). What remains to be done is to define the types. Rather than define types for all the items in G, we define them for just four of them—museum, art, smithsonian, and met.ny. For example, the type of museum might be

```
[       address:  string;
        director:  string;
        departments:  { string };
        budget:  real]
```

In contrast, the type of art (museum) might be

```
[       address:  string;
        director:  string;
        departments:  { string };
```

```
            budget:  real;
            old-master-collection:  { string };
            modern-art-collection:  { string };
            lithograph-collection:  { string };
            cartographic-collection:  { string }]
```

Note that the type of `art` is a subtype of the type associated with `museum`. The new fields in the type of `art` include items that are specific to art museums, but not to general museums. In the same vein, the type of `smithsonian` might be

```
[           address:  string;
            director:  string;
            departments:  { string };
            budget:  real;
            old-master-collection:  { string };
            modern-art-collection:  { string };
            lithograph-collection:  { string };
            cartographic-collection:  { string };
            animal-collection:  { string };
            mineral-collection:  { string };
            aquatic-collection:  { string };
            airplane-collection:  { string };
            space-collection:  { string }]
```

Observe that the `smithsonian`'s type contains fields such as `aquatic-collection` (which may be derived from the fact that the Smithsonian is also a subclass of `Natl.History` museums) and `airplane-collection` (which may be derived from the fact that the Smithsonian is also a subclass of `Science` museums).

In general, when constructing a class hierarchy, we would *not* explicitly list types derived from ancestors. This would mean, for example, that the type associated with `art` may simply be specified as

```
[           old-master-collection:  { string };
            modern-art-collection:  { string };
            lithograph-collection:  { string };
            cartographic-collection:  { string }]
```

This leaves the fields `address`, `director`, `departments`, and `budget` implicit, as they are derived anyway from an ancestor (i.e., `museum`) of the class `art`.

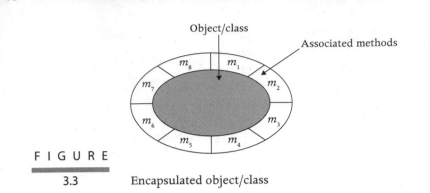

Object/class

Associated methods

3.3　　Encapsulated object/class

Though we have defined a class hierarchy, we have not explicitly specified what the members of a class are. Roughly speaking, the members of a class include all items "below" that class in the hierarchy.

Definition 3.5 Suppose $(G, \leq, \texttt{types})$ is a class hierarchy, and $g \in G$. The *members of class G* consist of all elements in the set $\{g' \in G \mid g' < G\}$.

Thus, for example, the members of the class art (museums) in Figure 3.2 are smithsonian, met, moma.

3.3　　Methods

We are now ready to address one of the most important aspects of object-oriented systems, methods. Given a class hierarchy $(G, \leq, \texttt{types})$, each class $g \in G$ may have its own type. While these types must be subtypes of g's ancestor(s), the type of g may include new fields not present in its ancestors. *Methods* are programs associated with any object/class $g \in G$ that manipulate the structures declared in g's type definition. In other words, in an object-oriented database, each class g has an associated set of programs, methods(g), that apply to that class. This simple fact achieves an important goal of object-oriented systems, *encapsulation*. The objects in a class can be manipulated only by methods applicable to that class, and no others. Thus, methods provide an elegant interface through which other classes/objects or other third-party programs may access an object or a class. Figure 3.3 shows this situation pictorially. Intuitively, the object or class can only be accessed by going "through" one of the methods associated with that object.

For example, returning to the Sample Multimedia Scenario given in Figure 3.1, we may have a function (not a method, as yet) called `FindDocs` that takes the name of a person as input and attempts to find all documents that are relevant to the person. Obviously, deciding which images are relevant to a person will be determined using an algorithm very different from that for a raw text document. Now, we may have a bunch of different methods:

- The class `documents` may have a method called `FindDocs` (referred to by us as $FindDocs_d$), which takes any name (type `string`) as input and returns a set of documents as output.

- The class `image` may have a method called `FindDocs` (referred to by us as $FindDocs_i$), which takes any name (type `string`) as input and returns a set of images as output.

- The class `Word` may have a method called `FindDocs` (referred to by us as $FindDocs_w$), which takes any name (type `string`) as input and returns a set of Word documents as output.

In this case, suppose the function `FindDocs` is invoked by the class `image`. Then the code associated with the function $FindDocs_i$ is executed, as there is a version of `FindDocs` that is *directly associated* with this class. On the other hand, consider invoking the method `FindDocs` in the class `PC_Word`. This class has no method called `FindDocs` *explicitly* associated with it. Thus, we must examine if one of its ancestors has `FindDocs` associated with it. The answer is yes, both the class `Word` and the class `Documents` have `FindDocs` associated with it. However, the class `Word` is more specific and applies "better" (informally speaking) to the case of PC Word documents, so we apply the function $FindDocs_w$ to objects in the class `PC_Word`.

3.3.1 I/O Types

If m is a method associated with class g, then m has an *input/output type* (often called its *signature*) that specifies the type structure of the inputs that method m (as defined in class g) expects and also specifies the output type. In general, m's input type is of the form $\tau_1 \times \cdots \times \tau_k$, where each τ_i, $1 \leq i \leq k$, is a type; its output type is τ_o for some type τ_o. Such a specification says that method m expects k inputs of types $\tau_1, \ldots, \tau_k$, respectively, and provides one output, τ_o.

For example, if we consider the method $FindDocs_w$ defined in the class `Word` above, then the signature of this method is

```
string → {wordfile}
```

specifying that it takes a string as input (e.g.,"John Smith") and returns a set of objects of type wordfile as output (which may be the set of all strings of the form α.doc, where α is an alphanumeric string of at most eight characters).

3.3.2 Overloading

In many cases, the same method may be defined in different classes. If the class g in which method m is defined is not clear from context (e.g., if m is defined in many classes), then we will use the notation m_g to denote the method m as defined in class g.

For example, the method FindDocs in the above example is defined in multiple classes, and hence is an overloaded method name.

3.3.3 Inheritance

As we have seen above, although a method (e.g., FindDocs) may be defined in a class g, it applies not just to that class, but all subclasses of class g as well. For example, the method FindDocs in our example is not explicitly defined in the class PC_Word; in this case, the method FindDocs, as defined in the class Word, is *inherited* by the subclass PC_Word. When discussing inheritance, there are two issues that need to be addressed: *structural similarity* and *conflict resolution*.

Structural Similarity of Methods

Suppose we consider two classes, g_1 and g_2, with $g_1 \leq g_2$. Suppose a method m is defined in both classes g_1 and g_2. For example, this is the situation with the method m = FindDocs and the classes g_1 = Word and g_2 = documents. We would like the method m to exhibit some structural similarity across these two classes. In particular, we require that if the input type of m in the subclass g_1 is $\tau_1 \times \cdots \times \tau_n$, and if the input type of m in the superclass g_2 is $\tau_1' \times \cdots \times \tau_n'$, then for all $1 \leq i \leq n$, τ_i is a subtype of τ_i'.

Notice that this requirement merely ensures that as we "climb up" the inheritance hierarchy, a method's domain increases in size. However, the version of the method defined in the subclass g_1 may be implemented very differently from (and may also return different answers than) the implementation of the method in the superclass g_2. For example, the "generic" method FindDocs defined in the class documents cannot take advantage of the fact that certain documents (e.g., HTML documents) have a specific structure that can be exploited when performing retrievals.

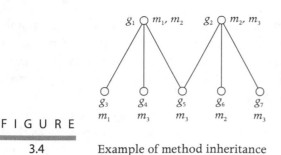

FIGURE

3.4

Example of method inheritance

In general, suppose g is a class. We use the notation $\uparrow g$ to denote the set $\{g' \in G \mid g \leq g'\}$. Class g *potentially inherits* method m from class $g^\star$ iff

1. $g^\star \in \uparrow g$ and method m is defined in $g^\star$ and

2. there is no class g° such that $g \leq g^\circ < g^\star$ and method m is defined in g°.

For example, Figure 3.4 shows a very simple inheritance hierarchy, where the methods associated with different classes are clearly marked next to each node. For example, in this class hierarchy:

1. $\uparrow g_1 = \{g_1\}$; $\uparrow g_3 = \{g_1, g_3\}$, $\uparrow g_5 = \{g_1, g_2, g_5\}$.

2. The class g_3 potentially inherits method m_1 from g_3 (i.e., from itself); it potentially inherits method m_2 from g_1. In both cases, there is exactly one class from which it potentially inherits the method, and hence there are no "conflicts."

3. In contrast, class g_5 potentially inherits method m_2 from both classes g_1 and g_2.

Conflict Resolution in Method Inheritance

As we have seen above, there is a possibility that a class can potentially inherit a method from two superclasses that are mutually incomparable (e.g., above we have $g_1 \not\leq g_2$ and $g_2 \not\leq g_1$.) We say that there is a *method inheritance conflict* with respect to class g and method m if the set of classes from which class g potentially inherits method m contains two or more elements.

A *conflict resolution policy* is a mapping, crp, that takes a set containing two or more classes as input and returns a single class from that set as output. For example, we may have that $\mathrm{crp}(\{g_1, g_2\}) = g_1$.

Conflict resolution can be done in one of a great many ways. A simple conflict resolution policy is that of *lexicographic ordering*. Here, if X is a set of classes, then we order the elements of X in ascending order of class-ids, using lexicographic ordering. $\text{crp}(X)$ is the first element within this total ordering. According to this strategy, $\text{crp}(\{g_1, g_2\}) = g_1$.

Alternatively, we could use a conflict resolution policy based on *recency*. Here, if X is a set of classes from which a class g can potentially inherit a method m, then $\text{crp}(X)$ would select that class $g' \in X$ whose method was most recently developed. Obviously, this conflict resolution strategy assumes the existence of some kind of time stamp associated with each method.

A third possibility is to associate an integer—a *priority*, denoted $pr(g)$—with each class g. The higher the priority, the more important that class is. A conflict resolution strategy based on priorities may now work as follows: Of all the classes in our set of classes X, from which g can inherit method m, pick the class with the highest priority. Of course, it is still possible that there are two or more such classes. One way to avoid this is to insist that all classes have different priorities. Another way is to check, when the class hierarchy is created, to ensure that this situation does not arise (this is a somewhat more complex task).

In general, the user/application developer can pick and implement any conflict resolution strategy that suits the needs of the application being developed.

In general, given a class g and a method m, class g *inherits* method m from the class $\text{crp}(X_{g,m})$, where $X_{g,m}$ is the set of all classes from which g *potentially inherits* method m.

3.4   Object Definition and Query Languages

The theory described in the preceding sections can, and has, been realized in many different ways, using a variety of syntactic forms. This has led to a wide diversity among object data management languages, each having its own unique syntax and assumptions. In order to alleviate this problem, there has been an industry effort in recent years to standardize such syntax. This group, called the Object Database Management Group (ODMG), has made a strong and dedicated effort toward standardizing the treatment of object-oriented databases. They have proposed, among other things, two important concepts: an object definition language (ODL) that may be used to define objects and an object query language (OQL) that may be used to query an object definition. We briefly review each of these below.

3.4.1   Object Definition Language (ODL)

The basic idea behind ODL is to provide a simple language within which both objects and object interfaces can be defined. Recall that in the object-oriented paradigm, each object has an associated set of methods. External programs wishing to access/manipulate the object must do so using the methods provided by the object. To do so, however, they must have access to the signatures (I/O types) of those objects. ODL provides a formal syntax for this purpose. *Note that ODL does not specify how the methods are implemented, just the I/O types of the methods.*

For example, let's return to the Sample Multimedia Scenario shown in Figure 3.1. An ODL definition of the object html is given by

```
interface html:documents                              (1)
( extent html_documents                               (2)
   keys url:persistent                                (3)
      {⟨properties⟩
      ⟨relationships⟩}
);
```

Line (1) above states that the type html is a subtype of the bigger type documents, explaining the parent-child relationship between documents and html in Figure 3.1. Line (2) states that the type html applies to all HTML documents; that is, it specifies that this type definition applies to all HTML documents in the object-oriented database. Line (3) specifies that the type HTML has a key attribute, called url, which is persistent—memory allocated to such persistent objects does not cause the object to "disappear" when the process that creates it terminates. In addition, the ODL definition of the object html contains two additional features, a list of *properties* and a list of *relationships*. Properties refer to attributes of the types. For example, expanding the above definition to include properties, we might write

```
interface html:documents                              (1)
( extent html_documents                               (2)
   keys url):persistent                               (3)
      { attribute string author;                      (4)
         attribute date date_created;                 (5)
         attribute date date_last_modified;           (6)
         ⟨relationships⟩
      }
```

Finally, relationships refers to the fact that the object might have a binary relationship with another class or type. ODL does not support *n*-ary relations for $n > 2$. For instance, an HTML document may have an associated relationship called writers specifying a set of individuals who have written the file, and another relationship called readers specifying a set of individuals who have read the file. These fit nicely into the relationships definition of an ODL type definition.

```
interface html:documents                               (1)
( extent html_documents                                (2)
    keys url):persistent                               (3)
        { attribute string author;                     (4)
            attribute date date_created;               (5)
            attribute date date_last_modified;         (6)
        relationship Set(Persons) author               (7)
                inverse Persons:written_work;
        relationship Set(Persons) reader               (8)
                inverse Persons:works_read;
        }
```

In the above definition, line (7) says that objects of type html have a relationship, called author, with a set of persons. Likewise, objects of type Persons have an inverse relationship, called written_work, that behaves as the inverse of the author relationship.

3.4.2 Object Query Language (OQL)

OQL was introduced by the ODMG group. OQL is a seamless extension of SQL. In other words, if Q is a query expressed in SQL, then Q is also a valid OQL query. However, SQL queries can only access "flat" relational tables. In contrast, objects may have a nested structure, as well as include fields that contain the *collection types*—sets, lists, and bags. OQL provides facilities to access such data types as well. Rather than go through a formal definition of the grammar underlying OQL, we will try to introduce it through a number of brief examples.

Suppose we return to the Sample Multimedia Scenario and issue the query, "Find all Word documents that have been authored by John Smith, and in each case, find all the hyperlinks of these documents." Unlike a standard relational query, this query returns an object having two fields, a name field and a set of links. In OQL, this query may be simply specified as follows:

```
SELECT   struct(field1:x.url, field2:x.link)
FROM     Word x
WHERE    x.author="John Smith"
```

This query is very simple. It first finds all objects x that are Word documents, and then identifies those Word documents that satisfy the conditions x.author="John Smith". For each such x, it returns a structure containing two fields: the url field of x and the link field of x. Note that the link field of x may be a linked list. Thus, an answer to this query may look like

http://www.somewhere.com/index.html	http://www.somewhere.com/file1.html
	http://www.somewhere.com/file2.html
	http://www.abc.com/file1.html.
http://www.cs.umd.edu/users/john/index.html	http://www.somewhere.com/index.html
	http://www.somewhere.com/file1.html
...	...

Should we wish to eliminate duplicates from the answer, we should replace SELECT in the above query by SELECT DISTINCT. Continuing with the above example, suppose we wish to find the authors of all the URLs identified in the preceding query. In other words, "Find the authors of all Word documents that are referenced by (i.e., have a hyperlink to) a document authored by John Smith." This may be done as follows:

```
 SELECT y.author
FROM
            (SELECT   x.link
            FROM      Word x
            WHERE     x.author="John Smith") y
```

This query is somewhat complicated for two reasons: first, it contains a nested query, and second, it contains this new variable y. What it does is very simple:

1. In general, the FROM clause identifies the extent of the class from which the selection is made. In the preceding query (top of page), the class is explicitly specified through the FROM Word x statement, which specifies that x is a variable ranging over the extent of the class Word (i.e., x ranges over all Word documents). In contrast, here the variable y occurring in the outer FROM statement ranges over a class whose extent is specified by the inner query (i.e., nested SELECT query).

2. Thus, this query says, "First find all Word documents authored by John Smith, and let y refer to any such object." This is accomplished by the inner `SELECT` statement.

3. Then return the `y.author` field for all such documents.

Suppose that now we wish to find all pairs of URLs that refer to each other via a hyperlink. This basically expresses a join query and may be expressed as follows:

```
SELECT  x.name, y.name
FROM    documents x,
        x.links y,
        y.links z
WHERE   x.url = z.url
```

Intuitively, this query iterates through all documents as follows: first find a document (x), then find a document (y) referenced by x through a hyperlink, then a document (z) referenced by y. If z's URL coincides with x's URL, then we know that y references x, and we can return the pair x, y as one answer to this query.

OQL allows us to use methods inside a query, as long as the application of the method satisfies the required type constraints. For example, suppose we wanted the most recent Word documents created by John Smith, and suppose we had a method called `mostrecent` defined in the class `Word` (or in a superclass of `Word`). Then we could express this query as

```
SELECT  x.url
FROM    mostrecent(SELECT x
        FROM Word
        WHERE x.author="John Smith")
```

Notice that the application of the function `mostrecent` applies to only documents of the class `Word`; that is, the application of the function `mostrecent` is consistent with the definition of `mostrecent`'s expected I/O types.

3.5   Object-Relational Systems

At this point in time, we have discussed both object-oriented databases and relational databases. Relational databases have proved very useful in querying flat data. But is it possible to extend the relational model of data to handle complex data, rather than flat data? The answer is yes, and the resulting paradigm is typically called an *object-relational database*.

Returning to our police example, consider the relation `bank` introduced in Section 2.1.2 and the relation `crime` described in Section 2.1.6. Currently, the bank relation has the scheme

(FNAME,LNAME,ACCTYPE,TRANS,AMOUNT,DAY,MTH,YR)

while the `crime` relation has the scheme

(SSN,FIRST,LAST,CONVICTION,DAY,MTH,YR)

Suppose we wished to extend both these schemes to also include an image. In the case of the `crime` relation, these images are obtained by taking a mugshot image of the convict (where we know the identity of the person in the image). In contrast, the images associated with the `bank` relation are obtained through surveillance cameras such as those located at automatic teller machines. In this case, we may not always know the identity of the person using the teller machine (for example, cards are sometimes used fraudulently at automatic teller machines by criminals who have illegally used someone's card and personal identification number).

In order to accommodate an additional image field in the database, it is adequate to merely extend the schemes of the two relations involved to include a PIC field as follows:

(FNAME,LNAME,ACCTYPE,TRANS,AMOUNT,DAY,MTH,YR,PIC)

(SSN,FIRST,LAST,CONVICTION,DAY,MTH,YR,PIC)

However, the situation gets complicated very rapidly. Let us now suppose that we have a tuple in the `bank` relation of the form

FNAME	LNAME	ACCTYPE	TRANS	AMOUNT	DAY	MTH	YR	PIC
Jill	Davis	savings	withdrawal	1400	1	jan	1993	image1

Suppose further that Jill Davis goes to the bank and reports that her bankcard was stolen from her and that she did not make this withdrawal. In this case, an obvious check to run is to examine the surveillance image, stored in the file `image1`, to see if it is in fact Jill Davis or not. Suppose Ms. Davis's assertion is correct, and it is apparent that the person depicted in `image1` is not her. A next logical step for the police to perform is to attempt to match the contents of image1 against the image contents of the crime database. In its simplest form, this requires execution of a query that says, "Select all tuples in the crime relation that "match" (using face recognition techniques) the image depicted in image1."

Relational database query languages such as SQL cannot support this query directly because the selection condition requires a comparison operator (match) that is not typically supported by a relational database. But an object database query language cannot be used either because the data is not stored in an object-oriented system.

This example provides a natural use of the concept of an object-relational database system. In our representation of the extended bank and crime relations, we have added an additional "object" field, namely, the field called PIC. All other fields/attributes in the bank and crime relations are alphanumeric fields, while the PIC field is an object field.

Suppose we have a set $\mathcal{O}$ of objects, each with associated properties and methods. An *object-relational scheme* is of the form

$$(A_1 : T_1, \ldots, A_n : T_n)$$

where A_i is an attribute name, and T_i is an object. Note that strings and integers/reals can also be considered to be object classes with operations on them like addition, subtraction, and Boolean comparisons. Thus, for instance, the schemes of the extended bank and crime relations can be written as

```
(FNAME:str,LNAME:str,ACCTYPE:int,TRANS:tt,AMOUNT:real,
         DAY:dom,MTH:mths,YR:int,PIC:image)
(SSN:ssntyp,FIRST:str,LAST:str,CONVICTION:str,DAY:dom,
         MTH:mths,YR:int,PIC:image)
```

Some of the fields are string (str) objects with associated operations, some are enumerated types (e.g., *dom* = [1, 31]), while some are objects (image).

For example, in the case of image objects, suppose we have a method called match that takes two images of the same size and matches them, and suppose we have a function called segment that takes an image as input and returns a set of images of size $(K \times K)$, for some fixed K. Then the following are examples of object conditions:

- match(image1,image2) > 0.7.
- match(image1,image2) > match(image3,image2).

- `match(image1,image2) < t.SAL`. (Though this condition may not make much sense from an intuitive point of view, it is a syntactically valid condition if `t.SAL` is a real valued field.)

We may now extend SQL to access the functions associated with objects and express our desired query as follows:

```
SELECT FNAME, LNAME
FROM crime C, bank B
WHERE match(image1,B.PIC) > 0.9
```

This query says, "Select the FNAME and LNAME fields of all tuples t in the crime relation such that the match function defined in the object image returns a value of over 90% when it matches image1 and the PIC field of t."

In general, if $m(arg1, \ldots, argn)$ is a valid method invocation, and x is either another method invocation or a value of the same type as the output type of method m, then $m(arg1, \ldots, argn) = x$ is an *object condition*. If x is a numeric value and the above condition holds, then $m(arg1, \ldots, argn) > x$, $m(arg1, \ldots, argn) \geq x$, and $m(arg1, \ldots, argn) \leq x$ are also object conditions.

A simple way to extend SQL to accommodate queries to object-relational databases is to allow the WHERE clause in an SQL query to contain object conditions in addition to the usual types of conditions allowed in SQL.

Every major relational database vendor (Oracle, Sybase, Informix, and IBM, in particular) has offerings that conform to the object-relational paradigm.

Informix offers a concept called a *datablade* architecture. Intuitively, a database mediates access to a collection of complex data objects, together with the functions needed to manipulate them. Informix offers a wide variety of datablades for a variety of objects including image database, face recognition, audio data handling, document processing, document cleaning, video processing, and spatial database accesses. For a comprehensive list, see *http://www.informix.com*.

IBM's DB2 database system has a similar component, called an *extender*. IBM has developed extenders for image processing and video processing, fingerprint data, spatial data, and document data. For a comprehensive list, see *http://www.software.ibm.com/data/db2/extenders/index.html*.

Oracle's offerings in this area include video support, a text analysis and summarizing program, and a spatial data option, together with OLAP (online analytic processing) options. *http://www.oracle.com* provides information on Oracle's object-relational database systems.

UniSQL (*http://www.unisql.edu*) and Omniscience (*http://www.omniscience.com*) are two other major vendors of object-relational technology.

3.6   Bibliographic Notes

Object-oriented databases arose from the need to represent data in an encapsulated form, as well as to represent nontraditional data that relational databases, because of their "flat" structure, was unable to handle well.

One of the early books on object-oriented databases is Kim [112], which provides an overview of early object database systems. Kifer, Kim, and Sagiv [108] provided general methods to query object-oriented databases. Kifer and Lausen [109, 110] proposed the important concept of F-logic that was used to capture the semantics of object-oriented databases.

Concurrently with the above efforts was the important O_2 effort at Inria, which is well described by the excellent collection of papers in [17]. In particular, [15] lays out the basic requirements that a system must satisfy in order to be called an "object-oriented database." The theoretical treatment provided in this chapter is based upon the elegant efforts of Kanellakis et al. [103]. Other excellent papers in this volume include [123] and [3].

Implementations of object databases are well described and discussed by Bertino and Martino [23]. In particular, they discuss specific systems such as GemStone, Iris, ObjectStore, O_2, ORION, and Vbase. Distributed object management is studied through a collection of papers in [156]. Finally, [232] provides an excellent collection of early papers in the area.

The emergence of the ODMG working group on object-oriented languages has been well described in [43], which provides an easy-to-read yet detailed description of ODL and OQL. This book is highly recommended if you are interested in further details of these languages.

Finally, object-relational systems have recently emerged as an important new paradigm for representing data. These systems take advantage of the highly structured relational form of data, but also allow a tight coupling with arbitrary object types. Stonebraker [199] provides a comprehensive introduction to object-relational systems as well as a detailed assessment of different commercial products.

3.7   Exercises and Projects

1. Write, in ODL, a definition of a class called word_document that has the following attributes and relationships:

(a) An attribute called `author` of type `person`, where `person` has the attributes `name` (string), `birthdate` (date), `mother` (person), `father` (person), and `siblings` (set of persons)

(b) An attribute called `date_created` of type date

(c) An attribute called `date_last_modified` of type date

(d) An attribute called `previous_versions` of type set of `words_documents`

(e) A relationship called `writers` specifying a set of people authorized to write the document

(f) A relationship called `readers` specifying a set of people authorized to read the document

2. Create an object hierarchy whose root is object `Image` and having children `tiff`, `gif`, and `bmp`. Each of these classes has a number of image files as children, all of the appropriate type. Construct a complete ODL specification for image databases of this type. In particular, each image file I must have the following attributes and relationships:

(a) An attribute called `date_created` of type date

(b) An attribute called `source`. A source may be either of type `person` (as in the preceding exercise) or an organization. Create a suitable type definition for the type `source`.

(c) A relationship that associates a set of people occurring in I with the image I, together with a description of where those people occur.

(d) A relationship that associates a set of other images containing at least one of the people occurring in image I with the image I.

3. Write, in OQL, the following queries to each of the two databases created in response to the preceding two questions:

(a) Find all people (from the object `person`), born on or after June 1, 1965.

(b) Find all people born on or after June 1, 1965, who have read a Word file created by John Smith.

(c) Find all pictures (from the class `images`) of people born on or after June 1, 1965, who have read a Word file created by John Smith.

(d) Find the names of all people who appear in at least three images in the class `images`.

(e) Suppose the class `persons` has a subclass called `suspects` as well as a class associating a country (e.g., `turkish`, `american`, `german`) with each person. Write a query that determines which German suspects have read a Word file written by John Smith.

4. Write, in pseudocode, an algorithm called `potentially_inherit`, that takes the following as input:

   (a) An inheritance graph $G = (V, E)$, where V is the set of objects, and E is the set of edges. $(a, b) \in E$ means that the class a is directly below class b

   (b) A method table MT containing a set of pairs of the form (m, c), where m is the name of a method and c is a class in V

   (c) A class $c \in G$

   (d) A method m

   The algorithm `potentially_inherit` must return the set of all classes from which class c potentially inherits method m as output. Use the definition of "potentially inherit" given in this chapter.

5. Write, in pseudocode, an algorithm called `inherits` that takes all the inputs in the preceding problem, plus one extra input—the name of a conflict resolution policy, `crp`—and returns a single class from which c inherits method m as output. (In the event that no such class c exists—that is, the set of classes from which class c potentially inherits method m is empty—then return the string `"Not applicable"`.)

6. Implement the algorithms `potentially_inherits` and `inherits` listed above. Implement a suite of three or four conflict resolution policies, such as the policies of lexicographic ordering, recency, and priority.

PART II   ORGANIZING MULTIMEDIA CONTENT

4 Multidimensional Data Structures

What new concepts will you learn in this chapter?
Most media data requires the ability to reason about both time and space. Such data is typically referred to as n-dimensional data, reflecting the fact that data has associated attributes drawn from an n-dimensional space. For instance, space is typically two-dimensional (x, y-coordinates) or three-dimensional (x, y, z-coordinates). Space-time usually has four dimensions (x, y, z, t-coordinates). You will study techniques for representing n-dimensional information.

What new abstractions are needed to realize these concepts?
Most techniques to store n-dimensional data do so by using "hierarchical" decompositions of space that are typically represented by various kinds of trees. The root of the tree implicitly represents an entire region. Any node represents a region, and its children represent a partition of that region into subregions.

What new techniques are needed to implement these abstractions?
There are various data structures that represent the above idea of hierarchical decomposition of space. We will study k-d trees, point quadtrees, MX-quadtrees, and R-trees. Each such data structure decomposes space in different ways, with concomitant advantages and disadvantages.

What technological features support these implementation methods?
You will be introduced to applications of many of these data structures in existing commercial database management systems and geographic information systems.

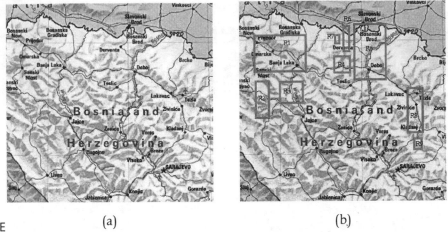

FIGURE

4.1   Example maps (a) with marked points and (b) with marked regions (see also color plate Figure 4.1)

4.1   Introduction

If we return to the Sample Multimedia Scenario given in Section 1.2, we observe that one of the data sources being consulted there is a geographic information source. Geographic data comes in many flavors. In its simplest form, a geographic information system (GIS) stores information about some physical region of the world. This stored information could be just a map (image) containing some salient features. In this case, the map is viewed as a two-dimensional image, and certain points on the map are considered to be of interest. These points are then stored in one of many specialized data structures. Figure 4.1(a) shows a simple map together with some points of interest that lie on the map. The points are marked with names (e.g., Banja Luka, Brcko). Alternatively, instead of having points of interest, the application may require that certain regions are of interest. In this case, data structures may be devised to store information about these regions. Figure 4.1(b) shows the same map with some marked rectangular regions of interest.

In this chapter, we will quickly overview how map data such as that shown in Figure 4.1 may be represented. We will review four well-known representations of spatial data—k-d trees, point quadtrees, MX-quadtrees, and R-trees. Each of these approaches has certain advantages and certain disadvantages, summarized in Section 4.6. Later, we will see that some of these structures are

INFO	XVAL	YVAL
LLINK	RLINK	

F I G U R E

4.2   Node structure for a 2-d tree

extremely useful in indexing images for retrieval by similarity (see Chapter 5), as well as for indexing video data (see Chapter 7).

4.2   *k*-d Trees

The *k*-d tree is used to store *k*-dimensional point data such as that shown in Figure 4.1(a). It is not used to store region data. Thus, a 2-d tree (i.e., $k = 2$) stores two-dimensional point data, a 3-d tree stores three-dimensional point data, and so on. In our examples in this section, we will deal with 2-d point data, and we will later indicate how this approach may be generalized to 3-d data.

4.2.1   Node Structure

In a 2-d tree, each node has a certain record structure. These records have the following type (see also Figure 4.2):

```
nodetype = record
    INFO: infotype;
    XVAL: real;
    YVAL: real;
    LLINK: ↑nodetype;
    RLINK: ↑nodetype
end
```

In particular, the INFO field of a node in a *k*-d tree can be any user-defined type whatsoever. The exact content of this field depends upon the application that the user has in mind. For example, the INFO field could be just a string field, depicting the name of a place, or it could be a record containing fields `name:string` and `population:integer`, or something else altogether. The fields XVAL and YVAL denote the coordinates of a point associated with the node. The LLINK and RLINK fields point to two children.

Suppose T is a pointer to the root of a 2-d tree. If N is a node in this tree, then the *level* of node N is defined inductively as

$$level(N) = \begin{cases} 0 & \text{if } N \text{ is the root of the tree} \\ level(P) + 1 & \text{if } N\text{'s parent is } P \end{cases}$$

Figure 4.4(e) (discussed in detail later) shows a simple 2-d tree, with the levels of each node marked at the side.

A 2-d tree is any binary tree satisfying the following conditions:

1. If N is a node in the tree such that $level(N)$ is even, then every node M in the subtree rooted at N.LLINK has the property that M.XVAL $<$ N.XVAL, and every node P in the subtree rooted at N.RLINK has the property that P.XVAL $\geq$ N.XVAL.

2. If N is a node in the tree such that $level(N)$ is odd, then every node M in the subtree rooted at N.LLINK has the property that M.YVAL $<$ N.YVAL, and every node P in the subtree rooted at N.RLINK has the property that P.YVAL $\geq$ N.YVAL.

4.2.2   Insertion and Search in 2-d Trees

An algorithm for *insertion* into a 2-d tree may easily be defined. Inserting a node N into the tree pointed to by T may be informally accomplished as follows. Check to see if N and T agree on their XVAL and YVAL fields. If so, just overwrite node T, and we are done. Otherwise, branch left if N.XVAL $<$ T.XVAL, and branch right otherwise. Suppose P denotes the child we are examining. If N and P agree on their XVAL and YVAL fields, just overwrite node P, and we are done; else branch left if N.YVAL $<$ P.YVAL, and branch right otherwise. Repeat this procedure, branching on XVALs when we are at even levels in the tree, and on YVALs when we are at odd levels in the tree. This algorithm is easily formalized.

Figure 4.3 shows a grid. The origin $(0, 0)$ is at the bottom-left corner of the grid. Each cell in the grid is of size 8, and hence the entire map is a grid of size (64×64). Suppose we wish to construct a 2-d tree by reading in the following

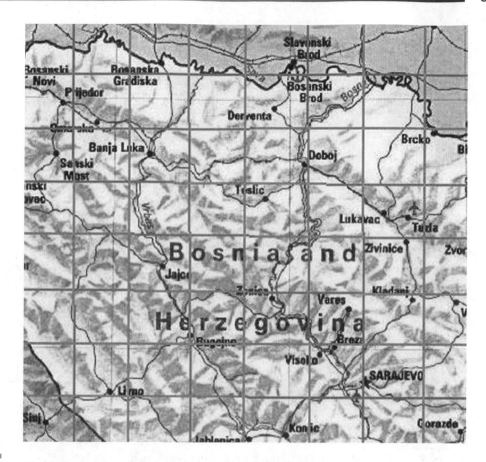

F I G U R E

4.3   Gridded map (see also color plate Figure 4.3)

nodes. In these cases, assume that the INFO field only contains the name of the place involved.

City	(XVAL, YVAL)
Banja Luka	(19, 45)
Derventa	(40, 50)
Teslic	(38, 38)
Tuzla	(54, 40)
Sinj	(4, 4)

Let us suppose that we read these points in one at a time in the order listed above. The 2-d tree is initially empty. Figure 4.4 shows the sequence of five

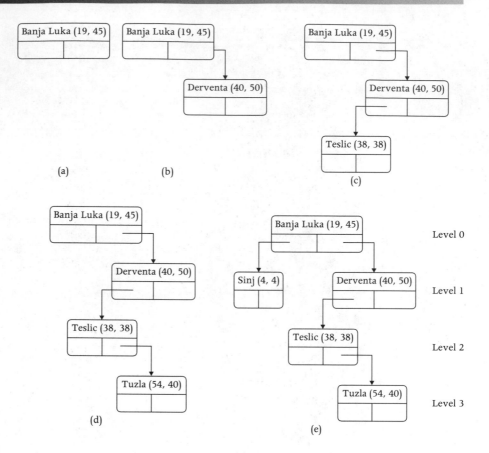

FIGURE
4.4

2-d trees representing part of the Bosnia map

trees resulting after each insertion. These trees are constructed as follows:

1. The insertion of Banja Luka results in a tree containing just one node, with INFO = Banja Luka, XVAL = 19, and YVAL = 45. The node labeled "Banja Luka" implicitly represents a region—the entire region of the map. In general, each node N represents a region $Reg(N)$. The node N's XVAL and YVAL fields determine a point in $Reg(N)$. This point, (N.XVAL, N.YVAL), splits $Reg(N)$ into two by either drawing a vertical line through the point within the region (if the node is at an even level) or by drawing a horizontal line through the point within the region (if the node is at an odd level).

2. When inserting Derventa, we must compare the XVAL fields of Derventa and Banja Luka. We branch right because Derventa's x-coordinate is 40,

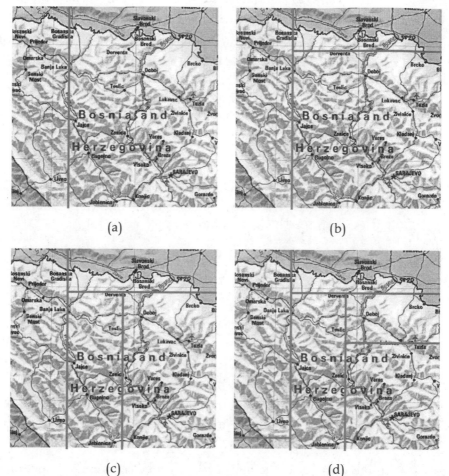

FIGURE

4.5

Splitting in the case of 2-d trees: splitting of region (a) by Banja Luka, (b) by Derventa, (c) by Teslic, and (d) by Tuzla and Sinj (see also color plate Figure 4.5)

which is larger than that of Banja Luka (19). This leads to the tree shown in Figure 4.4(b). Banja Luka splits the region it represents into two pieces by a vertical line—all points on the right have an x-coordinate greater than or equal to 19, while all points on the left of the line have an x-coordinate strictly less than 19. The region implicitly represented by Derventa is the one on the right of the vertical line in Figure 4.5(a). (In Figure 4.4, we represent points as pairs (x, y) and write these points next to a string representing the name of the point.)

3. When inserting Teslic, we first compare the XVAL fields of Teslic and Banja Luka. Teslic's XVAL field is 38, while Banja Luka's is 19, so we branch right. We then compare Teslic's YVAL field with Derventa's YVAL field. Teslic's YVAL field is 38, which is smaller than Derventa's YVAL field (50), so we must branch left, yielding the tree shown in Figure 4.4(c). Derventa splits the region it represents into two pieces by drawing a horizontal line. The region above the horizontal line represents all points whose x-coordinate is greater than or equal to 19 and whose y-coordinate is greater than or equal to 50. The region below the horizontal line represents all points whose x-coordinate is greater than or equal to 19 and whose y-coordinate is strictly less than 50. This split is shown in Figure 4.5(b).

4. When inserting Tuzla, we first compare the XVAL fields of Tuzla and Banja Luka. Tuzla's XVAL field is 54, while Banja Luka's is 19, so we branch right. We then compare Tuzla's YVAL field with Derventa's YVAL field. Tuzla's YVAL field is 40, which is smaller than Derventa's XVAL field (50), so we must branch left. We then compare Tuzla's XVAL field with Teslic's XVAL field. Tuzla's XVAL field is 54, which is larger than Teslic's XVAL field (38), so we must branch right. The result is shown in Figure 4.4(d). The region represented by Tuzla is shown in Figure 4.5(c).

5. Finally, when inserting the city Sinj, we must compare the XVAL fields of Sinj and Banja Luka. We branch left because Sinj's x-coordinate is smaller than that of Banja Luka. The result is shown in Figures 4.4(e) and 4.5(d).

In the worst case, the height of a 2-d tree containing k nodes in it is $(k - 1)$, and hence, in the worst case, searching the tree for a given node may take $O(k)$ time.

4.2.3   Deletion in 2-d Trees

The most complex part of dealing with a 2-d tree is deletion of points from the tree. Suppose T is a 2-d tree, and (x, y) refers to a point that we wish to delete from the tree. The first step in deletion is to search for the node N in T that has $N.\text{XVAL}=x$ and $N.\text{YVAL}=y$. If N is a leaf node, then the deletion of N is easy—we merely set the appropriate field (LLINK or RLINK) of N's parent to NIL and return N to available storage. However, the situation is somewhat more complex if N is an interior node. In this case, either the subtree rooted at N.LLINK (which we will denote by T_ℓ) or the subtree rooted at N.RLINK (which we will denote by T_r) is nonempty. What we would like to do is to find a node R from either T_ℓ or T_r that can replace node N and that can subsequently be deleted (recursively) from the subtree it resides in (either T_ℓ or T_r). Thus, the basic outline of our deletion algorithm, as applied to interior nodes N, consists of three steps:

Step 1: Find a candidate replacement node R that occurs in T_i for $i \in \{\ell, r\}$.

Step 2: Replace all of N's nonlink fields by those of R.

Step 3: Recursively delete R from T_i.

The above recursion is guaranteed to terminate because T_i for $i \in \{\ell, r\}$ has strictly smaller height than the original tree T from which we are deleting the node.

The critical step in the above algorithm is to find a suitable "candidate replacement node." The desired replacement node R must bear the same spatial relation to all nodes P in both T_ℓ and T_r that N bore to P; that is, if P is to the southwest of N, then P must be to the southwest of R, if P is to the northwest of N, then P must be to the northwest of R, and so on. This means that the desired replacement node R must satisfy the following properties:

1. Every node M in T_ℓ is such that M.XVAL $<$ R.XVAL if *level*(N) is even, and M.YVAL $<$ R.YVAL if *level*(N) is odd.

2. Every node M in T_r is such that M.XVAL $\geq$ R.XVAL if *level*(N) is even, and M.YVAL $\geq$ R.YVAL if *level*(N) is odd.

If T_r is not empty, and *level*(N) is even, then any node in T_r that has the *smallest* possible XVAL field in T_r is a candidate replacement node. For example, in Figure 4.4(e), if we take N to be the node containing Banja Luka, then the candidate replacement node from the right subtree is the node associated with Teslic, as this node has the smallest x coordinate from all nodes in Banja Luka's right subtree.

Likewise, if T_r is not empty, and *level*(N) is odd, then any node in T_r that has the *smallest* possible YVAL field in T_r is a candidate replacement node.

In general, finding a replacement node from the left subtree is possible only under some conditions. If *level*(N) is even, an appropriate replacement node in T_ℓ is any node whose XVAL field is the *largest* possible XVAL value in T_ℓ. Similarly, if *level*(N) is odd, then we may use any node in T_ℓ that has that maximal possible YVAL field as a replacement node. The problem with this approach is that there may be more than one node in T_ℓ that has such a maximal XVAL (or YVAL) field, and in this case, the second condition in the definition of 2-d trees would be violated by the three-step procedure outlined above. Thus, in general, if N is an interior node, and we wish to delete N from T, we prefer to find a replacement from the right subtree, since finding a candidate replacement from the left subtree may be infeasible.

This raises the question of what to do if node N has an empty right subtree (i.e., N.RLINK = NIL). In this case, we can choose as a replacement node, a node R from T_ℓ that has the smallest x-value in T_ℓ (if $level(N)$ is even) or the smallest y-value in T_ℓ (if $level(N)$ is odd). We then modify the three-step algorithm above a little bit by slightly changing its second step:

Step 2 (modified): Replace all of N's nonlink fields by those of R. Set N.RLINK = N.LLINK, and set N.LLINK = NIL.

4.2.4 Range Queries in 2-d Trees

A *range query* with respect to a 2-d tree T is a query that specifies a point (x_c, y_c) and a distance r. The *answer* to such a query is the set of all points (x, y) in the tree T such that (x, y) lies within distance r of (x_c, y_c). In other words, a range query defines a circle of radius r centered at location (x_c, y_c), and expects to find all points in the 2-d tree that lie within the circle.

When processing a range query, it is helpful to recall that each node N in a 2-d tree implicitly represents a region R_N. This is useful because if the circle specified in a query has no intersection with R_N, then there is no point searching the subtree rooted at node N. Let's first see what these regions might look like in the case of the five points shown in Figure 4.5(d).

1. The node labeled "Banja Luka" represents the region consisting of all points (x, y) for real numbers (x, y).

2. The node labeled "Derventa" represents the region consisting of all points (x, y) such that $x \geq 19$; that is, it can be captured by the expression $\{(x, y) \mid x \geq 19\}$.

3. The node labeled "Teslic" represents all points (x, y) such that $x \geq 19$ and $y < 50$; that is, it can be captured by the expression $\{(x, y) \mid x \geq 19 \ \& \ y < 50\}$.

4. The node labeled "Tuzla" represents all points (x, y) such that $x \geq 38$ and $y < 50$; that is, it can be captured by the expression $\{(x, y) \mid x \geq 38 \ \& \ y < 50\}$.

5. Finally, the node labeled "Sinj" represents all points (x, y) such that $x < 19$.

In general, each node N has at most four associated constraints that jointly define the region represented by that node:

1. XLB: This constraint represents the lower bound on x and has the form $x \geq c_1$.

2. XUB: This constraint represents the upper bound on x and has the form $x < c_2$.

3. YLB: This constraint represents the lower bound on y and has the form $y \geq c_3$.

4. YUB: This constraint represents the upper bound on y and has the form $y < c_4$.

It is possible to expand the definition of the data type `nodetype` to `newnodetype` by including these fields explicitly in the node definition:

```
newnodetype = record
    INFO: infotype;
    XVAL,YVAL: real;
    XLB, XUB, YLB, YUB: real ∪ {+∞, −∞};
    LLINK,RLINK: ↑newnodetype
end
```

When inserting nodes, all that needs to be done is the following:

1. The root of the tree has XLB and YLB set to $-\infty$, and XUB and YUB set to $+\infty$.

2. If node N has node P as its parent and *level*(P) is even, then

$$N.\text{XLB} = P.\text{XLB} \quad \text{if } N = P.\text{LLINK}$$
$$N.\text{XLB} = P.\text{XVAL} \quad \text{if } N = P.\text{RLINK}$$
$$N.\text{XUB} = P.\text{XVAL} \quad \text{if } N = P.\text{LLINK}$$
$$N.\text{XUB} = P.\text{XUB} \quad \text{if } N = P.\text{RLINK}$$
$$N.\text{YLB} = P.\text{YLB}$$
$$N.\text{YUB} = P.\text{YUB}$$

3. If node N has node P as its parent and *level*(P) is odd, then

N.YLB = P.YLB if N = P.LLINK

N.YLB = P.YVAL if N = P.RLINK

N.YUB = P.YVAL if N = P.LLINK

N.YUB = P.YUB if N = P.RLINK

N.XLB = P.XLB

N.XUB = P.XUB

Let's now consider the range query on our Bosnia map shown in Figure 4.6. Here, we are given a circle with center (35, 46) and radius 9.5. It is easy to verify that the two points that should be returned as the answer are Teslic and Derventa.

This query is processed as follows. The region represented by the root of our 2-d tree does intersect the circle, so we check whether Banja Luka is in the circle. It is not, hence we do not print it out. We then consider the two children of Banja Luka. The left child of Banja Luka represents all points (x, y) with $x < 19$; since this region has no intersection with our circle, we do not consider this subtree. On the other hand, the right child of Banja Luka represents all points (x, y) with $x \geq 19$, which certainly intersects our circle. Hence, we check if the right child (i.e., Derventa) is in the circle. It is, and so we return this node. We then examine the child of Derventa. The region represented by it is the set of all points (x, y) such that $x \geq 19$ and $y < 50$. This region intersects our circle, so we must check if the child is in the circle. It is, so we return this child (i.e., Teslic). We then check the child of Teslic (i.e., Tuzla). The region represented by it is the set of all points (x, y) such that $x \geq 38$ and $y < 50$, and this region certainly intersects our circle. Thus, we must check if Tuzla is in the circle. It is not, and we may stop at this point. It is important to note that the entire left subtree of Banja Luka was pruned away at the very beginning of this search. Had there been lots of nodes in the 2-d tree to the left of the vertical line through Banja Luka, none of these nodes would have ever been examined, leading to a substantial saving in time.

4.2.5 k-d Trees for $k \geq 2$

A 2-d tree is used to represent points in a two-dimensional space. A k-d tree, for $k \geq 2$, is used to represent points in a k-dimensional space. For example, a 3-d tree represents points of the form (x, y, z), a 4-d tree might represent points

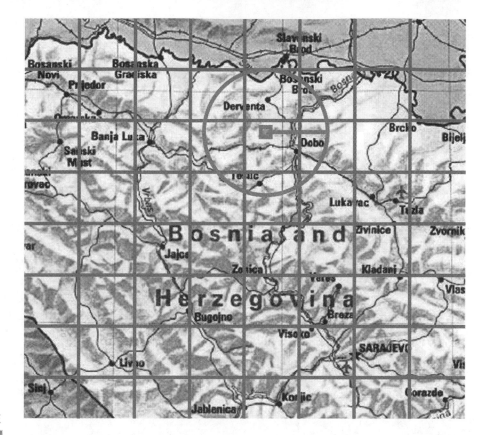

4.6

A simple range query with center (35, 46) and radius 9.5 (see also color plate Figure 4.6)

of the form (x, y, z, t), and so on. In general, a point in a k-dimensional space is of the form $(x_1, \ldots, x_k)$, where x_i is a real number.

In order to represent nodes of k-d trees, we will assume that the fields XVAL and YVAL used for 2-d trees are eliminated, and instead `nodetype` and/or `newnodetype` have a new field VAL that is an array of length k containing real numbers.

A tree T having this node structure is a k-d tree iff, for each node N in tree T, the following is the case:

1. Suppose $level(N) \bmod k = i$.

2. For each node M in N's left subtree, $M.\text{VAL}[i] < N.\text{VAL}[i]$.

3. For each node P in N's right subtree, $P.\text{VAL}[i] \geq N.\text{VAL}[i]$.

All algorithms for 2-d trees generalize in the obvious way to k-d trees for $k \geq 2$. Note that when $k = 1$, we get a standard binary search tree.

4.3 Point Quadtrees

The point quadtree, like the 2-d tree, is used to represent point data in two-dimensional spaces. Unlike the 2-d tree, point quadtrees always split regions into four parts. In a 2-d tree, node N splits a region into two by drawing one line through the point $(N.\text{XVAL}, N.\text{YVAL})$. This line may be either horizontal (if $level(N)$ is odd) or vertical (if $level(N)$ is even). In the case of a point quadtree, node N splits the region it represents by drawing both a horizontal and a vertical line through the point $(N.\text{XVAL}, N.\text{YVAL})$. These four parts are called the NW (northwest), SW (southwest), NE (northeast), and SE (southeast) quadrants determined by node N, and each of these quadrants corresponds to a child of node N. Thus, quadtree nodes may have up to four children each. Before proceeding any further, we provide a simple definition of the node structure of a point quadtree node:

```
qtnodetype = record
    INFO: infotype;
    XVAL: real;
    YVAL: real;
    NW,SW,NE,SE: ↑qtnodetype
end
```

4.3.1 Insertion/Search in Point Quadtrees

Let's now see informally how a point quadtree represents the set of five points (Banja Luka, Derventa, Teslic, Tuzla, and Sinj) that we had represented earlier with 2-d trees (see Figures 4.4 and 4.5). Figure 4.7 shows how the insertion of each point into the quadtree splits the region, while Figure 4.8 shows how the quadtree itself is constructed. Let's go over this process now.

1. Initially, the quadtree is empty, and the insertion of Banja Luka leads to the creation of a root node, labeled with the pair $(19, 45)$.

2. The insertion of Derventa causes the region represented by Banja Luka to be split into four parts by drawing a horizontal and vertical line through

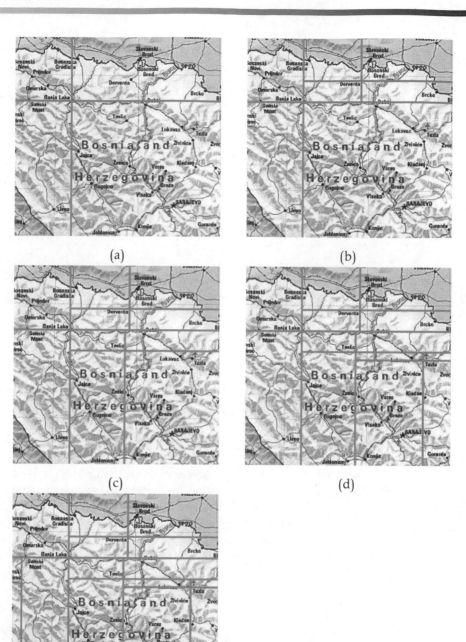

(a)

(b)

(c)

(d)

(e)

Splitting in the case of point quadtrees: splitting of region (a) by Banja Luka, (b) by Derventa, (c) by Teslic, (d) by Tuzla, and (e) by Sinj (see also color plate Figure 4.7)

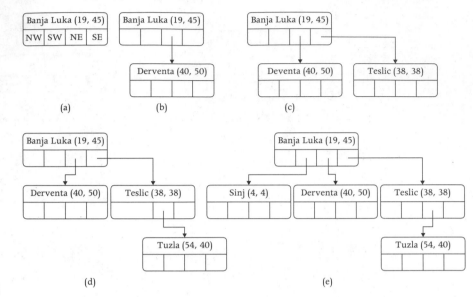

F I G U R E

4.8   The point quadtree

$(19, 45)$. Derventa, located at $(40, 50)$, falls in the NE quadrant (resulting from the split), leading to Banja Luka having Derventa as its NE child.

3. The insertion of Teslic is processed as follows. Teslic lies to the southeast of Banja Luka (with respect to the split alluded to above). Since that region currently has no points, we merely make Teslic the SE child of Banja Luka.

4. The insertion of Tuzla is more complicated. Here, we observe that Tuzla lies in the SE quadrant with respect to the split created by Banja Luka. Thus, we take the SE branch from Banja Luka. Subsequently, the SE quadrant (with respect to Banja Luka) is split by drawing a horizontal and a vertical line through the point Teslic. Of the four subquadrants that result, Tuzla is in the SE, and hence, Tuzla becomes the node pointed to by the SE link of Teslic.

5. Finally, the insertion of Sinj is straightforward because it lies in the SW quadrant associated with Banja Luka. Because that pointer is currently NIL, we just set it to a node containing the relevant information about Sinj.

Thus, in general, the height of a point quadtree containing n nodes can, in the worst case, be $(n - 1)$, which means that the insertion and search time can be linear in the number of nodes.

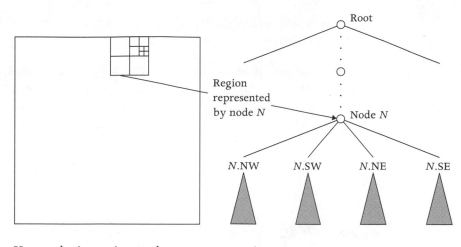

How nodes in a point quadtree represent regions

4.3.2 Deletion in Point Quadtrees

When deleting a node N from a point quadtree having root T, we need to try, as we did in the case of deletion in 2-d trees, to find an appropriate replacement node for nonleaf nodes. In the case of leaf nodes, of course, deletion is completely trivial: we just set the appropriate link field of node N's parent to NIL and return the node to available storage.

Deletion in point quadtrees is very complex, and Figure 4.9 may be used to illustrate why. First and foremost, each node in a point quadtree represents a region, and this region is defined somewhat differently than in the case of a 2-d tree. As in the case of 2-d trees, however, it suffices to associate four constraints of the form $x \geq c_1$, $x < c_2$, $y \geq c_3$, and $y < c_4$ for constants $c_1, \ldots, c_4$. Thus, as in the case of 2-d trees, where we expanded `nodetype` to `newnodetype`, we may expand the node structure `qtnodetype` to a new node structure `newqtnodetype` having the same types of fields (XLB, YLB, XUB, YUB) that we had seen earlier.

```
newqtnodetype = record
   INFO: infotype;
   XVAL,YVAL: real;
   XLB,YLB,XUB,YUB: real ∪{−∞,+∞};
   NW,SW,NE,SE: ↑newqtnodetype
end
```

When inserting a node N into the tree T, we need to ensure the following:

1. If N is the root of tree T, then $N.\text{XLB} = -\infty$, $N.\text{YLB} = -\infty$, $N.\text{XUB} = +\infty$, and $N.\text{YUB} = +\infty$.

2. If P is the parent of N, then the following table describes what N's XLB, YLB, XUB, and YUB fields should be, depending upon whether N is the NW, SW, NE, or SE child of P. We use the notation $w = (P.\text{XUB} - P.\text{XLB})$ and $h = (P.\text{YUB} - Y.\text{YLB})$.

Case	$N.\text{XLB}$	$N.\text{XUB}$	$N.\text{YLB}$	$N.\text{YUB}$
$N = P.\text{NW}$	$P.\text{XLB}$	$P.\text{XLB} + w \times 0.5$	$P.\text{YLB} + h \times 0.5$	$P.\text{YUB}$
$N = P.\text{SW}$	$P.\text{XLB}$	$P.\text{XLB} + w \times 0.5$	$P.\text{YLB}$	$P.\text{YLB} + h \times 0.5$
$N = P.\text{NE}$	$P.\text{XLB} + w \times 0.5$	$P.\text{XUB}$	$P.\text{YLB} + h \times 0.5$	$P.\text{YUB}$
$N = P.\text{SE}$	$P.\text{XLB} + w \times 0.5$	$P.\text{XUB}$	$P.\text{YLB}$	$P.\text{YLB} + h \times 0.5$

In order to successfully apply the deletion technique to a point quadtree when deleting an interior node N, we must find a replacement node R in one of the subtrees of N (i.e., in one of $N.\text{NW}$, $N.\text{SW}$, $N.\text{NE}$, or $N.\text{SE}$) such that every other node R_1 in $N.\text{NW}$ is to the northwest of R, every other node R_2 in $N.\text{SW}$ is to the southwest of R, every other node R_3 in $N.\text{NE}$ is to the northeast of R, and every other node R_4 in $N.\text{SE}$ is to the southeast of R.

Consider now the quadtree of Figures 4.8 and 4.9. Suppose we wish to delete Banja Luka from this quadtree. In this case, one such replacement node can, in fact, be found—Teslic. None of the other nodes satisfies the condition in the preceding paragraph.

However, in general, it may not always be possible to find such a replacement node. For example, consider the situation shown in Figure 4.10, where we have added "Bad Point" into the region. If such a point were present in our quadtree, then the deletion would be impossible because "Bad Point" would rule out Teslic's candidacy, and it would not be a viable candidate replacement node itself.

Thus, in the worst case, deletion of an interior node N may require reinsertion of some nodes in the subtrees pointed to by N.NE, N.SE, N.NW, and N.SW. Due to space restrictions, we will not go into the complex (but often not very useful) optimizations that can be made when deleting nodes from point quadtrees. Samet [180] provides an excellent overview that shows that in many cases, full reinsertion can be avoided. Instead, in Section 4.4, we will study another kind of quadtree, called an *MX-quadtree*, in which deletions are much easier to accomplish.

4.3.3 Range Queries in Point Quadtrees

Range queries in point quadtrees are treated in almost exactly the same way as they are treated in 2-d trees. Each node in a point quadtree represents a region, and the approach toward computing a range query avoids searching subtrees rooted at nodes whose associated region has no intersection with the circle defined by the range query. Roughly speaking, if we are searching a point quadtree rooted at T for all points in a circle C centered at location (x_c, y_c) and having radius r, the algorithm works as follows:

Algorithm 4.1
```
proc RangeQueryPointQuadtree(T:newqtnodetype, C:circle);
```

1. If region(T) ∩ C = Ø then Halt

2. else

   (a) If (T.XVAL,T.YVAL) ∈ C then print (T.XVAL,T.YVAL);
   (b) RangeQueryPointQuadtree(T.NW,C);
   (c) RangeQueryPointQuadtree(T.SW,C);
   (d) RangeQueryPointQuadtree(T.NE,C);
   (e) RangeQueryPointQuadtree(T.SE,C);

```
end proc
```

4.4 The MX-Quadtree

In the case of both 2-d trees and point quadtrees, the "shape" of the tree depends upon the order in which objects are inserted into the tree. In particular, the order affects the height of the tree, which, in turn, may affect the complexity of search and insertion operations. Also, for both 2-d trees and point quadtrees, each node N represents a region and splits the region into two (for 2-d trees) or four (for point quadtrees) subregions. The split may be uneven, depending upon exactly where the point (N.XVAL,N.YVAL) is located inside the region represented by node N.

In contrast, the aim behind MX-quadtrees was to ensure that the shape (and height) of the tree was *independent* of the number of nodes present in the tree, as well as the order of insertion of these nodes. Additionally, the MX-quadtree aimed at providing efficient deletion and search algorithms.

F I G U R E

4.10

Deletion in point quadtrees: a case where replacement nodes do not exist (see also color plate Figure 4.10)

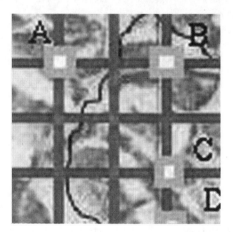

F I G U R E

4.11

A simple MX-quadtree grid (see also color plate Figure 4.11)

In short, the MX-quadtree works as follows: First, we assume that the map being represented is split up into a grid of size $(2^k \times 2^k)$ for some k. The application developer is free to choose k to reflect the desired granularity, but once k is chosen, it must be kept fixed. Figure 4.11 shows a small portion of the Bosnia map we have used earlier in this chapter, with four points marked on it. This grid is a $(2^2 \times 2^2)$ grid (i.e., $k = 2$).

MX-quadtrees have exactly the same node structure as point quadtrees; that is, they have the type `newqtnodetype`. There is one difference though—the root of an MX-quadtree represents the region specified by XLB = 0, XUB = 2^k, YLB = 0, YUB = 2^k. Furthermore, when a region is split, it is split down the middle. Thus, if N is a node, then the regions represented by the four children of N are described by the following table. In this table, w denotes the width of the region represented by N and is given by $w = N.\text{XUB} - N.\text{XLB}$. As all regions represented by MX-quadtree nodes are square regions, this width, w, is also equal to $N.\text{YUB} - N.\text{YLB}$.

Child	XLB	XUB	YLB	YUB
NW	$N.\text{XLB}$	$N.\text{XLB} + \frac{w}{2}$	$N.\text{YLB} + \frac{w}{2}$	$N.\text{YLB} + w$
SW	$N.\text{XLB}$	$N.\text{XLB} + \frac{w}{2}$	$N.\text{YLB}$	$N.\text{YLB} + \frac{w}{2}$
NE	$N.\text{XLB} + \frac{w}{2}$	$N.\text{XLB} + w$	$N.\text{YLB} + \frac{w}{2}$	$N.\text{YLB} + w$
SE	$N.\text{XLB} + \frac{w}{2}$	$N.\text{XLB} + w$	$N.\text{YLB}$	$N.\text{YLB} + \frac{w}{2}$

4.4.1 Insertion/Search in MX-Quadtrees

Let us now examine how we might insert points into an MX-quadtree. Each point (x, y) in an MX-quadtree represents the 1×1 region whose lower-left corner is (x, y). A point is inserted at the node representing the 1×1 region corresponding to that point. Suppose now that we wish to insert the points A, B, C, and D shown in Figure 4.12. We proceed as follows:

1. The insertion of point A with coordinates $(1, 3)$ causes the following: The root node represents the entire region, and A lies in its NW quadrant. Thus, the root's NW child corresponds to the 2×2 region whose lower-left corner is the point $(0, 2)$. The point A is in the NE subquadrant of this region. Figure 4.12(a) shows the MX-quadtree resulting after the insertion of A; Figure 4.13(a) shows the split of the regions involved. Note that point A is inserted at level 2 in the tree, and this level is identical to k. In general, points will always be inserted at level k in the MX-quadtree.

2. The insertion of point B with coordinates $(3,3)$ causes a branch to the NE quadrant as B. Thus, the root's NE child corresponds to the 2×2 region whose lower-left corner is the point $(2, 2)$. The point B is in the NE subquadrant of this region. Figures 4.12(b) and 4.13(b) show the resulting situation.

3. The insertion of point C with coordinates $(3,1)$ proceeds as follows: C is in the SE quadrant of the whole region. This causes us to create a new node

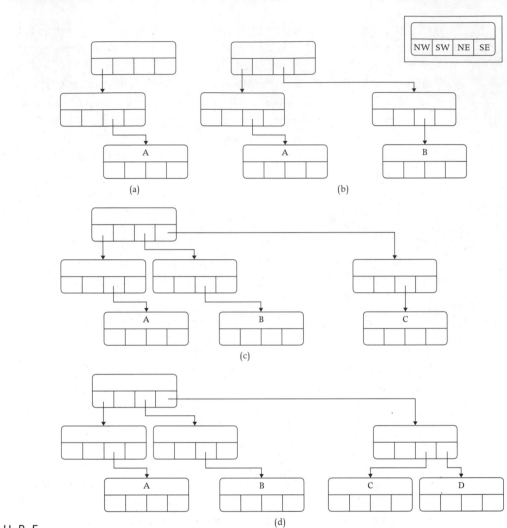

MX-quadtree for points A, B, C, and D

that is the SE child of the root. C is in the NE subquadrant of this node.
Figures 4.12(c) and 4.13(c) show the resulting situation.

4. Finally, Figures 4.12(d) and 4.13(d) show the result of inserting point D.

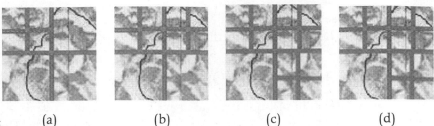

FIGURE

4.13

(a) (b) (c) (d)

Splitting of region by MX-quadtree (a) after insertion of A, (b) after insertion of B, (c) after insertion of C, and (d) after insertion of D (see also color plate Figure 4.13)

4.4.2 Deletion in MX-Quadtrees

Deletion in an MX-quadtree is a fairly simple operation because all points are represented at the leaf level. Notice that if N is an interior (i.e., nonleaf) node in an MX-quadtree whose root is pointed to by T, then the region implicitly represented by node N contains at least one point that is explicitly contained in the tree. If we wish to delete a point (x, y) from tree T, we try to preserve this property as follows. First, we set the appropriate link of N's parent to NIL. In other words, if M is N's parent, and if M.DIR points to N, then we set M.DIR = NIL and return N to available storage. We now check if the four link fields of M are all NIL. If so, we examine M's parent (let us call it P for now). As M is P's child, we find a link field DIR1 such that P.DIR1 = M. We then set P.DIR1 = NIL and (as before) check to see if P's four link fields are all NIL. If so, we continue this process. The entire process requires, at most, that we traverse the tree once from top to bottom (to find the node being deleted) and once more as we go up the tree, "collapsing" nodes. Thus, the entire process takes time $O(k)$.

Let us see how this process works when we consider the MX-quadtree in Figure 4.12(d). Suppose we wish to delete the node D. Deleting node D is no problem because we find it and set its parent's SE link field (the one pointing to D) to NIL. To determine if D's parent should be collapsed, we then check to see all four of its link fields are NIL. They are not, since C and D have the same common parent.

On the other hand, consider the deletion of the node A from the MX-quadtree in Figure 4.12(d). When we set the NE field of A's parent to NIL, we find that A's parent ends up with four empty link fields. Thus, the parent of A must be *collapsed*. When this happens, we examine A's parent's parent (which happens to be the root) and set the NW link of the root to NIL. We then check to see if the root has all its four link fields equal to NIL. This is not the case, and hence, since no further collapsing is possible, we are done.

4.4.3 Range Queries in MX-Quadtrees

Range queries in MX-quadtrees are handled in exactly the same way as in point quadtrees. There are only two differences between the two: The first is that *content* of the XLB, XUB, YLB, and YUB fields is different. The second difference is that, because points are stored at the leaf level, checking to see if a point is in the circle defined by the range query needs to be performed only at the leaf level.

4.4.4 PR-Quadtrees

The PR-quadtree is a variant of the MX-quadtree. You will notice that in an MX-quadtree all points are stored at leaves of the tree. Therefore, when considering an MX-quadtree representing a $(2^k \times 2^k)$ region, searching and inserting is an $O(k)$ process.

Recall that each node, N, in an MX-quadtree represents a region, $Reg(N)$. By expanding the data structure of a node to include a point in it, we can modify the splitting rule for MX-quadtrees by requiring that a node N be split iff $Reg(N)$ contains two or more points in it. If N contains one point, then that point is stored in node N itself instead of at a leaf node. This prevents us from expanding node N in such cases, and therefore reduces both insertion time and search time (as well as time required for range query execution).

4.5 R-Trees

In this section, we will introduce a new type of data structure, called an *R-tree*, that may be used to store *rectangular regions* of an image or a map, such as those shown in Figure 4.1(b). R-trees are particularly useful in storing very large amounts of data on disk. Because disk accesses are often painfully slow, R-trees provide a convenient way of minimizing the number of disk accesses made.

Each R-tree has an associated *order*, which is an integer K. Each nonleaf R-tree node contains a set of at most K rectangles and at least $\lceil K/2 \rceil$ rectangles (with the possible exception of the root). Intuitively, this says that each nonleaf node in the R-tree, with the exception of the root, must be at least half

4.14   Logical grouping of rectangles in an R-tree (see also color plate Figure 4.14)

full. This feature makes R-trees appropriate for disk-based retrieval because each disk access brings back a page containing several (i.e., at least $K/2$) rectangles. Additionally, by storing many rectangles per page, the height of the R-tree used to store a collection of rectangles is usually quite small (in comparison to extensions of quadtrees and k-d trees that handle rectangle data), thus diminishing the number of disk accesses required.

A rectangle is either a "real" rectangle (such as those shown in Figure 4.1(b)) or a *group rectangle* (such as those shown in Figure 4.14). Leaf nodes contain one "real" rectangle per node, while nonleaf nodes contain group rectangles.

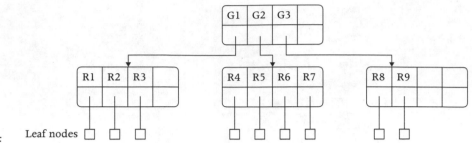

R-tree corresponding to the rectangles of Figure 4.14

Figure 4.14 shows one way of grouping together the rectangles of Figure 4.1(b) as follows:

Group	Rectangles
G1	R1, R2, R3
G2	R4, R5, R6, R7
G3	R8, R9

Figure 4.15 shows an R-tree of order 4 associated with the rectangles of Figure 4.14.

The structure of an R-tree node is defined as follows:

```
rtnodetype = record
    Rec₁, ... , Recₖ:  rectangle;
    P₁, ... , Pₖ:  ↑rtnodetype
end
```

We will not go into specific details about the data type `rectangle` above. Rectangles may be represented in one of any number of ways, and the precise representation is not important.

4.5.1   Insertion/Search in an R-Tree

When inserting a new rectangle (e.g., the rectangle R10 of Figure 4.16) into an R-tree, we proceed as follows:

1. We check to see which of the rectangles associated with the root needs to be expanded the least (in terms of area) in order to accommodate the rectangle being inserted. For example, if we are trying to insert the rectangle R10

shown in Figure 4.16 into the R-tree of Figure 4.15, then the easiest way of accomplishing this insertion would be by expanding group G1 because expanding any other group would cause a significant increase in the area covered by that group.

2. Thus, following the link associated with G1 (in the root, see Figure 4.15), we would insert R10 into the one available slot.

3. Now consider the insertion of the node R11. The group whose area would have to be minimally expanded in this case is G2. However, the G2 child of the root is full. Thus, there are several options, two of which are shown in Figure 4.17.

4. Of the two options shown in Figure 4.17, we prefer the option in Figure 4.17(b) because the total area of the group rectangles is smallest in this case.

5. Figure 4.18 shows an incorrect way of handling the insertion of rectangle R11. This approach is infeasible because the node representing the group containing the solitary rectangle R11 would be underfull (i.e., it would contain only one rectangle).

4.5.2   Deletion in R-Trees

In contrast, the deletion of objects from R-trees may cause a node in the R-tree to "underflow." Recall that an R-tree of order K must contain at least $\lceil K/2 \rceil$ rectangles (real or group) in it. When we delete a rectangle from an R-tree, we must ensure that that node is not underfull. For example, consider the R-tree of Figure 4.15. Suppose we wish to delete the rectangle R9. The node containing rectangle R9 would have only one node in it if we naively eliminated R9 from there, and hence that node would reflect an underflow condition. In this case, we must create a new logical grouping. One possibility is to reallocate the groups as follows:

Group	Rectangles
G1	R1, R2, R3
G2	R4, R6, R7
G3	R5, R8

In this case, the new R-tree is shown in Figure 4.19.

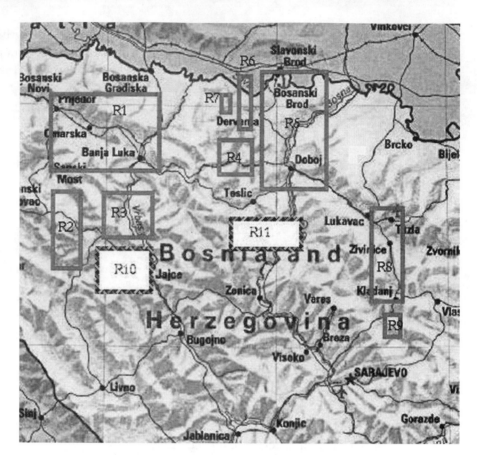

F I G U R E

4.16   Insertion of two rectangles (see also color plate Figure 4.16)

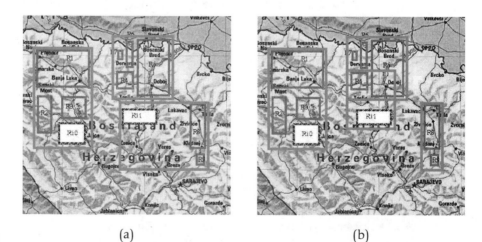

(a)   (b)

F I G U R E

4.17   Two ways of handling the insertion of rectangle R11 (see also color plate
             Figure 4.17)

F I G U R E

4.18

An incorrect way of handling the insertion of rectangle R11 (see also color plate Figure 4.18)

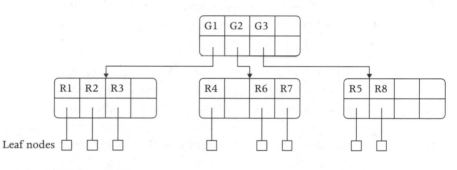

F I G U R E

4.19

Result of deletion of R9

4.6   Comparison of Different Data Structures

In this chapter, we have presented four types of data structures: k-d trees, point quadtrees, MX-quadtrees, and R-trees. Each of these has advantages and disadvantages:

- Point quadtrees are very easy to implement. However, in general, a point quadtree containing k nodes may have height k, which causes the complexity of both insertion and search in point quadtrees to be $O(k)$. In addition, each comparison requires comparisons on two coordinates, not just one. Deletion in point quadtrees is difficult because finding a candidate replacement node for the node being deleted is often difficult. Finally, range queries in point quadtrees take time $O(2\sqrt{n})$, where n is the number of records in the tree.

- k-d trees are very easy to implement. However, in general, a k-d tree containing k nodes may have height k, which causes the complexity of both insertion and search in k-d trees to be high. However, in practice, path lengths (from root to leaf) in k-d trees tend to be longer than those in point quadtrees because these trees are binary trees (as opposed to potentially having four children, as in the case of point quadtrees). In contrast to point quadtrees, the worst-case complexity of range searching in k-d trees is $O(k \times n^{1-\frac{1}{k}})$. When $k = 2$, this boils down to $O(2\sqrt{n})$, as for point quadtrees.

- In contrast, MX-quadtrees have a guaranteed height of at most $O(n)$, where the region being represented is composed of $2^n \times 2^n$ cells. In other words, insertion, deletion, and search in MX-quadtrees take time proportional to $O(n)$. Range search in MX-quadtrees is very efficient— $O(N + 2^h)$, where N is the number of points in the answer to the query and h is the height of the tree.

- The same applies to R-trees. However, because R-trees have a large number of rectangles potentially stored in each node, they are appropriate for disk accesses by reducing the height of the tree, thus leading to fewer disk accesses. This explains the wide popularity of R-trees and their scalability. However, by bucketing nodes in quadtrees, the same effect may be achieved.

- One disadvantage of R-trees is that the bounding rectangles associated with different nodes may overlap. Thus, when searching an R-tree, instead of following one path (as in the case of all quadtrees), we might follow multiple paths down the tree. This means that in some cases more disk accesses might be made by the R-tree than by quadtrees that bucket data. This distinction grows even more acute when range searches and nearest neighbor searches are considered.

In general, R-trees have been preferred over k-d trees and point quadtrees for multimedia applications because multimedia applications require massive amounts of storage, necessitating disk accesses. However, these advantages are easily realizable in the quadtree context as well by bucketing items together. When the indexes are small, using MX-quadtrees is a good idea. Samet [180] provides an excellent survey of different spatial data structures.

4.7   Selected Commercial Systems

There are now numerous products on the market that deal with techniques for the retrieval and storage of geographic data. Though many of the data structures presented in this chapter were originally conceived because of needs in the geographic information systems (GIS) community, they have subsequently led to substantial applications in the area of image indexing. Here we briefly present descriptions of commercially available spatial data options.

Informix's datablade architecture provides several datablades that handle spatial and geographic data. For example, the MapInfo Geocoding datablade allows users to geocode data. Geocoding basically involves the assignment of latitudinal and longitudinal elements to records that have spatial content. In addition, the Spatial datablade module offered by Informix presents scalable implementations of the R-tree data structure described in this chapter. For instance, it is stated that CitySearch (*http://www.citysearch.com*) uses this capability to allow users searching for a geographical location (e.g., for a restaurant) to zero in on it.

Likewise, the Oracle Universal Server provides a spatial data option that allows for the efficient storage, retrieval, and manipulation of geographic data. It uses a a special helical hyperspatial (HHCODE) data type to store locations in Oracle7 databases. HHCODEs are based on quadtree technology.

Intergraph (*http://www.intergraph.com*) provides a wide range of geographic information systems. For example, their Land Information System allows for the integration of survey data, imagery, title, and legal data, to name a few. Histories may be built of land use over a period of time. This is just one of several interesting GIS products offered by Intergraph, and you may wish to check out their extensive offerings.

Similarly, Sybase's partner, Vision International, provides a spatial data management system called VISION that acts like a datablade extension to Sybase databases. This program adds 10 SQS spatial data types (SDTs) and extends Transact SQL with SQS extensions such as WITHIN and OUTSIDE.

ESRI (*http://www.esri.com*) provides a range of spatial database products, including the well-known ARC/INFO system, which contains modules for specialized applications such as network analysis, terrain analysis, and so on. Their Spatial Database Engine, SDE 3.0, for example, works with geographic data stored in Oracle, Informix, Sybase, Microsoft SQL Server, and DB2 databases. Other products include the ArcView GIS and the MapObjects Internet Map Server program, which handles dynamic generation of maps.

There are numerous vendors who sell mapping products. You may wish to check out the following URLs:

www.mapquest.com   *www.ermapper.com*
www.lgc.com   *www.mapguide.com*
www.geosoft.co.uk   *www.etak.com*

Important ongoing efforts at standardization include efforts by the industrywide Open GIS Consortium (OGIS) and the U.S. National Spatial Data Infrastructure initiative (*http://nsdi.usgs.gov/nsdi* or *www.fgdc.gov/nsdi2.html*). The intention underlying these efforts is to develop a Spatial Data Transfer Standard (SDTS) that will work with industry database standards such as ODBC and CORBA. There is a pressing need for such standardization, given the wide range of specialized GIS data formats used today, numbering in the hundreds. A few of these include USGS DLG (digital line graph); DEM (digital elevation map); DTED (digital terrain elevation data); ITD (interim terrain data); CAMMS (computer-aided map mobility system); DOQ (digital orthographi quadrant) files; ARC/INFO arc, node, and polygon files; AutoCAD DXF files; SPOT (satellite) BIL files; Geosoft GXF; Landmark files; Geoquest IESX files; and PC-oriented raster files.

4.8   Bibliographic Notes

Samet's two-volume set forms one of the most comprehensive descriptions of the field of spatial data structures [180, 179]. It provides an excellent, highly detailed overview of the entire field of spatial data structures over the last 25–30 years. Samet's book provides a detailed bibliography consisting of contemporary methods for insertion, deletion, search, and range queries in k-d trees, point quadtrees, MX-quadtrees, and R-trees.

One significant area of importance not discussed in much detail by Samet is nearest neighbor searching. One of the early efforts in nearest neighbor searching was due to Fukunaga and Narendra [67]. Sproull [192] and Ramasubramanian and Paliwal [169] developed techniques for efficient searches for nearest neighbors in k-d trees. More recently, Roussopoulos, Kelley, and Vincent [173] have developed efficient algorithms for nearest neighbor retrievals in R-trees. Brinkhoff [29] also develop nearest neighbor algorithms in their GENESYS system. Arya et al. [14] develop a sophisticated optimal algorithm for finding nearest neighbors in metric spaces using Minkowski metrics. They define what it means for a point to be an approximate nearest neighbor and prove that their algorithm is an optimal algorithm for finding approximate nearest neighbors.

Hjaltason and Samet [94] have developed a very general and powerful algorithm that computes nearest neighbors in a data structure called the PMR-tree. Their algorithm applies also to the cases of a variety of the data structures described in this chapter.

If you are interested in seeing a visualized rendering of how many of the algorithms described in this chapter work, you may find the following Web site particularly useful: *http://www.cs.umd.edu/ brabec/quadtree/index.html*.

The MARCO (Map Retrieval by Content) system developed by Samet and Soffer [181] provides an elegant framework for converting raster map data into logical maps using some of the indexing techniques described in this chapter. Nearest neighbor searching in spatial data structures will play an important role later in the book; it forms the basis for retrieving objects that are "similar" (according to some distance metric chosen by an application) to a given query object.

4.9   Exercises and Projects

1. This exercise pertains to the design and analysis of k-d trees for the case when $k = 3$.

   (a) Define, using pseudocode, a simple data structure for nodes occurring in a 3-d tree. Assume that each of these nodes has a special field called INFO of type real.

   (b) Suppose you are given two real number values ℓ and r, with $\ell < r$. In addition, you are provided a pointer T to the root of a 3-d tree. Write, in pseudocode, an algorithm called SLICE that prints out the INFO field of all points (x, y, z) represented in the tree such that $\ell \leq x \leq r$.

   (c) Suppose you are given a point (x_c, y_c, z_c) denoting the center of a sphere, and a real number $rad > 0$ denoting the radius of the sphere as input. In addition, you are provided a pointer T to the root of a 3-d tree. Write, in pseudocode, an algorithm called 3DRANGE that prints out the INFO field of all points (x, y, z) represented in the tree such that (x, y, z) lies within the sphere specified by (x_c, y_c, z_c) and rad.

2. Write, in pseudocode, an algorithm to execute range queries on MX-quadtrees. Your algorithm, called RANGE, takes the following inputs: (1) a pointer T to

the root of an MX-quadtree, (2) an integer x denoting an x-coordinate, (3) an integer y denoting a y-coordinate, and (4) a distance $r > 0$. Your algorithm must print out all points (x_1, y_1) in the MX-quadtree pointed to by T that are strictly within r units of distance from the point (x, y). Note that the point (x, y) itself may not lie in the MX-quadtree.

3. Write, in pseudocode, an algorithm to execute slice queries on point quadtrees. Your algorithm, called POINTSLICE, takes the following inputs: (1) a pointer T to the root of a point quadtree, (2) a real number ℓ, and (3) another real $r > \ell$. Your algorithm must print out the INFO field of all points (x, y) represented in the point quadtree such that $\ell \le x \le r$.

4. Write, in pseudocode, an algorithm to execute range queries on R-trees. Your algorithm, called RTREERANGE, takes the following inputs: (1) a pointer T to the root of an R-tree, (2) an integer x denoting an x-coordinate, (3) an integer y denoting a y-coordinate, and (4) a distance $r > 0$. Your algorithm must print out the names of all rectangles in the R-tree pointed to by T that

(a) are entirely contained within the circle of radius r centered at (x, y) and

(b) have a nonempty intersection with the circle of radius r centered at (x, y).

5. Write, in pseudocode, an algorithm to execute slice queries on R-trees. Your algorithm, called RTREESLICE, takes the following inputs: (1) a pointer T to the root of an R-tree, (2) an integer ℓ, and (3) an integer r. Your algorithm must print out the names of all rectangles $\Re$ in the R-tree pointed to by T such that $\Re$'s left vertical edge is strictly greater than ℓ and $\Re$'s right vertical edge is strictly less than r.

5 Image Databases

What new concepts will you learn in this chapter?
You will learn what an image database is. You will be shown that querying image databases is often fundamentally different from querying textual databases and is further complicated by the usually imprecise techniques for image analysis.

What new abstractions are needed to realize these concepts?
You will be introduced to abstract definitions of image content. Describing the content of an image can be done either automatically or manually. In both cases, structures to store the results are needed, which you will be introduced to. In addition, you will be introduced to some automatic image-processing techniques.

What new techniques are needed to implement these abstractions?
Three generic techniques to implement image databases are presented. First, image databases may be implemented as extensions of the relational model, using the object-relational paradigm. Second, they may be implemented using n-dimensional data structures of the type described in the preceding chapter. Third, they may be implemented using image transformations.

What technological features support these implementation methods?
You will receive a quick overview of existing software to implement image database management operations on both the Unix and Windows software platforms.

Over the last few decades, a wide variety of government and industrial organizations have been collecting photographic and image data. For example, NASA's EOSDIS project has collected a tremendous amount of data pertaining to the earth. In the same vein, every U.S. citizen who has ever applied for a passport has his or her photograph on file somewhere—and the same is certainly true for most other countries as well. Likewise, hospitals regularly collect X ray and CAT scan data, leading to very large banks of such images. For the most part, many of these images are stored in nonelectronic forms, such as 4×6-inch photographs, or X rays. It is only recently, with the drop in prices of digitization equipment, that these images have started being digitized. As digitization becomes more and more widespread, we are confronted with a greater and greater need to manage such images efficiently.

In the relational model of data, we are typically confronted with a situation where queries are posed textually. In other words, the user types in a query and obtains an answer in response. However, consider the case of the police investigator as described in the Sample Multimedia Scenario in Chapter 1. The police investigator may have in front of him a surveillance photograph of someone whose identity he may not know, but wishes to determine. Thus, he may wish to ask a query of the form "Here's a picture of a person. Can you retrieve all pictures from the image database that are similar to this person and tell me the identities of the people in the pictures you return to me?" This query is fundamentally different from ordinary queries for two reasons. First, the query includes a picture as part of the query. Second, the query asks about "similar" pictures and hence uses a notion of "imprecise match," whose definition needs to be precisely articulated. (It is possible to reason precisely about imprecise data!)

In this chapter, we will use a small database of faces of people as a running example to illustrate the basic ideas. Figure 5.1 shows the different faces contained in this archive.

This chapter is organized as follows: First, in Section 5.1, we will introduce raw images and provide an abstract definition of such raw images. Later, we will introduce image transformations that convert raw images into a compressed form. For example, most commercial image data stored in standard formats, such as GIF, JPEG, and TIFF, represent images using such transformations. After this, we will introduce segmentation techniques that allow us to identify interesting properties of images. Then we will describe techniques to retrieve images by similarity. Finally, we will describe how images can be converted into a datablade that can be inserted or integrated into commercial relational DBMSs.

pic1.gif

pic2.gif

pic3.gif

pic4.gif

pic5.gif

pic6.gif

pic7.gif

FIGURE

5.1   A small database of faces

5.1   Raw Images

Informally speaking, the content of an image consists of all objects in that image that are deemed to be of interest from the point of view of an application. Such objects in an image could have a variety of associated *properties* such as the following:

1. A *shape descriptor* that describes the shape/location of the region within which the object is located inside a given image.

2. A *property descriptor* that describes the properties of the individual pixels (or groups of pixels) in the given image. Examples of such properties include red-green-blue (RGB) values of the pixel (or aggregated over a group of pixels), gray-scale levels in the case of black-and-white images, and so on. In general, it will be infeasible to associate properties with individual pixels, and hence *cells* (rectangular groups of pixels) will be used most of the time.

For example, consider the image file `pic1.gif` in Figure 5.1. This image has two objects of interest, corresponding to the two faces we see in that image. Let us call these two objects o_1 and o_2, respectively.

The image shows a rectangle around the faces. This rectangle specifies the shape descriptor of the face in question. In general, a shape is described by rectangles that bound the shape. However, there is no reason to believe that a shape descriptor should be composed of a single rectangle bounding the shape. Other possibilities include describing a shape by a polygon or by a collection of rectangles. However, in this example, we will assume that the shape descriptor of an image object is a rectangle whose sides are parallel to the *x*- and *y*-axes.

The property descriptor associated with a face typically consists of a set of pairs of the form `(PropName,PropValue)`. We assume the existence of a set `Prop` of properties. A property consists of two components—a *property name* (e.g., `Red`, `Green`, `Blue`) and a *property domain* that specifies the range of values that the property can assume (e.g., $\{0, \ldots, 8\}$).

For example, returning to the file `pic1.gif` in Figure 5.1, we could state that the object o_1, corresponding to the face to the left of the figure, has the following characteristics:

1. *Shape descriptor:* rectangle: XLB = 10; XUB = 60; YLB = 5; YUB = 50.

2. *Property descriptor:* As an example, the pixel at location $(14, 17)$ may have the following properties: `Red = 5; Green = 1; Blue = 3`.

Similarly, the object o_2, corresponding to the face on the right of the file `picl.gif` in Figure 5.1, may have the following characteristics:

1. *Shape descriptor:* rectangle: XLB = 80; XUB = 120; YLB = 20; YUB = 55.

2. *Property descriptor:* As an example, the pixel at location (90, 30) may have the following properties: Red = 2; Green = 7; Blue = 4.

Note that in general, instead of specifying properties for each pixel as in the above example, we may split a region of $(a \times b)$ pixels into $(m \times n)$ cells, where a mod $m = 0$, b mod $n = 0$, $m < a$, and $n < b$. This means that each cell above represents a contiguous rectangular region of $(a$ div $m) \times (b$ div $n)$ pixels. Thus, a cell is a rectangular collection of pixels.

Formally speaking, we have the following definitions that give precise, mathematical form to the above intuitions.

Definition 5.1 Every image I has an associated pair of positive integers (m, n), called the *grid resolution* of the image. This divides the image into $(m \times n)$ cells of equal size, called the *image grid*.

Each cell in a given gridded $(m \times n)$ image I consists of a collection of pixels.

Definition 5.2 A *cell property* is a triple (Name, Values, Method), where Name is a string denoting the property's name, Values is a set of values that the property may assume, and Method is an algorithm that tells us how to compute the property involved.

For example, consider the case of black-and-white images. A reasonable cell property in this case is

```
(bwcolor,{b,w},bwalgo)
```

where our property name is bwcolor and the possible values are b (black) and w (white), respectively. bwalgo may be an algorithm that takes a cell as input and returns either black (b) or white (w) as output, by somehow combining the black/white levels of the pixels in the cell.

On the other hand, with gray-scale images (with 0 = white and 1 = black), we may have the cell property

```
(graylevel,[0,1],grayalgo)
```

where our property name is graylevel, its possible values are real numbers in the [0, 1] interval, and the associated method grayalgo takes a cell as input and computes its gray level. As we saw in the case of R-trees, a cell may be characterized by the bounding edges of the cell, which in turn are described by four integers—XLB, XUB, YLB, and YUB. For example, if a cell describes the set of all pixels $\{(i,j) \mid \text{XLB} \leq i \leq \text{XUB} \ \& \ \text{YLB} \leq j \leq \text{YUB}\}$, then one example of our method may be computed by averaging

$$\texttt{grayalgo}(cell) = \frac{\sum_{\text{XLB} \leq i < \text{XUB}} \sum_{\text{YLB} \leq j < \text{YUB}} \texttt{findgray}(i,j)}{(\text{XUB} - \text{XLB}) \times (\text{YUB} - \text{YLB})}$$

where $\texttt{findgray}(i,j)$ merely returns the gray level of a pixel (i,j).

Alternatively, consider a color image. Here, we might have three properties:

```
(red,{0, ... ,7}), (green,{0, ... ,7}), (blue,{0, ... ,7})
```

Thus, if a cell has the properties

```
red = 3;  green = 7;  blue = 1
```

then this indicates a particular combination of the RGB attributes associated with that node.

In general, software engineers who are constructing an image database application must first decide which cell properties are of interest and then must articulate these properties to their satisfaction, and create methods associated with determining these properties.

Definition 5.3 An *object shape* is any set P of points such that if $p, q \in P$, then there exists a sequence of points $p_1, \ldots, p_n$ all in P such that

1. $p = p_1$ and $q = p_n$ and

2. for all $1 \leq i < n$, p_{i+1} is a neighbor of p_i; that is, if $p_i = (x_i, y_i)$ and $p_{i+1} = (x_{i+1}, y_{i+1})$, then (x_{i+1}, y_{i+1}) satisfies one of the following conditions:

$$
\begin{array}{ll}
(x_{i+1}, y_{i+1}) = (x_i + 1, y_i) & (x_{i+1}, y_{i+1}) = (x_i - 1, y_i) \\
(x_{i+1}, y_{i+1}) = (x_i, y_i + 1) & (x_{i+1}, y_{i+1}) = (x_i, y_i - 1) \\
(x_{i+1}, y_{i+1}) = (x_i + 1, y_i + 1) & (x_{i+1}, y_{i+1}) = (x_i + 1, y_i - 1) \\
(x_{i+1}, y_{i+1}) = (x_i - 1, y_i + 1) & (x_{i+1}, y_{i+1}) = (x_i - 1, y_i - 1)
\end{array}
$$

What the above definition says is that for a set of points to be considered a valid shape, given any two points in the shape, there must exist a path between those two points that is completely contained within the shape. For the sake of simplicity, in this book, we will only consider objects that have a *rectangular* shape.

Definition 5.4 A *rectangle* is an object shape, P, such that there exist integers XLB, XUB, YLB, YUB such that

$$P = \{(x, y) \mid \text{XLB} \leq x < \text{XUB} \ \& \ \text{YLB} \leq y < \text{YUB}\}$$

Definition 5.5 An *image database* (IDB) consists of a triple (GI, Prop, Rec) where

1. GI is a set of gridded images of the form (*Image*, m, n),

2. Prop is a set of cell properties, and

3. Rec is a mapping that associates, with each image, a set of rectangles denoting objects.

Note that when representing image data of the form described above, two major factors must be taken into account:

- First, images are often very large objects consisting of a $(p_1 \times p_2)$ pixel array. Explicitly storing properties on a pixel-by-pixel basis is usually infeasible. This has led to a family of *image compression* algorithms that attempt to compress the image into one containing fewer pixels. We will study such compression algorithms in Section 5.2.

- Second, given an image I (compressed or raw), there is a critical need to determine what "features" appear in the image. This is typically done by breaking up the image into a set of homogeneous (with respect to some property) rectangular regions, each of which is called a *segment*. The process of finding these segments is called *segmentation*. We will discuss segmentation in Section 5.3.

Once image data has been segmented, we need to support match operations that map either a whole image or a segmented portion of an image against another whole or segmented image. We will study techniques for supporting such matches in Section 5.4.

5.2   Compressed Image Representations

Consider a two-dimensional image I consisting of $(p_1 \times p_2)$ pixels. Then, typically, $I(x, y)$ is a number denoting one or more attributes of the pixel. For

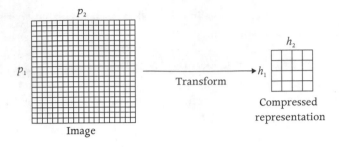

5.2   Transformation of an image into a vector

example, $I(x, y)$ may be a number between 0 and 255 (inclusive), denoting an encoding of the image's RGB values.

In general, reasoning about an image by considering all the pixels is not feasible because each of p_1, p_2 may be 1,024 or more, leading to over a million entries in the image matrix I. A common approach is to transform this matrix I into a *compressed representation* of the matrix, as shown in Figure 5.2. The creation of the compressed representation, $\mathrm{cr}(I)$, of image I consists of two parts:

1. *Size selection:* The size h of the compressed image is selected by the image database designer. The larger the size, the greater is the fidelity of the representation. However, as the size increases, so does the complexity of creating an index for manipulating such representations, and searching this index. Thus, an appropriate trade-off needs to be made. We will assume that the selected size of $\mathrm{cr}(I)$ is some pair of positive integers (h_1, h_2).

2. *Transform selection:* The user must select a transformation that is capable of converting the image into a compressed representation. In other words, he must select a transformation that, given the image I and any pair of numbers, $1 \leq i \leq h_1$ and $1 \leq j \leq h_2$, will determine what the value of $\mathrm{cr}(i, j)$ is. We will now briefly discuss two of the better-known transformations.

5.2.1   The Discrete Fourier Transform (DFT)

This is a very well-known transform, studied extensively in the literature. According to the discrete Fourier transform, we have

$$\mathrm{DFT}(x, y) = \frac{1}{p_1 p_2} \sum_{a=0}^{p_1-1} \sum_{b=0}^{p_2-1} \left(I(a, b) \times e^{-j\left(\frac{2\pi xa}{p_1} + \frac{2\pi yb}{p_2} \right)} \right)$$

where j is the well-known complex number $\sqrt{-1}$.

The DFT has many nice properties. For example, it is possible to get back the original image I from its DFT representation; that is, given a $(p_1 \times p_2)$ image I that is represented by DFT(I), we can apply an inverse of the DFT, denoted DFT^{-1}, that takes any pixel (x, y) in I as input and uses the values of DFT(x, y) to compute the values of the original image. This invertibility property is extremely useful. For example, suppose we have an image I, and we use the DFT to compress the image, thus obtaining a compressed image DFT(I). This compressed image may then be stored and/or manipulated in any number of ways. However, later, if we wish to uncompress the compressed image and recover the original image, then DFT^{-1} may be used to recover the original image. *It is important to note that not all compression schemes are 100% invertible, and thus some compression schemes may lead to loss of data/fidelity.* While the DFT is invertible in theory, practical realizations of it have often sacrificed this property by applying the DFT together with certain other noninvertible operations. In addition to the invertibility property, the DFT preserves Euclidean distance, which is important in image-matching applications where we may wish to use distance measures to represent similarity levels.

5.2.2 The Discrete Cosine Transform (DCT)

This is another well-known algorithm, and in fact forms the basis for the JPEG compression of images. Like DFT, the DCT is invertible, and is given by

$$\text{DCT}(i, j) = \frac{2}{\sqrt{p_1 \times p_2}} \alpha(i)$$

$$\times \alpha(j) \sum_{r=0}^{p_1-1} \sum_{s=0}^{p_2-1} \left(\cos \left(\frac{(2r + 1) \times \pi i}{2r} \right) \times \cos \left(\frac{(2s + 1) \times \pi j}{2s} \right) \right)$$

where

$$\alpha(i), \alpha(j) = \begin{cases} \frac{1}{\sqrt{2}} & \text{when } u, v = 0 \\ 1 & \text{otherwise} \end{cases}$$

The DCT can be quickly computed.

Both the DFT and the DCT have been modified in numerous ways to support different desired performance properties (e.g., speeding up the computation of the DCT/DFT or improving the quality of the compression). DCT has minor advantages over the DFT from the latter point of view, and a simple analysis of the summations involved shows that they are both approximately equal in the

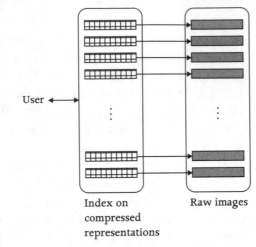

Index on
compressed
representations

Raw images

FIGURE

5.3   Transformed image index

time taken for computation. A new class of techniques for image compression is the class of wavelet transformations.

Suppose now that IDB is a collection of images and that the regions of interest in these images have been demarcated with rectangles (how to do this will be discussed later in Section 5.3). Suppose $r_1, \ldots, r_n$ are all such regions of interest. Then the set $\{cr(r_1), \ldots, cr(r_n)\}$ can easily be represented using any of the multidimensional indexing techniques (e.g., R-trees) discussed in Chapter 4; further techniques for indexing multidimensional data will be presented in Section 6.4. Figure 5.3 shows this situation.

5.3   Image Processing: Segmentation

Thus far in this chapter, we have proceeded under the optimistic assumption that the regions in an image, where features of interest lie, can be somehow identified, and then the content of these "interesting regions" is somehow determined. In this section, we will quickly overview how, given any image, we can separate the image into homogeneous regions called *segments*.

Suppose I is an image containing $(m \times n)$ cells. In the worst case, a cell could be a pixel, but as described earlier, in general, a cell is a rectangular set of pixels.

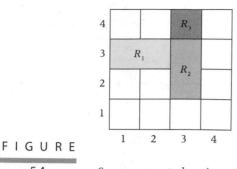

FIGURE

5.4 Some connected regions

A *connected region*, $\mathfrak{R}$, in image I, is a set of cells such that if cells (x_1, y_1), $(x_2, y_2) \in \mathfrak{R}$, there there exists a sequence of cells $C_1, \ldots, C_n$ in $\mathfrak{R}$ such that

1. $C_1 = (x_1, y_1)$ and

2. $C_n = (x_2, y_2)$ and

3. the Euclidean distance between cells C_i and C_{i+1} for all $1 \leq i < n$ is 1.

Figure 5.4 shows three regions, R_1, R_2, and R_3, each of which is a connected region. In addition:

1. $(R_1 \cup R_2)$ is a connected region.

2. $(R_2 \cup R_3)$ is a connected region.

3. $(R_1 \cup R_2 \cup R_3)$ is a connected region.

4. But $(R_1 \cup R_3)$ is *not* a connected region. The reason for this is that the Euclidean distance between the cell $(2, 3)$, which represents the rightmost of the two cells of R_1, and the cell $(3, 4)$, which represents the only cell of R_3, is $\sqrt{2} > 1$.

A *homogeneity predicate* associated with an image I is a function H that takes any connected region $\mathfrak{R}$ in image I as input and returns either "true" or "false." Here are some examples of simple homogeneity predicates:

1. Suppose δ is some real number between 0 and 1, inclusive, and we are considering black-and-white images. We may define a simple homogeneity predicate, H_δ^{bw}, as follows: $H_\delta^{bw}(R)$ returns "true" if over $(100 * \delta)\%$ of the cells in region R have the same color.

Now consider three regions, as described in the following table:

Region	Number of black pixels	Number of white pixels
R_1	800	200
R_2	900	100
R_3	100	900

Suppose we consider some different predicates, $H_{0.8}^{bw}$, $H_{0.89}^{bw}$, and $H_{0.92}^{bw}$. The following table shows us the results returned by these three homogeneity predicates on the above table:

Region	$H_{0.8}^{bw}$	$H_{0.89}^{bw}$	$H_{0.92}^{bw}$
R_1	true	false	false
R_2	true	true	false
R_3	true	true	false

Note, in particular, that according to this homogeneity predicate, it is only the number of pixels of identical color that matter, not which color predominates.

2. Suppose your image is now one where each pixel has a real value between 0 and 1, inclusive. This value is called the *bw-level*: 0 denotes "white," 1 denotes "black," and everything in between denotes a shade somewhere between black and white. Consider now a slightly different homogeneity predicate, where you have a function f that assigns numbers between 0 and 1, inclusive, to each cell. In addition, you have a "noise factor" $0 \leq \eta \leq 1$, and a threshold δ as in the preceding case. $H^{f,\eta,\delta}(R)$ is now "true" iff

$$\frac{\{(x,y) \mid |bw\text{-}level(x,y) - f(x,y)| < \eta\}}{(m \times n)} > \delta$$

In other words, what this homogeneity predicate does is to use a "baseline" function f and a maximal permissible noise level η. It considers the bw-level of cell (x,y) to be sufficiently similar to that predicted by f if

$$|bw\text{-}level(x,y) - f(x,y)| < \eta$$

that is, if the two differ by no more than η.

It then checks to see if sufficiently many cells (which is determined by the factor δ) in the region "match" the predictions made by f. If so, it considers the region R to be homogeneous, and returns "true." Otherwise, it returns "false."

3. A third scheme first classifies all bw-levels. For example, it may classify all bw-levels between 0 and 0.1 as 1, all bw-levels between 0.1 and 0.2 as 2, and so on, till the bw-levels between 0.9 and 1 are classified to be of level 10. As before, let δ lie between 0 and 1. $H^{class}(R)$ yields "true" iff over $(100 * \delta)\%$ of the cells in the region R fall into the same class.

4. A fourth homogeneity predicate, which we will denote by H^{dyn}, is a dynamic version of the H^{class} function. H^{class} sets up its classes a priori rather than dynamically. In contrast, we may say that region R is homogeneous, according to the predicate $H_{\delta}^{dyn,\eta}$, iff over $(100 * \delta)\%$ of the cells in the region R lie within a range of η of some real number r. Note that the precise identity of this real number is determined only at run time.

Other more complex, but very useful homogeneity predicates have been provided by many authors [24, 144].

Finally, note that homogeneity predicates do not necessarily have to be based on black/white levels, bw-levels, or gray levels. They are arbitrary predicates that, when given a region R, return "true" or "false" based on some computation that they perform. They may take into account factors such as depth, intensity, texture, color schemes, and so on, when determining homogeneity.

Given an image I represented as a set of $(m \times n)$ pixels, we define a *segmentation* of image I with respect to a homogeneity predicate P to be a set $R_1, \ldots, R_k$ of regions such that

1. $R_i \cap R_j = \emptyset$ for all $1 \leq i \neq j \leq k$,

2. $I = R_1 \cup \cdots \cup R_k$,

3. $H(R_i) =$"true" for all $1 \leq i \leq k$, and

4. for all distinct i, j, $1 \leq i, j \leq n$, such that $R_i \cup R_j$ is a connected region, it is the case that $H(R_i \cup R_j) =$"false."

F I G U R E

5.5   A segmentation of regions

For example, consider a simple (4×4) region containing the bw-levels shown in the table below:

Row/column	1	2	3	4
1	0.1	0.25	0.5	0.5
2	0.05	0.30	0.6	0.6
3	0.35	0.30	0.55	0.8
4	0.6	0.63	0.85	0.90

Consider now the homogeneity predicate $H_1^{dyn,0.03}$. This homogeneity predicate says that a region R is to be considered homogeneous iff there exists an r such that each and every cell in the region has a bw-level v such that

$$|v - r| \leq 0.03$$

According to this classification, it is easy to see that the following five regions constitute a valid segmentation of the above image with respect to $H_1^{dyn,0.03}$. Figure 5.5 shows the following segments diagrammatically.

$R_1 = \{(1,1),(1,2)\}$
$R_2 = \{(1,3),(2,1),(2,2),(2,3)\}$
$R_3 = \{(3,1),(3,2),(3,3),(4,1),(4,2)\}$
$R_4 = \{(3,4),(4,3),(4,4)\}$
$R_5 = \{(1,4),(2,4)\}$

The following is one simple method of finding a segmentation of an image with respect to a homogeneity predicate H:

1. *Split:* We start with the whole image. If it is homogeneous, then we are done, and the image is a valid segmentation of itself. Otherwise, we split the image into two parts and recursively repeat this process till we find a set $R_1, \ldots, R_n$ of regions that are homogeneous and satisfy all conditions, except the fourth, in the definition of homogeneity predicates.

2. *Merge:* We now check which of the R_is can be merged together. At the end of this step, we will obtain a valid segmentation $R'_1, \ldots, R'_k$ of the image, where $k \leq n$ and where each R'_i is the union of some of the R_js.

An algorithm encoding the above reasoning may be easily written by encoding three functions and a main function called segment as follows:

Algorithm 5.1

```
function segment(I:image);
    SOL = ∅;
    check_split(I);
    merge(SOL);
end function

function check_split(R);
    if H(R)="true" then addsol(R)
    else
        { X = split(R);
            check_split(X.part1);
            check_split(X.part2);
        }
end function

procedure addsol(R);
    SOL = SOL∪{R}
end procedure

function merge(S);
    while S ≠ ∅ do {
        Pick some Cand in S;
        merged = false;
        S = S -{Cand};
        Enumerate S as C₁, ... ,Cₖ;
```

```
        while i ≤ k do
        { if adjacent(Cand,Cᵢ) then
            { Cand = Cand∪ Cᵢ;
                S = S-{Cᵢ};
                merged = true;
            }
        else {i = i+1;
                if merged then S = S∪{Cand};
                merged = false
            }
        } };
end function
```

5.4   Similarity-Based Retrieval

At this point, we have studied techniques that take an image as input and that return a compressed version of the image as output, using image transformations such as the DCT, the DFT, or a wavelet transform. We have also seen how we may segment an image. An important question that still remains to be answered is the following: How do we determine whether the content of a segment (of a segmented image) is similar to another image (or a set of images) that we have?

There are many, many cases where we have a large image database, and the user wishes to ask a query like "Here is a picture of a person. Can you tell me who it is?" For example, consider a police investigator who has arrested an individual who claims to be John Smith (but whose driving license is phony). The police investigator may wish to query an FBI or local police department or an INS image database with a photo of the arrested individual, in order to determine who he really is.

There have been two broad approaches to similarity-based retrieval of images:

1. *Metric approach:* In this approach, there is assumed to be a distance metric d that can compare any two image objects. The closer two objects are in distance, the more similar they are considered to be. In this approach, the problem of similarity-based retrieval may be stated as "Given an input image i, find the "nearest" neighbor of i in the image archive." The metric-

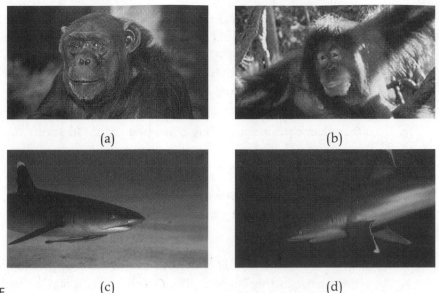

FIGURE
5.6

Which of these images are similar? (a) One monkey (chimpanzee) and (b) another monkey (orangutan); (c) one shark (tiger) and (d) another shark (gray reef) (see also color plate Figure 5.6)

based approach is by far the most widely followed approach in the database world.

2. *Transformation approach:* The metric approach assumes that the notion of similarity is "fixed"; that is, in any given application, only one notion of similarity is used to index the data (though different applications may use different notions of similarity). However, using the maxim "Beauty lies in the eye of the beholder" as a guide, we may wonder whether "Similarity lies in the eye of the beholder" as well. For instance, we have all encountered statements of the form "Oooh, the baby looks exactly like its father" by one person, and "He (the baby) looks more like his grandfather than his father" by another person. More confusing still is the fact that there may be legitimate reasons for such differences. For instance, consider the images shown in Figure 5.6(a) and (b). For most of us, these two images appear to be of similar animals (i.e., monkeys). However, an expert on primates would claim (correctly) that these are dissimilar images: (a) is a chimpanzee, while (b) is an orangutan. Similarly, the images shown in Figure 5.6(c) and (d) are similar to most of us, but dissimilar to an expert on sharks, who will rec-

ognize (c) as a tiger shark, which (to a marine biologist) is totally different from a gray reef shark (d). Likewise, in the domain of similarity between strings, the expressions "AI" and "intelligence" may be similar to a computer scientist, but totally dissimilar to an biologist (for whom "AI" stands for "artificial insemination").

Thus, the users should be able to specify what they consider to be similar, rather than the system forcing this upon them. In short, the transformational approach questions the claim that a given body of data (image, text, etc.) has a single associated notion of similarity.

We will now examine these two approaches in greater detail.

5.4.1   The Metric Approach

Suppose we consider a set *Obj* of objects, having pixel properties $p_1, \ldots, p_n$, as described earlier in this chapter. Thus, each object o may be viewed as a set $S(o)$ of $(n + 2)$-tuples of the form

$$(\texttt{xcoord}, \texttt{ycoord}, v_1, \ldots, v_n)$$

where v_i denotes the value of property p_i associated with the pixel coordinate (x, y). Obviously, $S(o)$ contains $w \times h$ of these $(n + 2)$-tuples, where w is the width of the rectangle associated with o and h is the height.

Usually, an object is either a whole image or a segment of an image. Thus, for example, given a face database consisting of pictures of people taken under different circumstances, an object may consist of faces.

In the metric-based approach, it is argued that dissimilarity is captured by a distance function d. A function d from some set X to the unit interval $[0, 1]$ is said to be a distance function if it satisfies the following axioms for all $x, y, z \in X$:

$$d(x, y) = d(y, x)$$
$$d(x, y) \leq d(x, z) + d(z, y)$$
$$d(x, x) = 0$$

Let d_{Obj} be a distance function on the space of all objects in our domain. However, as we have seen above, an object may be viewed as a set of points in a k-dimensional space for $k = (n + 2)$. This may cause the computation of d_{Obj} to be a rather complex process.

For example, suppose we just consider our set *Obj* to consist of (256×256) images having three attributes (red, green, blue), each of which assumes a value from the set $\{0, \ldots, 7\}$. Suppose we define a distance function d_1 between two images as follows:

$$d_1(o_1, o_2) = \sqrt{\sum_{i=1}^{256} \sum_{j=1}^{256} \left(\mathit{diff}_r[i, j] + \mathit{diff}_g[i, j] + \mathit{diff}_b[i, j] \right)}$$

$$\mathit{diff}_r[i, j] = \left(o_1[i, j].red - o_2[i, j].red \right)^2$$

$$\mathit{diff}_g[i, j] = \left(o_1[i, j].green - o_1[i, j].green \right)^2$$

$$\mathit{diff}_b[i, j] = \left(o_1[i, j].blue - o_1[i, j].blue \right)^2$$

Obviously, computing this is a cumbersome process because the double summation leads to 65,536 expressions being computed inside the sum. Furthermore, using an R-tree or a quad tree-like data structure causes the fan-out factor to potentially be very large—something that is typically not very desirable.

In order to alleviate this problem, some researchers have suggested an important alternative technique. Their technique is contingent upon the use of a "good" feature extraction function fe. Examples of such functions could include the DFT and the DCT. Using their approach, the feature extraction function fe would map objects into single points in a s-dimensional space, where s would typically be pretty small compared to $(n + 2)$. Thus, two reductions would be achieved:

1. Recall that an object o is a set of points in an $(n + 2)$-dimensional space. In contrast, $fe(o)$ is a single point.

2. $fe(o)$ is a point in an s-dimensional space where $s \ll (n + 2)$.

Figure 5.7 presents a visual rendering of the metric approach. The basic idea is to first map objects into points in an s-dimensional space, and then organize all objects using a spatial data structure such as an R-tree. However, the mapping should, intuitively, preserve distance: If o_1, o_2, o_3 are objects such that the distance $d(o_1, o_2) \leq d(o_1, o_3)$, then $d'(fe(o_1), fe(o_2)) \leq d'(fe(o_1), fe(o_3))$, where d is a metric on the original $(n + 2)$-dimensional space, and d' is a metric on the new s-dimensional space. In other words, the feature extraction map should preserve the distance relationships in the original space.

Subsequently, given a query object o, we convert o to $fe(o)$ and then try to find a point p in the s-dimensional space such that $d'(p, fe(o))$ is as small as possible. The formal algorithm for this process is given below. The formal algorithm uses the notation d to refer to the metric on the $(n + 2)$-dimensional space, and the notation d' to refer to the metric on the lower-dimensional space of dimensionality s.

Algorithm 5.2 `IndexCreation`
   Input: `Obj`, a set of objects.

1. `T=NIL. (* T is an empty quadtree, or R-tree for`
      `s-dimensional data *)`

2. `if Obj=∅ then return T and halt.`

3. `else`

   (a) Compute $fe(\mathsf{o})$.
   (b) Insert $fe(\mathsf{o})$ into `T`.
   (c) `Obj = Obj - {o}.`
   (d) `Go to 2.`

The formal process for finding the *best* answer to a query object is given by the following algorithm.

Algorithm 5.3 `FindMostSimilarObject`
   Input: a tree `T` of the above type. An object `o`.

1. `bestnode = NIL;`

2. `if T=NIL then return bestnode.  Halt`

3. `else`
   find the nearest neighbors of $fe(\mathsf{o})$ in `T` using a nearest neighbor search technique. If multiple such neighbors exist, return them all.

To find all objects that are similar to the query object within a given tolerance ϵ, we may use a range-query-based approach. The following approach assumes that for all o_1, o_2 in *Obj*,

$$d(o_1, o_2) \leq d'(fe(o_1), fe(o_2))$$

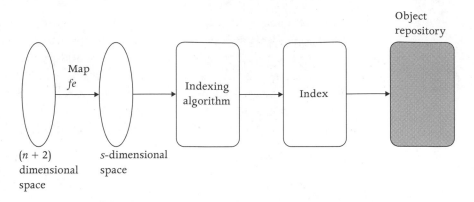

5.7   Data sources used in the Sample Multimedia Scenario

Algorithm 5.4 `FindSimilarObjects`
Input: a tree T of the above type. An object o. A tolerance $0 < \epsilon \leq 1$.

1. Execute a range query on tree T with center $fe(\mathtt{o})$ and radius ϵ.

2. Let $p_1, \ldots, p_r$ be all the points returned.

3. `for i = 1 to r do`

   (a) `if` $d(\mathtt{o}, fe^{-1}(p_i)) \leq \epsilon$ `then print` $fe^{-1}(p_i)$.

The above algorithm works only if the distance metric in the space of small dimensionality (i.e., dimension s) consistently overestimates (or equals) the distance metric d.

The algorithms in this section were originally proposed by Faloutsos [60] and his co-workers, who have also documented the use of these algorithms experimentally.

5.4.2   The Transformation Approach

The transformation-based approach is more general than (i.e., it subsumes) the metric approach. It is based on the principle that given two objects o_1, o_2, the level of dissimilarity between o_1 and o_2 is proportional to the (minimum) cost of transforming object o_1 into object o_2, or vice versa.

In this model, there is a set of *transformation operators*, $to_1, \ldots, to_r$. In the case of images, these operators may include *translation*, *rotation*, and *scaling* (e.g., reduction and magnification). An *extension operator* may also be included that modifies a shape by adding a new shape to it. Likewise, an *excision operator* may cull out a shape from an existing object. The user may choose to use only a subset of these operators. Furthermore, he may add new operators if he so wishes. Each operator has an associated cost function—the higher the cost, the less preferable it is to use the operation. For example, we may have an operation called `paint` that has four arguments—`paint(color1,val1,color2,val2)`, and we may specify that the cost of this operation is defined as

$$cost(\texttt{paint(color1,val1,color2,val2)})$$
$$= \textit{diff}(color1, color2)^3 + (val1 - val2)^2$$

where $\textit{diff}(red, green) = 3 = \textit{diff}(green, red)$, and so on.

The transformation of object o into object o' is a *sequence* of transformation operations $to_1, \ldots, to_r$ and a sequence of objects $o_1, \ldots, o_r$ such that

1. $to_1(o) = o_1$,

2. $to_i(o_{i-1}) = o_i$, and

3. $to(o_r) = o'$.

The cost of the above transformation sequence, TS, is given by

$$cost(TS) = \sum_{i=1}^{r} cost(to_i)$$

Note that there may be zero, one, or many transformation sequences that permit us to transform object o into object o'. Suppose $TSeq(o, o')$ is the set of all transformation sequences that convert o into o'. The dissimilarity between o and o', denoted $dis(o, o')$, with respect to a set TR of transformation operators and a set CF of cost functions is given by

$$dis(o, o') = min\{cost(TS) \mid TS \in TSeq(o, o') \cup TSeq(o', o)\}$$

For example, consider the two objects o_1 and o_2 in Figure 5.8, and consider some of the alternative ways of transforming one into the other.

1. TS_1: This transformation sequence consists of a nonuniform scaling operation (scale the blue part of o_1 50% in the vertical upward direction, leaving the horizontal unchanged), followed by another nonuniform scaling operation (scale the green part of object o_1 by a 100% increase in the vertical downward direction, with no change in the horizontal). The third operation applies the `paint` operation, painting the two pixels colored green to magenta. Figure 5.9 depicts the intermediate steps.

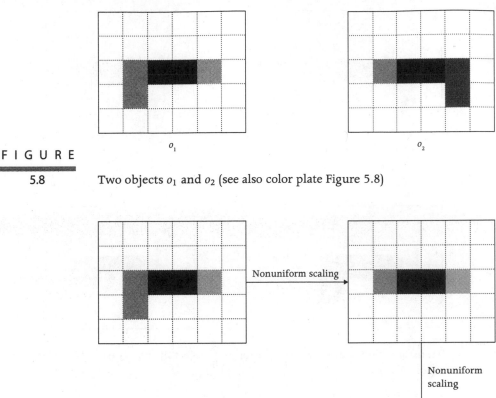

F I G U R E

5.8   Two objects o_1 and o_2 (see also color plate Figure 5.8)

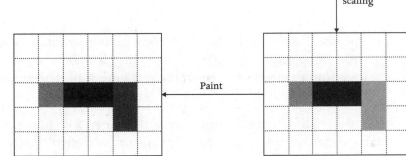

F I G U R E

5.9   Transformation sequence TS_1 transforming object o_1 into o_2 (see also color plate Figure 5.9)

2. TS_2: This transformation sequence consists of a nonuniform scaling opera-tion (scale the blue part of o_1 50% in the vertical upward direction, leaving the horizontal unchanged). Then we apply the `paint` operation, painting the green object magenta. (Notice that in the sequence TS_2, we had to paint only one pixel, but in the transformation sequence TS_1, we had to paint two

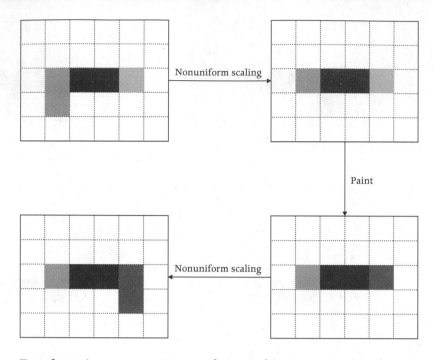

5.10   Transformation sequence TS_2 transforming object o_1 into o_2 (see also color plate
            Figure 5.10)

pixels). Finally, apply the nonuniform scaling operation (scale the magenta
part of object o_1 by a 100% increase in the vertical downward direction,
with no change in the horizontal). Figure 5.10 depicts the intermediate
steps.

If we assume that the cost functions associated with nonuniform scaling are
independent of color, and the `paint` operation merely counts the number of
pixels being painted, then it is easy to see that transformation TS_2 accomplishes
the desired transformation at a cheaper cost (since it paints one less pixel than
transformation TS_1).

The transformation model allows a great deal of flexibility over the metric
model in two ways:

1. Users can set up their own notion of similarity by specifying that certain
   transformation operators may or may not be used.

2. Users may associate, with each transformation operator, a *cost function* that
   assesses a cost to each application of the operation, depending upon the

arguments to the transformation operator. This allows users to personalize the notion of similarity for their needs.

The metric-based model has two advantages: first, by forcing the user to use one and only one (dis)similarity metric, the system can facilitate the indexing of data so as to optimize the one operation of finding the "nearest" neighbor (i.e., least dissimilar) object with respect to the query object specified by the user. Second, it is relatively easy to compute efficiently.

5.5   Alternative Image DB Paradigms

Against the backdrop of having discussed techniques for similarity-based retrieval on both whole and segmented images that are either compressed or uncompressed, we turn our attention to another question: How should we store a set of images so as to support image retrieval operations? In general, there are many ways of representing an image database:

- *Representing IDBs as relations:* The most straightforward way of representing image databases is as a set of relations. This is shown in Section 5.6.

- *Representing IDBs with spatial data structures:* The basic idea of this technique is simple. If all objects in an image are represented by rectangles (or generalizations of rectangles to higher dimensional spaces), then surely we can represent a set of (generalized) rectangles using a spatial data structure, such as the R-trees we studied in Section 4.5. This is shown in Section 5.7.

- *Representing IDBs using image transformations:* The basic idea behind this method is that an image containing $(1{,}024 \times 1{,}024)$ pixels, for example, is very large. However, there may be substantial similarities between different portions of the image. Can we represent the image by compressing its basic content into a single real-valued vector of length k (for some k selected by the application designer)? Typically, k is no more than 100 or 200, and the procedure to derive these k vector values is done through transforms such as the discrete Fourier transform or the discrete cosine transform. This approach was studied in Section 5.2.

When retrieving images, the characteristics of the image depend critically upon factors such as lighting conditions, camera positions, the position of the subject, and so on. For example, in the face database example, two different photographs of the same person may vary, depending upon a variety of factors, such as the time of the day at which the two photographs were taken, the lighting conditions under which the photographs were taken, the camera used, the exact position of the subject's head and facial expression, and so on.

Thus, image databases must be able to retrieve data based on similarity between the query image and images contained in the image database. In Section 5.4, we provided two alternative characterizations of similarity used in the literature and showed that, in both cases, the preceding representations are only partially successful. We also presented some specialized techniques for image retrieval by similarity. We assumed the existence of either a human, or a computer program, identifying regions in an image that are of interest (determining what objects are contained therein can be done using the techniques described in Section 5.4). If a human is to perform these tasks, then there is, of course, nothing more to be said. However, image-processing algorithms may be used to perform these tasks as well, with the underlying caveat that they are not always highly accurate.

5.6   Representing Image DBs with Relations

Any image database $\mathtt{IDB} = (\mathtt{GI}, \mathtt{Prop}, \mathtt{Rec})$ may be represented using the relational model as follows:

1. Create a relation called `images` having the scheme

    ```
    (Image, ObjId, XLB, XUB, YLB, YUB)
    ```

    where `Image` is the name of an image file; `ObjId` is a dummy name created for an object contained in the image; and `XLB, XUB, YLB, YUB` describe the rectangle in question. If R is a rectangle specified by `XLB, XUB, YLB, YUB` and R is in $\mathtt{Rec}(I)$, then there exists a tuple

    ```
    (I, newid, XLB, XUB, YLB, YUB)
    ```

    in the relation `images`. Figure 5.11 shows the relation `images` associated with the small face database shown in Figure 5.1. (Note that the creation of the relation `images` may be done by applying segmentation methods and matching techniques from image processing. These were discussed in detail in Sections 5.3 and 5.4.)

Image	ObjId	XLB	XUB	YLB	YUB
pic1.gif	o_1	10	60	5	50
pic1.gif	o_2	80	120	20	55
pic2.gif	o_3	20	65	20	75
pic3.gif	o_4	25	75	10	60
pic4.gif	o_5	20	60	30	80
pic5.gif	o_6	0	40	15	50
pic6.gif	o_7	20	75	15	80
pic6.gif	o_8	20	70	130	185
pic7.gif	o_9	15	70	15	75

FIGURE

5.11   The images relation

2. For each property $p \in$ Prop, create a relation R_p having the scheme

    (Image, XLB, XUB, YLB, YUB, Value)

Here, Image is the name of an image file. Unlike the preceding case though, XLB, XUB, YLB, and YUB denote a rectangular cell in the image, and Value specifies the value of the property p.

In general, properties of an image are of three types:

1. *Pixel-level properties:* Pixel-level properties of an image refer to properties such as the red-green-blue colors of individual pixels.

2. *Object/region-level properties:* Some of the objects in an image may have properties of their own. For example, the object o_1 of pic1.gif may have the properties: NAME and AGE, with corresponding values "Hatch, Jim" and 31, respectively.

3. *Image-level properties:* Properties of the image as a whole may include data such as when and where the image was captured, by whom, the type of equipment used, which users are authorized to access it, and so on.

Strictly speaking, given any property p in Prop, we may explicitly represent it as a relation R_p. However, in practice, explicitly representing each pixel value as a tuple in a relation is just plain dumb. Instead, we merely represent explicitly all object/region- and image-level properties as relations and do not explicitly represent pixel-level properties. They are explicit in the image anyway.

5.6.1 Querying Relational Representations of Image DBs

If we have stored the image data in a relational form, then we might be tempted to believe that "straight" SQL can be used to query these relations directly. It can, but only up to a point. To see why, let us consider a simple query, "Find all images in which Jim Hatch appears," and examine why straightforward SQL is not adequate. This query may be written as

```
SELECT   image
FROM     images I, name N
WHERE    I.objid = N.objid AND
         N.name = "Jim Hatch"
```

Unfortunately, the above query doesn't quite do the trick! The reason for this is that, in most large-scale applications, eliciting the contents of an image is done using image-processing algorithms. Sections 5.2 and 5.3 provided a brief description of how image-processing algorithms work (see [144] for an excellent overview of image processing). For now, we note that image-processing algorithms are usually only partially accurate. Thus, if the property NAME associated with an image is determined using an image-processing program, then we are forced to assume that these relations contain probabilistic attributes as well.

Without loss of generality, we may think of each object as having a value associated with each property $p \in$ Prop. Thus, each relation R_p associated with object/region-level properties as well as image-level properties has just two attributes: an object (or region) id and a value for the property. Thus, if we return to the objects in Figure 5.1, the relation name may have the form

ObjId	Name
o_1	Jim Hatch
o_2	John Lee
o_3	John Lee
o_4	Jim Hatch
o_5	Bill Bosco
o_6	Dave Dashell
o_7	Ken Yip
o_8	Bill Bosco
o_7	Ken Yip

The Need for Probabilities

However, an image-processing program that attempts to identify the people occurring in surveillance images may return multiple possible answers with different probabilities of a match. Thus, the two image objects identified as "Jim Hatch" may have some probabilistic attributes associated with the match. Thus, the relation name may need to be expanded to handle such a probabilistic attribute:

ObjId	Name	Prob
o_1	Jim Hatch	0.8
o_1	Dave Fox	0.2
o_2	John Lee	0.75
o_2	Ken Yip	0.15
o_3	John Lee	1
o_4	Jim Hatch	1
o_5	Bill Bosco	1
o_6	Dave Dashell	1
o_7	Ken Yip	0.7
o_7	John Lee	0.3
o_8	Bill Bosco	0.6
o_8	Dave Dashell	0.2
o_8	Jim Hatch	0.10
o_9	Ken Yip	1

Note that in the above probabilistic relation, we have a probability attached with the tuples. Intuitively, the first tuple in the above relation may be read as "The probability that 'Jim Hatch' is the name attribute of o_1 is 0.8." For o_2, the probabilistic relation states:

1. The probability that "John Lee" is the name attribute of o_2 is 0.75.

2. The probability that "Ken Yip" is the name attribute of o_2 is 0.15.

3. There is, in this case, a 10% missing probability.

Under this reading of the probabilistic tuples, things get a trifle more complex when we consider a complex query of the form "Find any image containing both Jim Hatch and Ken Yip." In this case, there are two candidate images—pic1.gif and pic6.gif. Why are these both candidates?

1. The image `pic1.gif` has two objects, o_1 and o_2. There is an 80% probability that o_1 is Jim Hatch and a 15% probability that o_2 is Ken Yip. Hence, this image must be a candidate.

2. The image `pic6.gif` has two objects, o_7 and o_8. There is a 70% probability that o_7 is Ken Yip and a 10% probability that o_8 is Jim Hatch. Hence, this image must be a candidate.

Given this reading, we are faced with the following questions:

1. What is the probability that `pic1.gif` contains both Jim Hatch and Ken Yip? Is the answer the product of the two probabilities—that is, is it $(0.8 \times 0.15) = 0.12$?

2. What is the probability that `pic6.gif` contains both Jim Hatch and Ken Yip? Is the answer $(0.7 \times 0.1) = 0.07$?

You may be tempted to infer that this is the "correct" answer. Unfortunately, things are not quite so simple. To see why, consider a hypothetical image `pic8.gif` with two objects, o_{10} and o_{11}, in it, and suppose our table above is expanded by the insertion of the following new tuples identified by the image-processing algorithm:

ObjId	Name	Prob
o_{10}	Ken Yip	0.5
o_{10}	Jim Hatch	0.4
o_{11}	Jim Hatch	0.8
o_{11}	John Lee	0.1

If we are ignorant[1] about the dependencies between different events (as we are in the above case), then we are forced to confront four possibilities:

- *Possibility 1:* o_{10} is Ken Yip, and o_{11} is Jim Hatch.

---

[1]Note that, in many cases, we might know that the events in question are independent, in which case we can merely multiply probabilities. In this book, our probabilistic relational data model is based on no assumptions being made about the relationship between events, leading to a probabilistic treatment pioneered by Boole [26]. Lakshmanan et al. [121] show how arbitrary probabilistic knowledge may be used to generate new probabilistic relational algebras. Their framework applies to the "ignorance" assumption used in this chapter, as well as a host of other probabilistic assumptions, such as independence, positive correlation, negative correlation, and so on.

- *Possibility 2:* o_{10} is Ken Yip, and o_{11} is not Jim Hatch.

- *Possibility 3:* o_{10} is not Ken Yip, but o_{11} is Jim Hatch.

- *Possibility 4:* o_{10} is not Ken Yip, and o_{11} is not Jim Hatch.

Using the probabilistic data provided in the preceding table, we must assess the four possibilities listed above and find out, for each of these possibilities, the probability that that possibility is in fact the right one! As possibilities 1–4 are mutually incompatible, the probability that `pic8.gif` is an answer to our query is identical to the sum of the probabilities (to be determined) of possibility 1.

Suppose p_i denotes the probability of possibility i, $1 \leq i \leq 4$. Then, we can say that

$$p_1 + p_2 = 0.5$$
$$p_3 + p_4 = 0.5$$
$$p_1 + p_3 = 0.8$$
$$p_2 + p_4 = 0.2$$
$$p_1 + p_2 + p_3 + p_4 = 1$$

The first equation follows from the fact that o_{10} is Ken Yip according to possibilities 1 and 2, and we know from the table that the probability of o_{10} being Ken Yip is 0.5.

The second equation follows from the fact that o_{10} is someone other than Ken Yip according to possibilities 3 and 4, and we know from the table that the probability of o_{10} not being Ken Yip is 0.5.

The third equation follows from the fact that o_{11} is Jim Hatch according to possibilities 1 and 3, and we know from the table that the probability of o_{11} being Jim Hatch is 0.8.

Finally, the fourth equation follows from the fact that o_{11} is someone other than Jim Hatch according to possibilities 2 and 4, and we know from the table that the probability of o_{11} not being Jim Hatch is 0.2.

In order to determine the probability that `pic8.gif` contains both Ken Yip and Jim Hatch, we must attempt to solve the above system of linear equations for p_1, keeping in mind that all possible scenarios are covered by our four possibilities. The result we obtain, using a linear programming engine, is that p_1's probability is not uniquely determinable. It could be as low as 0.3 or as high as 0.5, or anywhere in between. In particular, note that merely multiplying the probability of 0.5 associated with Ken Yip being object o_{10} and the probability value 0.8 of Jim Hatch being object o_{11} leads to a probability of 0.4, which is certainly inside this interval, but does not accurately capture the four possibilities listed above.

Unfortunately, this result, though correct, poses a fundamental new problem. In the relational model of data, the answer to any query may be stored as a relation itself. In the case of relations with probabilistic attributes, we would like the results of queries to themselves be probabilistic relations. However, a probabilistic relation had one single probability attribute to start off with, but the results of queries caused us to end up with *probability intervals* such as the interval $[0.3, 0.5]$ we just derived above.

The Need for Probability Intervals

The above example shows that if we wish to store information of the form "Object o occurring in image i is X with probability p," we run into trouble. In contrast, as we shall see below, replacing the *point probability* with an interval $[\ell, u]$ allows us to escape this problem. This approach also has an additional advantage. When an image-processing program identifies an object o in image i as X with probability p, then if we take into account the fact that there is a margin of error ϵ in such an identification, we end up, naturally, with the interval probability $[p - \epsilon, p + \epsilon]$.

Thus, in general, let us return to the table associated with the probabilistic version of the relation name given in the preceding section, expand it by including pic8.gif, and assume a margin of error of $\pm 3\%$. Thus, if we had a probability of p in that table, then we replace that probability by the interval $[max(0, p - 0.03), min(1, p + 0.03)]$ to obtain the following table:

ObjId	Name	Prob (Lower)	Prob (Upper)
o_1	Jim Hatch	0.77	0.83
o_1	Dave Fox	0.17	0.23
o_2	John Lee	0.72	0.78
o_2	Ken Yip	0.12	0.18
o_3	John Lee	0.97	1.00
o_4	Jim Hatch	0.97	1.00
o_5	Bill Bosco	0.97	1.00
o_6	Dave Dashell	0.97	1.00
o_7	Ken Yip	0.67	0.73
o_7	John Lee	0.27	0.33
o_8	Bill Bosco	0.57	0.63
o_8	Dave Dashell	0.17	0.23
o_8	Jim Hatch	0.07	0.13
o_9	Ken Yip	0.97	1.00
o_{10}	Ken Yip	0.47	0.53
o_{10}	Jim Hatch	0.37	0.43
o_{11}	Jim Hatch	0.77	0.83
o_{11}	John Lee	0.07	0.13

Let's now return to the query "Find an image that contains both Ken Yip and Jim Hatch." Let's reexamine the image pic8.gif and see what the probability of this image containing both Ken Yip and Jim Hatch is. In this case, using the same reasoning and notation as we did for interval probabilities, we may write down the following constraints:

$$0.47 \leq p_1 + p_2 \leq 0.53$$
$$0.47 \leq p_3 + p_4 \leq 0.53$$
$$0.77 \leq p_1 + p_3 \leq 0.83$$
$$0.17 \leq p_2 + p_4 \leq 0.23$$
$$p_1 + p_2 + p_3 + p_4 = 1$$

Let us quickly see how the third and fourth inequalities above were obtained. The third inequality is derived from our knowledge that Jim Hatch is object o_{11} with probability between 77 and 83%. As in the case of point probabilities, there are two possibilities (i.e., possibilities 1 and 3) in which object o_{11} is in fact Jim Hatch. Thus, $p_1 + p_3$ must lie within the 77–83% interval.

The fourth inequality is derived from our knowledge that object o_{11} is someone other than Jim Hatch with probability 17–23%, since $100 - 83 = 17$ and $100 - 77 = 23$. There are two possibilities (i.e., possibilities 2 and 4) in which object o_{11} is not Jim Hatch. Thus, $p_2 + p_4$ must lie within the 17–23% interval.

Solving the above linear program for minimal and maximal values of the variable p_1, we obtain 0.24 and 0.53, respectively.

A General Approach

Let us define a *probabilistic relation* over a scheme $(A_1, \ldots, A_n)$ to be an ordinary relation over the scheme $(A_1, \ldots, A_n, \mathsf{LB}, \mathsf{UB})$ where the domain of the LB and UB attributes is the unit interval $[0, 1]$ of real numbers. In particular, the relation `name` is a probabilistic relation that has three attributes,

```
(ImageId, ObjectId, Name)
```

of the sort we have already seen thus far. The `name` relation satisfies some integrity constraints:

$$(\forall t_1, t_2)\ t_1.\mathsf{ObjId}=t_2.\mathsf{ObjId} \rightarrow t_1.\mathsf{ImageId} = t_2.\mathsf{ImageId}$$

This constraint states that an `ObjectId` can be associated with only one image; that is, distinct images have distinct `ObjectIds`. The following constraint says that the LB field of any tuple is always smaller than or equal to the UB field:

$$(\forall t)\qquad t.\mathsf{LB} \le t.\mathsf{UB}$$

An *image database* consists of a probabilistic relation called `name` of the above form, together with a set of *ordinary* (i.e., nonprobabilistic) relations $R_1, \ldots, R_k$ corresponding to image properties. The reason for this distinction is because the only operation that leads to uncertainty in image databases is the identification of the objects in the images, and this is automatically captured by the `name` relations. Properties of images, such as red, green, blue values, and other attributes such as the camera used and the time/date the image was taken can usually be determined with certainty.

A *membership query* in an image database is a query of the form "Find all images in the image database that contain objects named $s_1, \ldots, s_n$."

This query can be expressed in ordinary SQL as

```
SELECT   ImageId
FROM     name T₁, ... ,Tₙ
WHERE    T₁.Name=s₁ AND ··· AND Tₙ.Name=sₙ AND
         T₁.ImageId=T₂.ImageId AND ··· AND T₁.ImageId=Tₙ.ImageId
```

The result of this membership query is a table containing three fields—the `ImageId` field that is explicitly listed in the query, an `LB` field, and a `UB` field. (im, ℓ, u) is in the result iff for each $1 \leq j \leq n$, there exists a tuple $t_j \in$ name such that

1. `t.ImageId` $= im$,

2. `t.LB` $= \ell_i$ and `t.UB` $= u_i$, and

3. $[\ell, u] = [\ell_1, u_1] \otimes [\ell_2, u_2] \otimes \cdots \otimes [\ell_n, u_n]$

where

$$[x, y] \otimes [x', y'] = [max(0, x + x' - 1), min(y, y')]$$

It turns out, by a long and complex reasoning process (see Ng and Subrahmanian [145] and Zaniolo et al. [231]) that the $\otimes$ operator above yields the same result as solving the linear program described previously. Thus, by virtue of the Ng-Subrahmanian result, image databases can be efficiently implemented using the simple $\otimes$ operator described above.

A simple enhancement to SQL to handle the above is to include a special operator called `HAS`. To find all images that contain objects named $s_1, \ldots, s_n$, we merely need to write the query

```
name HAS s_1, ..., s_n
```

The semantics of this special structure is realized through the more complex SQL query we wrote and described earlier.

The syntax of ordinary SQL may then be extended to allow the conditions of the form

```
name HAS s_1, ..., s_n
```

as a part of the `WHERE` clause. For example, the query below uses the bank relation in Chapter 2, plus the `HAS` construct just introduced above, to "Find all people who have had deposits of over $9,000, and who have been photographed with Denis Jones."

```
SELECT  I.ImageId
FROM    name I, bank B
WHERE   I HAS B.name, "Denis Jones" AND
        B.trans = deposit AND B.amount > 9000 AND
        B.name = I.name
```

5.7 Representing Image DBs with R-Trees

Image databases may also be represented as R-trees. If we look at all the examples we have seen thus far, we notice that objects are typically represented as rectangles. Thus, one way to represent an image database is as follows:

1. Create a relation called occursin with two attributes (ImageId,ObjId) specifying which objects appear in which images.

2. Create one R-tree that stores all the rectangles. If the same rectangle (say, with XLB = 5, XUB = 15, YLB = 20, YUB = 30) appears in two images, then we have an overflow list associated with that node in the R-tree.

3. Each rectangle has an associated set of fields that specifies the object/region-level properties of that rectangle. These fields contain information about the "content" of the rectangle.

To see how this representation works, we will describe how the small face database of Figure 5.1 is stored using the R-tree technique.

First, the occursin relation is the following table:

pic1.gif	o_1
pic1.gif	o_2
pic2.gif	o_3
pic3.gif	o_4
pic4.gif	o_5
pic5.gif	o_6
pic6.gif	o_7
pic6.gif	o_8
pic7.gif	o_9

The nodes in the R-tree representation associated with this database may have the following structure:

```
facenode = record
    Rec₁,Rec₂,Rec₃:  rectangle;
    P₁,P₂,P₃:  ↑rtnodetype
end
```

```
rectangle = record
   XLB,XUB,YLB,YUB: integer;
   objlist:  ↑objnode;
   day,mth, yr:  integer;
   camera_type:  string;
   other_info:  data_record; (* stores info about rectangle *)
   place:  string
end

objnode = record
   objid:  string;
   imageid:  string;
   data:  ↑infotype    (* stores arbitrary information
                 about the object *)
   nxt:  ↑objnode
end

infotype - record
   objname:  string;
   objdata:  objdata_record;
   Lp, Up:  real:  (* lower and upper probability bounds *)
   Next:  ↑infotype
end
```

In the definition of `objnode` above, `Lp` and `Up` denote the lower bound and upper bound, respectively, of the probability that this identification is correct.

Let us consider a really simple image database, consisting just of the photographs `pic1.gif`, `pic2.gif`, and `pic3.gif` of Figure 5.1. Suppose these photographs contain the objects o_1, o_2, o_3, and o_4 with the probability intervals specified earlier in the interval probabilistic version of the `name` relation. Figure 5.12 shows the R-tree used to represent these three images and the four objects involved. The R-tree of Figure 5.12 is constructed by the following steps:

1. *Get rectangles:* First, we construct a small table describing all the rectangles that occur and the images they occur in. Figure 5.13 shows the four rectangles o_1, o_2, o_3, and o_4. Note that even though these rectangles were obtained from different images, we are superimposing all of them within a single image.

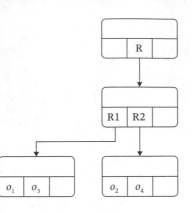

FIGURE

5.12 R-tree representing simple face database

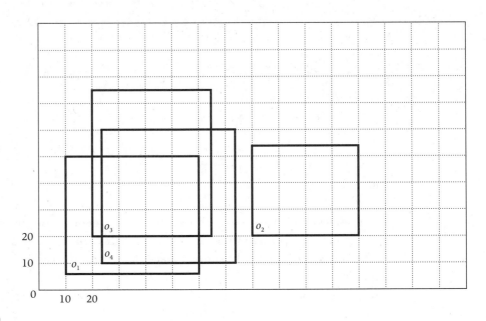

FIGURE

5.13 Superimposed rectangles representing face objects

ObjId	ImageId	XLB	XUB	YLB	YUB
o_1	pic1.gif	10	60	5	50
o_2	pic1.gif	80	120	20	55
o_3	pic2.gif	20	65	20	75
o_4	pic3.gif	25	75	10	60

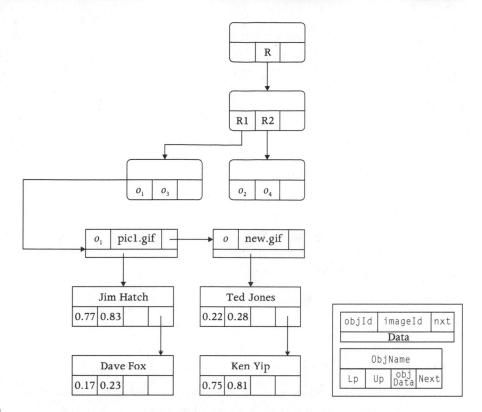

5.14 Fleshed-out R-tree (with objects o and o_1 fleshed out)

2. *Create R-tree:* We then create an R-tree representing the above rectangles (shown in Figure 5.12). At this stage the object nodes in the R-tree may still not be filled in completely.

3. *Flesh out objects:* We then flesh out and appropriately fill in the fields of the various objects stored in the R-tree. Figure 5.14 shows the contents of the different nodes when a new object o is added to the system, and this new object has exactly the same XLB, XUB, YLB, YUB fields as object o_1. The only difference between object o_1 and the new object o is that the latter occurs in a different image.

5.7.1 Representing Image DBs with Generalized R-Trees

The representation of image data with R-trees just described above does not provide an efficient way to perform nearest neighbor searches. The reason for this is that each object o has an associated rectangle, R_o. However, this rectangle is a rectangle in 2-space, as shown in Figure 5.14. This representation stores the attributes of each object in its "Data" field. As the "Data" field is not used in creating the R-tree index, this means that retrievals based on these fields are inefficient, thus making nearest neighbor searching very cumbersome.

There are two straightforward extensions of R-trees that may be used to solve this problem. The first is based on the notion of generalized R-trees (gR-trees) described below. The second is based on telescoping vector trees (TV-trees) that we will study later in Section 6.4.

Recall that an object o can be represented by a region in an $(n + 2)$-dimensional space, where each object has n features and the other two dimensions represent the rectangle bounding the object. A *generalized rectangle* for a space of dimensionality g (specifically consider $g = n + 2$) may be defined by a set of constraints of the form:

$$\ell_1 \leq x_1 \leq u_1$$
$$\ell_2 \leq x_2 \leq u_2$$
$$\ldots$$
$$\ell_g \leq x_g \leq u_g$$

Note that when $g = 2$, we have $n = 0$, and in this case, an ordinary 2-dimensional rectangle is a special case of this definition.

If we now have a set *Obj* of objects, we may represent this set of objects by a set of $(n + 2)$-dimensional constraints. A generalized R-tree (gR-tree) of order K is exactly like an R-tree except for the following factors:

- First, each node N represents a generalized bounding rectangle $GBR(N)$ of dimensionality $(n+2)$, which is represented by $2 \times (n+2)$ real number fields, one for the lower bound and upper bound, respectively, of each dimension.

- When a node N is split, the union of the generalized bounding rectangles associated with its children equals the generalized bounding rectangle associated with N.

- Each node (other than the root and the leaves) contains at most K generalized bounding rectangles and at least $\lceil K/2 \rceil$ generalized rectangles.

- As usual, all $(n + 2)$-dimensional "data" rectangles are stored in leaves.

Thus, gR-trees are defined in exactly the same way as R-trees, except that nodes now contain a set of generalized bounding rectangles rather than a set of 2-dimensional bounding rectangles. Obviously, the structure of a node is expanded to describe the upper and lower bounds of the $(n + 2)$ dimensions. Nearest neighbor searching may now be efficiently performed as follows.

Suppose R_Q is a query rectangle (which may represent an image object). We want to find all rectangles in a gR-tree T that are as close to R_Q as possible (where closeness is defined by a metric d on points). We extend the metric d to apply to rectangles as follows:

$$d(R, R') = \min\{d(p, p') \mid p \in R, p' \in R'\}.$$

Our search now proceeds as shown in the following algorithm.

Algorithm 5.5

```
NN_Search_GR(T,R_Q) SOL = NIL;      (* no solution so far *);
Todo = List containing T only;
Bestdist =∞; (* distance of best solution from R_Q *);
while Todo ≠ NIL do
{
   F = first element of Todo;
   Todo = delete F from Todo;
   if d(GBR(F),R_Q)) < Bestdist then
   {
       Compute children N₁, ... ,Nᵣ of F;
       if Nᵢ's are leaves of T then
       {
           N_min = any Nᵢ at minimal distance from R_Q;
           Ndist = d(GBR(Nᵢ),R_Q));
           if Ndist < Bestdist then
           {
               Bestdist = Ndist; SOL = N_min;
           }
       }
       else Todo = insert all Nᵢ's into Todo in order of distance from R_Q;
   }
}
Return SOL;
end
```

Later, in Section 6.4, we will develop an alternative data structure called a TV-tree to handle storage of objects involving high-dimensional data.

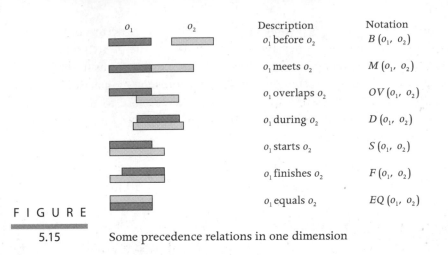

	Description	Notation
o_1 o_2	o_1 before o_2	$B(o_1, o_2)$
	o_1 meets o_2	$M(o_1, o_2)$
	o_1 overlaps o_2	$OV(o_1, o_2)$
	o_1 during o_2	$D(o_1, o_2)$
	o_1 starts o_2	$S(o_1, o_2)$
	o_1 finishes o_2	$F(o_1, o_2)$
	o_1 equals o_2	$EQ(o_1, o_2)$

FIGURE

5.15   Some precedence relations in one dimension

5.8   Retrieving Images by Spatial Layout

Finally, before concluding this section, we present a simple outline of another kind of retrieval operation that users may wish to perform on images. Given an image I and two objects (represented by rectangles) o_1 and o_2 in I, a user may wish to ask queries like the following:

1. Is o_1 to the south of o_2?

2. Is o_1 to the southeast of o_2?

3. Is o_1 to the left of o_2?

4. Are o_1 and o_2 overlapping?

These are just four simple queries that a user may wish to ask that allude to the spatial layout of objects in an image. In order to answer such queries effectively, it turns out that first, some precedence relations need to be introduced.

Figure 5.15 shows some elementary precedence relations that may be defined between objects when they are compared along one dimension (e.g., the x-dimension in Figure 5.15). The notations are explained in the figure.

Extending precedence relations along one dimension to two dimensions is straightforward. If we use the notation $o[x]$ and $o[y]$ to denote the projection of object o on the x- and y-axes, respectively, then it is easy to capture our spatial relationships as follows:

1. We say o_1 is South of o_2 iff $B(o_1[y], o_2[y])$ and one of $D(o_1[x], o_2[x])$ or $D(o_2[x], o_1[x])$

or $S(o_1[x], o_2[x])$ or $S(o_2[x], o_1[x])$
or $F(o_1[x], o_2[x])$ or $F(o_2[x], o_1[x])$
or $EQ(o_1[x], o_2[x])$
holds.

2. Likewise, we say that o_1 is to the Left of o_2 iff either $B(o_1[x], o_2[x])$ or $M(o_1[x], o_2[x])$ holds.

Similar definitions can be given for properties such as North, West, East, Northwest, Southwest, Northeast, Southeast, Right, Below, Above, Equal, Inside, Cover, Overlap, and Disjoint.

You will observe that the multidimensional data structures of Chapter 4 can easily support all the spatial operations described in this section.

5.9   Implementations

Current database management systems that support image databases do so largely in terms of an object-oriented implementation. They assume that images are objects, in the strict sense of object-oriented databases, and that the class of image objects has certain methods available such as the following:

1. rotate(ImageId,dir,angle) takes an image and rotates it in either the clockwise or counterclockwise direction for a specified angle, and returns the resulting image as output.

2. segment(ImageId,H_Pred) takes an image and a homogeneity predicate as input and returns all regions in a segmentation of the image with respect to the homogeneity predicate *H_Pred* as output. Note here that the result is a *set* of regions, not just one region.

3. edit(image,editop) takes an image and an edit operation and returns the image after performing the edit operation. Examples of edit operations include changing the background color, changing the texture of the image, replacing certain colors by certain other colors, and inverting the image (e.g., making the foreground black and the background white, when it had previously been the opposite).

Most current image databases work in the following way:

1. They assume that whole images are being compared (thus avoiding the need for segmentation).

2. They assume that, given any image, they can associate a few salient properties (such as image color, shape, texture, etc.) with the image. These properties are stored as a vector of n fields.

3. For an image database, an index is created, consisting of these n-dimensional vectors. Thus, each image I is represented as a point v_I in n-space. Such an index is typically a multidimensional extension of a point quadtree or an R-tree.

4. When the user asks a query of the form "Find all images similar to the query image Q," they proceed by attempting to find all vectors v_I such that the (perhaps weighted) Euclidean distance between vectors v_I and v_Q is below some specified threshold. All such Is are then returned.

5.10   Selected Commercial Systems

Camrax's (*http://www.camrax.com*) Knoware image databases include a variety of image-based database applications for artwork, real estate, and personnel management systems. There is also a comprehensive image index.

One of the world leaders in the development of image databases is Informix, in partnerships with various commercial vendors. Informix's datablade architecture allows several image-oriented datablades to be plugged in and accessed from any Informix system.

The Informix commercial DBMS system supports image datablades that allow users of the Informix server to query databases that include images indexed using specialized techniques. These datablades build on object-relational technology and support a wide variety of image operations, including conversion, storage, and enhancement. Manipulation operations include scaling, shearing, rotation, and image merging.

Informix also has a visual image retrieval datablade (VIR) that supports both audio and video retrieval based on content. When applied to images, this datablade allows the retrieval of images based on attributes such as shape, color, texture, and composition.

Informix's face recognition datablade module, developed by Excalibur Technologies, uses feature vectors to build indexes based on various facial features. The system also stores spatial information about such features. It allows client programs to access this database. Informix information may be obtained from *http://www.informix.com*.

IBM's DB2 system has an image extender that builds upon the Query by Image Content project to facilitate retrieval of data based on attributes of images such as colors, texture, and so on. In their framework, you can select a picture, and then ask to find pictures in the archive that are similar to the selected picture. All information on IBM's DB2 system extenders can be found at *http://www.software.ibm.com/data/db2/extenders/index.html*.

In addition, IBM has an extender for storing fingerprint data. For instance, consider the Sample Multimedia Scenario. Clearly, any law enforcement agency interested in catching drug criminals would like to maintain fingerprint data on file. IBM's fingerprint extender provides facilities to index fingerprints based on identifying patterns and orientation of the fingerprint. Fingerprints may then be searched on these patterns.

Genesys (*http://www.icspdx.com/genesys*) has announced an image extender. The image extender from Genesys works with the Genesys image server to handle image-processing requests.

5.11 Bibliographic Notes

One of the first efforts at describing image databases was made by Grosky [78, 79], who proposed architectural schemes to represent image data. Grosky also proposed an initial extension of SQL for querying image databases. Roussopoulos, Faloutsos, and Sellis [172] proposed a language called PSQL that allowed a wide variety of search operations including *point* functions (e.g., nearest and furthest), *segment* functions (e.g., length and slope), *region* functions (e.g., area and perimeter), and hybrids of these functions. They show how these operators can be efficiently implemented using a data structure called the R^+-tree, defined in Sellis, Roussopoulos, and Faloutsos [183]. Sistla, Yu, and Haddad [190] and Li, Ozsu, and Szafron [125] provide detailed techniques to evaluate certain kinds of spatial layout queries.

Detailed software code for the DFT and the DCT can be obtained from the FFTPACK libraries at *http://netlib.org/fftpack/*. C programs implementing the DCT may be obtained from *http://www.evitech.fi/ACADEMIC/Materials/Karenl/mm/MMdct.html*. Finally, fast algorithms for DCT have been developed by Sherlock and Monro [186]. The new technique of wavelets for image representations is well presented by Daubechies [51].

The concept of similarity between image objects goes back to Tversky [209, 210] who proposed a two-valued "Feature Contrast" paradigm that characterizes the similarity of two objects in terms of the contrasts between their respectively features. While most work on databases assumes that similarity is a symmetric property, Tversky's work attacks this assumption based on psychological evidence from people. Tversky's point of view is corroborated by Rosh [170]. Almost all work in databases, on the other hand, assumes explicitly that similarity is somehow defined as an antimonotonic function of distance; that is, if the objects of interest form a metric space with respect to a metric d, then $d(x, y) \leq d(x, z)$ implies that $S(x, y) \geq S(x, z)$, where S denotes some binary similarity function. In an excellent survey paper, Santini and Jain [182] provide a detailed overview of similarity. They propose a fuzzy-logic-based approach to similarity that extends Tversky's binary (i.e., two-valued) concept of Feature Contrast.

Algorithms for image segmentation have been extensively studied by many researchers. Nalwa [144] provides an excellent introduction to the field. The split-merge algorithm described here is a variant of the segmentation procedure based on tree traversals of Horowitz and Pavlidis [96]. Several predicates for checking homogeneity have been proposed by researchers. One of the most sophisticated of these is the variable-order surface fitting technique of Besl and Jain [24]. Haralick and Shapiro [89] also provide details of various segmentation algorithms.

The treatment of spatial layout relations given in this chapter is based on the work of Li, Ozsu, and Szafron [125]. Sistla, Yu, and Haddad [190] have developed *logical* axioms for capturing spatial relationships in pictures. They show that their axioms are complete for the two-dimensional case, but are not complete in the three-dimensional case.

Several systems for image retrieval exist. The QBIC system developed at IBM applies to both image data and video data [147]. The QBISM system for image retrieval in medical domains builds upon the experiences with QBIC and provides techniques based on z-ordering for random access of volume (3-d) data [13]. The CHABOT system uses simple color and text analysis strategies for image retrieval [151]. The MACS system allows querying and integration not just of image data, but also heterogeneous data sources including video [28]. The MACS+HERMES system includes accessing images annotated textually and with captions, as well as accessing face recognition algorithms to manipulate a face database. Srihari [193] develops techniques to retrieve captioned images.

5.12   Exercises and Projects

1. Write an algorithm that takes a point (x, y), a pointer T to the root of a point quadtree, and a positive integer n as input, and returns a sequence $p_1, \ldots, p_n$ of n points as output such that $p_1, \ldots, p_n$ are the n closest points in tree T to the point (x, y). $p_1, \ldots, p_n$ should be printed out in nondescending order of their distance from the point (x, y).

2. Repeat the above problem for the case of MX-quadtrees, and compare the relative times taken. Which is faster in the worst case? Why?

3. Given a point p and a rectangle R, let's define the *rectangular distance*, $rd(p, R)$, between p and R, to be

    $$min\{d(p, p') \mid p' \text{ is a point in } R\}$$

    Now, given a pointer T to the root of an R-tree, a point (x, y), and a positive integer n, write an algorithm that returns a sequence of the n closest rectangles $R_1, \ldots, R_n$ to (x, y) in nondescending order of their distance from the point (x, y).

4. Provide definitions, in predicate logic, for the following spatial layout operations: North, West, East, Northwest, Southwest, Northeast, Southeast, Right, Below, Above, Equal, Inside, Cover, Overlap, Disjoint.

5. As a project, develop a software package that implements the transformation-based approach to retrieval by similarity. In particular, your package must contain the following capabilities that can be encoded as functions:

    (a) Develop a syntax in which transformation operators can be represented. Then develop a program, called TransformationLibraryManager, that takes as input, perhaps through a user interface or from a file, a transformation operator specified in your syntax, and appends it to the library through a TLMinsert routine. Similarly, write a TLMsearch routine that, given the name of an instantiated operator, will return an appropriately instantiated version of the operator.

    (b) Develop a syntax in which cost functions can be represented. Then write a program, called CostFunctionServer, that has a Costinsert routine that takes as input, perhaps through a user interface or from a file, a cost function specified in your syntax, and appends it to a library of cost functions. CostFunctionServer must also have a function, called EvaluateCall, that takes an instantiated transformation operator as input and returns the cost of this operator as output, using the cost functions represented using your syntax.

(c) Develop a program, called `ObjectConvertor`, that takes two objects o_1 and o_2 as input and that uses `TransformationLibraryManager` and `CostFunctionServer` to construct a least-cost transformation sequence between o_1 and o_2.

(d) Demonstrate your system's operation using the simple example of transformation sequences in Figure 5.10. In particular, specify all the operations for this example in your syntax, as well as all the cost functions.

6 Text/Document Databases

What new concepts will you learn in this chapter?
You will learn what a text database is. You will learn what the problems in querying a text database are. You will be introduced to two concepts—*precision* and *recall*, which specify how to measure the performance of a text retrieval algorithm.

What new abstractions are needed to realize these concepts?
Documents are characterized by the words occurring in them. However, the same word may mean different things when used in different contexts (called *polysemy*). Alternatively, different words may mean the same thing (called *synonymy*). You will learn about techniques for clustering "similar" documents. A query is nothing but a small document, and the result of a query is a set of documents similar to it.

What new techniques are needed to implement these abstractions?
You will learn about *latent semantic indexing* (LSI)—a technique to implement ways of matching query documents against documents in the archive. The underlying mathematical basis for LSI is called *singular-valued decomposition* (SVD). You will learn about the basic ideas of SVDs in this chapter.

What technological features support these implementation methods?
You will receive a quick overview of existing text database management systems on both the Unix and Windows software platforms.

DocumentID	String
d_1	Jose Orojuelo's Operations in Bosnia
d_2	The Medellin Cartel's Financial Organization
d_3	The Cali Cartel's Distribution Network
d_4	Banking Operations and Money Laundering
d_5	Profile of Hector Gomez
d_6	Connections between Terrorism and Asian Dope Operations
d_7	Hector Gomez: How He Gave Agents the Slip in Cali
d_8	Sex, Drugs, and Videotape
d_9	The Iranian Connection
d_{10}	Boating and Drugs: Slips Owned by the Cali Cartel

FIGURE
6.1   Some document titles

Ever since their invention, one of the fundamental uses of computers has been to store textual documents, usually in the form of text files (formatted or otherwise). Initial efforts in this area revolved around a very simple idea: a document D was thought of as being represented by a string. For example, the string could be the entire document, or just the document title, or the entire document abstract. A document database was just a collection of such strings indexed in a suitable manner. For example, if the document representation uses the title of the documents to index the documents (as in Figure 6.1), then a suitable method is used to index this collection of strings. When a user wanted to find documents related to a topic T, the search program tried to find the documents in the document database that contained the string T. This led to a good deal of research on efficient string-matching and substring-finding algorithms. Unfortunately, this approach proved rather naive for two fundamental reasons:

1. *Synonymy:* It may well be the case that given a topic T, the word T does not occur anywhere in a document D, even though the document D is in fact closely related to the topic T in question. For example, suppose we are considering only the document titles listed in Figure 6.1. Suppose the index is constructed from these titles, rather than from the entire document, and a user asks the following queries:

   (a) "Find all documents related to the topic *money laundering*." As neither of these words appears in the title of document d_2, that document would be missed by any string match algorithm.

(b) "Find all documents related to the topic *drugs.*" The situation here is even worse because document d_6 would be missed (the word *dope*, which is more or less synonymous with *drugs*, would be missed by syntactic string matching). Similarly documents d_2 and d_3 would also be missed—both should certainly be returned since they are about drug cartels.

In this case, the problem is that the index may contain one or more words used to describe each document, but it is impossible to anticipate, and index a priori, all possible query words that an unknown user might want to search for.

2. *Polysemy:* Another fundamental problem is that the same word may mean many different things in different contexts. For example, the word *bank* could mean a number of different things: a financial institution, a river bank, to rely on ("bank on"), and so on. Clearly, when asked to retrieve documents relating to finances, we are not interested in an article having the title "Otters on the Banks of the Colorado River" or the title "Divorce: Don't Bank on Your Spouse!" returned to us as part of the answer, even though the word *bank* forms a legitimate component of these titles.

In this chapter, we will first introduce two basic measures for evaluating the performance of text retrieval systems—precision and recall. We will then describe a very recent approach, called Latent Semantic Indexing (LSI), for accessing large text databases based on "semantic content." LSI has recently proven to be one of the most successful methods for indexing large textual archives. This technique allows us to eliminate words and phrases that do not allow us to distinguish between different documents, and also allows us to identify words that do distinguish between different documents. It also identifies similar words. The LSI technique effectively associates a bounded-size vector *vec(d)* of term frequencies with any document *d*. This vector is then used for all retrievals. This topic forms the heart of this chapter. As a document *d* is now represented by a vector *vec(d)*, the problem of storing a document database (in the LSI paradigm) is essentially equivalent to that of storing a set of such vectors of relatively high dimension (usually the vector has about 200 fields).

We next describe a specialized data structure, called a telescoping vector tree (TV-tree), that is useful for LSI. When a user wishes to retrieve all documents about a certain topic (i.e., he specifies a set of keywords), the query *Q* is considered to be a document d_Q, and this document also has an associated vector $vec(d_Q)$. We then search the TV-tree data structure to find the *n* nearest

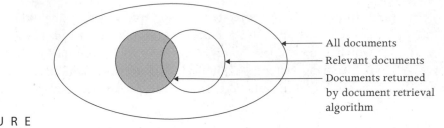

Document retrieval: relevance predicate and actual results

neighbors of the query document vector $vec(d_Q)$ with respect to a specific distance metric. These are then returned. Later, in Section 6.5, we will quickly overview some alternative techniques for querying text databases.

6.1   Precision and Recall

Suppose D is a finite set of documents, and suppose $\mathcal{A}$ is any algorithm that takes a topic string t as input and returns a set $\mathcal{A}(t)$ of documents as output; that is, $\mathcal{A}(t) \subseteq D$. Intuitively, one may think of $\mathcal{A}$ as encoding an algorithm or technique for document retrieval.

Suppose that, in addition, we have a predicate *relevant* with two arguments: a topic t and a document d. Intuitively, if $relevant(t, d)$ is true, then this means that document d is considered relevant to topic t. We are not concerned with exactly how the relevance predicate is implemented. For instance, the relevance predicate may have been handcrafted by a human being on a specific test set $D_{test} \subseteq D$ of documents and a similar test set T_{test} of topics.

Figure 6.2 shows an illustration of this situation. The unshaded circle in Figure 6.2 shows all documents that are relevant to a query topic t, while the shaded circle shows those documents that are in fact returned by the document retrieval algorithm when it is requested to retrieve documents pertaining to a topic t.

We say that the *precision* of algorithm $\mathcal{A}$ with respect to the predicate *relevant* and test set D_{test} is $P_t\%$ for topic $t \in T_{test}$ iff

$$P_t = 100 \times \frac{1 + card(\{d \in D_{test} \mid d \in \mathcal{A}(t) \wedge relevant(t, d) \text{ is true}\})}{1 + card(\{d \in D_{test} \mid d \in \mathcal{A}(t)\})}$$

(To avoid division by zero, we add one to both the numerator and denominator above.) We say that the precision of algorithm $\mathcal{A}$ with respect to the predicate *relevant*, the document test set D_{test}, and the topic test set T_{test} is $P\%$ iff

$$P = \frac{\sum_{t \in T_{test}} P_t}{card(T_{test})}$$

In other words, the precision of an algorithm $\mathcal{A}$ for information retrieval, with respect to suitable test sets and relevance definitions, is measured by determining how many of the answers returned by the algorithm are in fact correct. Thus, in Figure 6.2, we should count the number of objects in the intersection of the two circles (and add one to it), and then divide this number by the number of objects in the shaded circle (with one added to it).

In contrast, the *recall* of an algorithm $\mathcal{A}$ is a measure of how many of the right documents are in fact retrieved by the query. Precision asks the question "How many of the documents retrieved by algorithm $\mathcal{A}$ are correct?" Recall asks the question "How many of the documents that should have been retrieved by algorithm $\mathcal{A}$ were in fact retrieved?"

Using the same notation as for precision, the recall R_t associated with a topic t is given by the following formula:

$$R_t = 100 \times \frac{1 + card(\{d \in D_{test} \mid d \in \mathcal{A}(t) \wedge \ relevant(t, d) \text{ is true}\})}{1 + card(\{d \in D_{test} \mid relevant(t, d) \text{ is true}\})}$$

The overall recall rate R associated with test sets D_{test} of documents and T_{test} of topics is given by

$$R = \frac{\sum_{t \in T_{test}} R_t}{card(T_{test})}$$

In other words, in Figure 6.2, we need to count all the documents in the intersection of the two regions (and add one to this number) and divide it by the number of elements in the unshaded region (with one added to it).

For example, suppose the number of objects in each region of Figure 6.2 is as shown in Figure 6.3. Then, the precision of retrieval for this specific topic is given by

$$\frac{20 + 1}{20 + 150 + 1} = \frac{21}{171}$$

By the same reasoning, the recall for this specific topic is given by

$$\frac{20 + 1}{20 + 50 + 1} = \frac{21}{71}$$

Precision and recall form the two best-known ways of measuring "how good" an algorithm for text retrieval is. In many cases, an algorithm with a

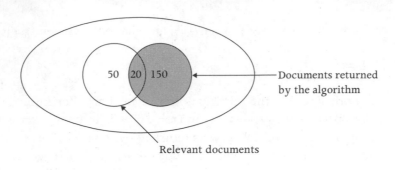

Documents returned
by the algorithm

Relevant documents

F I G U R E

6.3   Precision and recall: an example

very high precision may have very poor recall. For instance, an algorithm that returns absolutely nothing would have a precision of 100%, but such an algorithm may not be very useful. On the other hand, it is equally possible that an algorithm with a very high recall rate may have very poor precision. The algorithm that always returns every document has 100% recall, but it is not of very much use.

6.2   Stop Lists, Word Stems, and Frequency Tables

In this section, we introduce some basic techniques that are used in most document/text retrieval systems.

A *stop list* associated with a document set D is a set StopL of words that are deemed "irrelevant," even though they may appear frequently. For example, the SMART system developed at Cornell University uses a stop list of 439 words. Examples of words that could appear in stop lists include *the*, *and*, *for*, *with*, and so on. Obviously, stop lists may vary as D varies. For instance, if D is a set of documents associated with the University of Maryland's Computer Science technical reports, then it may be useful to place the word *computer* on the stop list associated with this document base. In contrast, the word *computer* may not be on the stop list of a collection of documents about *archeology*. As you may have guessed, the purpose of a stop list is to eliminate words that are "useless" from the point of view of searching/indexing.

Often, several words are small syntactic variants of each other. For example, the words *drug*, *drugged*, and *drugs* are all similar in the sense that they share a common *word stem*—drug. A document d_1 containing the word *drugged* is as likely to be about drugs as an identical document d_2 obtained from d_1 by replacing all occurrences of *drugged* in d_1 by *drug*. By reducing different words to their stems, we implicitly group together words that are derived from the same stem. Thus, instead of indexing documents based on three different words—*drug*, *drugged*, and *drugs*—we would use only one of these words, the stem *drug*, to index on.

Suppose D is a set of N documents, and T is a set of M words/terms occurring in the documents of D. Assume that no words on the stop list for D occur in T, and that all words in T have been stemmed. The *frequency table*, `FreqT`, associated with D and T is an $(M \times N)$ matrix such that `FreqT`(i, j) equals the number of occurrences of the word t_i in document d_j.

For example, consider the document set $D = \{d_8, d_9, d_{10}\}$ shown in Figure 6.1. In addition, suppose we have one extra document, d_{11}, having the title "Drugs, drugs, drugs." The words involved in these four document titles are *sex*, *drug*, *videotape*, *iran*, *connection*, *boat*, *slip*, *own*, *cali*, and *cartel*. Note that words such as *and* and *the* are not listed in this list because they are assumed to occur in the stop list for D. Likewise, words such as *owned* have been replaced by their stem, *own*. The frequency table for these four documents is

Term/document	d_8	d_9	d_{10}	d_{11}
sex	1	0	0	0
drug	1	0	1	3
videotape	1	0	0	0
iran	0	1	0	0
connection	0	1	0	0
boat	0	0	1	0
slip	0	0	1	0
own	0	0	1	0
cali	0	0	1	0
cartel	0	0	1	0

Thus, in a frequency table `FreqT`, each document d_j is represented by the jth column of `FreqT`. Likewise, the occurrence of each term/word t_i is represented by row i. But why are frequencies important? What do they convey? To informally answer these questions, let's take a very simple example, containing several hypothetical documents. For the sake of simplicity, we only show five terms.

Term/document	d_1	d_2	d_3	d_4	d_5	d_6
t_1	615	390	10	10	18	65
t_2	15	4	76	217	91	816
t_3	2	8	815	142	765	1
t_4	312	511	677	11	711	2
t_5	45	33	516	64	491	59

If we examine these documents, we notice that d_1 and d_2 are similar because the distribution of the words in d_1 mirrors the distribution of the words for d_2. Both contain lots of occurrences of t_1 and t_4, relatively few occurrences of t_2 and t_3, and moderately many occurrences of t_5. In the same vein, d_3 and d_5 are similar. However, d_4 and d_6 stand out as sharply different.

But shouldn't the relative lengths of the documents involved be taken into account? Merely counting words does not indicate the importance of the words in the document. For example, if a word occurs three times in a 10-word document, then it might be considered important. On the other hand, occurring three times in a million-word document may reduce its significance. Thus, in frequency tables, we are usually interested in the ratio of the number of occurrences of a word in a document to the number of words in the document altogether. In addition to the above measures, many other measures of the importance of terms/words have been proposed in the literature. However, for the sake of brevity, we will not go into them here. For the rest of this chapter, we will merely assume that $\mathtt{FreqT}(i, j)$ is some real number greater than or equal to zero, and that its precise value is determined in one of the two ways outlined above. You should note that several other definitions of $\mathtt{FreqT}(i, j)$ have been proposed in the literature, and the two definitions given here are representative of this body of definitions.

Suppose now that the user wishes to retrieve the top n documents in a document database D that are "relevant" to a query Q. For example, the user may say, "Find the 25 documents that are maximally relevant with respect to banking operations and drugs." In this case, the query Q is trying to retrieve documents relevant to two keywords, which after stemming are *bank* and *drug*. If we think of the query Q as a document, then we are looking for the columns in $\mathtt{FreqT}$ that are as "close" as possible to the vector associated with Q. Closeness is defined in terms of a metric such as the following:

1. *Term distance:* Suppose $vec_Q(i)$ denotes the number of occurrences of term t_i in Q. Then the term distance between Q and document d_r is given by

$$\sqrt{\sum_{j=1}^{M} \left(vec_Q(j) - \mathtt{FreqT}(j,r) \right)^2}$$

Of course, this is a rather arbitrary metric.

2. *Cosine distance:* This metric is used extensively in the document database world and may be described as follows:

$$\frac{\sum_{j=1}^{M}(vec_Q(j) \times \mathtt{FreqT}(j,r))}{\sqrt{\sum_{j=1}^{M} vec_Q(j)^2} \times \sqrt{\sum_{j=1}^{M} \mathtt{FreqT}(j,r)^2}}$$

Here, we compute the product of the vectors associated with the query Q and document d_i, and divide it by the product of the root sum squares of the vectors involved.

In the worst case, we will require $O(N)$ comparisons, one for each document, and each comparison will take time $O(M)$, one for each term. Hence, in total, we will spend time $O(M \times N)$ to find the best solutions. However, even for the very small database consisting just of the University of Maryland Computer Science Department's technical reports since 1990, $(M \times N)$ is likely to run into hundreds of millions, perhaps even billions, of comparisons. The technique of latent semantic indexing (LSI) is intended to reduce this time substantially.

6.3 Latent Semantic Indexing

The basic idea behind latent semantic indexing is that similar documents have similar word frequencies. However, in general, for any nontrivial document database, the number of documents M and the number of terms N is very large. If we wish to index university technical reports using the full text, we will very quickly realize that the number of terms is likely to run into the hundreds of thousands, if not the millions. Given that several hundred thousand technical reports exist today, this makes the size of the frequency table prohibitively large $(M \times N)$, running into the hundreds of millions of entries. Manipulating such large tables is highly nontrivial.

What LSI tries to do is to use a technique called *singular value decomposition* (SVD), well known in matrix theory, to reduce the size of the frequency table to something much smaller than $(M \times N)$. In general, any such reduction leads to some loss of information, and hence we must ensure that SVDs are as "information-efficient" as possible; that is, they must miss only the least significant parts of the frequency table. In other words, the LSI technique takes an $(M \times N)$ matrix, and represents it as a much smaller $(K \times K)$ matrix. This is done by eliminating some rows and some columns of the original frequency matrix. Usually, K is taken to be around 200 for large document collections.

Recall that each column in the frequency matrix represents a document. LSI considers each document to be a vector of length K by merely retaining the K most significant rows of the frequency table. These "most significant" rows are those rows that did not get eliminated when the $(K \times K)$ matrix was created. In short, we may now summarize the basic steps behind LSI as follows:

1. *Table creation*: Create frequency matrix `FreqT`.

2. *SVD construction*: Compute the singular valued decompositions (A, S, B) of `FreqT` by splitting `FreqT` into three matrices A, S, B (Section 6.3.1).

3. *Vector identification*: For each document d, let $vec(d)$ be the set of all terms in `FreqT` whose corresponding rows have not been eliminated in the singular matrix S.

4. *Index creation:* Store the set of all $vec(d)$'s, indexed by any one of a number of techniques (in Section 6.4, we will discuss one such technique, called a TV-tree).

When asked to retrieve a document similar to a query document d_Q, we merely look at the index structure created above and try to find the document d in the archive such that $vec(d_Q)$ is closest to $vec(d)$ with respect to a selected metric on vectors.

6.3.1   Background on Singular Valued Decompositions

Recall that a matrix $\mathcal{M}$ is said to be of order $(m \times n)$ if it has m rows and n columns. If $\mathcal{M}_1$ and $\mathcal{M}_2$ are matrices of order $(m_1 \times n_1)$ and $(m_2 \times n_2)$, respectively, then we say that the product, $(\mathcal{M}_1 \times \mathcal{M}_2)$, is *well defined* iff $n_1 = m_2$. The order of the product matrix $(\mathcal{M}_1 \times \mathcal{M}_2)$ is $(m_1 \times n_2)$. For example, consider the two matrices A and B given below:

$$A = \begin{pmatrix} 3 & 2 \\ 4 & 8 \end{pmatrix} \qquad B = \begin{pmatrix} 1 & 4 & 3 \\ 2 & 4 & 6 \end{pmatrix}$$

A is of order (2×2), and B is of order (2×3). Hence, $(A \times B)$ is well defined and is of order (2×3).

In general, suppose the product $(\mathcal{M}_1 \times \mathcal{M}_2)$ of two matrices is well defined. If

$$\mathcal{M}_1 = \begin{pmatrix} a_1^1 & a_2^1 & \cdots & a_{m_1}^1 \\ a_1^2 & a_2^2 & \cdots & a_{m_1}^2 \\ \cdots & \cdots & \cdots & \cdots \\ a_1^{n_1} & a_2^{n_1} & \cdots & a_{m_1}^{n_1} \end{pmatrix} \qquad \mathcal{M}_2 = \begin{pmatrix} b_1^1 & b_2^1 & \cdots & b_{m_2}^1 \\ b_1^2 & b_2^2 & \cdots & b_{m_2}^2 \\ \cdots & \cdots & \cdots & \cdots \\ b_1^{n_2} & b_2^{n_2} & \cdots & b_{m_2}^{n_2} \end{pmatrix}$$

then the product $(\mathcal{M}_1 \times \mathcal{M}_2)$ is the matrix

$$(\mathcal{M}_1 \times \mathcal{M}_2) = \begin{pmatrix} c_1^1 & c_2^1 & \cdots & c_{m_1}^1 \\ c_1^2 & c_2^2 & \cdots & c_{m_1}^2 \\ \cdots & \cdots & \cdots & \cdots \\ c_1^{n_2} & c_2^{n_2} & \cdots & c_{m_1}^{n_2} \end{pmatrix}$$

where

$$c_j^i = \sum_{r=1}^{n_1} \left(a_r^i \times b_j^r \right)$$

For example,

$$\begin{pmatrix} 3 & 2 \\ 4 & 8 \end{pmatrix} \times \begin{pmatrix} 1 & 4 & 3 \\ 2 & 4 & 6 \end{pmatrix} = \begin{pmatrix} 7 & 20 & 21 \\ 20 & 48 & 60 \end{pmatrix}$$

Given a matrix $\mathcal{M}$ of order $(m \times n)$, the *transpose* of $\mathcal{M}$, denoted $\mathcal{M}^T$, is obtained by converting each row of $\mathcal{M}$ into a column of $\mathcal{M}^T$. Thus, the first row of $\mathcal{M}$ becomes the first column of $\mathcal{M}^T$, the second row of $\mathcal{M}$ becomes the second column of $\mathcal{M}^T$, and so on, until the mth row of $\mathcal{M}$ becomes the mth column of $\mathcal{M}^T$. Thus, $\mathcal{M}^T$ is an $(n \times m)$ matrix. For example,

$$\begin{pmatrix} 7 & 20 & 21 \\ 20 & 48 & 60 \end{pmatrix}^T = \begin{pmatrix} 7 & 20 \\ 20 & 48 \\ 21 & 60 \end{pmatrix}$$

We will use the expression *vector* to refer to a matrix of order $(1 \times m)$. Two vectors x and y of the same order are said to be *orthogonal* iff $x^T y = 0$. For example, suppose we have the following vectors:

$$x = (10, 5, 20)$$
$$y = (1, 2, -1)$$

These two vectors are orthogonal because

$$x^T y = \begin{pmatrix} 10 \\ 5 \\ 20 \end{pmatrix} \times (1 \quad 2 \quad -1) = \begin{pmatrix} 0 \\ 0 \\ 0 \end{pmatrix}$$

Matrix $\mathcal{M}$ is said to be orthogonal iff $(\mathcal{M}^T \times \mathcal{M})$ is the identity matrix (i.e., the matrix whose diagonal entries are 1). For example, consider the matrix

$$\mathcal{M} = \begin{pmatrix} 1 & 1 \\ 0 & 0 \end{pmatrix}$$

It is easy to see that $\mathcal{M}^T \times \mathcal{M}$ yields the identity matrix, and hence this matrix is orthogonal.

Matrix $\mathcal{M}$ is said to be a *diagonal matrix* iff the order of $\mathcal{M}$ is $(m \times m)$, and for all $1 \leq i, j \leq m$,

$$i \neq j \rightarrow \mathcal{M}(i, j) = 0$$

In other words, $\mathcal{M}$ is a diagonal matrix iff it is a square matrix and all its nondiagonal entries are zero. Note that there is no requirement that diagonal entries be nonzero; they could either be zero or nonzero. For example, both matrices A and B below are diagonal matrices, but C is not:

$$A = \begin{pmatrix} 1 & 0 & 0 \\ 0 & 4 & 0 \\ 0 & 0 & 5 \end{pmatrix} \qquad B = \begin{pmatrix} 1 & 0 & 0 \\ 0 & 0 & 0 \\ 0 & 0 & 0 \end{pmatrix} \qquad C = \begin{pmatrix} 1 & 1 \\ 0 & 0 \end{pmatrix}$$

A diagonal matrix $\mathcal{M}$ of order $(m \times m)$ is said to be *nonincreasing* iff for all $1 \leq i, j \leq m$,

$$i \leq j \rightarrow \mathcal{M}(i, i) \geq \mathcal{M}(j, j)$$

In other words, as we "walk down" the diagonal from the top to the bottom, the values decrease. For instance, in the above example, B is a nonincreasing diagonal matrix, but A is not.

Suppose FreqT is any frequency table (which, of course, is a matrix of order $M \times N$). A *singular value decomposition* of FreqT is a triple (A, S, B) where

1. FreqT $= (A \times S \times B^T)$,

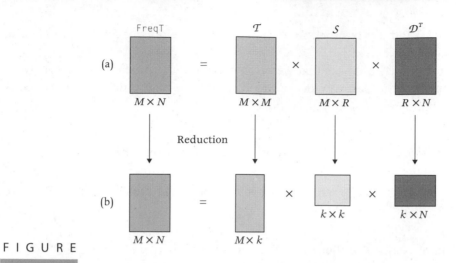

FIGURE

6.4   Size reduction through SVD

2. A is an $(M \times M)$ orthogonal matrix such that $A^T A = I$,

3. B is an $(N \times N)$ orthogonal matrix such that $B^T B = I$,

4. S is a diagonal matrix called a *singular matrix*.

It is well known that given any matrix $\mathcal{M}$ of order $(m \times n)$, it is possible to find a singular value decomposition (A, S, B) of $\mathcal{M}$ such that S is a nonincreasing diagonal matrix. For example, the singular value decomposition of

$$\begin{pmatrix} 1.44 & 3.08 \\ 3.92 & 1.44 \end{pmatrix}$$

is given by

$$\begin{pmatrix} 0.6 & -0.8 \\ 0.8 & 0.6 \end{pmatrix} \begin{pmatrix} 5 & 0 \\ 0 & 2 \end{pmatrix} \begin{pmatrix} 0.8 & 0.6 \\ 0.6 & -0.8 \end{pmatrix}$$

Here, the singular values are 5 and 2, and it is easy to see that the singular matrix is nonincreasing.

The basic idea behind LSI is that given a frequency matrix FreqT, we can decompose it into an SVD $\mathcal{T}S\mathcal{D}^T$, where S is nonincreasing. Figure 6.4(a) shows this equivalence. However, if FreqT is of size $(M \times N)$, then $\mathcal{T}$ is of size

$(M \times M)$ and $\mathcal{S}$ is of order $(M \times R)$, where R is the rank of FreqT, and $\mathcal{D}^T$ is of order $(R \times N)$.

The beauty of LSI is that we can now shrink the problem substantially by eliminating the least significant singular values from the singular matrix $\mathcal{S}$, as shown in Figure 6.4(b). This is done as follows:

1. Choose an integer k that is substantially smaller than R.

2. Replace $\mathcal{S}$ by $\mathcal{S}^\star$, which is a $(k \times k)$ matrix, such that $\mathcal{S}^\star(i, j) = \mathcal{S}(i, j)$ for $1 \leq i, j \leq k$.

3. Replace the $(R \times N)$ matrix $\mathcal{D}^T$ by the $(k \times N)$ matrix $\mathcal{D}^{\star T}$, where $\mathcal{D}^{\star T}(i, j) = \mathcal{D}^T(i, j)$ if $1 \leq i \leq k$ and $1 \leq j \leq N$.

4. Replace the $(M \times M)$ matrix $\mathcal{T}$ by an $(M \times K)$ matrix $\mathcal{T}^\star$ in a similar way.

In other words, LSI throws away the least significant values and retains the rest of the matrix involved. The product $\mathcal{T}^\star \mathcal{S}^\star \mathcal{D}^{\star T}$ is denoted by Freq*. The key claim underlying the LSI technique is that if k is chosen judiciously, then the k rows appearing in the singular matrix $\mathcal{S}^\star$ represent the k "most important" (from the point of view of retrieval) terms occurring in the *entire* document collection.

To see how LSI reduces dimensions in this way, let us take a simple example. Suppose FreqT has the SVD

$$\begin{pmatrix} a_1^1 & a_2^1 & a_3^1 & a_4^1 & a_5^1 \\ a_1^2 & a_2^2 & a_3^2 & a_4^2 & a_5^2 \\ \vdots & \vdots & \vdots & \vdots & \vdots \\ a_1^M & a_2^M & a_3^M & a_4^M & a_5^M \end{pmatrix} \begin{pmatrix} 20 & 0 & 0 & 0 & 0 \\ 0 & 16 & 0 & 0 & 0 \\ 0 & 0 & 12 & 0 & 0 \\ 0 & 0 & 0 & 0.08 & 0 \\ 0 & 0 & 0 & 0 & 0.004 \end{pmatrix} \begin{pmatrix} b_1^1 & b_2^1 & b_3^1 & \cdots & b_N^1 \\ b_1^2 & b_2^2 & b_3^2 & \cdots & b_N^2 \\ \vdots & \vdots & \vdots & \ddots & \vdots \\ b_1^5 & b_2^5 & b_3^5 & \cdots & b_N^5 \end{pmatrix}$$

The designer of the document retrieval system may have set three as the threshold (when we examine the singular matrix in the above decomposition, we notice that the fourth and fifth singular values are very small compared to the others). Thus, the document database system designer may very well choose to reduce the size of the matrix by eliminating the last two rows and columns of this singular matrix. The result is

$$
\begin{pmatrix}
a_1^1 & a_2^1 & a_3^1 \\
a_1^2 & a_2^2 & a_3^2 \\
\vdots & \vdots & \vdots \\
a_1^M & a_2^M & a_3^M
\end{pmatrix}
\begin{pmatrix}
20 & 0 & 0 \\
0 & 16 & 0 \\
0 & 0 & 12
\end{pmatrix}
\begin{pmatrix}
b_1^1 & b_2^1 & b_3^1 & \cdots & b_N^1 \\
b_1^2 & b_2^2 & b_3^2 & \cdots & b_N^2 \\
b_1^3 & b_2^3 & b_3^3 & \cdots & b_N^3
\end{pmatrix}
$$

Typically, the size of the singular matrix in reasonably large domains is about 200. Let's examine what this means:

1. The size of the original frequency table is $(M \times N)$, where M is the number of terms and N is the number of documents. We may easily have $M = 1$ million and $N = 10,000$, even for just a small document database such as that consisting of the University of Maryland's Computer Science technical reports.

2. Now for the size of the three matrices after we have reduced the size of the singular matrix to, say, 200:

   - The first matrix's size is $M \times R$. With the above numbers, this is 1 million $\times$ 200 = 200 million entries.
   - The singular matrix's size is 200 $\times$ 200 = 40,000 entries. (In fact, of these 40,000 entries, only 200 at most need to be stored; all the other entries are zero.)
   - The last matrix's size is $R \times N$. With the above numbers, this is 200 $\times$ 10, 000 = 2 million entries.

   Adding up the above, we get a total of approximately 202 million entries in the tables after SVDs are applied.

3. In contrast, $(M \times N)$ is close to 10 billion; in other words, the SVD trick reduced the space utilized to about one-fiftieth of that required by the original frequency table.

Caution: The above analysis is somewhat oversimplified and potentially magnifies the gains that the SVD decomposition affords. In many cases, the original $M \times N$ matrix is a *sparse matrix*, which can often be stored using far fewer entries than $M \times N$. In such cases, it is possible that the SVD decomposition actually increases the amount of storage required.

The actual computation of the SVD associated with a matrix is a complex question in matrix theory, so we will not go into the details here. Fortunately, we do not need to do so, since well-known SVD algorithms are available freely through packages such as MATLAB and the LAPACK library from *http://usi.utah.edu/software/math/pub/LAPACK/lug/node55.html*.

6.3.2   Document Retrieval Using SVDs

Suppose we have already created an SVD representation, $\mathcal{TS}^\star \times \mathcal{D}^{\star T}$, of a frequency table. In this section, we look at this representation and answer a couple of simple questions: Given two documents d_1 and d_2 in the archive, how "similar" are they? Given a query string/document Q, what are the n documents in the archive that are "most relevant" for the query?

Before we proceed any further, let's review the concept of a dot product of two vectors (of equal length). Suppose $\mathbf{x} = (x_1, \ldots, x_w)$ and $\mathbf{y} = (y_1, \ldots, y_w)$ are two real-valued vectors. Then the *dot product* of $\mathbf{x}$ and $\mathbf{y}$, denoted $\mathbf{x} \odot \mathbf{y}$, is given by

$$\mathbf{x} \odot \mathbf{y} = \sum_{i=1}^{w} x_i \times y_i$$

Similarity of Two Documents

Suppose d_i and d_j are two documents. The similarity of these two documents with respect to the SVD representation, $\mathcal{TS}^\star \times \mathcal{D}^{\star T}$, of a frequency table is given by computing the dot product of the two columns in the matrix $\mathcal{D}^{\star T}$ associated with these two documents:

$$\sum_{z=1}^{R} \mathcal{D}^{\star T}[i, z] \times \mathcal{D}^{\star T}[j, z]$$

Here, the singular matrix, after reduction, is of size $(R \times R)$. Note that instead of comparing all M terms for these two documents, we are only comparing R, which, as we have already seen earlier, is significantly smaller than M and is usually set to about 200.

Finding the Top p Matches for a Query Q

Suppose Q is a query. We treat Q as a document and create a vector vec_Q for it, as before. However, there is one difference: only the R significant terms are considered, not all N. When we are asked to find the top p matches for Q, we are trying to find p documents $d_{\alpha(1)}, \ldots, d_{\alpha(p)}$ such that

1. for all $1 \leq i \leq j \leq p$, the similarity between vec_Q and $d_{\alpha(i)}$ is greater than or equal to the similarity between vec_Q and $d_{\alpha(j)}$, and

2. there is no other document d_z such that the similarity between d_z and vec_Q exceeds that of $d_{\alpha(p)}$.

This can be accomplished by using any indexing structure for R-dimensional spaces. Such indexing structures include R-trees and k-d trees, which we have already studied in preceding chapters. However, in general, indexing structures such as R-trees and k-d trees do not work well for high-dimensional data (say, 20 dimensions or more). For this purpose, somewhat better techniques are required. The TV-tree described in the next section is a somewhat more appropriate indexing structure for such high-dimensional data.

6.4   TV-Trees

The basic objective behind TV-trees (telescopic vector trees) is that access to point data in very large dimensional spaces should be highly efficient. As we have already seen in this chapter, a document d may be viewed as a vector $\vec{d}$ of length k, where the singular valued matrix, after decomposition, is of size $(k \times k)$. Thus, each document may be thought of as a point in a k-dimensional space. A *document database*, of the sort described in the preceding sections, may be thought of as a collection of such points, indexed appropriately.

When a user presents a query Q, he is in effect specifying, as we have seen earlier, a vector $vec(Q)$ of length k. We are required to find the p documents in the database that are maximally relevant to Q. In effect, this boils down to attempting to find the k nearest neighbors of the query Q present in the document database. The TV-tree is a data structure that borrows from R-trees in this effort.

The TV-tree attempts to dynamically and flexibly decide how to branch, based on the data that is being examined. The idea is that if lots of vectors all agree on certain attributes (e.g., if lots of documents all have many common terms), then we must organize our index by branching on those terms (i.e., fields of the vectors) that *distinguish* between these vectors/documents. For example, in a document database consisting of the set of all the University of Maryland's Computer Science technical reports, words such as *database* may be satisfied by several thousand documents. To distinguish further among reports containing the word *database*, we need to organize our index in such a way that we can branch on the occurrence or lack of some other word that is more discriminating.

6.4.1 Organization of a TV-Tree

Before defining a TV-tree to store k-dimensional points, we need to specify two parameters:

1. NumChild: the maximal number of children that any node in the TV-tree is allowed to have

2. α: a number, greater than zero and less than or equal to k, called the *number of active dimensions*

We will use the notation TV(k, NumChild, α) to denote a TV-tree used to store k-dimensional data, with NumChild as the maximal number of children, and α as the number of active dimensions. As in the case of R-trees, each node in a TV-tree represents a region. For this purpose, each node N in a TV-tree contains three fields:

1. $N.Center$: This represents a point in k-dimensional space.

2. $N.Radius$: This is a real number greater than zero.

3. $N.ActiveDims$: This is a list of at most α dimensions. Each of these dimensions is a number between 1 and k. Thus, $N.ActiveDims$ is a subset of $\{1, \ldots, k\}$ of cardinality α or less.

Suppose $\mathbf{x}$ and $\mathbf{y}$ are points in k-dimensional space, and *ActiveDims* is some set of active dimensions. The *active distance* between $\mathbf{x}$ and $\mathbf{y}$, denoted act_dist($\mathbf{x}, \mathbf{y}$), is given by

$$\texttt{act\_dist}(\mathbf{x}, \mathbf{y}) = \sqrt{\sum_{i \in ActiveDims} \mathbf{x}_i^2 - \mathbf{y}_i^2}$$

Here, $\mathbf{x}_i$ and $\mathbf{y}_i$ denote the value of the ith dimension of $\mathbf{x}$ and $\mathbf{y}$, respectively.

For example, suppose $k = 200$, $\alpha = 5$, and the set *ActiveDims* $= \{1, 2, 3, 4, 5\}$. Suppose

$$\mathbf{x} = (10, 5, 11, 13, 7, x_6, x_7, \ldots, x_{200})$$
$$\mathbf{y} = (2, 4, 14, 8, 6, y_6, y_7, \ldots, y_{200})$$

Then the active distance between $\mathbf{x}$ and $\mathbf{y}$ is given by

$$\texttt{act\_dist}(\mathbf{x}, \mathbf{y}) = \sqrt{(10 - 2)^2 + (5 - 4)^2 + (11 - 14)^2 + (13 - 8)^2 + (7 - 6)^2}$$
$$= \sqrt{100}$$
$$= 10$$

Note that the active distance between two vectors ignores all fields that are not active.

Given a node N in a TV-tree, the node represents the region containing all points $\mathbf{x}$ such that the active distance (with respect to the active dimensions in $N.ActiveDims$) between $\mathbf{x}$ and $N.Center$ is less than or equal to $N.Radius$.

For example, if we had a node N with its center at

$$N.Center = (10, 5, 11, 13, 7, 0, 0, 0, 0, \ldots, 0)$$

and $N.ActiveDims = \{1, 2, 3, 4, 5\}$, then this node represents the region consisting of all points $\mathbf{x}$ such that

$$\sqrt{(\mathbf{x}_1 - 10)^2 + (\mathbf{x}_2 - 5)^2 + (\mathbf{x} - 11)^2 + (\mathbf{x}_4 - 13)^2 + (\mathbf{x}_5 - 7)^2} \leq N.Radius$$

We use the notation $Region(N)$ to denote the region represented by a node N in a TV-tree.

In addition to the *Center, Radius,* and *ActiveDims* fields, a node N in a TV-tree also contains an array, `Child`, of `NumChild` pointers to other nodes of the same type.

As in the case of R-trees, TV-trees have the following properties:

1. All data is stored at the leaf nodes.

2. Each node in a TV-tree (except for the root and the leaves) must be at least half full, that is, at least half the `Child` pointers must be non-NIL.

3. If N is a node, and $N_1, \ldots, N_r$ are all its children, then

$$Region(N) = \bigcup_{i=1}^{r} Region(N_i)$$

6.4.2 Insertion into TV-Trees

Let us consider the case where we have a five-dimensional space (i.e., this is a situation where we have just five terms drawn from our collection of documents), and we wish to insert some vectors into our TV-tree, $TV(5, 3, 2)$. Furthermore, suppose our entire space is a hyper-sphere centered at $(0, 0, 0, 0, 0)$ with radius 50. Initially, the TV-tree is empty.

1. Suppose the first vector to be introduced is $(5, 3, 20, 1, 5)$. This is handled straightforwardly by the creation of a root node with the following characteristics:

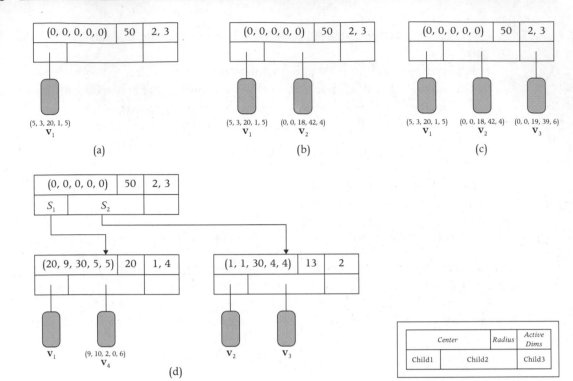

FIGURE

6.5   Insertion into a TV-tree (splitting)

(a) *Root.Center* $= (0, 0, 0, 0, 0)$.

(b) *Root.Radius* $= 50$.

(c) In this case, the root is also a leaf, with a pointer to the information relevant to the point $v_1 = (5, 3, 20, 1, 5)$.

(d) Suppose *Root.ActiveDims* $= \{2, 3\}$.

Figure 6.5(a) demonstrates this situation.

2. Suppose the next vector to be introduced is $v_2 = (0, 0, 18, 42, 4)$. In this case, too, we can create another leaf as indicated above. Figure 6.5(b) depicts this situation.

3. Suppose we subsequently introduce the vector $v_3 = (0, 0, 19, 39, 6)$. Figure 6.5(c) depicts this situation. At this stage, the root node is full, and it can have no more children.

4. Suppose we now introduce the vector $v_4 = (9, 10, 2, 0, 16)$. Now things get interesting. The region represented by the root contains more than three entries, thus exceeding the capacity of the root (i.e., the root can have no more children). At this stage, we must *split* the root. There are many strategies to split the root. Ideally, what we would like to do is to take the four vectors involved and group them together into two groups. An alternative way of viewing this is to split the region represented by the root into two parts such that each part contains two of the four vectors involved. Later in this section, we will discuss some alternative splitting strategies. But for now, all we need to worry about is that the split should cause similar nodes to stay together. Suppose our splitting strategy causes v_1 and v_4 to be in one part, and v_2 and v_3 to be in the other; after all, v_2 and v_3 are "similar" by virtue of being near each other according to our notion of "active distance." The tree that results is shown in Figure 6.5(d). The values for the radius and center fields of the children have been filled in arbitrarily for now; later in this section, we will show how they can be determined. Notice that the root now has two children, S_1 and S_2, and each of these children represents a region, as shown in Figure 6.5(d). *Note that all leaf nodes are now at level 2 in the tree.*

5. Suppose now that we wish to add the node $v_5 = (18, 5, 27, 9, 9)$. To determine which of the two children of the root v_5 should be added into, we must perform the operation of *branch selection* (or determining which way to branch). Figure 6.6(a) shows that we chose to branch to the first child, rather than to the second. A detailed description of branch selection follows this example.

6. Suppose we now wish to add another vector, $v_6 = (0, 0, 29, 0, 3)$. Again, we must perform branch selection, and this time we may choose to branch right, as shown in Figure 6.6(b).

7. This process can be continued as we proceed, adding more and more nodes.

In general, there are three key steps that determine how to insert a new vector v into a TV-tree:

1. *Branch selection:* When we insert a new vector into the TV-tree, and we are at node N (with children N_i, for $1 \leq i \leq$ NumChild), we need to determine which of these children to insert the key into.

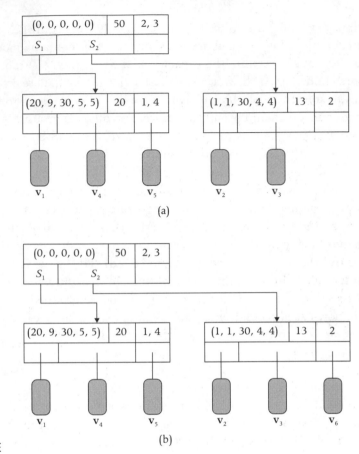

(a)

(b)

6.6   Insertion into a TV-tree (branch selection)

2. *Splitting:* We use this approach when we are at a leaf node that is full and cannot accommodate the vector **v** we are inserting. This step causes a split in that node.

3. *Telescoping:* Suppose a node N is split into subnodes N_1 and N_2. In this case, it may well turn out that the vectors in $Region(N_1)$ all agree on not just the active dimensions of the parent N, but a few more as well. The addition of these extra dimensions is called *telescoping*. Telescoping may also involve the *removal* of some active dimensions, as we shall see later.

Branch Selection

Consider a situation where we have a node N with $1 \leq j \leq$ NumChild children, denoted $N_1, \ldots, N_{\text{NumChild}}$. Let's use the notation $exp_j(\mathbf{v})$ to denote the amount we must expand $N_j.Radius$ so that $\mathbf{v}$'s active distance from $N_j.Center$ is less than or equal to $(N_j.Radius + exp_j(\mathbf{v}))$, i.e.,

$$exp_j(\mathbf{v}) = \begin{cases} 0 & \text{if act\_dist}(\mathbf{v}, R_j.Center) \leq R_j.Radius \\ \text{act\_dist}(\mathbf{v}, R_j.Center) - R_j.Radius & \text{otherwise} \end{cases}$$

First, we select all js such that $exp_j(\mathbf{v})$ is minimized. In other words, if we have nodes $N_1, \ldots, N_5$ with exp values $10, 40, 19, 10$, and 32, respectively, the two candidates selected for possible insertion are N_1 and N_4 because their expansion is minimal. If a tie occurs, as in the above case, pick the node such that the distance from the center of that node to $\mathbf{v}$ is minimized.

Splitting

We saw that when we attempt to insert a vector $\mathbf{v}$ into a leaf node N that is already full, then we need to split the node. We must create subnodes N_1 and N_2, and each vector in node N must fall into one of the regions represented by these two subnodes. We can split the vectors in leaf N into two groups (G_1, H_1). In this case, we may be able to enclose all vectors in G_1 within a region with center c_1 and radius r_1, and all vectors in H_1 within a region with center c_2 and radius r_2. Many such splits are possible in general. We say split (G_1, H_1) is *finer* than split (G_2, H_2) iff the sum of the radii $(r_1 + r_1')$ is smaller than the sum of the radii $(r_2 + r_2')$. However, this may not be enough to uniquely identify a "finest" split. If there is a tie, we use another parameter to distinguish. If (G_1, H_1) and (G_2, H_2) are splits such that neither is finer than the other and no other split is finer than each of them, then we say that (G_1, H_1) is *more conservative* than (G_2, H_2) iff

$$r_1 + r_1' - \text{act\_dist}(c_1, c_1') \leq r_2 + r_2' - \text{act\_dist}(c_2, c_2')$$

In general, split (G, H) is the selected split iff

1. there is no split (G', H') that is strictly finer than (G, H) and

2. (G^*, H^*) is as fine as (G, H), then (G^*, H^*) is not more conservative than (G, H).

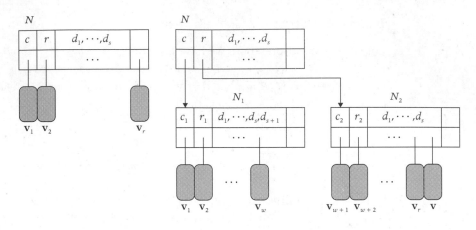

6.7   Telescoping when splitting

Telescoping

Telescoping primarily occurs because of insertion. Suppose N is the node into which we are to insert a vector $\mathbf{v}$. The insertion of $\mathbf{v}$ may cause two types of changes to N: it may cause N to be split into two subnodes N_1 and N_2, or it may "modify" the set of active dimensions of node N (e.g., if vector $\mathbf{v}$ does not agree on the active dimensions with other vectors stored at node N).

When node N gets split into two subnodes N_1 and N_2, the set of vectors at either node N_1 or node N_2 (but not both) must be a subset of the set of vectors at node N before the insertion. Suppose N_1 has this property. It may well be the case then that the vectors in N_1 agree not only on the active dimensions of N, but on some other dimensions as well. In this case, we can expand the set of active dimensions of node N by adding these new dimensions. Figure 6.7 shows a node N that is being split into two subnodes N_1 and N_2. All vectors $\mathbf{v}_1, \ldots, \mathbf{v}_r$ in node N agree on the active dimensions $d_1, \ldots, d_s$, where $s < \alpha$. Suppose now that node N_1 contains only vectors $\mathbf{v}_1, \ldots, \mathbf{v}_w$ and node N_2 contains only vectors $\mathbf{v}_{w+1}, \ldots, \mathbf{v}_r, \mathbf{v}$ (where $\mathbf{v}$ is the vector being inserted). If $\mathbf{v}_1, \ldots, \mathbf{v}_w$ agree not just on dimensions $d_1, \ldots, d_s$, but also on another dimension d_{s+1}, then we can expand the set of active dimensions for node N_1 as shown in Figure 6.7. (In fact if the split is really nice, such a telescopic expansion may be possible on both nodes N_1 and N_2.)

Telescoping also occurs when a vector is added to a node N, but no split occurs. If N originally contained the vectors $\mathbf{v}_1, \ldots, \mathbf{v}_r$, and $\mathbf{v}$ is the vector being added, even though vectors $\mathbf{v}_1, \ldots, \mathbf{v}_r$ originally agreed on the active dimensions $d_1, \ldots, d_s$ of node N, now they agree only on a subset (for example, $d_2, \ldots, d_s$). Hence, the set of active dimensions of node N must be contracted to reflect this fact.

6.4.3 Searching in TV-Trees

Searching for a vector **v** within a TV-tree merely reverses the insertion process. When searching for a document represented by vector **v** in a TV-tree rooted at T, we proceed as follows:

```
Algorithm 6.1  Search(T,v)
   if Leaf(T) then { Return (T.Center=v); Halt }
(* check above if the point represented by the leaf equals v
and return Boolean value *)
else
   { if v∈ Region(T) then
       Return V_{i=1}^{NumChild} Search(T.child[i],v)
   }
end
```

In the above algorithm, $\vee$ represents logical "or".

6.4.4 Nearest Neighbor Retrievals in TV-Trees

Finally, the most important problem from the point of view of document retrieval is that of finding the p nearest neighbors. Given a query Q represented by its vector $vec(Q)$, a TV-tree rooted at T representing the vectors associated with a set of documents, and an integer $p > 0$, we wish to find the top p "matches" for query Q in the document database. Before defining the algorithm, we introduce an elementary concept.

Suppose N is a node. Let $min(N, \mathbf{v})$ and $max(N, \mathbf{v})$ be the minimal and maximal distances of **v** from some point in $Region(N)$. These two quantities merely look at $N.Center$ and $N.Radius$ to determine how near or far a point in the region represented by N could possibly be from the query representation $vec(Q)$. These quantities may be computed very easily:

$$min(N, \mathbf{v}) = \begin{cases} 0 & \text{if } \mathbf{v} \in Region(N) \\ \mathtt{act\_dist}(\mathbf{v}, N.Center) - N.Radius & \text{otherwise} \end{cases}$$

$$max(N, \mathbf{v}) = \mathtt{act\_dist}(\mathbf{v}, N.Center) + N.Radius$$

We can easily compute the p closest neighbors as follows. Maintain an array *SOL* of length p (i.e., with indices running 1 through p). The intention is that the "best" match will be in location *SOL*[1], the second best in location *SOL*[2], and so on. Initially, array *SOL* contains some dummy values (e.g., ∞) that do not denote any document. The algorithm `NNSearch` uses a routine called `Insert` that takes a vector *vec* and an array *SOL* maintained in nondescending order of active distance from *vec* as input; in other words, if $1 \leq i \leq j \leq p$, then the active distance of *SOL*[i] from *vec* is less than or equal to the active distance of *SOL*[j] from *vec*. `Insert` returns the array *SOL* with *vec* inserted in it at the right place and with the pth element of *SOL* eliminated as output.

```
Algorithm 6.2  NNSearch(T,v,p)
    for i=1 to p do SOL[i]=∞;
NNSearch1(T,v,p);
end (* end of program NNSearch *)
procedure NNSearch1(T,v,p);
    if Leaf(T) & act_dist(T.val,v) < SOL[p] then
        Insert T.val into SOL;
    else
        {
            if Leaf(T) then r=0;
            else { Let N₁, ... ,Nᵣ be the children of T;
                Order the Nᵢs in ascending order with respect to
                    min(Nᵢ,v); Let N_{η(1)}, ... ,N_{η(r)} be the resulting order;
            };
            done = false; i=1;
            while ((i≤ r) ∧ ¬ done) do
                {
                    NNSearch(N_{η(i)},v, p);
                    if SOL[p] < min(N_{η(i+1)},v) then
                        done = true;
                    i=i+1;
                }; (* end of while *)
        } (* end of else *)
Return SOL;
end proc (* end of subroutine NNSearch1 *)
```

6.5   Other Retrieval Techniques

LSI has proven to be one of the most effective ways of indexing text archives. However, we would be remiss if we did not mention a number of other, less sophisticated techniques that have been studied in the literature prior to, and concurrently with, the LSI technique.

6.5.1   Inverted Indices

The inverted index is perhaps the most widely used method in industry for indexing text document databases. The idea is very simple:

1. A document record contains two fields—a `doc_id` and a `postings_list`. Intuitively, the postings list is a list of terms (or pointers to terms) that occur in the document. Obviously, only relevant terms occur in postings lists. The postings list may be sorted using a suitable *relevance measure*.

2. A `term record` consists of two similar fields—a `term` field (string) and a `postings_list`. Here, the postings list specifies which documents the term appeared in.

3. Two hash tables are maintained—a `DocTable` and a `TermTable`. The `DocTable` is constructed by hashing on the `doc_id` key; the `TermTable` is obtained by hashing on the `term` key.

To find all documents associated with a term, we merely return the postings list. To find all documents associated with a set of terms, we merely perform an intersection operation on such postings lists.

As inverted lists are very easy to implement, they have been adopted in many commercial systems, such as MEDLARS and DIALOG. However, they suffer from several disadvantages: They do not account satisfactorily for synonymy and polysemy. Postings lists can get rather long, and the storage requirements may be very large. In Chapter 9, we will study inverted indexes (enhanced to handle multimedia data) in detail.

6.5.2   Signature Files

The basic idea behind a signature file is to associate a signature s_d with each document d. Informally speaking, a *signature* is a representation of an ordered list of terms that describe the document.

The list of terms from which s_d is derived is obtained after performing a frequency analysis, stemming, and using stop lists. Suppose this list consists of the ordered list of words $w_1, w_2, \ldots, w_r$. Intuitively, this means that word w_1 is most important when describing the document, word w_2 is second most important, and so forth. The signature of the document d is a bit representation of this list, usually obtained by encoding the list after using hashing, and then superimposing a coding scheme.

6.6   Selected Commercial Systems

Informix's datablade architecture provides a wide range of text database products that may be used in conjunction with their Universal Server's datablade architecture. For example, the ArborText Document Objects datablade module provides a variety of services on SGML text objects, including validation of the document object, storage and retrieval of documents as well as portions of documents, and search techniques.

Other datablade modules for text processing include the Open Text Livelink Library for document management and Excalibur Technologies Corporation Text DataBlade Module. Details on these technologies were unavailable when this book was being written.

Oracle provides a text database package, called ConText, that provides text retrieval and management capabilities built on top of the Oracle Universal Server. ConText performs full text retrievals using SQL. It also can automatically extract themes from text and create summaries.

IBM's DB2 system has a Text Extender that can be plugged into their DB2 server to support full text retrieval of multilingual documents. This extender supports searching on keywords, synonyms, and word/phrase variations.

6.7   Bibliographic Notes

Perhaps the most comprehensive work on text databases is the excellent book by Witten, Moffat, and Bell [221]—the serious reader is referred to that work for a comprehensive overview of text databases The technique of latent semantic indexing was introduced by Deerwester et al. [53] in a reasonably easy-to-read paper that skips a detailed mathematical analysis. Dumais [58] provides further details on LSI, while a fairly detailed, mathematical analysis of LSI may be found in Berry, Dumais, and O'Brien [20]. Recently, Kolda and

O'Leary [115, 114] have observed that SVD decompositions are often larger than the original matrix when the original matrix is sparse. To avoid this problem, they have suggested an alternative decomposition, called the *semi-discrete decomposition* (SDD), and have shown, using MEDLINE data, that SDD improves upon SVDs by using less storage, yet often performing equally well in response to retrieval requests. They note that the one-time cost of setup for SDDs is higher than for SVDs. The basic matrix theoretic background needed for understanding both SVDs and SDDs may be found in Golub and Van Loan [74]. For the mathematically strong, who are interested in a quick rundown of definitions needed to understand SVDs, we recommend Stewart [198]. Program code to compute SVDs of matrices may be found in Press et al. [162].

TV-trees were introduced by Lin, Jagadish, and Faloutsos [127]. They present a description of how TV-trees may be used to support operations on high-dimensional data. The treatment of TV-trees in this book is a slight variant of the version they originally proposed. White and Jain [218] have proposed a data structure called the SS-tree for effectively indexing high-dimensional data. They showed that their approach significantly outperformed earlier approaches based on the $R^\star$ tree, a data structure introduced in [18]. Subsequently, they have introduced a modified version of the k-d tree called a VAM k-d tree, as well as a modified version of the R-tree called a VAMSplit R-tree [218].

Recently, Berchtold, Keim, and Kriegel [19] have introduced a new data structure for storing very high dimensional data, called the X-tree, that outperforms the TV-tree.

Inverted indexes have been studied extensively. Salton and McGill [178] is the classic reference for modern information retrieval and provides a description of inverted indexes. More recently, Faloutsos and Jagadish [61] have proposed the use of B-trees to implement postings lists. Their approach works well in the case when the postings lists obey Zipf's distribution—most words occur rarely, but a few words occur very frequently. Because such indexes may be very large, fast insertion algorithms on inverted indexes have been proposed by Tomasic, Garcia-Molina, and Shoens [206] and Brown, Callan, and Croft [30].

Signature files have been studied in detail by Tsichritzis and Christodoulakis [208]. Superimposed coding methods have been studied by Sacks-Davis and Ramamohanrao [176].

6.8   Exercises and Projects

1. Consider a very simple frequency table, FreqT, given by

$$
FreqT = \begin{pmatrix}
11 & 2 & 36 & 1 & 15 & 29 & 0 \\
1 & 21 & 3 & 11 & 45 & 3 & 17 \\
13 & 4 & 39 & 3 & 18 & 26 & 3 \\
10 & 54 & 11 & 2 & 16 & 34 & 1 \\
11 & 1 & 0 & 14 & 2 & 0 & 29
\end{pmatrix}
$$

Do not use SVDs in this exercise.

(a) How many terms and how many documents are represented in the above frequency matrix?

(b) Compute a table containing columns (*DocA, DocB, Similarity*). For each distinct pair, d_i, d_j, of documents in the archive, there should be a triple (d_i, d_j, s) in the table, where s represents the similarity between d_i and d_j.

(c) Consider now a query Q requesting the two best documents in the above collection that associate the following weights with each term: $(33, 5, 42, 8, 2)$. What should be the answer returned?

(d) Write, in pseudocode, an algorithm to compute the answer to Q above.

2. Write, in pseudocode, an algorithm that takes a frequency matrix FreqT and a query Q's vector as input and returns the top 10 matches in the document base for the query Q as output. Assume the existence of a routine called ComputeSVD that takes a frequency table as input and returns three matrices corresponding to the three matrices in singular valued decompositions as output. Make sure you specify the I/O type of this function.

3. Write, in pseudocode, an algorithm to implement insertion in a TV-tree. Your algorithm should include the following subroutines:

(a) SelectBranch selects a branch.

(b) Split splits a node.

(c) SetActive sets the active dimensions of all nodes in the subtree rooted at a given node.

4. Write, in pseudocode, an algorithm to delete a document (vector) from a TV-tree.

5. As a project, write a program that implements inverted indexes. Your program must contain the following routines:

(a) CreateIndex(Dir,StopList) takes a directory name and a file called StopList (in that directory) as input. It returns an inverted index as output. The DocTable includes all files in the directory Dir, except for the StopList file. The TermTable includes only all words occurring in the directory that start with the letter *C* (lower- or uppercase).

(b) Find(Word,Weight,N) finds the top N documents in the index associated with the word specified in the input.

(c) Find(WordFile,N) is similar to the above, but there is one difference. Instead of taking a single word as part of the input, it takes a file called WordFile as input. This file has, on each line, a word (string) and a weight (integer). It then attempts to find, using the inverted index, the top N matches for this query.

7   Video Databases

CHAPTER

What new concepts will you learn in this chapter?
You will learn what a video database is. You will learn what kinds of queries may be posed to a video library, and how they may be efficiently implemented.

What new abstractions are needed to realize these concepts?
In simplistic terms, a video is nothing more than a sequence of images. You will learn how information about sequences of images can be efficiently stored. You will be shown how it is possible to query such image sequences.

What new techniques are needed to implement these abstractions?
You will learn about two kinds of data structures, called the *frame segment tree* and the *R-segment tree*, that may be used to store image data.

What technological features support these implementation methods?
You will learn about the basic storage mechanism used in the MPEG video standard. You will also learn about existing video database tools on the market.

If we return to the Sample Multimedia Scenario involving the police investigation described at the beginning of Chapter 1, we will observe that one of the
data sources being accessed is video data. The need to access video data arises
in a wide range of applications, and typically the access patterns vary considerably from one application to another. Some possible video access patterns are
the following:

- *Retrieving a specified video:* In many applications, such as movies-on-
  demand systems, users accessing the video database explicitly specify the
  movie they wish to see. For example, the user might state: "Show me *The
  Sound of Music*," and the task of the video database system is to physically
  retrieve all the movie blocks associated with that movie and deliver a jitter-
  free, smooth presentation of it to the user's output device. Techniques to
  handle such queries vary, depending on both the storage medium on which
  the video data resides and where on the network the video data is stored (in
  the case of networked systems). Such techniques will be described in detail
  in Part III of this book.

- *Identifying and retrieving video segments:* In other applications, the user
  might express a query such as "Find all videos (in the Sample Multimedia Scenario of this book) in which Denis Dopeman is seen next to a plane
  at an airport in the desert." For instance, the airport in question may have
  been under routine surveillance (suspected drug entry point), and a police
  investigator may be interested in finding corroborating evidence linking
  Dopeman to suspected drug shipments. In this query, we must identify
  not only a relevant video (from a potentially huge archive of surveillance
  videos), but must also clearly identify the segment of the video where Dopeman appears with a plane in the background. Techniques to handle this
  type of application will be studied in this chapter.

We will first specify how to store the content of a single video, and then
specify how to store the content of a collection of videos.

7.1 Organizing Content of a Single Video

When representing the content of a single video, we must ask ourselves the
following questions:

1. Which aspects of the video are likely to be of interest to the users who
   access the video archive?

2. How can these aspects of the video be stored efficiently, so as to minimize the time needed to answer user queries?

3. What should query languages for video data look like, and how should the relational model of data be extended to handle video information?

4. Can the content extraction process be automated, and if so, how can the reliability of such content extraction techniques be taken into account when processing queries?

In this chapter, we will answer each of these four questions.

7.1.1 Video Content: Which Aspects of a Video to Store?

Suppose we wish to describe the content of an arbitrary video v. Let's take a few simple examples first, before providing an abstract definition of video content.

An Educational Video Example Consider an eight-hour, one-day lecture of a short course given by a professor on the topic "multimedia databases." In this case, the video contains a set of items of interest, which could include the following:

1. *People*, such as the professor, any guest lecturer (or lecturers) who speak at selected times in the course, and any students who might ask questions or distinguish themselves in other ways. For instance, Prof. Felix might be one such person, and Erica, a student, might be another.

2. *Activities* that occur in the class, such as *lecturing* (on a particular topic, by a particular individual), *questioning* (by a particular student), or *answering* a question posed by a particular student. Other activities could involve general group discussions or coffee breaks.

Examples of activities include *lecturing(quadtrees, Prof. Felix)*, indicating an activity involving Prof. Felix lecturing on quadtrees, and *questioning(Erica, Prof. Felix)*, indicating that Prof. Felix was questioned by Erica. In both of these cases, an activity has certain attributes. For example, the activity *lecturing* has two attributes:

1. Topic, which is *quadtrees* in the *lecturing(quadtrees, Prof. Felix)* example

2. Lecturer, which is *Prof. Felix* in the *lecturing(quadtrees, Prof. Felix)* example

The Sample Multimedia Scenario If we return to the Sample Multimedia Scenario involving the police investigator, we realize that a single four-hour videotape containing surveillance data of a suspected drug-running airfield might involve a variety of items of interest:

1. *People*, such as Denis Dopeman, a pilot, and members of the ground staff

2. *Inanimate objects*, such as airplanes, cars, trucks, warehouses, or airport hangars

3. *Activities*, such as *plane_landing* (specifying that a plane with certain markings landed on the airfield), or *car_on_runway* (specifying that a car with a certain license plate was seen on the runway), or *seen* (specifying that a certain person was seen)

Examples of such activities could include

1. *plane_landing(cessna,zz8016,150KHz)*, specifying the activity relating to the landing of a Cessna airplane with aviation markings "zz8016" and broadcasting on frequency 150 KHz

2. *car_on_runway(ford_taurus,black,va,zzk7152)*, specifying the activity involving a black Ford Taurus with Virginia license plate ZZK 7152 being on the runway

3. *seen(denis_dopeman)*, specifying the activity involving the appearance of Denis Dopeman at the airfield

A Movie Example Suppose we consider the content of a movie such as *The Sound of Music*. A movie such as this is characterized by its characters (e.g., Maria), the attributes of these characters (e.g., the fact that the character Maria was played by Julie Andrews), and the activities engaged in by these characters, such as *singing* and *dancing*. Thus, once again, we notice that the items of interest in a movie such as *The Sound of Music* include the following:

1. *People*, such as Maria, Count Von Trapp, and others

2. *Inanimate objects*, such as the piano in Count Von Trapp's house

3. *Animate objects*, such as the ducks and birds in the pond

4. *Activities*, such as *singing* and *dancing*, with their associated list of attributes. For example, the activity *singing* may have two attributes: Singer, specifying which person is singing, and Song, specifying the name of the song.

When we examine the above examples, we notice that they all share certain common characteristics. For example, in each case, given any frame f in the video, the frame f has a set of associated objects and associated activities. For instance, in the Sample Multimedia Scenario, a given video frame f may contain the object Denis Dopeman and the activity *plane_landing*. *Notice that the common, recurring theme that occurs in each video frame is that there is an associated set of objects and activities.* Objects may have certain properties, and these properties may vary from one frame to another. Likewise, activities may also have associated properties that vary from one frame to another. With these observations in mind, we are now ready to start formally defining a video database through a sequence of definitions.

Definition 7.1 A *property* is a pair (pname, Values), where pname is the *name* of the property and Values is a set. An *instance* of a property (pname, Values) is an expression of the form pname $= v$, where $v \in$ Values.

Examples of properties include the following:

1. (*height*, $\mathbf{R}^+$) consists of the "height" property with positive real values.

2. (*primarycolors*, {*red, green, blue*}) consists of a property called *primarycolors* with values *red, green, blue*.

3. (*license_plate*, X) could represent the property specifying the license plate of a car. Here, X could be the set *State* $\times$ *Alpha*$_3$ $\times$ *Num*$_4$ where *State* is the set of abbreviations of all states in the United States, *Alpha*$_3$ refers to all three-letter alphabetic strings, and *Num*$_4$ refers to the set of all four-digit numbers. For instance, the property instance given as

   $$license\_plate = (VA, ZUH, 7132)$$

   refers to a Virginia vehicle with license plate ZUH 7132.

4. (*shirtcolor*, *Colors*) may be a property where *shirtcolor* is the color of a shirt, and *Colors* is an enumerated list of colors.

Definition 7.2 An *object scheme* is a pair (fd, fi) where

1. fd is a set of *frame-dependent* properties,

2. fi is a set of *frame-independent* properties, and

3. fi and fd are disjoint sets.

Note that both fd and fi are disjoint sets of properties. If (pname, Values) is a property in fd, then this means that the property named pname may assume different instances, depending upon the video frame being considered. For instance, suppose we consider the property *shirtcolor*. This property may vary depending upon which frame in the movie is being considered.

Definition 7.3 An *object instance* is a triple (oid, os, ip) where

1. oid is a string called the object-id,

2. os = (fd, fi) is an object scheme, and

3. ip is a set of statements such that

   (a) for each property (pname, Values) in fi, ip contains at most one property instance of (pname, Values), and

   (b) for each property (pname, Values) in fd, and each frame f of the video, ip contains at most one property instance of (pname, Values). This property instance is denoted by the expression $pname = v \text{ IN } f$.

Sample Multimedia Scenario Revisited Let us consider the very simple sequence of five video frames shown in Figure 7.1. These five frames show, through sketches, a surveillance video of the house of Denis Dopeman. In the first frame, we see a woman, Jane Shady, appear at the path leading to Dopeman's door. She is carrying a briefcase. The next frame shows her halfway up the path to the door, at which point the door opens, and Dopeman appears at the door. The third frame depicts Shady and Dopeman standing next to each other at the door; Shady is still carrying the briefcase. In the fourth frame, Shady is walking back, and Dopeman has the briefcase. In the fifth frame, the door is shut, and Shady is at the beginning of the path to Dopeman's door.

In order to represent the contents of this sequence of five video frames, we may do so by selecting four objects—Denis Dopeman, Jane Shady, the briefcase, and Denis Dopeman's house. These four objects may have three associated object structures:

1. We might have an object structure called (Person, fd_1, fi_1), where

   (a) fd_1 contains the properties has, specifying objects that the person has (e.g., Jane Shady has the briefcase in frame 1), and at, specifying where the person is located (e.g., in frame 1, Jane Shady is at the path leading to Denis Dopeman's door).

   (b) fi_1 contains the properties age, specifying the age of the person; height, specifying the person's height in centimeters, and so on.

2. We might have another object called (House, fd$_2$, fi$_2$), where fi$_2$ contains the properties address, type (e.g., brick, woodframe, etc.), color, and so on. Here, fd$_2$ might only contain properties of the form door (with values open/closed).

3. Finally, we might have an object called (briefcase, fd$_3$, fi$_3$), where fd$_3$ is empty, and fi$_3$ contains the properties color, length, width, and so on.

The table below provides a succinct description of the content of the video, restricted only to the objects of interest. It does make a simplifying assumption—that it takes only one frame for Jane Shady to walk from one location to another. In practice, it might take longer, but this can be handled by making the example somewhat more complicated.

Frame	Objects	Frame-dependent properties
1	Jane Shady	has(briefcase), at(path_front)
	dopeman_house	door(closed)
	briefcase	
2	Jane Shady	has(briefcase), at(path_middle)
	Denis Dopeman	at(door)
	dopeman_house	door(open)
	briefcase	
3	Jane Shady	has(briefcase), at(door)
	Denis Dopeman	at(door)
	dopeman_house	door(open)
	briefcase	
4	Jane Shady	at(door)
	Denis Dopeman	has(briefcase),at(door)
	dopeman_house	door(open)
	briefcase	
5	Jane Shady	at(path_middle)
	dopeman_house	door(closed)
	briefcase	

In addition, each object might have frame-independent properties such as those summarized in the table below:

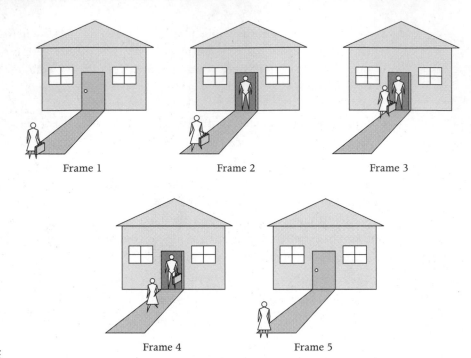

Frame 1   Frame 2   Frame 3

Frame 4   Frame 5

FIGURE

7.1   Sketch of video frames in the Sample Multimedia Scenario

Object	Frame-independent properties	Value
Jane Shady	age	35
	height	170 cm
dopeman_house	address	6717 Pimmit Drive Falls Church, VA 22047
	type	brick
	color	brown
Denis Dopeman	age	56
	height	186 cm
briefcase	color	black
	length	40 cm
	width	31 cm

At this stage, we have given a fairly comprehensive description of objects and object representations in a single video. However, the three examples for video data in this chapter (an educational video, the Sample Multimedia Scenario, and a movie example), all had two parts to them—objects and activities. We are now ready to describe what activities are.

Definition 7.4 An *activity scheme*, ACT_SCH, is a finite set of properties such that if (pname, Values$_1$) and (pname, Values$_2$) are both in ACT_SCH, then Values$_1$ = Values$_2$.

For example, consider the activity ExchangeObject, such as the exchange of objects between Jane Shady and Denis Dopeman in the preceding example. This activity has a three-pair scheme:

1. (Giver, Person): This pair specifies that the activity ExchangeObject has a property called Giver, specifying who is transferring the object in question. The property Giver is of type Person. Person is the set of all persons.

2. (Receiver, Person): This pair specifies that the activity ExchangeObject has a property called Receiver, specifying who is receiving the object in question.

3. (Item, Thing): This pair specifies the item being exchanged. Thing is the set of all exchangeable items.

Thus, the exchange of the briefcase that occurred between Jane Shady and Denis Dopeman can be captured as an activity scheme with Giver = Jane Shady, Receiver = Denis Dopeman, and Item = briefcase.

Definition 7.5 An *activity* is a pair consisting of

1. AcID, the name of the activity of scheme ACT_SCH, and

2. for each pair (pname, Values) ∈ ACT_SCH, an equation of the form pname = v, where v ∈ Values.

Informally speaking, any activity has an associated activity scheme, and each property of the activity has an associated value from its set of possible values. Let's quickly provide some examples of activities, based on the educational video example, the Sample Multimedia Scenario, and the movie example.

The Educational Video Example Revisited Let us return to the educational video example, and consider some of the activities we had informally discussed previously:

1. The activity Lecturing may have the scheme

    {(Lecturer, Person), (Topic, String)}

and may contain the equations

Lecturer = Prof. Felix
  Topic = Video Databases

2. Likewise, the activity Questioning may have the scheme

    {(Questioner, Person), (Questionee, Person),
                    (Question, String), (Answer, String)}

and may contain the equations

Questioner = Erica
Questionee = Prof. Felix
  Question = How many children does a quadtree node have?
    Answer = At most 4.

The Sample Multimedia Scenario Revisited Now let's consider the activity ExchangeObject in the Sample Multimedia Scenario. This activity has three associated (pname, Values) pairs:

  {(Giver, Person), (Receiver, Person), (Item, Object)}

as described earlier, and an event may consist of the specific equations

    Giver = Jane Shady
Receiver = Denis Dopeman
  Object = briefcase

Strictly speaking, in the last equality, we would use an oid denoting the briefcase's id, rather than the string "briefcase" (there may be many different briefcases with different associated properties).

The Movie Example Revisited If we return to the movie example and consider the activity Singing, this activity may have the activity scheme

  {(Singer, Person), (Song, String)}

An example of a concrete activity/event may use the above activity scheme and may contain the equations

Singer = Maria

Song = "You Are 16"

Given a single video v, we are now ready to formally define what we mean by the "content" of the video v.

Definition 7.6 Let us suppose that framenum(v) specifies the total number of frames of video v. The *content* of v consists of a triple (OBJ, AC, λ) where

1. OBJ = $\{oid_1, \ldots, oid_n\}$ is a finite set of object instances,

2. AC = $\{AcID_1, \ldots, AcID_k\}$ is a finite set of activities/events, and

3. λ is a map from $\{1, \ldots, framenum(v)\}$ to $2^{OBJ \cup AC}$.

Intuitively, the content of a video v is described, theoretically, by a triple (OBJ, AC, λ) where

1. OBJ represents the set of objects of interest in the video,

2. AC represents the set of activities of interest in the video, and

3. λ tells us which objects and which activities are associated with any given frame f of the video.

You might wonder whether we need to specify λ for each individual frame. Clearly this would be inefficient because a typical 90-minute movie, running 30 frames per second (as is common in the commercial video world today), would consist of approximately $90 \times 60 \times 30 = 162{,}000$ frames, and representing the set of events/objects associated with each individual frame may be computationally infeasible. We will address this topic later in this chapter; for now, we merely note this fact and provide a formal definition of the content of a video v. Later we will develop *compact representations* of this content.

7.2 Querying Content of Video Libraries

In the preceding section, we have specified what information constitutes the content of a single video. In this section, we will describe techniques to query video libraries. Informally speaking, a video library is just a description specifying

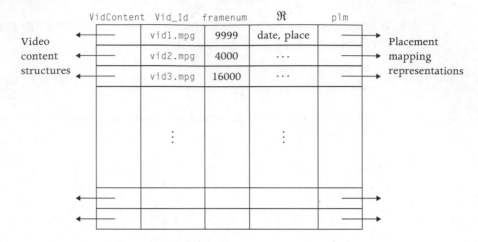

	VidContent	Vid_Id	framenum	$\Re$	plm	
Video content structures		vid1.mpg	9999	date, place		Placement mapping representations
		vid2.mpg	4000	...		
		vid3.mpg	16000	...		
			⋮	⋮		

FIGURE

7.2   Organization of a simple video library

1. *which* videos are in the library,

2. *what* constitutes the content of each of the above videos, and

3. *where* the videos are located physically.

In this chapter, we will focus primarily on the first two issues; detailed techniques for physical storage and retrieval of video data will be discussed in Part III of this book (each chapter of Part III will discuss video retrieval from a different physical storage device, such as disks, tapes, and CD-ROMs).

Definition 7.7 A *video library*, VidLib, consists of a finite set of 5-tuples (VidContent, Vid_Id, framenum, $\Re$, plm), where

1. VidContent is the content of the video,

2. Vid_Id is the name of the video,

3. framenum is the number of frames in the video,

4. $\Re$ is a set of relations about videos as a whole, and

5. plm is a *placement mapping* that specifies the address of different parts of the video (described in detail in Part III).

Figure 7.2 shows the organization of a very simple video library. In this representation, the video library, VidLib, consists of a set of 5-tuples. The second element in the tuple is the name of the video. The third is the number of frames in the video. The fourth element is a set of relations $\Re = \{R_1, \ldots, R_k\}$, each of which has an attribute called `Vid_Id` in its scheme. Intuitively, each relation R_i is maintained in a standard relational database as an ordinary relation and contains information about the video as a whole (e.g., there may be a relation called `cast` having scheme (`Vid_Id,Role,Person`) specifying, for each video v, who played roles such as `director`, `producer`, `sound track composer`, etc.).

The first element is a pointer to an as-yet-undefined representation of the content of the video. The fifth component of the tuple is a pointer to a representation of the placement mapping (which will be studied in Part III).

We will now first define query languages for querying video libraries and retrieving video. Subsequently, we will define index structures to represent video content and show how to implement the queries using those index structures.

7.2.1   Query Languages for Video Libraries

When querying a video library, `VidLib`, we are interested primarily in the following types of queries:

1. *Segment retrievals:* Find all segments, from one or more videos in the library, that satisfy a given condition. An example of such a query is "Find all video segments where an exchange of a briefcase occurred at Denis Dopeman's house."

2. *Object retrievals:* Given a video v and a segment $[s, e]$ (start frame through end frame) of the video, find all objects that occurred in either all frames between s and e (inclusive) or some frame between s and e (inclusive). An example of such a query is "Find all people who appeared sometime between frames 50 and 75 of the surveillance video `dopeman_stakeout_1.mpg`."

3. *Activity retrievals:* Given a video v and a segment $[s, e]$ (start frame through end frame) of the video, find all activities that occurred in either all frames between s and e (inclusive) or some frame between s and e (inclusive). An example of such a query is "Find all activities that occurred between frames 50 and 75 of the surveillance video `dopeman_stakeout_1.mpg`."

4. *Property-based retrievals:* In such queries, we are told to find all videos and video segments in which objects/activities with certain properties occur. An example of such a query is "Find all videos v and segments $[s, e]$ in video v such that some object `oid` (some activity `AcID`) occurred in it, and

oid.pname ∈ *Set*, where (pname, Values) is in the object scheme of object oid and *Set* ⊆ Values (AcID.pname ∈ *Set*, where (pname, Values) is in the activity scheme of activity AcID and *Set* ⊆ Values)."

Once the above elementary queries can be expressed, Boolean combinations of the above are also easily expressible through straightforward extensions of these core functionalities.

Video Functions

We will now see how the query language SQL may be extended to query video data through the ability to invoke *video functions*. Informally speaking, a video function is a function that an SQL query might access. These video functions are of the following types:

1. FindVideoWithObject(o): Given the name of a data object *o*, this function returns a set of triples of the form

   (VideoId, StartFrame, EndFrame)

   as output, such that if (v, s, e) is a triple returned in the output, then video *v*'s segment starting at frame *s* and ending at frame *e* has the object *o* in all frames between and including *s* and *e*.

2. FindVideoWithActivity(a): This does exactly the same as above, except that it returns all triples (v, s, e) such that video *v*'s segment starting at frame *s* and ending at frame *e* has the activity *a* in it. For each property *p*, the notation *a.p* specifies the value of that property.

3. FindVideoWithActivityandProp(a,p,z): This does exactly the same as above, except that it returns all triples (v, s, e) such that video *v*'s segment starting at frame *s* and ending at frame *e* has the activity *a* in it with *z* as the value of property *p*.

4. FindVideoWithObjectandProp(o,p,z): This does exactly the same as above, except that it returns all triples (v, s, e) such that video *v*'s segment starting at frame *s* and ending at frame *e* has the object *o* in it with *z* as the value of property *p*.

5. FindObjectsInVideo(v,s,e): Given the name of a video, and a start and end frame, this returns all objects that appear in all segments of the video between *s* and *e* (inclusive).

6. `FindActivitiesInVideo(v,s,e)`: Identical to the above, except it applies to activities, not objects.

7. `FindActivitiesAndPropsinVideo(v,s,e)`: Given the name of a video, and a start and end frame, this returns a set of records of the form

    `activityname:prop1 = entity1;prop2 = entity2;`
    `...;propk = entityk`

    comprising all activities, and their associated roles, that occur in all times between s and e of video v.

8. `FindObjectsAndPropsinVideo(v,s,e)`: Identical to the above, except that it applies to objects, not to activities.

    A standard SQL query has the form:

    ```
    SELECT   field1,...,fieldn
    FROM     relation1 ⟨R1⟩, relation2 ⟨R2⟩,..., relationk ⟨Rk⟩
    WHERE    Condition
    ```

    In addition to SQL's standard constructs, we will allow each of the above three clauses (`SELECT`, `FROM`, `WHERE`) to have, in addition to what SQL supports already, the following parameters:

1. The `SELECT` statement may contain entries of the form

    `Vid_Id : [s,e]`

    denoting the selection of a video with id `Vid_Id`, and with the relevant segment comprised of frames between s and e inclusive.

2. The `FROM` statement may contain entries of the form

    `video : ⟨source⟩⟨V⟩`

    which says that V is a variable ranging over videos from the source named.

3. The `WHERE` condition allows statements of the form

    term `IN` *func_call*

    where

(a) *term* is either a variable, an object, an activity, or a property value

(b) *func_call* is any of the eight video functions listed above

Here are some simple examples of queries to a video library. Consider the simple query "Find all videos and their relevant segments from video library $VidLib_1$ that contain Denis Dopeman." This query can be expressed as

```
SELECT  vid:[s,e]
FROM    video:VidLib₁
WHERE   (vid,s,e) IN FindVideoWithObject(Denis Dopeman)
```

Now consider a slightly more complex query: "Find all videos and their relevant segments from video library $VidLib_1$ that contain Denis Dopeman and Jane Shady." This query can be expressed as

```
SELECT  vid:[s,e]
FROM    video:VidLib₁
WHERE   (vid,s,e) IN FindVideoWithObject(Denis Dopeman) AND
        (vid,s,e) IN FindVideoWithObject(Jane Shady)
```

Now consider an even more complex query: "Find all videos and their relevant segments from video library $VidLib_1$ that contain Denis Dopeman getting a briefcase from Jane Shady." This query can be expressed as

```
SELECT  vid:[s,e]
FROM    video:VidLib₁
WHERE   (vid,s,e) IN FindVideoWithObject(Denis Dopeman) AND
        (vid,s,e) IN FindVideoWithObject(Jane Shady) AND
        (vid,s,e) IN FindVideoWithActivityandProp
                (ExchangeObject,Item,Briefcase) AND
        (vid,s,e) IN FindVideoWithActivityandProp
                (ExchangeObject,Giver,Jane Shady) AND
        (vid,s,e) IN FindVideoWithActivityandProp
                (ExchangeObject,Receiver,Denis Dopeman)
```

Now consider a somewhat different query that asks: "Find all videos and people seen with Denis Dopeman." This query has to be expressed somewhat differently from the preceding queries.

```
SELECT  vid:[s,e], Object
FROM    video:VidLib₁
WHERE   (vid,s,e) IN FindVideoWithObject(Denis Dopeman) AND
```

```
Object IN FindObjectsInVideo(vid,s,e) AND
Object ≠ Denis Dopeman AND
type of(Object,Person)
```

In this query, `type of` is assumed to be an ordinary relation. What is interesting about this query language is that ordinary SQL is being augmented, in a minimally invasive manner, to query video libraries. If we were merely interested in the identities of all people who appear in videos with Denis Dopeman, then we would merely modify the SELECT condition in the above query to read

```
SELECT  Object
```

and keep the rest of the query as is. The resulting query would still need to access the video sources to compute the answer, but would not explicitly return video clips to the user as part of the answer (though such video clips would be identified during the internal processing of the query).

7.2.2   Indexing Video Content

At this stage, we have formally defined

- what constitutes the content of a video,

- what constitutes a video library, and

- what constitutes an appropriate video query language to query video libraries, using SQL as a base language extended with video capabilities.

One of the reasons for the success of the relational model of data is the ability to index very large collections of tuples to facilitate retrievals on certain attributes (called *primary* and *secondary* keys). Likewise, in the case of spatial data structures, indexes on locations played a critical role. In this section, we consider the problem of developing data structures to organize video data so as to optimize the processing of the eight types of video functions listed earlier. We would like to reiterate that, in general, it is impossible to store video content on a frame-by-frame basis because a single 90-minute video contains 162,000 frames! Thus, we need to develop *compact representations* of the concept of video content described earlier in this chapter. In the rest of this section, we will present two such data structures: frame segment trees and R-segment trees (or RS-trees).

7.2.3   Frame Segment Trees

The table depicting the events that occurred in Figure 7.1 had the following form: for each frame f in the video, the "contents" of that frame were described in the table. In practice, however, an activity usually spans several contiguous frames. After all, in the Sample Multimedia Scenario, it may take 10 seconds for Jane Shady to reach the middle of the path from the end of the path, and this translates to 300 frames, all contiguous, that represent one activity. Likewise, Prof. Felix, when giving a lecture in the educational video example, is unlikely to spend just one-thirtieth of a second on a topic; more likely, he might spend 30 minutes describing the concept of "Object Structure and Objects," which translates to a contiguous segment of $(30 \times 60 \times 30) = 54,000$ frames, again all contiguous. Thus, it may make much more sense to store data in terms of *video segments*.

Definition 7.8 A *frame sequence* is a pair $[i, j)$, where $1 \leq i \leq j \leq n$. $[i, j)$ represents the set of all frames between i (inclusive) and j (noninclusive). In other words, $[i, j) = \{k \mid i \leq k < j\}$. i is said to be the *start* of the frame sequence $[i, j)$, and j is said to be the *end*.

For example, the frame sequence $[6, 12)$ denotes the set of frames $\{6, 7, 8, 9, 10, 11\}$.

Definition 7.9 We may define a partial *ordering*, $\sqsubseteq$, on the set of all frame sequences as follows: $[i_1, j_1) \sqsubseteq [i_2, j_2)$ iff $i_1 < j_1 \leq i_2 < j_2$. Intuitively, $[i_1, j_1) \sqsubseteq [i_2, j_2)$ means that the sequence of frames denoted by $[i_1, j_1)$ precedes the sequence of frames denoted by $[i_2, j_2)$. As usual, we use $[i_1, j_1) \sqsubset [i_2, j_2)$ to denote that $[i_1, j_1) \sqsubseteq [i_2, j_2)$ and $j_1 \neq i_2$.

For example, consider frame sequences $fs_1 = [10, 15)$, $fs_2 = [8, 10)$, and $fs_3 = [11, 13)$. Then it is easy to see that $fs_2 \sqsubseteq fs_1$ and $fs_2 \sqsubseteq fs_3$. However, it is not the case that $fs_1 \sqsubseteq fs_3$ because fs_1 does not completely precede fs_3.

Definition 7.10 A set X of frame sequences is said to be *well-ordered* iff

1. X is finite (i.e., $X = \{[i_1, j_1), \ldots, [i_r, j_r)\}$ for some integer r) and

2. $[i_1, j_1) \sqsubseteq [i_2, j_2) \sqsubseteq \ldots \sqsubseteq [i_r, j_r)$.

   Intuitively, a well-ordered set of frame sequences is a set that can be enumerated in ascending order with respect to the ordering $\sqsubseteq$. For example, the set $X = \{[1, 4), [9, 13), [33, 90)\}$ is a well-ordered set of frame sequences because $[1, 4) \sqsubseteq [9, 13) \sqsubseteq [33, 90)$. On the other hand, $X' = \{[1, 7), [5, 8)\}$ is not well-ordered because $[1, 7) \not\sqsubseteq [5, 8)$ and $[5, 8) \not\sqsubseteq [1, 7)$.

Definition 7.11 A set X of frame sequences is said to be *solid* iff

1. X is well-ordered, and

2. there is no pair of frame sequences in X of the form $[i_1, i_2)$ and $[i_2, i_3)$.

For instance, if we take $X = \{[1, 5), [5, 7), [9, 11)\}$, then X is not solid, even though it is well-ordered. It may be converted into an equivalent solid set of frame sequences by replacing X by $\{[1, 7), [9, 11)\}$, which is solid. Intuitively, the requirement of solidity says that if we have two abutting frame sequences $[i, j)$ and $[j, k)$, then these should be merged to form the frame sequence $[i, k)$.

When attempting to create a compact representation of the content, $(\texttt{OBJ}, \texttt{AC}, \lambda)$, of a video, as defined earlier in the chapter, we need to represent the map λ, which associates a set of objects and activities with each video frame, in a concise manner. Doing so in terms of segments is often helpful.

Definition 7.12 Suppose $(\texttt{OBJ}, \texttt{AC}, \lambda)$ represents the content of a video v. A *segment association map* σ_v associated with video v is the map defined as follows:

1. σ_v's domain is $\texttt{OBJ} \cup \texttt{AC}$ and

2. σ_v returns, for each $x \in \texttt{OBJ} \cup \texttt{AC}$, a solid set of frame sequences, denoted $\sigma_v(x)$, such that

   (a) if $[s, e) \in \sigma_v(x)$, then for all $s \le f < e$, it is the case that $x \in \lambda(f)$, and
   (b) for all frames f and all $x \in \texttt{OBJ} \cup \texttt{AC}$, if $x \in \lambda(f)$, then there exists a frame sequence $[s, e) \in \sigma_v(x)$ such that $f \in [s, e)$.

In short, if $(\texttt{OBJ}, \texttt{AC}, \lambda)$ is the content of video v, then replacing the map λ by the map σ_v (which is equivalent in content) may often represent a substantial saving. To see why, consider the very simple example shown in Figure 7.3. In this figure, the x-axis represents frame numbers, while the y-axis specifies the names of certain objects. These objects have no frame-dependent properties, and hence the only thing to be represented is when they appear in the video. No activities are encoded in this example.

When we consider this figure, we notice that there is a total of 5,000 frames. The following table summarizes the number of frames that each object appears in:

Object	Number of frames
object1	1,250
object2	1,500
object3	3,250
object4	1,000
object5	2,750

Thus, were we to explicitly represent the mapping λ associated with the content of this video, we would need to have a total of 9,750 tuples. Rather than do this, we are much better off if we merely try to represent the information in the following table. Unlike the 9,750 tuples in the previous representation, this segment table contains just 16 tuples—a significantly smaller number!

Object	Segment
object1	250–750
object1	1,750–2,500
object2	250–1,000
object2	2,250–2,500
object2	2,750–3,250
object3	0–250
object3	500–750
object3	1,000–1,750
object3	2,500–2,750
object3	3,250–5,000
object4	1,500–2,250
object4	4,500–5,000
object5	250–750
object5	1,250–2,750
object5	3,500–3,750
object5	4,500–5,000

However, in practice, even this table can get unmanageably big. In general, if there are n objects $o_1, \ldots, o_n$ in our video v, and m activities $a_1, \ldots, a_m$, then we will have a total of

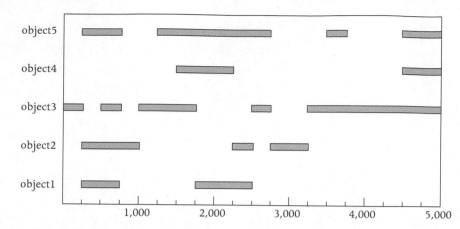

F I G U R E

7.3
    An example of a video's content

$$\sum_{i=1}^{n} \left(card(\sigma_v(o_i)) \right) + \sum_{j=1}^{m} \left(card(\sigma_v(a_j)) \right)$$

entries in the table *just for one single video*. Though this may not be too large, in general, the tables of the sort described above are not well suited to answering queries that manipulate segments. An index structure called a *frame segment tree* may be used to store such data. This data structure takes advantage of the fact (clearly visible from Figure 7.3) that the segment association map, σ_v, associates a set of line segments with each object and activity.

The basic idea behind frame segment trees is very simple. First create two arrays:

1. OBJECTARRAY: The object array is an array whose *i*th element denotes video object number *i* (denoted by o*i*). Associated with any element of this array is an *ordered linked list* of pointers to nodes in the frame segment tree. For example, we will see later in Figure 7.7 that the linked list associated with object number 1 (o1) contains four pointers to nodes 17, 18, 23, and 24. These are the nodes in the frame segment tree (that will be described in detail below, and that can be seen in Figure 7.4) that are labeled with object number 1.

2. ACTIVITYARRAY: Like the object array, the activity array is an array whose *i*th element denotes video activity *i* (denoted by a*i*). Each element of this array, like the OBJECTARRAY, has an *ordered linked list* of pointers to nodes in the frame segment tree.

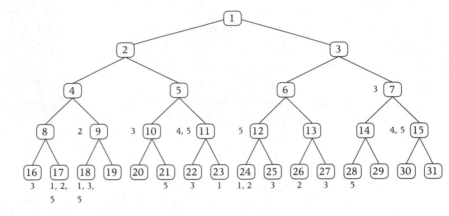

FIGURE

7.4   Frame segment tree with objects associated with nodes

Next, the frame segment tree is constructed from the segment table given above in two steps.

In step (1), let $[s_1, e_1), \ldots, [s_w, e_w)$ be all the intervals in the "Segment" column of the segment table. Let $q_1, \ldots, q_z$ be an enumeration, in ascending order, of all members of $\{s_i, e_i \mid 1 \leq i \leq w\}$, with duplicates eliminated. If z is not an exponent of 2, then do as follows: let r be the smallest integer such that $2^r > z$ and $2^r > \texttt{framenum}(v)$. Add new elements $q_{z+1}, \ldots, q_{2^r}$ such that $q_{2^r} = \texttt{framenum}(v) + 1$ and $q_{z+j} = q_z + j$ (for $j > 0$ such that $z + j < 2^r$). Now we may proceed under the assumption that z is an exponent of 2 (i.e., $z = 2^r$ for some r).

In step (2), the frame segment tree is a binary tree constructed as follows:

1. Each node in the frame segment tree represents a frame sequence $[x, y)$, starting at frame x and including all frames up to, but not including, frame y.

2. Every leaf is at level r. The leftmost leaf denotes the interval $[z_1, z_2)$, the second from the left represents the interval $[z_2, z_3)$, the third from the left represents the interval $[z_3, z_4)$, and so on. If N is a node with two children representing the intervals $[p_1, p_2), [p_2, p_3)$, then N represents the interval $[p_1, p_3)$. Thus, the root of the segment tree represents the interval $[q_1, q_z)$ if q_z is an exponent of 2; otherwise it represents the interval $[q_1, \infty)$.

3. The number inside each node may be viewed as the address of that node.

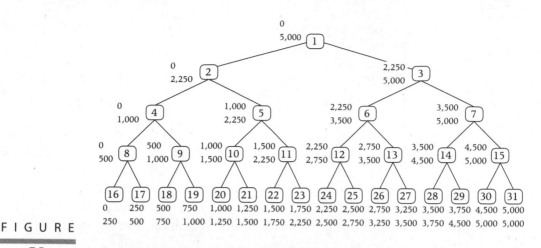

Segment tree with intervals associated with nodes

4. The set of numbers placed next to a node denotes the id numbers of video objects and activities that appear in the entire frame sequence associated with that node. Thus, for example, if a node N represents the frame sequence $[i, j)$, and object o occurs in all frames in $[i, j)$, then object o labels node N (unless object o labels an ancestor of node N in the tree).

Let's see how the frame segment tree can be used to represent the content of Figure 7.3. To do so, we must show what OBJECTARRAY contains and what the frame segment tree contains (in this example, there are no activities, and hence the ACTIVITYARRAY is empty). Figure 7.7 shows the contents of OBJECT-ARRAY. The nodes in OBJECTARRAY refer to nodes in the frame segment tree of Figure 7.5.

In step 1, we sort the end points of all intervals in Figure 7.3, obtaining the following sequence:

0, 250, 500, 750, 1,000, 1,250, 1,500, 1,750, 2,250, 2,500,

2,750, 3,250, 3,500, 3,750, 4,500, 5,000

This sequence has 16 elements in it, leading to the segment tree in Figure 7.5. Each node in the segment tree contains five fields:

1. An LB field, denoting the lower bound of the segment that node represents

2. A UB field, denoting the upper bound of the segment that node represents

3. An OBJ field that points to a linked list of pointers to entries in OBJECT-ARRAY. If a pointer to object*i* appears in this linked list, then it means that

objecti appears in the video *throughout the entire duration of the interval* [LB,UB).

4. An RCHILD field.

5. An LCHILD field.

In Figure 7.5, each node has a number that reflects the address of the node, as well as a pair of numbers written either below it or to its left. This pair is the interval [LB, UB).

Now for step 2. Figure 7.4 shows the same tree as in Figure 7.5, except that the numbers on the left of (or below) each node denote the objects that are associated with that node. We label a node in the frame segment tree with objecti if there exists a frame sequence $fs \in \sigma_v(\text{object}i)$ such that $fs \supseteq int$ where *int* is the interval associated with that node (as shown, for example, in Figure 7.5). What this means, in practice, is that for each object objecti and each frame sequence $fs \in \sigma_v(\text{object}i)$, we must find nodes in the tree whose associated events are covered by fs.

Let us see how this works in the case of object1. In this case, $\sigma_v(\text{object}1) = \{[250, 750), [1750, 2500)\}$.

The insertion of $I = [250, 750)$ proceeds as follows:

1. I does not cover the root, so we consider the left and right subchild. There is no intersection between I and the right subchild, so we can safely ignore the right subchild and recursively invoke our insertion routine on the left.

2. I does not cover node 2, so we consider the left and right subchilds (nodes 4 and 5). I does not intersect the interval associated with 5, so we ignore it and consider the left subtree rooted at node 4.

3. I does not cover node 4, so we consider the left and right subchilds (nodes 8 and 9). I intersects the intervals represented by both nodes 8 and 9, so we must call them recursively.

4. When processing node 8, we notice that I does not completely cover it. Furthermore, as it does not intersect the region associated with the left child (node 16), we merely process the right child recursively and notice that I covers the interval represented by node 17. Thus, node 17 is labeled with object 1.

5. When processing node 9, we notice that I does not completely cover it. Furthermore, as it does not intersect the interval associated with the right

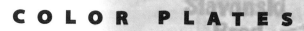

a

b

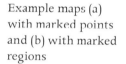

FIGURE 4.1

Example maps (a) with marked points and (b) with marked regions

FIGURE 4.3

Gridded map

FIGURE 5.9

Transformation
sequence TS_1 trans-
forming object o_1
into o_2

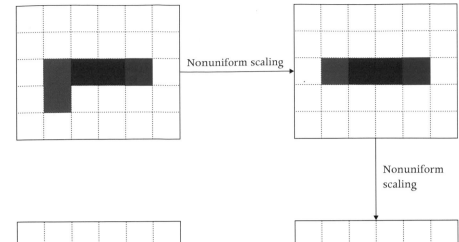

Nonuniform scaling

Nonuniform
scaling

Paint

FIGURE 5.10

Transformation
sequence TS_2 trans-
forming object o_1
into o_2

Nonuniform scaling

Paint

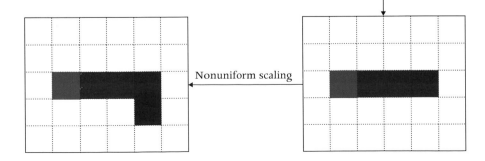

Nonuniform scaling

FIGURE 9.8

Example screen
showing annotation
of image objects

FIGURE 13.9

CHIMP object cre-
ation/search win-
dows

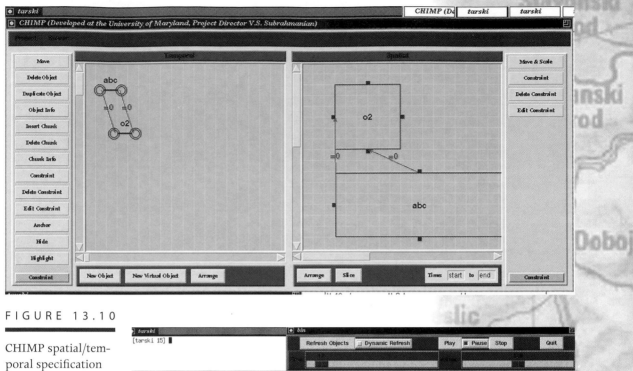

FIGURE 13.10

CHIMP spatial/temporal specification window

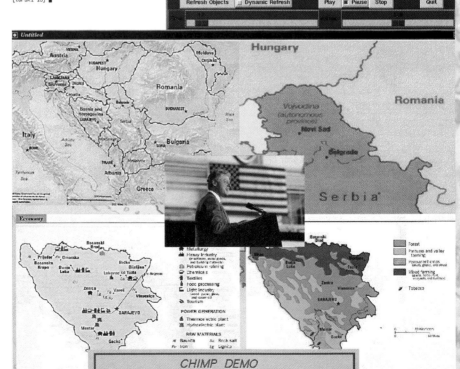

FIGURE 13.11

CHIMP presentation playout snapshot

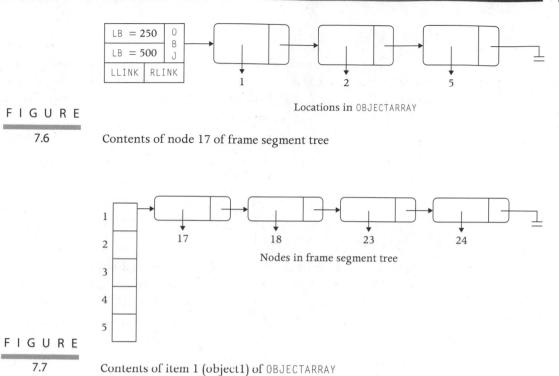

Contents of node 17 of frame segment tree

Contents of item 1 (object1) of OBJECTARRAY

child (node 19), we merely process the left child recursively and notice that *I* covers the interval represented by node 18. Thus, node 18 is labeled with object 1.

The insertion of $J = [1750, 2500)$ proceeds in an analogous manner, leading to nodes 23 and 24 being marked with object1.

When we say a node *N* is being "marked" with an object*i*, what we mean, in fact, is that we append to the front of the list N.OBJ, a node pointing to the OBJECTARRAY's *i*th location. Figure 7.6 shows the contents of node 17.

We now need to update the OBJECTARRAY appropriately as follows. For each object*i*, the *i*th entry in the array OBJECTARRAY contains a linked list of pointers to nodes in the frame segment tree. For example, consider the entry in the OBJECTARRAY associated with object1. As we saw above, nodes 17, 18, 23, and 24 are marked with object1. Hence, the linked list associated with object1 in the OBJECTARRAY contains nodes pointing to nodes 17, 18, 23, and 24. This is shown in Figure 7.7.

Operations on Frame Segment Trees

As shown in Figure 7.2, associated with each video v is a video content structure, which, for now, consists of a frame segment tree, an object array, and an activity array. In particular, if our video library, VidLib, contains videos $v_1, \ldots, v_n$, then it is sufficient to associate the following:

1. A single table called INTOBJECTARRAY having the scheme (VID_ID, OBJ, PTR), where the tuple (v, o, ptr) is in INTOBJECTARRAY iff the pair (o, ptr) is in the OBJECTARRAY associated with video v

2. A single table called INTACTIVITYARRAY having the scheme (VID_ID, ACT, PTR), where the tuple (v, a, ptr) is in INTOBJECTARRAY iff the pair (a, ptr) is in the ACTIVITYARRAY associated with video v

3. For each v_i, a frame segment tree, $fst(v_i)$ is associated with video v_i. The only difference here is that pointers from the frame segment tree point to locations in INTOBJECTARRAY and INTACTIVITYARRAY, rather than to OBJECTARRAY and ACTIVITYARRAY as described earlier.

Earlier in this chapter, we showed how SQL could be extended through the addition of eight specific operations that act on video. We will now describe how these eight functions can be implemented on frame segment trees:

1. FindVideoWithObject(o): This is fairly simple. All we need to do is to perform a selection operation on INTOBJECTARRAY having the form:

```
SELECT  VIDEO_ID
FROM    INTOBJECTARRAY
WHERE   OBJ = o
```

2. FindVideoWithActivity(a): Similar to the above.

3. FindVideoWithActivityandProp(a,p,z): In this case, we merely perform a somewhat different selection operation:

```
SELECT  VIDEO_ID
FROM    INTACTIVITYARRAY t
WHERE   ACT = a AND t.p = z
```

4. FindVideoWithObjectandProp(o,p,z): Similar to the above.

5. FindObjectsInVideo(v,s,e): The queries given above don't need to access the frame segment tree. In this case, however, we must access the frame segment tree associated with v. Suppose R denotes the root of this frame segment tree. We proceed as follows:

```
Algorithm 7.1  FindObjectsInVideo(R,s,e)
   S = NIL; (* no objects found so far *)
if R = NIL then { Return S; Halt }
else
   { if [R.LB,R.UB) ⊆ [s,e) then S = append(S,preorder(R))
     else
     { if [R.LB,R.UB) ∩ [s,e) ≠ ∅ then
       { S = append(S,R.obj);
         S = append(S,FindObjectsInVideo(R.LLINK,s,e));
         S = append(S,FindObjectsInVideo(R.RLINK,s,e));
       }
     }
   }
return(S); end
```

In the above algorithm, preorder(N) traverses the entire subtree rooted at node N in preorder, and, when visiting any node N', it appends the OBJ field of N' to a list. At the end, the entire list L is returned. At the beginning of the preorder function, list L is NIL.

Basically, the above algorithm works as follows: to find all objects that occur in frames s through e of video v, we examine the segment tree as follows, by first starting from the root. The root represents the interval $[R.LB, R.UB)$. If this interval is a subset of $[s, e)$, then we must visit each node in the tree and output all objects labeling nodes in the tree. If this is not the case, but $[R.LB, R.UB)$ intersects $[s, e)$, then clearly each object labeling node R must be in the interval $[s, e)$ because each object labeling node R occurs in *all* frames in the interval $[R.LB, R.UB)$. If this is not the case either, then we must recursively repeat this procedure on the left and the right subtree of R.

6. FindActivitiesInVideo(v,s,e): Similar to the above.

7. FindActivitiesAndPropsinVideo(v,s,e): Similar to the above.

8. FindObjectsAndPropsinVideo(v,s,e): Similar to the above.

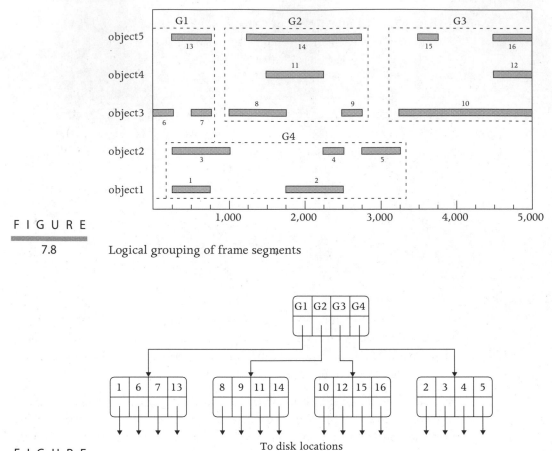

7.8   Logical grouping of frame segments

F I G U R E

7.9   RS-tree representing frame segments of the Sample Multimedia Scenario

7.2.4   The R-Segment Tree (RS-Tree)

The R-segment tree is very similar to the frame segment tree, with one major distinction. Although the concepts of OBJECTARRAY and ACTIVITYARRAY remain the same as before, instead of using a segment tree to represent the frame sequences (such as those shown in Figure 7.3), we take advantage of the fact that a sequence $[s, e)$ is a *rectangle* of length $(e - s)$ and of width 0. We already know from Chapter 4 how to represent a set of rectangles using an R-tree. For example, consider the objects in Figure 7.3. Figure 7.8 shows how the frame sequences associated with these objects may be logically grouped together, and Figure 7.9 shows how the set of frame sequences associated with these objects may be arranged in an R-tree. In this case, each R-tree node will have a special structure to specify, for each rectangle, which object or activity is associated with it. The algorithms given for manipulating the frame segment tree can be easily adapted to work with the RS-tree. The main advantage that an RS-tree has over a frame segment tree is that it is suitable for retrieving pages from disk, since each disk access brings back a page containing not one rectangle, but several proximate rectangles.

7.3 Video Segmentation

Throughout this chapter, we have assumed a *logical delineation* of video data in which the video is "broken up" into homogeneous segments. However, we have not discussed precisely how this is done. The aim of this section is to briefly overview image-processing techniques that accomplish this.

Usually, a video is created by taking a set of *shots* and composing them together using specified *composition operators*. A shot is usually a piece of video taken with a fixed set of cameras, each of which has a constant relative velocity. Thus, for instance, a shot may be composed of a synthetic view obtained from two cameras—one stationary, the other with constant velocity of 2 mph relative to the scene being filmed. For instance, in our drug enforcement example, there may be a fixed camera that focuses on Denis Dopeman's door, and another fixed camera that monitors the path to the door. In general, a shot may have many associated attributes, such as the duration of the shot, the type(s) of camera(s) uscd, and so on.

A *shot composition operator*, often referred to as an *edit effect*, is an operation that takes two shots, S_1 and S_2, and a duration t as input and merges the two shots into a composite shot within time t. Thus, for example, suppose we wish to compose together two shots S_1 and S_2, and suppose these two shots have durations t_1 and t_2, respectively. If f is a shot composition operator, then

$$f(S_1, S_2, t)$$

creates a segment of video of length $(t_1 + t_2 + t)$. S_1 is first shown and then undergoes a continuous transformation over a time interval t, leading to the presentation of S_2 next. $f(S_1, S_2, t)$ then is a continuous sequence of video. In general, a video as a whole may be represented as

$$f_n(\ldots f_2(f_1(S_1, S_2, t_1), S_3, t_2) \ldots, S_{n+1}, t_n)$$

Thus, a video is typically created by composing together a set of video shots using a finite set of video composition operations. Examples of such video composition operations include the following:

- *Shot concatenation:* This is the simplest type of composition operation. It merely concatenates the two shots (even if the transition is not smooth). If shotcat is a shot concatenation operator, then t must be zero; that is, whenever we invoke shotcat(S_1, S_2, t), the third argument t must be set to zero.

- *Spatial composition:* The best-known type of spatial composition operation is a *translate* operation, which causes two successive shots to be overlayed one on top of the other. For instance, suppose we want to show shot S_1 first, followed by shot S_2. This is done by first overlaying shot S_1 on top of shot S_2 and then moving (i.e., translating) shot S_1 away, thus exposing shot S_2.

- *Chromatic composition:* There are two well-known kinds of chromatic compositions—*fades* and *dissolves*. Both these operations are chromatic scaling operations that try to continuously transform each pixel (x, y) in the first shot into the corresponding pixel in the second shot. The smoothness of this transformation depends both upon the degree of difference between the two shots and the amount of time available for the composition operation.

Video segmentation techniques attempt to take a video as input and determine when shots have been concatenated, when they have been spatially composed, and when they have been chromatically composed; that is, given a video V, express the video V in the form

$$V = f_n(\ldots f_2(f_1(S_1, S_2, t_1), S_3, t_2) \ldots, S_{n+1}, t_n)$$

In other words, given video V, find n and shots $S_1, \ldots, S_{n+1}$, times $t_1, \ldots, t_n$, and composition operations $f_1, \ldots, f_n$ such that the above equation holds.

Techniques to do this are well described in various sources (Hampapur, Jain, and Weymouth; Tonomura et al.; Zhang, Kankanhalli, and Smoliar [88, 207, 233]). These methods can be quite successful when we know in advance that the video has been produced under a small set of known conditions, but are not equally successful in unrestricted conditions.

1	2	3	4	5	6	7	8	9	10	11	12	13	14	15	16	17	18	19	20	
I	B	B	P	B	B	I	B	B	P	B	B	I	B	B	P	B	B	I	B	⋯

F I G U R E

7.10   MPEG-1 stream

7.4   Video Standards

Though, in general, industry standards do not constitute part of the basic foundations of multimedia settings, we would be remiss if we did not, at least briefly, explain the basic ideas underlying the MPEG standard.

All video compression standards attempt to compress videos by performing an *intra-frame* analysis: Each frame is divided up into blocks, and different frames are compared to see which data is "redundant" in the two frames. The redundant data is then dropped to achieve a level of compression. The quality of a compression technique is measured by three basic parameters:

- *Fidelity of the color map*: How many colors of the original video are still present when the compressed video is decompressed?

- *Pixel resolution per frame*: How many pixels per frame of the video have been dropped?

- *Number of frames per second:* How many frames have been dropped?

There are numerous different standards for video compression, such as MPEG, Cinepak, and MPEG-2.

MPEG-1 videos are stored as a sequence of I-, P-, and B-frames (Figure 7.10). I-frames are independent images called *intra frames*. Basically, an I-frame is a still image. A P-frame is computed from the closest I-frame preceding it by interpolation using the discrete cosine transform (DCT). For example, if we consider frame 4 in Figure 7.10, we have a P-frame that is computed by interpolation from the I-frame constituting frame 1. A P-frame may also be computed by interpolation from the closest P-frame preceding it. For example, if we look at Figure 7.11, the P-frame at frame 7 may be obtained from the P-frame at frame 4 by interpolation.

B-frames are computed by interpolating from the two closest P- or I-frames. For example, in Figure 7.10, we compute the B-frame at frame 6 by interpolating from frame 4 (P) and frame 7 (I).

In general, given a sequence of B-, P-, and I-frames, we must proceed as follows: first decode the I-frames, then decode the P-frames, and finally decode

1	2	3	4	5	6	7	8	9	10	11	12	13	14	15	16	17	18	19	20
I	B	B	P	B	B	P	B	B	P	B	B	I	B	B	P	B	B	P	B	$\cdots$

FIGURE 7.11   Another MPEG-1 stream

the B-frames. For example, consider the sequence of frames [1, 13) in Figure 7.10. We may proceed by decoding the first I-frame (1), then decoding the P-frame (4), then the two B-frames (2 and 3), then the next I-frame (7), then the two B-frames (5 and 6), and so on. Often, once a frame has been decoded, it can be displayed while the next frame determined by it by interpolation is being computed.

The MPEG-2 standard was created as a successor to MPEG-1 because the quality of MPEG-1 is not adequate for TV broadcasts. MPEG-2 uses a higher pixel resolution and a higher data rate, thus making it superior to MPEG-1 in terms of the quality of the video as seen by the user. However, it requires higher bandwidth, thus making it feasible for only some applications. The MPEG-3 standard, created to support high-definition TV (HDTV), requires even higher sampling rates and frames per second than MPEG-2.

Having briefly described the basic ideas underlying MPEG, a note of caution is in order. Any technique dealing with multimedia data must try to modularize dependence on standards because standards evolve over time, and today's standards will become outdated in the future. By modularizing dependence on standards, MMDBMSs can "plug and play" by replacing a component relevant to an old standard with a new one. For instance, MPEG-1 is already under challenge by new standards, MPEG-2, -3, and -4. If existing MMDBMSs were hardwired to MPEG-1, then upgrading to these new standards would prove difficult.

7.5   Selected Commercial Products

Informix's (*http://www.informix.com*) datablade architecture provides one of the widest array of video database products through the incorporation of a wide variety of video database modules.

For example, their Video Foundation datablade module allows for the management of video content and metadata. This datablade stores metadata using a layered/stratified approach within the Informix Universal Server, while the media content itself is stored on a variety of store devices. Users may pick any video they like (or even a clip) and play it.

Another datablade, called VXTreme, allows for the creation of both audio and video data. It can apparently deliver videos over the network (see also Chapter 14) in a streamed, real-time fashion.

Informix also has a Scene Change datablade developed by Excalibur, which is very useful for video applications. Scene changes are a critical aspect of any video. Once scenes are identified using this datablade, the content of the scenes may be individually described, extracted, and indexed.

Oracle offers a video server on top of the Oracle Universal Server. This video server provides concurrent delivery of full-motion video and supports full remote control operations.

IBM's DB2 system has a video extender that allows for the import of video clips as well as for querying the video clip based on information such as the format, the name/number or description of the video, and the last time the video was modified. Information on all of IBM's extenders is available at *http://www.software.ibm.com/data/db2/extenders/index.html*.

7.6   Bibliographic Notes

Gibbs, Breiteneder, and Tsichritzis [72] studied how stream-based temporal multimedia data may be modeled using object-based methods. Hjelsvold and Midtstraum [95] developed a "generic" data model for capturing video content and structure. Their idea is that video should be included as a data type in relational databases; that is, systems such as PARADOX and INGRES should be augmented to handle video data. They provide a temporal query framework. Oomoto and Tanaka [152] have developed a language called VideoSQL for accessing video data.

Other work on video includes work by Davenport, Smith, and Pincever [52], who argue that segmenting video should not be done at the frame level. This is consistent with the treatment in this chapter, in the sense that both frame segment trees and RS-trees allow segments to be of variable length. Samet's book [180] provides an excellent overview of segment trees.

All the above techniques assume that the content of videos has somehow been elicited from the raw video. Other works on video indexing include specific disk-based techniques [46, 21]), methods dealing with compression/image processing [12], synchronization structures [100], and developing ways of handling/presenting continuous data [174].

The MPEG video standard is well explained in LeGall [124].

7.7 Exercises and Projects

1. Using the Sample Multimedia Scenario involving Jane Shady and Denis Dopeman given in this chapter, express the following queries in the video extension of SQL described here:

   (a) Find all video segments in which Jane Shady and Denis Dopeman's house appear together.

   (b) Find the color of each briefcase in any frame containing Jane Shady and a briefcase.

   (c) Find the color of each briefcase in any frame containing Jane Shady, Denis Dopeman, and the activity where Jane Shady is giving the briefcase to Denis Dopeman.

   (d) Find all objects that appear in a frame with Denis Dopeman.

2. Suppose you are given a segment table, and you are asked to find all pairs (o_1, o_2) of objects that appear together in some frame. In other words, you are required to return the set of all pairs (o_1, o_2) of objects such that there exists a frame f in which o_1 and o_2 appear together. Write, in pseudocode, an algorithm that computes this. What is the complexity of your algorithm?

3. Write an algorithm that takes a set O of objects and a video library VidLib (as shown in Figure 7.2) as input and returns a solid set of frame sequences $X = \{[s_1, e_1], \ldots, [s_n, e_n]\}$, such that all objects in O appear in all frames of X as output. You must write two algorithms, one for the case where the video content structure is a frame segment tree, and another for the case where we have an RS-tree.

4. For each of the eight basic video functions described in this chapter, analyze the worst-case complexity of implementing those functions on top of

   (a) frame segment trees

   (b) an RS-tree

5. This project pertains to the design and implementation of RS-trees. To successfully complete this project, we encourage you to review material both in this chapter and in Section 4.5.

   (a) Design and implement an algorithm that reads a segment table containing objects as input and that returns an RS-tree and an OBJECTARRAY containing the relevant information as output.

   (b) Implement each of the eight functions listed below on top of the RS-tree constructed above:

     i. `FindVideoWithObject(o)`

    ii. `FindVideoWithActivity(a)`

   iii. `FindVideoWithActivityandProp(a,p,z)`

   iv. `FindVideoWithObjectandProp(o,p,z)`

    v. `FindObjectsInVideo(v,s,e)`

   vi. `FindActivitiesInVideo(v,s,e)`

  vii. `FindActivitiesAndPropsinVideo(v,s,e)`

 viii. `FindObjectsAndPropsinVideo(v,s,e)`

(c) Design a graphical user interface from which the user can execute each of the functions listed above.

(d) Demonstrate the operation of your algorithm by showing how it accesses a small video of 80–100 frames.

8 Audio Databases

What new concepts will you learn in this chapter?
You will learn what an audio database is. Audio signals are certain kinds of continuous analytic functions. You will learn how to compress such signals into discrete representations and index their content.

What new abstractions are needed to realize these concepts?
Audio signals are typically continuous waveforms whose discretization is achieved using transformations such as the one-dimensional discrete cosine transform (DCT) and the discrete Fourier transform (DFT). You will learn about these transforms.

What new techniques are needed to implement these abstractions?
You will learn how TV-trees, defined in Chapter 6, may be used to index audio data, in much the same way they were used to index text.

What technological features support these implementation methods?
You will receive a quick overview of existing audio database management systems on both the Unix and Windows software platforms.

8.1 Introduction

Although audio data has been around for quite a long while and has existed in magnetic media since the advent of magnetic recording devices, there has been surprisingly little work on audio databases. Nonetheless, audio data plays an important role in many application areas. For example:

1. Returning to the Sample Multimedia Scenario, we will notice that our police investigators may conduct telephone surveillance of various criminal elements. For instance, they may have placed legally authorized wiretaps on the phones of suspected drug dealers and may be interested in knowing the identities of individuals calling these suspects. In such cases, accessing an audio archive identifying the voices of known individuals is extremely useful. Similarly, a police investigator monitoring a particular phone call may say to himself, "That voice sounds familiar." He may then request that all audio clips containing a voice similar to the voice currently being heard be retrieved from the archive.

2. In the same vein, a musician may be looking for certain musical patterns. For example, the composer Richard Wagner made extensive use of a certain musical construct called a *leitmotif* ("leading motive") in his operas. Certain music segments were repeated, over and over again, at certain selected dramatically appropriate intervals in the opera. A student of music, while listening to a Wagnerian opera, may halt it at a certain point and ask the query "Find all segments in the rest of the opera that are similar to the piece I just heard." This is a case of similarity-based retrieval in music.

In the next section, we will present a general model of audio data. Subsequently, in Section 8.3, we will show that audio data, too, may be compressed, using the discrete Fourier transform and the discrete cosine transform, and that retrieval of audio data can also be viewed as retrieval from a large-dimensional vector space.

8.2 A General Model of Audio Data

As in the case of images and video data, audio data content can be characterized in two basic ways (that can later lead to hybrids): by using metadata explaining the content of an audio file or by extracting pertinent features of

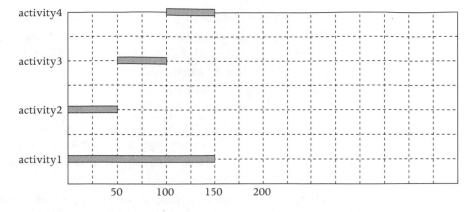

FIGURE

8.1   Sample audio data segments

audio data using signal-processing techniques. In this chapter, we will briefly overview both techniques.

8.2.1   Metadata to Represent Audio Content

Consider a single audio file containing, say, a Wagnerian opera. In this case, just as we did earlier with video data, we may associate a set of line segments (each referring to a time period) covering the entire opera, and we may associate with each line segment a set of activities that occur in the time periods denoted by those line segments.

For example, Figure 8.1 shows the line segments associated with part of an opera. Here, activity1 may be Act 1 of the opera, activity2 may be Act 1, Scene 1, and so on. Each activity may have an associated set of fields. For example:

1. `Singers`: This may be a set valued field containing records having a `Role`, `SingerType`, and `SingerName` field. For example, if the triple (`Lohengrin`, `Tenor`, `Rene Kollo`) appears as a member of the set valued field `Singers` associated with a segment [5, 9], then Rene Kollo, a tenor, is singing the role of Lohengrin during the time segment [5, 9] of the opera.

2. `Score`: This may be a field of type `music_doc` that points to a relevant part of the music score associated with the time segment [5, 9].

3. `Transcript`: This may be a field of type `document` that points to the relevant part of the libretto (words being sung) during the time segment [5, 9].

In general, the metadata used to represent audio content may be viewed as a set of objects spread out over a time line, exactly like video. Objects, individuals, features, and activities all occur in audio exactly as they did in video. The only difference is that in audio they are heard but not seen, while in video they are both seen and heard. Thus, we may index the metadata associated with audio in exactly the same way as we indexed video, and the same query-processing techniques may be used over again.

Most existing sound databases use metadata-based indexing schemes. For instance, a simple movie sound database can be accessed at *http://www.hollywood.com*, and sounds from different movies can be queried. Similarly, the site *http://www.discjockey.com* provides information for would-be disc jockeys to set up their own sound clip database using metadata expressed as textual fields such as `title`, `artist`, `year`, and `tempo`. Another annotation-based framework is at *http://www.lib.shizuoka.ac.jp* and describes a queryable cartoon database called Animation DB.

8.2.2 Signal-Based Audio Content

The use of metadata is reliable and recommended when there is a way to create the metadata. Thus, for instance, if we are creating audio databases of radio broadcasts and music recordings, there is almost no problem in creating the metadata. However, in other applications (e.g., the police wiretaps on the phone of a suspected drug dealer), creation of metadata is somewhat more complex because the identities of the individuals speaking may not be known, and even the content of the conversation may be unclear (e.g., if a scrambling device is being used).

In such cases, the concept of *content* (which was described by metadata before) is described in terms of signal-processing methods. In effect, the audio data is considered as a signal, $\phi(x)$, over time x. Different *features* of the signal ϕ are extracted, indexed, and stored for efficient retrieval. Metadata may still be used to complement the signal data and may include information on where the audio sensors were located, what type they are, when the recordings were made, and so on. Figure 8.2 shows two sample audio signals.

A wave (such as the sound waves shown in Figure 8.2) consists of a periodic collection of *crests* (or peaks) and *troughs* (or valleys). The *period of vibration* of a wave, denoted T, is defined as the time taken for a particle in the wave to return to its starting position. For example, consider the point A in Figure 8.2(a). This point moves along the wave in the direction indicated by the dotted line.

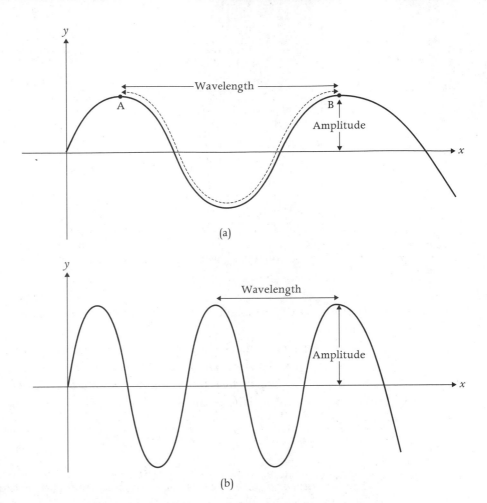

8.2   Sample audio signals

The next time it reaches the correct position is when it reaches location B. T is the time this takes to occur.

The *frequency*, f, of a wave is defined as the number of vibrations per second. Thus,

$$f = \frac{1}{T}$$

The frequency of a wave is typically expressed in Hertz (or kilohertz). Thus, when we say that a wave has a frequency of 10 kHz, we mean that it has 10,000 vibrations per second, which in turn means that the quantity T is $\frac{1}{10,000}$. Gen-

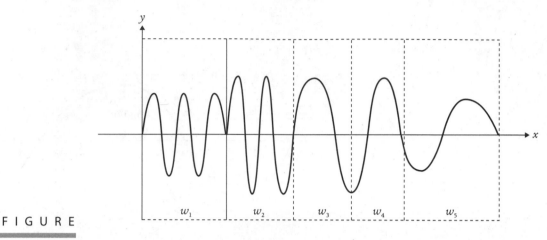

FIGURE

8.3 Windowing of nonhomogeneous audio signal

erally speaking, the human ear can hear sounds in the frequency range 15 Hz to 20 kHz.

The *velocity*, v, of the wave is the speed at which the crests and troughs move to the right. Thus, when we say that the wave moves at a velocity of v, we mean that the crests move to the right at the rate of v meters per second. It is easy to see that if w denotes the wavelength of the wave, then

$$v = \frac{w}{T}$$
$$= w \times f$$

The *amplitude*, a, of a wave is the maximum intensity of the signal associated with the wave; that is, it is the value (on the y-axis) of the crest of the signal, as shown in Figure 8.2.

Thus, the wave in Figure 8.2(a) has a lower frequency than the wave in Figure 8.2(b), a higher period of vibration, a lower amplitude, and a greater wavelength.

The most common way of content-based indexing of audio data is to consider a signal over time and break it up into small windows of time. The signal may exhibit considerable variations across different windows; however, if the window sizes are small, the signal is likely to be fairly homogeneous within that window. For example, Figure 8.3 shows a nonhomogeneous audio signal and how it may be split into five windows. Each window is homogeneous in the sense that it has a constant amplitude, wavelength, and wave velocity; however, two different windows exhibit considerable variations in wave patterns.

Audio databases may be indexed using an audio signal in the following way:

1. *Segmentation*: Split up the audio signal into relatively homogeneous windows. This may be done in one of two ways. One possibility is that the application developer can specify, a priori, a window size w (in seconds or milliseconds) and assume that the wave's properties within that window are obtained by averaging. The second possibility is that the user can segment the audio signal in much the same way as we segmented images, using a homogeneity predicate H. The only difference is that this homogeneity predicate applies to the one-dimensional case, rather than to the two-dimensional case (for images).

2. *Feature extraction*: Once segmentation is performed, the audio signal may be viewed as a sequence of n windows, $w_1, \ldots, w_n$. For each window, we extract some features associated with the audio signal. If k features are extracted, then an audio signal may be considered to be a sequence of n points in a k-dimensional space. We may then index this sequence of n points. Some of the best known and most widely used features for indexing are the following:

   (a) *Intensity:* The intensity of a wave may be thought of as the power of the signal generated by the wave. Without going into the technical details of how this value is computed (consult a textbook on wave mechanics, such as Flint [65], for this purpose), we may define the intensity of an audio signal as

   $$I = 2 \times \pi^2 \times f^2 \times \mu \times a^2 \times v$$

   where f is the frequency of the wave (in Hertz), μ is the density of the material through which the sound is being propagated (in kilograms per cubic meter), a is the amplitude of the wave (in meters), and v is the velocity of the wave (in meters per second). The intensity is in watts per square meter.

   (b) *Loudness:* Though higher-intensity waves are perceived by the human ear to be louder than lower-intensity waves, loudness does not increase linearly with intensity. For instance, if two waves are both below the human hearing range, then their loudness is zero, even though one wave may be significantly lower than the other in intensity. Thus, suppose L_0 denotes the loudness associated with the lowest frequency that a human ear can detect (about 15 Hz), and suppose we are looking at a wave of intensity I. Then the loudness of I, in decibels, is given by

$$L = 10 \times \log \left(\frac{I}{L_0} \right)$$

Notice that when $I = L_0$, then $L = 10 \times \log(1) = 0$.

(c) *Pitch:* The pitch, $p(f, a)$, of an audio signal is computed as a derived quantity from the frequency f and amplitude a of the signal. Typically, given any window of the sort shown in Figure 8.3, the pitch is computed using a gcd algorithm in terms of the frequency and amplitude.

(d) *Brightness:* The brightness of a signal ϕ in a window w is a measure of how "clear" the sound is. For instance, a muffled sound is less bright than the sound of breaking glass.

In addition to the above properties, several other derived features, such as variance and correlation of an audio signal at various points in the signal, may be expressed in terms of the basic audio signal. We will not go into these here.

In general, when we wish to index the content of an audio signal, we proceed with the following two steps:

1. Find a set $w_1, \ldots, w_n$ of window segments.

2. For each window w_i, store a vector consisting of K acoustical attributes such as those listed above.

Thus, from the point of view of signals, an audio database may be (naively) viewed as a set of $(K + 3)$-tuples consisting of the audio source (e.g., the audio file involved), the window (within that audio file), the duration of the window, and the K feature values associated with that window.

8.3   Capturing Audio Content through Discrete Transformations

When considering the human frequency range of 15 Hz to about 20 kHz, even a relatively short audio recording (say, of about 10 minutes) may have as many as 100,000 windows, assuming that each window represents a fairly smooth signal.

Just as in the case of images, where we attempted to reduce an image composed of a very large number of cells to a manageable number of cells, we would like to use compression techniques to reduce the number of windows. This is routinely done in audio processing through the use of the discrete Fourier transform (DFT), and the discrete cosine transform (DCT), suitably adapted. Suppose we have a total of n windows after segmenting the audio signal, but we wish to store this in an array, A, of size N, where N is considerably smaller than n. Obviously each array entry is a record containing fields such as amplitude, loudness, pitch, and so on. For each field f, we may compute a value for $A[i].f$, $1 \leq i \leq n$, as follows, using the DFT. (We could use the DCT instead.)

$$A[r].f = \sum_{n=0}^{N-1} \phi(j).f \; exp \left(\frac{-2\pi \times j \times r \times n}{N} \right)$$

Here, $\phi(j).f$ refers to the value of property f at time j of the signal ϕ. As usual, the symbol j denotes the complex number $\sqrt{-1}$.

8.4   Indexing Audio Data

The indexing of signal-based audio data may now be accomplished in a fairly straightforward way. Suppose we have a set $\phi_1, \ldots, \phi_K$ of signals in our audio archive. Let N be an integer specifying the number of windows that the application developer wishes to assign for each audio signal ϕ_i. Once N is selected, this means that we wish to store a set of N-dimensional vectors. However, by just looking at a vector, it is difficult to determine which audio signal it was derived from. Thus, we will assume that each vector is of length $(N + 1)$; the extra field at the end contains the index i of the audio signal ϕ_i from which that vector was derived. We may now develop an audio database by following the steps enumerated below, using the concept of a TV-tree introduced in Chapter 6 to index high-dimensional data.

```
Algorithm 8.1  CreateAudioIndex(K,N)
   Index = NIL; (* index is initially empty *)
for i=1 to K do
   {
       for j=0 to (N-1) do Aⁱ[j] = DFT(φᵢ);
       Aⁱ[N]=i;
```

```
        (* insert vector Aⁱ[j] into TV-tree *)
      Index = insert(Aⁱ[j],Index)
  }
end
```

In the above algorithm, `Index` refers to a TV-tree that we have already studied in Chapter 6. In fact, `Index` could just as easily be a k-d tree for the value $k = N$ because, in general, N is usually fairly small (usually 5 or 6, and almost never more than 10). Thus, when a user asks a query of the form "Find all audio sources that are similar to a given sound," all we need to do is to apply the DFT to the sound provided in the query, and then perform a nearest neighbor search on the index being used. This is fairly straightforward to do, and we have already studied it earlier on in the book.

8.5   Selected Commercial Systems

Audio databases are still in their infancy. Informix's datablade architecture includes MuscleFish's audio database management system, which allows users to access audio database based on fuzzy, content-based retrievals. In addition, it also includes an audio browser.

IBM's DB2 system is nicely enhanced with audio technology in many ways. For instance, the DB2 system is neatly coupled to an audio system that allows leaving voice messages on answering machines. This has obvious applications to marketing. DB2 also has interesting extenders (the IBM equivalent of Informix's "datablade") for audio data. DB2 can import and maintain audio clips, and allows for querying audio archives as well. For instance, a clip can be searched by either name or description, or by data such as the format of the audio or when it was last updated.

8.6   Bibliographic Notes

The design and implementation of content-based audio archives is just emerging. The MuscleFish research group have created an excellent overview of the field, backed by a commercial content-based retrieval engine [224, 25]. They provide a system for audio indexing by content using several parameters, such as smoothness and bandwidth, that are not described here, and they also provide a browser for audio files. Demonstrations will be found at *http://www.musclefish.com.*

An excellent framework for rendering text into audio, called ASTER, has recently been developed by Raman [168] but it does not provide an audio retrieval/indexing system.

Feiter and Gunzel [63] provide techniques for audio indexing using neural networks, though the scalability of the approach remains unclear because neural nets are not well known for their indexing techniques.

An emerging area of development is the placement of audio data on disks, CD-ROMs, and other tertiary storage devices to facilitate content-based retrieval [229]. We will discuss this matter in greater detail in Chapter 11.

8.7   Exercises and Projects

1. Design a set of primitive function calls that may be used to implement core audio retrieval operations. These functions may be designed in the same manner as we had previously done for video data.

2. For each core function you have designed above, develop a data structure that extends the data structure used in the `CreateAudioIndex` function (Algorithm 8.1). Show how your core functions can be implemented on this index.

3. Design an extension of SQL called `AudioSQL` that can be used to query audio databases. You can create this language using the similar language we have designed earlier on for querying video data as a starting point. This language should have the ability to access the functions you designed in Exercise 1 above.

4. Develop an indexing scheme for metadata about audio information. You may modify the metadata indexing scheme for video described earlier in Chapter 7.

5. As a project, implement a small audio database system that implements all the above functions. Create a small sound index by using sounds corresponding to properties such as male laughter (you may be able to obtain such a sound database from *http://www.musclefish.com* after obtaining relevant copyright permissions).

9 Multimedia Databases

What new concepts will you learn in this chapter?
You will learn how to design a multimedia database using homegrown, third-party, and legacy sources. You will also learn how such a multimedia database can be queried and how such queries can be efficiently executed.

What new abstractions are needed to realize these concepts?
You will be introduced to three architectures. The first organizes all media sources in a single common format. The second allows all media sources to exist in their native form. The third is a hybrid of the other two. The advantages and disadvantages of these three representations are discussed.

What new techniques are needed to implement these abstractions?
You will be introduced to a formal mathematical concept called a *media abstraction*. You will be introduced to the concept of an inverted index, and you will be shown how inverted indexes, suitably enhanced, can support queries to databases involving the architectures above. You will also learn how queries may be efficiently relaxed, thus facilitating dynamic user interaction.

What technological features support these implementation methods?
You will receive a quick overview of existing multimedia database management systems on both the Unix and Windows software platforms.

In the preceding chapters, we have studied how to represent and organize the content of different types of individual media data. For instance, the concept of an image database involves representing different kinds of images, the concept of a video database involves representing different types of videos, and the concept of a document database involves representing different types of documents. While images, videos, and documents are types of media data, our view of a multimedia database is that of a collection of media objects of different types. In other words, a multimedia database consists of some images, some videos, some documents, and some audio files, as well as, perhaps, more traditional data types such as relational data and object-oriented data representations. In the next section, we will present a detailed overview of the architecture of the content of a multimedia database system.

9.1   Design and Architecture of a Multimedia Database

When designing a multimedia database system that represents a wide variety of media types, we are forced to confront several questions concerning both the organization of the content of the media data, as well as the physical layout of the media data on storage devices. The first of these concerns is briefly discussed below; Part III of the book discusses the second.

9.1.1   Architectures for Content Organization

Let's consider three architectures for the organization of the content of a multimedia database system:

1. *The principle of autonomy*: Should we choose to group together all images, all videos, and all documents, and index each of them in a way that is maximally efficient for the expected types of accesses we plan to make on those objects? We call this the principle of autonomy because it ensures that each media type (e.g., image, video, etc.) is organized in a media-specific manner suitable for that media type. Figure 9.1 shows a conceptual diagram of different kinds of media data organized according to the principle of autonomy.

2. *The principle of uniformity*: Alternatively, should we try to find a single abstract structure $\mathcal{A}$ that can be used to index *all* the above media types, and that can thus be used to create a "unified index" that can then be used to access the different media objects? In other words, can we represent the

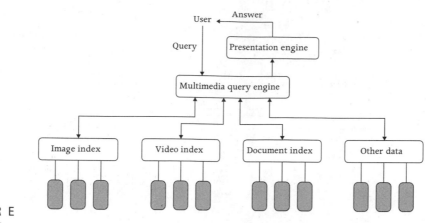

FIGURE 9.1 Architecture of a multimedia database under the principle of autonomy

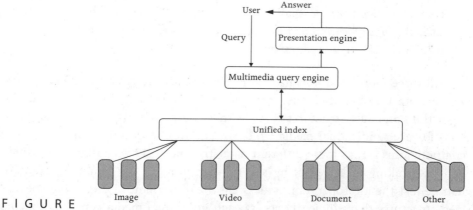

FIGURE 9.2 Architecture of a multimedia database under the principle of uniformity

content of all the different media objects (image, video, document, audio, etc.) within a single data structure, and then develop algorithms to query that data structure? Figure 9.2 shows a conceptual diagram of different kinds of media data organized according to the principle of uniformity.

3. *The principle of hybrid organization*: A third possibility is to use a hybrid of the previous two principles. In effect, according to this principle, certain media types use their own indexes, while others use the "unified" index. Exactly which media types use which type of index depends upon various

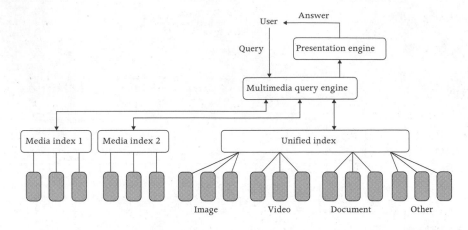

F I G U R E

9.3   Architecture of a multimedia database under the principle of hybrid organization

characteristics that we shall discuss shortly. Figure 9.3 shows a conceptual diagram of different kinds of media data organized according to the principle of hybrid organization.

All three representations have a number of advantages and disadvantages. The architecture based on the principle of autonomy requires the creation of algorithms and data structures (such as those described in the preceding chapters) for each individual media type. In addition, techniques are needed to compute joins across these different data structures. This could be a complex and painstaking task, requiring several man-years of programming effort to handle just the interoperation issues. On the other hand, by creating specialized structures that efficiently access each individual media type, multimedia databases organized according to the principle of autonomy may lead to relatively fast query-processing times. Furthermore, in the case of many *legacy data banks*, where data structures and algorithms for a specific media archive already exist, the principle of autonomy may well be the architecture of choice. Object-oriented techniques are well suited to implementing the principle of autonomy, by treating each media data source as an object whose methods are accessible to the global multimedia database.

In contrast to the principle of autonomy, the principle of uniformity requires that we find a common data structure that can store information about the content of images, videos, documents, audio, and so on. This requires that we examine the content of each of these media types and attempt to abstract out the common part of them all, and then build an index based on the common part thus identified. In industry, the principle of uniformity has been extensively used through the device of annotations, or metadata, where some information about the content of each media source is expressed in a common metalanguage, and this metadata is then indexed appropriately. The main advantages of the principle of uniformity are that it is very easy to implement, and the resulting algorithms are often very fast. The main disadvantage is that the annotations must be created in some way—either manually or automatically. A manual creation process may be expensive and time consuming. Furthermore, some information may be lost if the language for the annotations is not expressive enough to capture all aspects of the content. For example, image content annotation languages may lose information on the texture of individual pixels or groups of pixels. Similarly, audio content annotation languages may lose information about the amplitude and frequency of a signal at certain strategic points. An automatic process to create annotations, however, could be tricky, since an automatic content extraction program may be subject to substantial error.

The principle of hybrid organization takes advantage of the "good features" of the previous two architectures, while concurrently eliminating some of their disadvantages. Suppose we wish to create a multimedia database consisting of media types $\mathcal{M}_1, \ldots, \mathcal{M}_n$. We start by splitting this set into two parts:

1. Those media types that are legacy sources and that have an existing index and algorithms to manipulate the index. In this case, we would like to take advantage of this existing index and software code.

2. Those media types that are not legacy sources and that have no existing index (and hence no algorithms to manipulate the index). In this case, using the approach of uniform representation is to be recommended (unless the loss of detailed physical information, such as texture of individual pixels, is critical to the application).

We then create the necessary code to perform the joins across multiple data sources using their native indexes. This approach leads to a maximal leveraging of existing code, while minimizing the additional effort to be expended because existing domain-specific indexes are utilized. For example, a user may wish to ask the query "Find all images and audio clips in which John Smith's boss is seen (image) and heard (audio) talking to Denis Dopeman." This query involves a multiindex join, accessing an image database (through an image index), an audio database (through an audio index), and a relational database (through a relational index). It may be expressed as

```
SELECT   Name, Image, Audio
FROM     employee E, ImageDB I, AudioDB A
WHERE    E.Name = "John Smith" AND
         I CONTAINS E.boss AND
         A CONTAINS E.boss, AND
         A CONTAINS Denis Dopeman
```

In earlier chapters, we have already explained, in effect, how to organize indexes based on the principle of autonomy. Section 9.2 will show how to organize multimedia archives based on the principle of uniformity. Section 9.4.2 will present methods to query multimedia archives based on the principle of hybrid organization. Because this latter possibility also covers querying multiple indexes based on the principle of autonomy, this covers all the above cases.

9.2   Organizing Multimedia Data Based on the Principle of Uniformity

The basic idea underlying the principle of uniformity is that from a semantical point of view, the "content" of a multimedia data source is often independent of the source itself. For example, let's reconsider our (by now familiar) law enforcement example. In this example, we may be able to make statements (in English) of the following form:

1. The image `photo1.gif` shows Jane Shady, Denis Dopeman, and an unidentified third person, in Medellín, Colombia. The picture was taken on January 5, 1997.

2. The video clip `video1.mpg` shows Jane Shady giving Denis Dopeman a briefcase (in frames 50–100). The video was obtained from surveillance set up at Denis Dopeman's house in Rockville, Maryland, in October 1996.

3. The document `dopeman.txt` contains background information on Denis Dopeman, obtained from his FBI file.

Each of these three assertions says something about the content of a media object (image, video, document). In contrast to the treatments in Chapters 5, 6, and 7 though, the content is described *semantically*, rather than in terms of pixel-level or grid-level properties, which are typically lower-level properties. One of the most successful approaches to multimedia databases—and the one that is most widely used in industry today—uses statements of the above form as *metadata*. Thus, suppose we have a set of media objects $o_1, \ldots, o_n$. We associate some metadata $\text{md}(o_i)$ with each media object o_i. The exact form of this metadata will be discussed later. Thus, the metadata associated with objects $o_1, \ldots, o_n$ is $\text{md}(o_1), \ldots, \text{md}(o_n)$. We then index the metadata $\text{md}(o_1), \ldots, \text{md}(o_n)$ in a way that provides efficient ways of implementing the expected accesses that users will make.

Clearly, the success of such an effort depends fundamentally on our ability to ensure that, for each media object o_i, the metadata $\text{md}(o_i)$ is succinct but reflects "just what the user is looking for." The smaller the amount of textual metadata, the easier it is for us to index it and perform retrieval operations. However, the smaller the amount of metadata, the more likely it is that the user will need to iteratively refine queries, as can be seen from the following sample interaction:

USER: Find me either videos or photographs showing Denis Dopeman and Jane Shady exchanging a package.

SYSTEM: Sorry, I don't have it. (The system may have a video/picture of Denis Dopeman and Jane Shady exchanging a briefcase, but does not return it because it does not know that a briefcase is a "package.")

USER: Find me either videos or photographs showing Denis Dopeman and Jane Shady exchanging some item.

SYSTEM: OK, frames 50–100 of the video clip `video1.mpg` satisfy your requirement.

There are tradeoffs with the use of the uniform representation approach (which represents, using metadata, some but not all aspects of the media objects in the database). But it does have the following advantages:

1. The metadata can often be stored in relatively standard relational or object-oriented structures and can be queried through simple extensions of languages such as SQL.

2. Writing software code to manipulate such metadata is often easy.

3. Writing small programs that interact with feature extraction algorithms (such as those described in Chapters 5, 6, and 7) and that create the metadata is fairly straightforward for a competent programmer.

We will now describe a basic representation of such metadata.

9.3   Media Abstractions

A media abstraction is a formal structure that may be used to capture media content. Intuitively, a media abstraction defines a data structure that may then be populated with data representing information about the content of a media source.

Before defining a media abstraction formally, we must ask ourselves a question: If we consider the content of media data of different types, what is it that is common to all these media types, and what is it that is different? We may then exploit the commonality across media types to build a "shell" or "skeletal" data structure. This skeletal data structure provides a common core or foundation that we can then extend to include characteristics that distinguish one media type from another.

The common characteristics that media content from different media types share are the following: In each case, we have a set of individual objects whose content is being described (e.g., image, video clip, etc.). Within each object, certain features occur (e.g., the people in the image, the activity occurring in it, etc.). The features that occur within these objects have one or more attributes, and there may exist some relationships between the different features (e.g., spatial relationships between different objects in an image). Some of these attributes or relations may depend upon the object; others may be independent of the object (e.g., the color of Bill Clinton's tie may depend upon an image, but the fact that he is a man is independent of the image). We now present the definition of a media abstraction that formally describes this common core.

Definition 9.1 A *media abstraction* is an 8-tuple

$$(\mathcal{S}, fe, \text{ATTR}, \lambda, \Re, \mathcal{F}, \text{Var}_1, \text{Var}_2)$$

where

- $\mathcal{S}$ is a set of objects called *states*,

- fe is a set of objects called *features*,

- ATTR is a set of objects called *attribute values*,

- $\lambda : \mathcal{S} \to 2^{fe}$ is a map from states to sets of features,

- $\Re$ is a set of relations on $fe^i \times \text{ATTR}^j \times \mathcal{S}$ for $i, j \geq 0$,

- $\mathcal{F}$ is a set of relations of $\mathcal{S}$,

- Var_1 is a set of objects, called *variables*, ranging over $\mathcal{S}$, and

- Var_2 is a set of variables ranging over *fe*.

We now present some intuitions that underlie the somewhat complicated definition presented above. Later, we will show how many different types of media data may be viewed as instances of a media abstraction.

- A *state* is the smallest chunk of media data that we wish to consider. For instance, in an image database, each image may be viewed as a state. If this view is adopted, then we are making a commitment to consider images as basic indivisible objects, whose properties are of interest (and hence, we will not be considering properties of individual pixels if this view is adopted). In the case of videos, for example, a state may be any consecutive sequence of frames of the form $[10 \times i, 10 \times (i+1))$, reflecting a chunk of 10 frames starting at a frame number that is divisible by 10.

- A *feature* is any object in a state that is deemed to be of interest to the multimedia database application that is being built. For example, if we consider the image `photo1.gif` showing Jane Shady, Denis Dopeman, and an unidentified person, the features of interest in this image are Jane Shady, Denis Dopeman, and Person_113 (for example). Similarly, if we examine clips 50–100 of the video file `video1.mpg`, the features of interest might be Jane Shady, Denis Dopeman, and the briefcase.

- The features that occur in a state may have some *attributes* of interest to the application. For example, if Jane Shady is getting out of a car, the attributes of the car (e.g., license plates, car make and model, color, etc.) may be well worth recording. Similarly, a media object may itself have some attributes of interest. This may include information such as the date, time, and location at which the images were shot.

- λ is a *feature extraction* map that tells us which features occur in which states. We have already provided techniques by which features may be extracted from images and documents in Chapters 5, 6, and 7. In such cases, λ is nothing more than an implementation of such feature identification techniques. In other cases, λ may be a graphical user interface that a user interacts with to identify the content of a media object. It is important to note that λ is rich enough to capture both possibilities.

- $\Re$ is a set of relations on $fe^i \times \text{ATTR}^j \times \mathcal{S}$—these relations are *state-dependent*. For instance, consider an image such as `photo1.gif`. There may be a state-dependent relation called `left_of` containing triples of the form

    ```
    (Jane Shady,Denis Dopeman,photo1.gif)
    ```

    Alternatively, we may have a relation called `background` containing pairs of the form

    ```
    (photo1.gif,White House)
    ```

    indicating that the background depicted in the image `photo1.gif` is the White House. Similarly, we may have a relation called `age` that is state-independent and that may contain a tuple such as

    ```
    (Jane Shady,36)
    ```

    which states that Jane Shady's age is 36. Strictly speaking in state-independent relations, we should state the argument, but as this argument is going to apply to all possible states, we omit it above.

- $\mathcal{F}$ may contain, for example, relations that take two states as input such as `before`. For instance, if the tuple (`photo1.gif`, `photo2.gif`) is in the `before` relation, then `photo1.gif` was taken before `photo2.gif`, and so on.

Before proceeding any further, let us see how we may treat certain objects as instances of the definition of a media abstraction.

Image Data Viewed as a Media Abstraction Suppose we consider the very simple image database composed of the images in Figure 5.1. This simple database corresponds to the following media abstraction:

1. The set of states consists of $\{$`pic1.gif`$,\ldots,$`pic7.gif`$\}$.

2. The set of features consists of the names of the people shown in the photographs, say, Bob, Jim, Bill, Charlie, and Ed.

3. The extraction map λ tells us, for each state, which features occur in that state. The table following contains this description:

State	Feature
pic1.gif	Bob, Jim
pic2.gif	Jim
pic3.gif	Bob
pic4.gif	Bill
pic5.gif	Charlie
pic6.gif	Ed, Bill
pic7.gif	Ed

It is important to note that even though we are presenting the results of λ as a table (for the sake of simplicity), we may choose to index this information in a very different way.

4. The set of relations may contain just two relations: a state-dependent relation called left_of and a state-independent relation called father, with the obvious meanings.

5. The set of interstate relations may be empty.

Video Data Viewed as a Media Abstraction Suppose we consider the very simple video database composed of the frames in Figure 7.1. This simple video database may be viewed as a media abstraction as follows:

1. The set of states consists just of frames 1 through 5.

2. The set of features consists of Jane Shady, Denis Dopeman, Dopeman's house, and briefcase.

3. The extraction map λ is described by the following simple table:

State	Feature
frame 1	Dopeman's house, briefcase, Jane Shady
frame 2	Dopeman's house, briefcase, Jane Shady, Denis Dopeman
frame 3	Dopeman's house, briefcase, Jane Shady, Denis Dopeman
frame 4	Dopeman's house, briefcase, Jane Shady, Denis Dopeman
frame 5	Dopeman's house, Jane Shady

As in the case of image databases, the extraction map λ may be represented in a different format internally, for purposes of efficient indexing and retrieval.

4. We may have the following simple state-dependent relations:

   (a) have is a state-dependent relation specifying who has an object in a given state. This may be given by the following simple table:

Person	Object	State
Jane Shady	briefcase	1
Jane Shady	briefcase	2
Jane Shady	briefcase	3
Denis Dopeman	briefcase	4

   (b) spouse is a state-independent relation specifying the name of the spouse of an individual. This may be given by the following simple table:

Person	Spouse
Jane Shady	Peter Shady
Denis Dopeman	Debra Dopewoman

5. There may be just one interstate relation, called before(s1,s2), which holds iff state s1 occurs before state s2.

In the same way as described above, it is easy to see that other media types, such as audio and document data, can be represented as instances of the general definition of a media abstraction. In its simplest form, a multimedia database is a collection of media abstractions.

Definition 9.2 A *simple multimedia database* is a finite set, $\mathcal{M}$, of media abstractions.

For example, a simple multimedia database may consist of the video file video1.mpg and the image file photo1.gif. In this case, it contains two instances of media abstractions.

However, a simple multimedia database is rather naive in some respects. For example, a media abstraction may list "church" as a feature; however, when searching for "cathedrals" or "monuments," we may not find the church because the system does not know that cathedrals and churches are (more or less) synonymous, and that all churches are monuments (but not vice versa). The former ("church" vs. "cathedral") is reminiscent of the problem of synonymy in document databases; the latter is reminiscent of inheritance hierarchies in object databases.

A further parameter to keep in mind is that users often search for media objects containing one or more features, and then refine the search later when they find that the media objects returned by their query, though correct, do not correspond precisely to what they wanted. You may have experienced this phenomenon when searching the Web using a search engine such as Lycos, Infoseek, or Alta Vista. For example, you might conduct a search for "Alexandria" and receive a thousand hits as a response, covering everything from Alexandria, Virginia; companies located in Alexandria, Virginia; to Alexandria, Egypt; to persons whose names are Alexandria. If your real interest is in Alexandria, Virginia, you may narrow the search.

Conversely, there are also cases where the user may wish to widen the search. A search for the string "Venkatramanan Siva Subrahmanian" may yield no hits (because it is too specific)—I tried this with both Infoseek and Alta Vista and found no hits—but widening the search by searching for just "Subrahmanian" may reveal several hits.

Finally, a user may issue a query such as "Find all images where Jane Shady and Denis Dopeman are present with a St. Bernard"; if there are no hits, the user may wish to modify the query a bit by saying, "Hmmm. A Newfoundland is very much like a St. Bernard; maybe I should modify this question by replacing the search for St. Bernards by a search for Newfoundlands instead." This corresponds to a query modification by *substitution* of certain constants (e.g., "St. Bernard") by other constants (e.g., "Newfoundland").

Examples of the above sort motivate the need for a somewhat more sophisticated definition of a multimedia database that takes into account synonymy and inheritance relationships between features.

Definition 9.3 A *structured multimedia database system* (SMDS) is a 5-tuple $(\{\mathcal{M}_1, \ldots, \mathcal{M}_n\}, \equiv, \leq, \mathsf{inh}, \mathsf{subst})$, where

- $\mathcal{M}_i = (\mathcal{S}^i, fe^i, \mathsf{ATTR}^i, \lambda^i, \mathfrak{R}^i, \mathcal{F}^i, \mathsf{Var}_1^i, \mathsf{Var}_2^i)$ is a media abstraction,

- $\equiv$ is an equivalence relation on $\mathcal{F} = \bigcup_{i=1}^{n} fe^i$,

- $\leq$ is a partial ordering on the set $\mathcal{F}/\equiv$ of equivalence classes on $\mathcal{F}$,

- $\mathsf{inh} : \mathcal{F}/\equiv \rightarrow 2^{\mathcal{F}/\equiv}$ such that $[f_1] \in \mathsf{inh}([f_2])$ implies that $[f_1] \leq [f_2]$ (thus, inh is a map that associates with each feature f, a set of features that are "below" f according to the $\leq$-ordering on features), and

- subst is a map from $\bigcup_{i=1}^{n} \mathsf{ATTR}^i$ to $2^{\bigcup_{i=1}^{n} \mathsf{ATTR}^i}$.

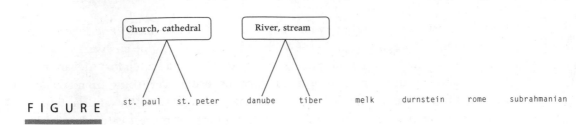

FIGURE
9.4

The $\leq$ relation in an SMDS

For example, consider a very simple multimedia database system containing the few media objects listed below:

Media	Object	Part/frame	Feature(s)
image	photo1.gif	-	church, durnstein, danube, subrahmanian
image	photo2.gif	-	cathedral, melk, subrahmanian
image	photo3.gif	-	church, st. paul, rome
video	video1.mpg	1–5	church, durnstein, stream
video	video1.mpg	6–10	stream
audio	audio1.wav	1–20	st. peter, tiber, rome

Notice that the annotations (metadata) associated with the video are somewhat different from the metadata associated with the images and with the audio (names of rivers are not listed, for example). To formally describe this as an SMDS, we need to specify what the 5-tuple $(\{\mathcal{M}_1, \ldots, \mathcal{M}_n\}, \equiv, \leq, \text{inh}, \text{subst})$ is. This may be done as follows:

- We have three media abstractions, one each associated with image, video, and audio data.

- The set of features $\mathcal{F}$ contains church, durnstein, danube, subrahmanian, cathedral, melk, st. paul, rome, stream, st. peter, tiber.

- $\equiv$ says that

  church $\equiv$ cathedral

  river $\equiv$ stream

- The $\leq$ relation (shown in Figure 9.4) says that

  [tiber] $\leq$ [*river*]

  [danube] $\leq$ [*river*]

$$[\text{st. paul}] \leq [church]$$
$$[\text{st. peter}] \leq [church]$$

- We will assume that subst makes no assignments for now.

The above definitions provide a *declarative* rendering of the concept of a simple structured multimedia database system. However, it does not, as yet, provide indexing structures by which a multimedia database system may be organized/archived. Before presenting such indexing structures, we provide a simple query language that may be used to query multimedia data. We present a query language first because we can provide efficient index methods only if we know up-front what kind of user queries need to be efficiently handled.

9.4   Query Languages for Retrieving Multimedia Data

In this section, we present a simple query language for retrieving multimedia data that builds on top of SQL. We have already shown that media abstractions may be used to represent different kinds of media data using the uniform representation architecture. In this section, we will first present an extension of SQL for querying data under the uniform representation architecture (Section 9.4.1). Later, we will show how this paradigm may be further extended to handle queries to databases using the hybrid representation architecture. As in the case of the SQL-like language we presented in Chapter 7 for querying video data, the new extensions of SQL we present are simple and noninvasive.

9.4.1   Querying SMDSs (Uniform Representation)

All SMDSs involve the following basic functions that a user might ask:

1. FindType(Obj): This function takes a media object Obj as input and returns the output type of the object. For example:

$$\text{FindType(im1.gif)} = gif$$
$$\text{FindType(movie1.mpg)} = mpg$$

2. FindObjWithFeature(f): This function takes a feature f as input and returns the set of all media objects that contain that feature as output. For

example:

```
FindObjWithFeature(john)
        = {im1.gif, im2.gif, im3.gif, video1.mpg:[1,5]}
FindObjWithFeature(mary)
        = {video1.mpg:[1,5], video1.mpg:[15,50]}
```

3. `FindObjWithFeatureandAttr(f,a,v)`: This function takes a feature `f`, an attribute name `a` associated with that feature, and a value `v` as input. It returns all objects *o* that contain the feature and where the value of the attribute `a` in object *o* is `v`. Here are some simple invocations of this function:

   (a) `FindObjWithFeatureandAttr(Jane Shady,suit,blue)`: This query asks to find all media objects in which Jane Shady appears in a blue suit.
   (b) `FindObjWithFeatureandAttr(Elephant,bow,red)`: This query asks to find all media objects in which an elephant wearing a red bow appears.

4. `FindFeaturesinObj(Obj)`: This query asks to find all features that occur within a given media object. It returns the set of all such features as output. Here are some simple invocations of this function:

   (a) `FindFeaturesinObj(im1.gif)`: This asks for all features within the image file `im1.gif`. It may return the objects John and Lisa as output.
   (b) `FindFeaturesinObj(video1.mpg:[1,5])`: This asks for all features within the first five frames of the video file `video1.mpg`. The answer may include objects such as Mary and John.

5. `FindFeaturesandAttrinObj(Obj)`: This query is exactly like the previous query except that it returns a relation having the scheme

   `(Feature,Attribute,Value)`

   where the triple (f, a, v) occurs in the output relation iff feature f occurs in the query `FindFeaturesinObj(Obj)`, and feature f's attribute a is defined and has value v.

   For example, the invocation `FindFeaturesandAttrinObj(im1.gif)` may return the following table:

Feature	Attribute	Value
John	age	32
John	address	32 Pico Lane, Mclean, VA 22050
Mary	age	46
Mary	address	16 Shaw Road, Dumfries, VA 22908
Mary	employer	XYZ Corp.
Mary	boss	David

Note that the query language for SMDSs is being constructed in exactly the same way that we constructed the query language for video databases in Chapter 7. There, too, we defined a set of basic functions that could be applied to the video data domain, and then we showed how SQL could be extended to handle these basic functions. We now do likewise for SMDSs.

Our SMDS-SQL extension of SQL will include all valid ordinary SQL statements. In addition, the following enhancements will be allowed to occur in SQL's (SELECT, FROM, WHERE) constructs:

1. The SELECT statement may contain *media entities*. A media entity is defined as follows:

   (a) If m is a continuous media object, and i and j are integers, then $m : [i, j]$ is a media entity denoting the set of all frames of media object m that lie between (and inclusive of) segments i and j.

   (b) If m is not a continuous media object, then m is a media entity.

   (c) If m is a media entity, and a is an attribute of m, then $m.a$ is a media entity.

2. The FROM statement may contain entries of the form

   $\langle media \rangle \ \langle source \rangle \langle M \rangle$

   which says that only media objects associated with the named media type and named data source are to be considered when processing the query, and that M is a variable ranging over such media objects.

3. As in Chapter 7, the WHERE statement allows (in addition to standard SQL constructs), expressions of the form

   term IN *func_call*

   where

(a) *term* is either a variable (in which case it ranges over the output type of *func_call*) or an object having the same output type as *func_call* and

(b) *func_call* is any of the five function calls listed above.

We are now ready to present several examples of SMDS-SQL.

1. "Find all image/video objects containing both Jane Shady and Denis Dopeman." This can be expressed as the SMDS-SQL query:

```
SELECT   M
FROM     smds source1 M
WHERE    (FindType(M)=Video OR FindType(M)=Image) AND
         M IN FindObjWithFeature(Denis Dopeman) AND
         M IN FindObjWithFeature(Jane Shady)
```

2. "Find all image/video objects containing Jane Shady wearing a purple suit." This can be expressed as the SMDS-SQL query

```
SELECT   M
FROM     smds source1 M
WHERE    (FindType(M)=Video OR FindType(M)=Image) AND
         M IN FindObjWithFeatureandAttr(Jane Shady,suit,purple)
```

3. "Find all images containing both Jane Shady and Denis Dopeman, with Jane Shady to the left of Denis Dopeman." This can be expressed as the SMDS-SQL query

```
SELECT   M
FROM     smds source1 M
WHERE    FindType(M)=Image AND
         M IN FindObjWithFeature(Denis Dopeman) AND
         M IN FindObjWithFeature(Jane Shady) AND
         left(Jane Shady,Denis Dopeman,M)
```

It is important to note here that the ternary relation left used in the above query is a relation in the image database media abstraction.

4. "Find all images containing Jane Shady and a person who appears in a video with Denis Dopeman." Unlike the preceding queries, this query involves computing a joinlike operation across different data domains. In order to do this, we use existential variables such as the Person in the query below, which is used to refer to the existence of an unknown person whose identity is to be determined.

```
SELECT  M,Person
FROM    smds source1 M,M1
WHERE   FindType(M)=Image AND
        FindType(M1)=Video AND
        M IN FindObjWithFeature(Jane Shady) AND
        M1 IN FindObjWithFeature(Denis Dopeman) AND
        Person IN FindFeaturesinObj(M) AND
        Person IN FindFeaturesinObj(M1) AND
        Person≠Jane Shady AND Person≠Denis Dopeman
```

An alternative way to phrase this query is to rewrite it as

```
SELECT  M,R
FROM    smds source1 M,M1
WHERE   FindType(M)=Image AND
        FindType(M1)=Video AND
        M IN FindObjWithFeature(Jane Shady) AND
        M1 IN FindObjWithFeature(Denis Dopeman) AND
        R = (FindFeaturesinObj(M) INTERSECT
           FindFeaturesinObj(M1)) MINUS
           {Denis Dopeman, Jane Shady}
```

5. "Find all images containing Jane Shady and a person wearing a purple suit who also appears in a video with Denis Dopeman."

```
SELECT  M,Person
FROM    smds source1 M,M1
WHERE   FindType(M)=Image AND
        FindType(M1)=Video AND
        M IN FindObjWithFeature(Jane Shady) AND
        M1 IN FindObjWithFeature(Denis Dopeman) AND
        Person IN FindFeaturesinObj(M) AND
        M IN FindObjWithFeatureandAttr(Person,suit,purple) AND
        Person IN FindFeaturesinObj(M1) AND
        Person≠Jane Shady AND Person≠Denis Dopeman
```

9.4.2 Querying Hybrid Representations of Multimedia Data

In the preceding section, we have presented the language SMDS-SQL as a paradigm for the querying of multimedia objects stored in the uniform representation. In this section, we will show how this may be extended to query processing in the presence of the hybrid representation.

When considering query languages for processing queries in the hybrid representation, we must ask ourselves the question "What is it about the hybrid representation that causes our query language to change?" The answer, of course, is rooted in the fact that in the uniform representation, all the data sources being queried are SMDSs, while in the hybrid representation, different (non-SMDS) representations may be used that are more appropriate, for the given domain, than an SMDS representation. For example, consider the video domain. SMDSs do not immediately distinguish between activities and features (though this can, in fact, be simulated) and roles. A hybrid media representation basically consists of two parts—a set of media objects that use the uniform representation (which we have already treated in the preceding section) and a set of media types that use their own specialized access structures and query language. Thus, in order to extend SMDS-SQL to a full-fledged, hybrid-multimedia SQL (HM-SQL), we need to do two things:

1. HM-SQL must have the ability to express queries in each of the specialized languages used by these non-SMDS sources.

2. HM-SQL must have the ability to express joins and other similar binary algebraic operations between SMDS sources and non-SMDS sources.

We will treat each of these requirements in turn, by extending the standard SELECT, FROM, WHERE constructs of SQL. To do so, we assume first that each non-SMDS media source MS has its own associated query language QL(MS). The query language HM-SQL is exactly like SQL except that the SELECT, FROM, WHERE clauses are extended in the following manner:

1. The SELECT and FROM clauses are treated in exactly the same way as in SMDS-SQL.

2. As in Chapter 7, the WHERE statement allows (in addition to standard SQL constructs), expressions of the form

   term IN MS : *func_call*

   where

   (a) *term* is either a variable (in which case it ranges over the output type of *func_call*) or an object having the same output type as *func_call* as defined in the media source MS and

(b) either MS = SMDS, and *func_call* is one of the five SMDS functions described earlier, or MS is not an SMDS media source, and *func_call* is a query in QL(MS).

Thus, HM-SQL is exactly like SMDS-SQL except for two differences:

1. *func_call*s occurring in the WHERE clause must be explicitly annotated with the media source involved.

2. Queries from the query languages of the individual (non-SMDS) media source implementations may be embedded within an HM-SQL query. This latter feature makes HM-SQL very powerful, indeed, because it is, in principle, able to express queries in other, third-party or legacy media implementations.

Here are some examples of queries expressed in HM-SQL:

1. Suppose we have two video data sources, video1 and video2, where the former is implemented via an SMDS and the latter is implemented via the video database formalism of Chapter 7. Suppose we wish to ask the very simple query: "Find all video clips containing Denis Dopeman from both video sources, video1 and video2." This query may be expressed in HM-SQL as follows:

```
SELECT  M
FROM    smds video1, videodb video2
WHERE   M IN smds:FindObjWithFeature(Denis Dopeman) OR
        M IN videodb:FindVideoWithObject(Denis Dopeman)
```

In this query, we are basically finding all Ms that are returned either by a call to the SMDS or by a call to the specialized video database implementation of Chapter 7.

2. Suppose, in addition to the above, that we have an image database (idb), implemented using specialized non-SMDS operators, and suppose this image database has a query operation getpic(obj) that takes an object as input and returns a pair consisting of a picture (file) and a relevance ranking as output. Suppose we now wish to search all three sources (video1, video2, idb) for a picture of Denis Dopeman. To do this, we may execute the following HM-SQL query:

```
(SELECT M
FROM     smds video1, videodb video2
WHERE    M IN smds:FindObjWithFeature(Denis Dopeman) OR
         M IN videodb:FindVideoWithObject(Denis Dopeman))
UNION
(SELECT M.file
FROM     imagedb idb M
WHERE    M IN imagedb:getpic(Denis Dopeman))
```

3. Suppose we wish to find all people seen with Denis Dopeman in either video1, video2, or idb. We can do so through the following query:

```
(SELECT P1
FROM     smds video1 V1
WHERE    V1 IN smds:FindObjWithFeature(Denis Dopeman) AND
         P1 IN smds:FindFeaturesinObj(V1) AND
         P1 ≠ Denis Dopeman)
UNION
(SELECT P2
FROM     videodb video2 V2
WHERE    V2 IN smds:FindObjWithFeature(Denis Dopeman) AND
         P2 IN videodb:FindObjectsinVideo(V2) AND
         P2 ≠ Denis Dopeman)
UNION
(SELECT *
FROM     imagedb idb I2
WHERE    P2 IN imagedb:getpic(Denis Dopeman) AND
         P2 IN imagedb:getfeatures(I2) AND
         P2 ≠ Denis Dopeman)
```

9.5   Indexing SMDSs with Enhanced Inverted Indices

In the preceding section, we have seen how we may express queries to multimedia databases using both the uniform representation and the hybrid representation. Non-SMDS sources are indexed using their own specialized indexing scheme (which may include the methods described in Chapters 4 through 8 of this book). As we briefly saw in Section 6.5.1, inverted indices form an easy-to-implement mechanism for indexing large document bases. In the same way, inverted indices, suitably modified, may be used as an initial step toward indexing SMDSs. In this section, we will describe, in detail, how the inverted index method may be used for query processing in SMDSs. In the next section, we will show how query relaxation techniques may be effectively built on top of this method.

Given an SMDS $(\{\mathcal{M}_1, \ldots, \mathcal{M}_n\}, \equiv, \leq, \text{inh}, \text{subst})$ where

$$\mathcal{M}_i = (\mathcal{S}^i, fe^i, \text{ATTR}^i, \lambda^i, \Re^i, \mathcal{F}^i, \text{Var}_1^i, \text{Var}_2^i)$$

we must show how we can organize this data into an efficient indexing mechanism. The data structure shown in Figure 9.5 shows one possible inverted index organization for this data. The basic idea is very simple:

1. `featuretable`: This is a hash table whose entries are features in $\bigcup_{i=1}^n fe^i$. Each hash table location i contains a bucket of `featurenodes` that hash to location i.

2. `statetable`: This is a hash table whose entries are states in $\bigcup_{i=1}^n \mathcal{S}^i$. Like the `featuretable`, the `statetable` contains a bucket of `statenodes` that hash to the specified location.

3. `featurenodes`: Each `featurenode` contains the following:
   - the name of the feature (e.g., "Denis Dopeman")
   - a list of children nodes (if f_1 and f_2 are features in $\bigcup_{i=1}^n fe^i$, we say that f_2 is a child of f_1 iff $f_2 \leq f_1$ and there is no other feature $f_3 \in \bigcup_{i=1}^n fe^i$ such that $f_2 < f_3 < f_1$)
   - a list of pointers to `statenodes` (see below) that contain the relevant feature (in the case of an image database, this would be a pointer to the nodes associated with images that contain the feature in question, e.g., Denis Dopeman)
   - a list of pointers to other `featurenodes` that are appropriate substitutes for the `featurenode` in question. Specifically, if we consider a `featurenode` associated with feature f, then a pointer to feature g is in this list iff g `inh`(f)

4. `statenodes`: A `statenode` consists of just two components: a pointer to a file containing the media object (image, video, audio, document, etc.) that the state in question refers to, and a linked list whose members point to `featurenodes`. Intuitively, there is a pointer to a `featurenode` f iff the feature in question is in the state.

```
type featurenode = record of /* nodes in feature graph */
    name : string; /* name of feature */
    children: ^node1; /* points to a list of pointers to the children */
    statelist: ^node2; /* points to a list of pointers to states that */
                        /* contain this feature */
    replacelist: ^node3; /* points to a list of descendants whose */
                          /* associated states can be deemed to have */
                          /* the feature associated with this node */
    end record;

type node1=record of
    element: ^featurenode; /* points to a child of a featurenode */
    next :    ^node1; /* points to next child */
    end record;

type node2=record of
    state: ^statenode; /* pointer to the list associated with a state */
    link:  ^node2;  /* next node */
    end record;

type node3=record of
    feat: ^featurenode; /* pointer to a node that can be deemed to */
                        /* have the feature associated with the */
                        /* current node */
    link1: ^node3;
    end record;

type statenode=record of
    rep:   ^framerep;
    flist: ^node4;
    end record;

type node4=record of
    f : ^featurenode;
    link2: ^node4;
    end record;
```

FIGURE

9.5   Data structure for SMDS

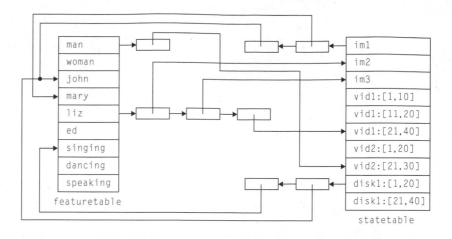

F I G U R E

9.6   Example of an enhanced inverted index structure (shown partially)

As an example, consider a very simple toy SMDS containing three media abstractions—images, video, and audio—with the following content:

Media abstraction	State	Features
image	im1	john, mary
	im2	john, mary, liz
	im3	liz, mary
video	vid1:[1,10]	john, singing
	vid1:[11,20]	john, mary, dancing
	vid1:[21,40]	john, mary, liz, singing, dancing
	vid2:[1,20]	ed, speaking
	vid2:[21,30]	man, speaking
audio	disk1:[1,20]	john, singing
	disk1:[21,40]	woman, speaking

Note that in the above example description, video is represented in terms of SMDSs rather than the specialized data structures of Chapter 7. In order to index this information so as to optimize retrieval, we need to maintain the following structures (shown in Figure 9.6).

1. Figure 9.6 shows one possible statetable (though for simplicity we are not specifying the hash function used) and a possible featuretable. Each of the 10 states above is stored in the state table, as are the 9 features. In

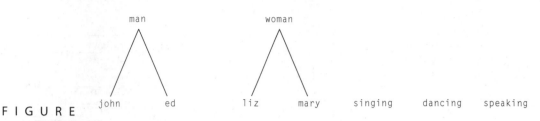

9.7   Example of the ≤ hierarchy on features

particular, note that "singing" and "dancing" are considered to be features (as opposed to activities for the non-SMDS structures in Chapter 7).

2. The ≤ ordering on features is shown in Figure 9.7. Note that the ordering is quite simple.

3. We have shown the featurelist associated with the states iml and disk1: [1,20]. Other featurelists are not shown for the sake of simplicity.

4. Likewise, we have shown the statelists associated with the features man and liz.

5. The relations associated with these media abstractions may be stored within standard relational databases.

Queries to such an enhanced inverted index structure are of three basic types, which may be easily answered as follows:

1. "Given a feature f, find all states that contain that feature." To answer this query, we proceed as follows:

Algorithm 9.1 FindObjWithFeature(f);

1. SOL = ∅.

2. Hash feature f and resolve collisions (if any) till feature f is located (at location i, say) in the featuretable.

3. SOL = append(SOL,featuretable[i].statelist).

4. Forall children f' of some member of [f] do
   SOL = append(SOL,FindObjWithFeature(f')).

5. Return SOL.

This assumes that if f' is a descendant of f, then f' occurs in every state in which f occurs. We may easily modify the above algorithm if this assumption is not valid.

2. "Given a state s, find all features in that state." This algorithm is somewhat simpler than the preceding one. It can be easily implemented as follows:

   (a) Hash state s and resolve collisions (if any) till state s is located (at location i, say) in the `statetable`.
   (b) Return `statetable[i].Featurelist`.

3. "Given a state s and a feature f, check if state s contains feature f." This algorithm is even easier than the preceding one.

   (a) Hash state s and resolve collisions (if any) till state s is located (at location i, say) in the `statetable`;
   (b) If f is in `statetable[i].Featurelist`, then return true, else return false.

Notice that there is an asymmetry between the treatment of the first and second queries because there is a partial ordering on the set of features, while there is no partial ordering on the set of states. Let us see how the above algorithms may be used to answer some simple queries.

Finding States with a Specified Feature Suppose the user wishes to find all states containing the object `John`. In this case, the `FindObjWithFeature(John)` function call is made. The string `John` is first hashed, leading to the third location in the `featuretable` of Figure 9.6. Subsequently, `SOL` is assigned the set containing the states

```
im1, im2, vid1:[1,10], vid1:[11,20], vid1:[21,40], disk1:[1,20]
```

We then check to see (from Figure 9.7) whether there are any features below `John` in the $\leq$ ordering. There are not, and hence we are done.

Finding States with a Specified Feature Using $\leq$-ordering Suppose now that the user wishes to find all states containing the object `man`. In this case, the `FindObjWithFeature(man)` function call is made. The string `man` is first hashed, leading to the first location in the `featuretable` of Figure 9.6. Subsequently, `SOL` is assigned the set containing the single state `vid2:[21,30]`. We then check to see (from Figure 9.7) whether there are any features below man in the $\leq$ ordering on features. There are two—John and Ed. We execute the function call `FindObjWithFeature(john)` (as described in the preceding example): the result of this function call is appended to SOL, leading to SOL being set to

$$\texttt{im1, im2, vid1:[1,10], vid1:[11,20], vid1:[21,40],}$$
$$\texttt{vid2:[21,30], disk1:[1,20]}$$

We likewise execute the function call `FindObjWithFeature(ed)`: the result of this function call contains the single state `vid2:[1,20]`, which is appended to SOL, leading to SOL having the set value

$$\texttt{im1, im2, vid1:[1,10], vid1:[11,20], vid1:[21,40],}$$
$$\texttt{vid2:[1,10], vid2:[21,30], disk1:[1,20]}$$

This set is the value returned by the algorithm.

It is easy to see that the four basic queries can be implemented very efficiently, as well as very easily, by any competent programmer. This is a major advantage of the inverted-index-based approach.

Using the four basic functions described above, together with the relations in Section 9.4, we may process very complex queries, such as those described earlier, using the above index structure.

9.6   Query Relaxation/Expansion

Thus far, when processing media abstractions, we have not dealt with the `subst` component. The `inh` and `subst` components are used to determine how queries must be relaxed.

Query relaxation is a key aspect of multimedia databases because users may not always specify their queries in a manner that is consistent with the representation of media data content. Though this problem exists even in the relational world, it is more acute in the case of multimedia systems because there is inherent ambiguity when features are identified. For example, image-processing programs do not guarantee the correctness of their results, and in the same vein, text-processing systems suffer from the problems of synonymy and polysemy that make it difficult to retrieve data based on user queries.

The basic idea behind query relaxation is that when a user poses a query Q, we somehow modify that query Q into a set $\{Q_1, \ldots, Q_k\}$ of queries. This set is partially ordered and contains the original query Q as the maximal element of the ordering. We may think of this as a hierarchy with top element Q. If Q' is a child of Q'', then this means that Q' is obtained from Q'' by making a modification or relaxation.

Thus, query relaxation depends on two questions: What are the modification operations that are allowed to modify queries? And what is the ordering on the set of modified queries? The `inh` and `subst` components of an SMDS are used to determine the answers to these two questions.

For example, in step (4) of Algorithm 9.1, we have already seen how when we search for states containing a feature f, we try to find all states containing any feature f' such that $f' \leq f$. However, in many cases, this may be rather cumbersome. After all, our $\leq$ relation may contain a chain of the form

$$\texttt{john\_rthumb} \leq \texttt{john\_rfingers} \leq \texttt{john\_rhand} \leq \texttt{john\_arm} \leq \texttt{john}$$

In this case, if asked for a picture of John, is it reasonable to return a picture containing a close up of John's right thumb? It would appear not.

In general, the relation `inh` says that we do not necessarily look all the way below feature f when trying to find all states containing feature f. Instead, we merely try to find all states containing some feature f', where $f' \in \texttt{inh}(f)$. This requires that we modify Algorithm 9.1 in the following simple way:

Algorithm 9.2
```
FindObjWithFeatureandInh(f,inh);
```

1. `SOL` $= \emptyset$.

2. Hash feature `f` and resolve collisions (if any) till feature `f` is located (at location `i`, say) in the `featuretable`.

3. `SOL = append(SOL,featuretable[i].statelist)`.

4. `Forall` children `f'` of some member of `inh([f])` do
   `SOL = append(SOL,FindObjWithFeatureandInh(f', ∅))`.

5. `Return SOL`.

This algorithm is identical to Algorithm 9.1 except for the explicit specification of the inheritance functions being used, and the underlined part of step (4), which says that instead of recursively invoking the algorithm with all descendants of members of $[f]$, we only invoke those descendants that are in

inh(f). When this algorithm is called initially, we call it with the original `inh`
relation. In the recursive calls, however, we use the empty `inh` relation.

In general, given a query Q written in the SQL notation we have introduced
earlier in this chapter, we will associate with query Q a set of "relaxations" of Q.

Definition 9.4 Suppose Q_1 and Q_2 are queries. We say that Q_1 is a *feature
relaxation* of Q_2, denoted $Q_1 \sqsubseteq Q_2$, iff there exist features $f_1, f_2 \in \bigcup_{i=1}^{n} fe^i$ such
that

- $Q_1 \preceq Q_2[f_1/f_2]$ (where the notation $Q_2[f_1/f_2]$ denotes the replacement of all
  occurrences of f_1 in Q_2 by f_2) and

- $f_2 \in$ `inh`($[f_1]$).

The notation $Q_1 \preceq Q_2$ above is used to denote the fact that Q_1 can be obtained from Q_2 by replacing a set $\{a_1, \ldots, a_n\}$, $n \succeq 0$, of attributes occurring
in Q_2 by $\{a'_1, \ldots, a'_n\}$, respectively, where $a'_i \in$ `subst`(a_i).

For example, consider the HM-SQL query Q_2

```
SELECT  M
FROM    smds video1, videodb video2
WHERE   M IN smds:FindObjWithFeature(Denis Dopeman) OR
        M IN videodb:FindVideoWithObject(Denis Dopeman)
```

that we saw earlier. If David Johns (which might be an alias for Denis Dopeman)
is in `inh`(Denis Dopeman), then the query Q_1 given by

```
SELECT  M
FROM    smds video1, videodb video2
WHERE   M IN smds:FindObjWithFeature(David Johns) OR
        M IN videodb:FindVideoWithObject(David Johns)
```

is a feature relaxation of Q_2.

Feature relaxations basically allow a query to be modified by replacing features by other features in accordance with the `inh` specification. However,
it is entirely possible that we can relax a query by allowing substitution of
attributes for other attributes. For instance, consider the query Q_3 given by

```
SELECT  M
FROM    smds
WHERE   M IN smds:FindObjWithFeature(Denis Dopeman) AND
        M IN smds:FindObjWithFeatureandAttr(package,color,black)
```

This query asks for media objects containing Denis Dopeman and a black package. Suppose we know that `briefcase` $\leq$ `package`, and that `briefcase inh(package)`, and that `grey` $\in$ `subst(black)`. Then consider the following three queries. Query Q_4 is given by

```
SELECT   M
FROM     smds
WHERE    M IN smds:FindObjWithFeature(Denis Dopeman) AND
         M IN smds:FindObjWithFeatureandAttr(briefcase,color,black)
```

Query Q_5 is given by

```
SELECT   M
FROM     smds
WHERE    M IN smds:FindObjWithFeature(Denis Dopeman) AND
         M IN smds:FindObjWithFeatureandAttr(package,color,grey)
```

Query Q_6 is given by

```
SELECT   M
FROM     smds
WHERE    M IN smds:FindObjWithFeature(Denis Dopeman) AND
         M IN smds:FindObjWithFeatureandAttr(briefcase,color,grey)
```

In the above three queries,

- we obtained Q_4 by replacing occurrences of `package` in Q_3 with `briefcase` (feature replacement),

- we obtained Q_5 by replacing occurrences of `black` with `grey` (attribute replacement), and

- we obtained Q_6 by replacing occurrences of `black` with `grey` and occurrences of `package` with `briefcase` (feature and attribute replacement).

Notice that we will allow an attribute value a to be replaced by an attribute value b iff $b \in$ `subst`(a). Examination of query Q_6 reveals that it is an intuitively "larger" relaxation than either query Q_4 or Q_5, and hence (in an intuitive sense) is semantically further from the initial query Q_3. Thus, we would like to process query Q_6 only if the preceding queries fail to yield the desired answers. These intuitions are formalized below.

Definition 9.5 Query Q_1 is said to be a *attribute relaxation* of Q_2, denoted $Q_1 \sqsubseteq_a Q_2$, iff there exist attributes $a_1, a_2 \in \bigcup_{i=1}^{n} \text{ATTR}^i$ such that $Q_1 = S_2[a_1/a_2]$ and $a_2 \in \text{subst}(a_1)$.

Thus, for instance, using the queries $Q_3, \ldots, Q_6$ above, it is easy to see that $Q_5 \sqsubseteq_a Q_3$, because Q_5 is obtained from Q_3 by replacing `black` with `grey`.

Definition 9.6 *Relaxation* of queries is defined inductively as follows:

- If Q_1 is a feature relaxation of Q_2, then Q_1 is a relaxation of Q_2.

- If Q_1 is an attribute relaxation of Q_2, then Q_1 is a relaxation of Q_2.

- If Q_1 is a relaxation of Q_3, and Q_3 is a relaxation of Q_2, then Q_1 is a relaxation of Q_2.

Given a query Q, we use the notation `Relax`(Q) to denote the set of all relaxations of query Q (with respect to some SMDS).

In general, as we have seen earlier in this section, some relaxations of a query are "closer" to the query than others because they modify the original query less. We will assume that there exists a partial ordering, $\preceq$, on `Relax`(Q). One such partial ordering, $\preceq_1$, is to simply require that if Q_1 and Q_2 are in `Relax`(Q), then $Q_1 \preceq_1 Q_2$ iff Q_1 is either a feature/attribute relaxation of Q_2, or if $Q_1 \preceq_1 Q_3$ and $Q_3 \preceq_1 Q_2$ for some Q_3. This partial ordering is "fair" to both feature relaxations and attribute relaxations in the sense that it does not state that one is more important than the other. Independent research has gone into the specification of different relaxation policies that allow biased/weighted orderings (Marcus and Subrahmanian [136]). In particular, these authors argue that SMDSs must satisfy certain intuitive conditions. Such SMDSs are called *tree-closed SMDSs*, and they are defined as follows.

Definition 9.7 Suppose $(\{\mathcal{M}_1, \ldots, \mathcal{M}_n\}, \leq, \mathrm{inh}, \mathrm{subst})$ is a structured multimedia database system. This SMDS is said to be *closed* iff the following three conditions hold:

1. $(\forall a, b \in \bigcup_{i=1}^n fe^i) a \in \mathrm{inh}(b) \Rightarrow a \leq b$.

2. $(\forall a, b, c \in \bigcup_{i=1}^n fe^i)\, c \leq b \leq a\ \&\ c \in \mathrm{inh}(a) \Rightarrow c \in \mathrm{inh}(b)\ \&\ b \in \mathrm{inh}(a)$.

3. $(\forall s \in \bigcup_{i=1}^n \mathcal{S}^i)(\forall a, b, c \in \bigcup_{i=1}^n fe^i)\, c \leq b \leq a\ \&\ c \in \bigcup_{j=1}^n \mathcal{N}^j(s)\ \&\ a \in \bigcup_{j=1}^n \mathcal{N}^j(s) \Rightarrow b \in \bigcup_{j=1}^n \mathcal{N}^j(s)$. (We assume that if $\mathcal{N}^j$ is not defined on s, then the function call $\mathcal{N}^j(s)$ returns the empty set.)

The third part of the above definition says that if c is a subfeature of b, and b is a subfeature of a, and state s possesses both features a and c, then state s must also possess the intermediate feature b.

Definition 9.8 A *tree-closed* SMDS (TC-SMDS) is a closed SMDS such that the set of features in $\bigcup_{i=1}^{n} fe^i$ can be represented as a tree.[1]

Marcus and Subrahmanian [136] prove that TC-SMDSs can express everything that ordinary SMDSs can (i.e., the restrictions to "closedness" and trees does not limit expressive power). By using tree-closed SMDSs, they show that we can substantially reduce the space needed for an inverted-index-based storage scheme, as well as improve the speed of query processing.

9.7   Conclusions

When faced with the problem of creating a multimedia database, we must take into account the following two questions:

- What kinds of media data should this multimedia database provide access to?

- Do legacy algorithms already exist (and are they available) to index this data *reliably and accurately* using content-based indexing methods?

The answers to these two questions divide the data into two parts—those for which reliable and accurate automatic indexing techniques exist, and those for which they do not. All media that falls into the latter category may be easily represented through an SMDS structure. For example, the Media Abstraction Creation System (MACS), developed by Brink, Marcus, and Subrahmanian [28, 27], provides a simple user interface through which the metadata inherently present in a media abstraction may be created. Figure 9.8 shows such an interface. Using this interface, the creator of the metadata description in an SMDS can explicitly specify what metadata is present in a media object, such as an image. In this particular image, we are being told that the image in question contains a feature called "John Miller" with 75% certainty.

For media that fall into the category for which software tools for automatic indexing exist, we can first create indexes (using that software), and then use the HM-SQL language to perform queries that access both the SMDS archive and the specialized multimedia processing indexes.

---

[1]As usual, we assume that all partially ordered sets can be represented as Hasse diagrams, and thus, the poset $(\bigcup_{i=1}^{n} fe^i, \leq)$ is tree-closed iff the corresponding Hasse diagram is a tree.

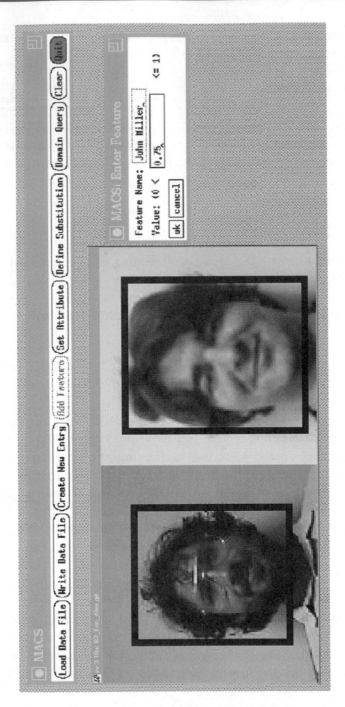

FIGURE

9.8 Example screen showing annotation of image objects (see also color plate Figure 9.8)

9.8 Selected Commercial Systems

Informix's datablade architecture includes content management datablades from Mortice Kern Systems. The content management datablade allows access to a wide variety of media data, including images, documents, and Web pages, as well as various user-defined types based on binary large objects.

MediaWay (*http://www.mediaway.com*) offers a similar product, called MediaDB, that provides a client-server architecture for the storage, querying, and retrieval of both relational data and a variety of media data, including image, audio, video, and text data.

9.9 Bibliographic Notes

There is now a great deal of ongoing work on multimedia systems, both within and outside the database community. Most of this work deals with integration of specific types of media data; for example, there are systems that integrate certain compressed video representation schemes with other compressed audio representation schemes. Marcus and Subrahmanian [137, 136] were the first to propose a single theoretical framework for integrating multimedia data that abstracts away the essential features of diverse media and data representations, making it possible, in principle, to integrate multimedia data without knowing in advance what the structure of the data might be. The work on SMDSs described in this chapter is based on work reported in Marcus and Subrahmanian [136]. In particular, Marcus and Subrahmanian [137, 136] proposed a logic-based language to handle the querying of SMDSs, and Marcus [135] showed how SQL could just as easily be extended to handle this. Brink, Marcus, and Subrahmanian [28] showed how SMDSs could be implemented through their MACS system.

Grosky's early work proposed a version of SQL that could be used to query pictorial databases using feature-based approaches [78, 79]. He describes *complex* features—intuitively, complex features have subfeatures [79]. In connection with the work in this chapter, given a feature f, the set of features "below" f (with respect to the notion of "belowness" defined by the ordering $\leq$ on features) may be thought of as the subfeatures associated with f. This concept is used in this chapter to define a mathematically solid way of relaxing queries and to define optimal answers.

Likewise, Gibbs, Breiteneder, and Tsichritzis [72] studied how stream-based temporal multimedia data may be modeled using object-based methods. According to their framework, an "artifact" is an object produced in a specific medium; for instance, prints, TV news programs, and music recordings are all artifacts. "Media objects" are digital representations of artifacts. In terms of our framework, the set of media objects in an SMDS is essentially the same as $\bigcup_{i=1}^{n} S^i$, using the notation developed in this paper.

Woelk and Kim [223] have developed an object-oriented implementation of multimedia capabilities on top of the ORION object-oriented database system. A key feature of their work is that it is closely tied to an object-oriented implementation. This is not strictly necessary: like most systems, implementations can take any one of a variety of forms, and we have attempted to keep the model as amenable to different implementations as possible.

9.10   Exercises and Projects

1. Develop a simple framework with which a multimedia database developer may specify the `inh` and `subst` relations. Your framework should include a mathematical definition of how `inh` and `subst` are represented, as well as data structures corresponding to these mathematical structures. Using these data structures, show how the following operations are implemented:

   (a) `FindInh(f)`: Given a feature f, find all features f' such that $f' \in inh(f)$.

   (b) `FindSubst(a)`: Given an attribute value a, find all attributes a' such that $a' \in subst(a)$.

   (c) `FindRelaxations(Q,N)`: Given a query Q and an integer $N > 0$, find all relaxations Q' of Q that are obtained by applying at most N substitutions (of attributes for attributes, or features for features).

2. The set of relaxations, `Relax(Q)`, of query Q can have many possible partial orderings. Define a partial ordering, $\preceq_2$, on `Relax(Q)` such that feature relaxations have lower preference than attribute relaxations. Thus, for instance, the application of the substitution `briefcase` for `package` would have priority over the application of the feature substitution `John Davis` for `Denis Dopeman`.

3. Using the partial ordering you defined in the preceding exercise, develop an algorithm that will take a query Q as input and return all answers to an optimal relaxation of Q as output. Query Q' is said to be an optimal relaxation of Q iff

   (a) $Q' \in$ `Relax`(Q),

(b) Q' has at least one answer, and

(c) there is no other query Q'' that satisfies the previous two conditions such that $Q' \preceq Q'' \preceq Q$.

4. Develop an enhancement of the inverted index data structure presented in this chapter that accommodates uncertainty. For example, suppose metadata for an image database is being generated by someone. The person may not know who a particular individual in an image is, or they might know that the individual is either person A or person B, each with certainty 50%. Expand the indexing structure to accommodate this kind of information.

5. Use the index structure developed in the preceding exercise to solve the following problem. Suppose the function `FindObjWithFeature(f)` is modified to have two arguments, f and an integer $N > 0$. Return the N objects that contain feature f with the highest possible certainty as output.

PART III

PHYSICAL STORAGE AND RETRIEVAL

Retrieving Multimedia Data from Disks

What new concepts will you learn in this chapter?
You will learn how disk arrays access data. You will learn how disk arrays may be used to support video-on-demand applications involving interactive video operations such as rewind, fast forward, pause, and play.

What new abstractions are needed to realize these concepts?
Disk servers may be viewed as resource managers. The resources they manage include disk bandwidth and buffer space, among others. The problem of processing client requests by a media-on-demand server may be viewed, at a high level, as a real-time resource allocation problem.

What new techniques are needed to implement these abstractions?
Resource management and scheduling have been studied extensively for over 50 years in operations research. Many of these techniques are applicable here. Media-on-demand systems, however, exhibit two aspects that make them different from operations research approaches—the need for continuity in the retrieval schedules and the real-time requirement.

What technological features support these implementation methods?
We will study architectures such as the RAID (redundant array of inexpensive disks) for disk-based storage management.

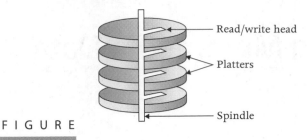

Read/write head

Platters

Spindle

F I G U R E

10.1   Layout of a disk drive (side view)

Multimedia data is often very large. A single image may take up several megabytes, while a single 90-minute video might occupy several gigabytes of disk space, even when it is highly compressed. Hence, it is imperative that media data be stored in secondary and tertiary storage devices such as disks, CD-ROMs, and tapes. In this chapter, we will concentrate primarily on storage of multimedia data on disk. Later chapters will concentrate on CD-ROMs and tapes.

Unlike traditional database applications, the retrieval of dynamic multimedia data such as audio and video requires that it be *continuous*—the segments of video must be retrieved and presented to the user in a manner that has no jitter or delays. Since images and static multimedia objects can be retrieved from disk in a standard fashion using B-tree, R-tree, and quadtree-like indexes, in this chapter, we will focus primarily on the needs of continuous media (audio and video) storage and retrieval.

The organization of this chapter is as follows. First, in Section 10.1, we will provide a brief overview of disk drives and disk-based storage. Then, in Section 10.2, we will define various techniques used to "lay out" or "place" continuous data on disk. In Section 10.3, we will provide a formal model of disk servers (and collections of disk servers). Section 10.4 then describes an algorithm to implement disk servers so that they can support standard operations such as play, fast-forward, rewind, and pause when the video data involved is stored on disk.

10.1   An Overview of Disks

Figure 10.1 shows a side view of the layout of a standard disk drive; Figure 10.2 shows a top view. The disk drive consists of a central *spindle* around

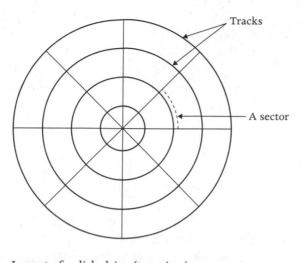

Tracks

A sector

FIGURE

10.2   Layout of a disk drive (top view)

which a set of disk *platters* are arranged. Attached to the central spindle are disk *arms*, each of which contains a read/write head. One arm is positioned above each disk platter.

Each disk platter consists of a number of concentric *tracks* corresponding to the circles shown in Figure 10.2. The platters in Figure 10.2 have four tracks. The data stored on disk is written onto these tracks. Consequently, the read heads need to read the tracks.

Suppose we are intersected in track number *i* for some *i*. Each platter in our disk device contains such a track. The set of such tracks, one from each platter, is called a *cylinder* and has the obvious geometric interpretation.

Furthermore, each disk platter is divided into *k regions* for some fixed *k*. Each region represents a wedge of the platter with angle 360/*k*. For example, Figure 10.2 shows a platter consisting of eight regions, each representing a wedge of angle 45 degrees.

Figure 10.3 shows a detailed view of a wedge. That part of a track that intersects a wedge is called a *sector*. Clearly, if we have *n* tracks altogether, then we will have *n* sectors per wedge. In most disk drives, the storage capacity is stated in megabytes per sector. Thus, even though sectors that are further away from the spindle are longer than sectors belonging to inner tracks, all sectors have the same capacity. There are other types of disk drives that allow storage in megabytes per centimeter; thus, in these disk systems, sectors in outer tracks

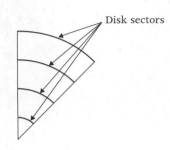

Disk sectors

F I G U R E

10.3   A detailed view of a wedge

have a larger storage capacity than those in inner tracks. However, these disk systems are beyond the scope of this book.

As we mentioned above, and as shown in Figure 10.1, associated with each disk platter is a disk arm that contains a *read/write head* to read from and write to the platter. When a disk address is to be accessed, the *disk controllers* (the programs that control the position of the disk head relative to the disk) start by pursuing two steps:

1. *Seek operations:* Find the track (and hence the cylinder) on which the address is located. The time taken for the disk arm to position the read/write head over the track in question is called the *seek time*. The seek time can be broken up into four phases: the acceleration phase, when the arm accelerates toward its final destination; the constant velocity or coast phase, when it reaches a constant velocity of motion; the deceleration phase, when the arm slows down while approaching the destination; and a settle phase, when its velocity is close to zero and the arm is trying to position the head just over the appropriate track. Short seeks, where the head moves just a bit, are dominated by the settle phase; long seeks are dominated by the coast phase.

2. *Rotational operation:* Once the head is positioned over the right track, the disk spindle rotates so that the sector containing the desired physical address is located directly under the read/write head. The time taken for this operation is called *rotational latency*.

Associated with each disk arm is a read/write head that contains the necessary hardware to read data from a sector or write data onto a sector. Associated with any disk drive is a quantity called the *transfer rate* of the disk (sometimes also called *bandwidth*), which indicates the number of megabytes per second that can be read by the read head. Strictly speaking, the transfer rates of most disks are different for reads and writes. In this chapter, whenever we refer to transfer rates, we will refer to the read transfer rates. When describing write transfer rates, we will explicitly say so.

The best-known and most widely used disk drives are called *constant angular velocity* (CAV) disk drives. In these drives, the disk rotates at a constant angular velocity. Notice that, as a consequence, the amount of time it takes to move from sector *a* to sector *b* is not dependent upon which track is being considered, even though the length of a sector increases as we go further away from the spindle. In this chapter, we will primarily concentrate on CAV drives.

The time taken to read a sector into the buffer involves the seek time, plus the rotational latency, plus the time taken to actually transfer the data. We will use the symbols given in the table below to compute this quantity:

Symbol	Meaning
tnum	total number of tracks
rnum	total number of regions
itd	distance between two tracks (intertrack distance)
ss	spin speed of disk in rotations per minute
rv	average radial velocity = average movement of disk head along arm
dtr	transfer rate of the disk
rd	recording density in megabytes per sector

Suppose we wish to read sector i (on track t_i) on a given platter, and the read head on that platter is currently over sector j in track t_j. Then

$$Readtime(i, j) = \frac{rd}{dtr} + spintime(i, j) + Sk(t_i, t_j)$$

where $spintime(i, j)$ is the amount of time required to spin from sector i to sector j, and $Sk(t_i, t_j)$ is the amount of time for the read head to move from track t_i to track t_j. The first term denotes the time required (in seconds) to read a sector. The second term denotes the rotational latency. The third term denotes the seek time. The seek time required to find track i from track j (assuming the head is currently positioned at track j) is given crudely by

$$Sk(t_i, t_j) = \frac{abs(t_i - t_j)}{rv}$$

where $abs(t_i - t_j)$ denotes the number of tracks to be traversed, and rv denotes the average velocity of the read head along the arm (strictly speaking, the quantity rv can be further broken up and expressed in terms of the acceleration/coast/deceleration/settle cycle mentioned earlier, but for the sake of simplicity, we will not go into that).

Similarly,

$$spintime(i,j) = \text{abs}((i - j) \bmod rnum) \times \frac{360}{rnum} \times \frac{1}{rv}$$

where $\text{abs}((i - j) \bmod rnum)$ denotes how many sectors away our target sector (the one to be read) is located. The term $360/rnum$ specifies how many degrees (angular) each wedge of the disk is composed of. Thus, the quantity $\text{abs}((i - j) \bmod rnum) \times 360/rnum$ specifies the total amount of rotation needed to bring our target sector under the read head. Dividing this by the angular velocity gives us the total spin time or rotational latency.

10.2 RAID Arrays and Placement Methods

In recent years, one of the most successful disk-based storage methods has been the RAID (redundant array of inexpensive disks) paradigm. RAID provides several architectures by which many relatively inexpensive disks can be used together to provide scalable performance. We now describe three well-known RAID architectures. In the discussion that follows, the term "block" is used to denote the smallest chunk of data that we are interested in reading or writing. Thus, any body of data may be divided up into several contiguous blocks. For example, a video being shown at 30 frames per second may be broken up into blocks composed of 1,800 frames (1 minute).

10.2.1 RAID-0 Architecture

This is the simplest form of RAID architecture. In this architecture, we have a set of n disks, labeled $0, 1, \ldots, (n - 1)$, that are accessed through a single disk controller.

A k-*stripe* is a set of k drives, for some integer $k \leq n$ that divides n. Intuitively, once n and k are fixed, we can, in effect, logically (not necessarily physically) split the set of disk drives into n/k clusters, consisting of k drives each.

When storing a set $b_0, b_1, \ldots, b_{r-1}$ of contiguous blocks in terms of a k-striped layout, we do the following. We store block b_0 on disk 0, block b_1 on disk 1, block b_2 on disk 2, and so on. In general, we store block b_i on disk

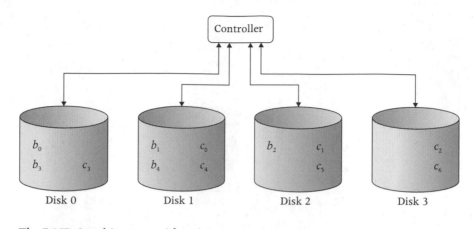

10.4   The RAID-0 architecture with striping

$i \bmod r$. Furthermore, a stripe could start at disk j rather than at disk 0, in which case, block b_i would be stored on disk $((i + j) \bmod r)$.

Figure 10.4 provides a simple layout of two movies. The blocks of the first movie are denoted by b_0, b_1, b_2, b_3, b_4. These are striped with $k = 3$ starting at disk 0. Thus, block b_0 is placed on disk 0, block b_1 is placed on disk 1, and block b_2 is placed on disk 2. Block b_3 is now placed back on disk 0, and block b_4 is placed on disk 1.

The second movie has six blocks, denoted by $c_0, \ldots, c_5$, and these are striped with $k = 4$ and starting at disk 1 (i.e., $j = 1$). Thus, block c_0 is placed on disk 1, block c_1 is placed on disk 2, and so on.

When we stripe a movie across k disks, it is as though the transfer rate of the disk has increased k-fold. The reason for this is that data can be read, in parallel, from each of the disks. For example, the controller can directly read blocks b_0, b_1, and b_2 in parallel from the three disks containing those blocks. Thus, the larger k is, the better the transfer rate of the disk. However, we should not increase k arbitrarily because the actual transfer rate is limited by the buffer size as well as the output bandwidth of the channel/bus to which the disk array is connected. Furthermore, in practice k-fold increases are almost never obtained due to various performance attenuations.

A major disadvantage with the RAID-0 architecture is that of reliability. If a disk crashes, then the system as a whole crashes.

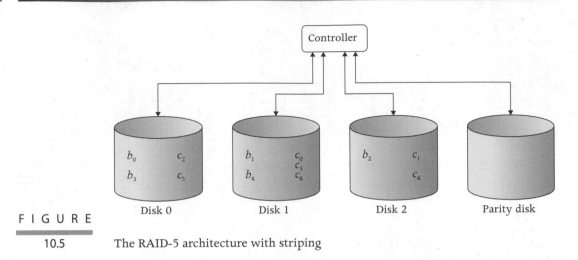

10.5   The RAID-5 architecture with striping

10.2.2 RAID-1 Architecture

The RAID-1 architecture basically uses only half the available disks. In other words, if there are N disks available altogether, then $n = N/2$ disks are utilized. For each disk, there is a *mirror disk*. Striping is done across the n disks as before. RAID-1 is predicated on the assumption that there is a very low probability that a disk and its mirror will fail simultaneously. When we wish to read from a disk, we read from the disk (if it is active) or we read from its mirrored disk (if the disk has crashed). When writing to a disk, we must write on both the disk and its mirror.

The obvious disadvantage of the RAID-1 architecture is that only 50% storage utilization is achieved—this is the price paid for the desired reliability.

10.2.3 RAID-5 Architecture

The RAID-5 architecture is perhaps the best suited for database applications. It reflects a simple but elegant trade-off between efficient utilization of available storage and excellent reliability. In the RAID-5 architecture, each cluster of k disks has one disk reserved as a *parity disk*. For now, let's suppose that $k = n$; that is, we have only one cluster, as shown in Figure 10.5. Let us further assume that these disks are numbered $0, 1, \ldots, (n-1)$.

In this case, movie blocks are striped across $(n-1)$ of the n disks available, and disk number $(n-1)$ is reserved as a parity disk. The parity disk is derived from the other disks as follows: Suppose we use $D_i.j$ to denote the value of the jth bit of disk i and suppose disk $(n-1)$ is the parity disk. If the symbol $\oplus$

denotes the exclusive-or operator, then

$$D_{n-1}.j = D_0.j \oplus \cdots \oplus D_{n-2}.j.$$

In other words, the jth bit of the parity disk is obtained by taking the exclusive-or of the jth bits of all the other disks. Recall that the exclusive-or operator is associative—that is, $(a \oplus b) \oplus c = a \oplus (b \oplus c)$—and hence, there is no need for parentheses above.

The main advantage of having a parity disk is that whenever a disk crash occurs, it is possible to compute the content of the crashed disk by examining the contents of the other disks and of the parity disk; if disk d crashes, for $0 \leq d \leq (n-2)$, then we can compute, for each bit j, the value of $D_d.j$ from the values of $D_0.j, \ldots, D_{d-1}.j, D_{d+1}.j, \ldots, d_{n-1}.j$.

To see how this is possible, consider a simple example where we have three disks plus a fourth parity disk. In this case, the truth table for exclusive-or is

D_1	D_2	D_3	(Parity disk) $D_p = D_1 \oplus D_2 \oplus D_3$
1	1	1	0
1	1	0	1
1	0	1	0
1	0	0	1
0	1	1	0
0	1	0	1
0	0	1	1
0	0	0	0

Let's now suppose that disk D_2 crashes and we wish to find the value for a specific bit j. We read the value of bit j in disks D_1, D_3, and the parity disk D_p. For example, these values might be $0, 1, 1$, respectively. We then examine the above truth table to see which row has $D_1 = 0, D_3 = 1$ and $D_p = 1$. The second-to-last row in the table satisfies this condition. From this, we can infer the value of this bit in disk D_2 to be 0. It turns out that this is always possible for all $n > 1$.

Thus, the RAID-5 architecture has the advantage over RAID-1 that only one disk per cluster is used for data recovery when disk crashes occur. A disadvantage is that every time we write on a disk, we must also update the parity bits in the parity disk that are affected by the write. A further disadvantage is that the RAID-5 architecture does not work effectively if either the parity disk crashes, or two or more disks crash simultaneously.

10.3   A Model of Heterogeneous Disk Servers

One fundamental problem in dealing with continuous media data such as video and audio is that when a user wishes to retrieve continuous data, the retrieval request may involve retrieving multiple pages from disk, and these pages may be scattered across many sectors of the disk. For example, suppose the user's request involves retrieving and presenting pages $p_1, \ldots, p_k$, and suppose each page p_i lies on sector s_i of track t_i of platter pl_i. In most applications, the user wishes to see pages $p_1, \ldots, p_k$ displayed in a continuous, jitter-free fashion, on their output device (screen or speakers). To solve this problem, what is typically done is to write these pages into a buffer, and then to have the buffer flushed when the process that is consuming the data obtains/reads a page. In this section, we will discuss techniques for scheduling read transactions from disks, and techniques for delivering continuous data to users when multiple heterogeneous disk servers are used to store a movie.

Figure 10.6 provides a table containing notation that we will use when describing the characteristics of a set of disk servers. When using this notation, we assume that we have n disk servers, $d_1, \ldots, d_n$ and k movies $m_1, \ldots, m_k$. Each movie is divided up into blocks. Informally speaking, a movie block is a contiguous set of movie frames. The size of a movie block is arbitrary but fixed; we may select a movie block to be any number of frames that we like, but once we make the selection, we are stuck with it. For example, we may select a movie block to consist of 30 frames (many of today's display devices display 30 frames per second), or we may select it to be a 3-minute block of 5,400 frames. These are just two examples of what a block could be; in general, it could be any number of frames. Now we will explain the notation in Figure 10.6 in detail:

1. bnum($\mathcal{M}_i$): This quantity denotes the total number of blocks associated with a movie $\mathcal{M}_i$. For instance, if a block represents 1 minute of a movie (1,800 frames), and if a movie $\mathcal{M}_1$ is 77 minutes long, then bnum($\mathcal{M}_1$) = 77.

2. buf(i): Each disk server has a certain amount of buffer space. When the disk head reads data from the disk, this data is written into the buffer (as shown in Figure 10.7). Because the amount of buffer space is limited in most disk servers (e.g., 4 MB is typical), once data is written into the buffer, it must be read (by a client) before it gets overwritten by a subsequent disk read operation. In short, the disk read operation reads from the disk and writes onto the buffer. A client is responsible for reading the data on the buffer before it is overwritten.

Symbol	Meaning
$\text{bnum}(\mathcal{M}_i)$	number of blocks in movie $\mathcal{M}_i$
$\text{buf}(i)$	total buffer space associated with disk server i
$\text{cyctime}(i, t)$	total cycle time for server i at time t
$\text{dtr}(i)$	total disk bandwidth associated with disk server i
$\text{switchtime}(i, t)$	time required for disk server i to switch from one client's job to another client's job at time t
$\text{cons}(i, t)$	consumption rate of client C_i at time t
$\text{data}(i, t)$	event specification for the client C_i at time t
$\text{timealloc}(i, j, t)$	time slice allocated to client j at time t
$\text{active}(t)$	set of all clients that are active at time t
$\text{d\_active}(i, t)$	set of all clients that have been assigned a nonzero time allocation by disk server i
$\wp(\mathcal{M}_i, b)$	set of servers that contain block b of movie $\mathcal{M}_i$ according to placement mapping $\wp$
$\mu_t(i)$	set of servers handling requests by client C_i at time t
$\text{bufreq}(j, i, t)$	buffer space needed at server i to match the consumption rate of client j
$\mathcal{S}(t)$	state of a movie-on-demand system

FIGURE

10.6   Notation and terminology

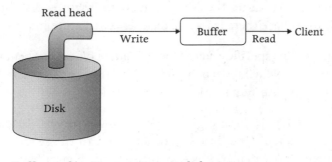

FIGURE

10.7   Buffer read/write operations in disks

3. $\text{cyctime}(i, t)$: Suppose we are examining disk server s_i, and it is currently serving clients $C_1, \ldots, C_k$. Then the server s_i schedules its read operations to first read C_1's job, then C_2's job, and so on till it reads C_k's job (in general, a permutation of the C_i's is used). This process of first reading C_1's job, then

C_2's job, and so on till C_k's job is read, is termed a *cycle*. The cycle time, $\texttt{cyctime}(i, t)$, denotes the amount of time needed for one complete cycle of read operations to be executed by server s_i at time t. Note that $\texttt{cyctime}(i, t)$ can vary with t because the set of clients (and number of clients) being served by server s_i may vary with time.

4. $\texttt{dtr}(i)$: This expression is the disk transfer rate (also termed *disk bandwidth*) and refers to the number of megabytes per second that the disk is able to read. The precise transfer rate varies with the actual sequence of read operations being executed because the seek time and rotational latency depend upon the actual tracks/sectors of the disk that are being read. Thus, in most cases, when a disk vendor quotes a transfer rate, that transfer rate is usually either an average or a maximum transfer rate.

5. $\texttt{switchtime}(i, t)$: We saw before that the cycle time, $\texttt{cyctime}(i, t)$, denotes the amount of time needed for one complete cycle of read operations to be executed by server s_i at time t. However, in general, reading client C_{i+1}'s desired sectors involves a seek/rotational operation to bring this sector under the read head. We use the notation $\texttt{switchtime}(i, t)$ to denote the total time such switches require within a single cycle.

6. $\texttt{cons}(i, t)$: This refers to the data consumption rate at which client C_i is consuming/reading data at time t. Informally speaking, the consumption rate of the client specifies exactly how fast the client is reading data from the buffer. The faster the client reads data from the disk buffer, the more free buffer space there is for the disk server to write into the buffer.

7. $\texttt{data}(i, t)$: This specifies exactly which movie blocks are being read by client C_i at time t. We will go much further into the specification of $\texttt{data}(i, t)$ and present a precise syntax and semantics for it.

8. $\texttt{timealloc}(i, j, t)$: In any given cycle of disk server i, each client C_j has a time, denoted $\texttt{timealloc}(i, j, t)$, allocated to the read request that that client has. In particular, it is easy to see that we must have

$$\texttt{cyctime}(i, t) \geq \left(\sum_j \texttt{timealloc}(i, j, t) \right) + \left(n_{i,t} \times \texttt{switchtime}(i, t) \right)$$

where $n_{i,t}$ denotes the total number of clients being served by server i at time t. Figure 10.8 shows the relationship between the quantities $\texttt{cyctime}(i, t)$, $\texttt{timealloc}(i, j, t)$, and $\texttt{switchtime}(i, t)$.

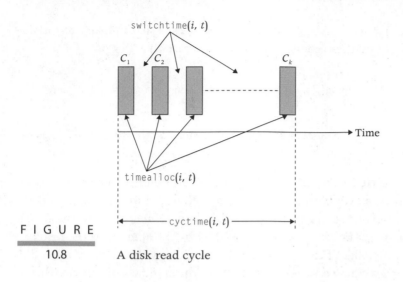

10.8   A disk read cycle

9. $\texttt{active}(t)$: This is the set of all clients that are active at time t. A client is said to be *active* at a given point in time if that client is "in" the system and is currently performing any of the following operations: play, fast-forward, rewind, or pause.

10. $\texttt{d\_active}(i, t)$: This is the set of all clients that are being served by server s_i at time t. It is easy to see that

$$\texttt{active}(t) = \bigcup_i \texttt{d\_active}(i, t)$$

Note that it is entirely possible that two servers are serving a given client at the same time; that is, it may be the case that $\texttt{d\_active}(i, t) \cap \texttt{d\_active}(j, t) \neq \emptyset$ when $i \neq j$. If $s \in \texttt{d\_active}(i, t)$, then s must allocate a period of time greater than zero to process client C_i's request.

11. $\wp(\mathcal{M}_i, b)$: The function $\wp$ is called a *placement mapping*. $\wp(\mathcal{M}_i, b)$ denotes the set of all servers that contain block b of movie $\mathcal{M}_i$. It is entirely possible that block b of movie $\mathcal{M}_i$ is in zero, one, or several servers.

12. $\mu_t(i)$: This set denotes which servers in the system are handling the requests of client C_i. In particular, it is easy to see that

$$\mu_t(i) = \{s \mid C_i \in \texttt{d\_active}(s, t)\}$$

13. $\texttt{bufreq}(j, i, t)$: This specifies the amount of buffer that is required at server s_i so that data that client C_j needs to read doesn't get overwritten. If

d_active$(i, t) = \{C_1, \ldots, C_k\}$, then it is easy to see that in order to satisfy the requests of all these clients, it must be the case that

$$\text{buf}(i) \geq \sum_{j=1}^{k} \text{bufreq}(j, i, t)$$

14. $\mathcal{S}(t)$ is the state of the system at time t. The state of the system consists of values assigned to each of the 13 components listed above.

In the above discussion, recall that at any given point in time t, data(i, t) refers to the set of movie blocks that are being requested by client C_i. In general, data(i, t) is a set of pairs of the form (m, b), where m is a movie and b is a block in that movie. The set data(i, t) is specified by the client; it is the responsibility of the controller of the disk array to determine which disk will handle the request. Let's see how easy it is to specify all the standard operations that a user may wish to perform when viewing a movie:

1. *Play—normal viewing*: Consider an ordinary user who is viewing a movie in "normal" mode. That is, he doesn't hit any buttons on his remote control viewing device. If this user is watching movies at a rate of r blocks per time unit, and the first block of the movie m that he is watching is block b, then

   data$(i, t) = \{(m,b),(m,b+1), \ldots ,m(b+r\text{-}1)\}$

2. *Fast-forward*: Suppose the user wishes to start viewing block b of movie m, and then wishes to fast-forward. Fast-forwarding is typically implemented by skipping frames. The longer the skip, the more frames are dropped, and the higher the fast-forward rate. Technically, suppose ffs is a positive integer called the *fast forward step*. This means that the blocks that the user sees are

   $b, (b + \text{ffs}), (b + 2 \times \text{ffs}), \ldots$

Assuming as above that he can watch r blocks per time unit, we have

   data$(i, t) = \{(m, b + i \times \text{ffs}) \mid i < r \; \& \; (b + i \times \text{ffs}) < \text{bnum}(m)\}$

Figure 10.9(a) shows what happens when the user is watching block 30 of a movie and fast-forwards at the rate of ffs $= 4$, when $r = 4$. In this case, he is in fact requesting blocks

   $30, (30 + 4), (30 + 8), (30 + 12)$

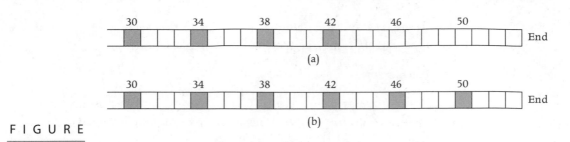

FIGURE

10.9

The *step* approach to modeling fast-forward and rewind operations

These blocks are denoted by shaded areas in Figure 10.9.

Figure 10.9(b) shows what happens when $r = 8$. In this case, the user's consumption rate is higher than in Figure 10.9(a), and he is requesting blocks

$$30, 34, 38, 42, 46, 50, 54, 60$$

However, this movie only has 53 blocks, and hence

$$data(i, t) = \{30, 34, 38, 42, 46, 50\}$$

3. *Rewind*: As in the case of fast-forward, we have an associated *rewind step*, which we will denote by rws. If the user wishes to start watching block b of movie m, and rewind at the rewind rate rws and watch r blocks, then

$$data(i, t) = \{(m, b - i \times rws) \mid i < r \,\&\, (b - i \times rws) \geq 1\}$$

4. *Pause*: If, when the user pauses, he was watching block b of movie m, then

$$data(i, t) = \{(m, b)\}$$

If we look at the above four examples, we notice that we can reformulate the definition of $data(i, t)$ so that it can be made more succinct. This is important because the disk controller must handle a set, $data(i, t)$, from *each* client of the movie-on-demand system as a whole. A succinct specification in each case makes the task of the controller that much easier (and more efficient as well).

The key observation here is that each client C_i wishes to view r_i blocks of the movie. Exactly which blocks of the movie the user wishes to view is determined by a number that we will call a *step*. This concept of a step generalizes both entities, ffs and rws, alluded to earlier in this section. In general, we observe that $data(i, t)$ may be specified by a single 4-tuple:

$$(m, b, len, step)$$

where m and b are as before, $len > 0$ is an integer, and $step$ is any arbitrary integer (which could be positive or negative or zero). When we have

$$data(i, t) = (m, b, len, step)$$

then this means that client C_i wishes to view the following blocks of movie m:

$$b, (b + step), (b + 2 \times step), \ldots, (b + (len - 1) \times step)$$

By choosing the value of $step$ appropriately, we can capture all the VCR-like operations described earlier:

1. *Play—normal viewing*: In this case, $step = 1$.

2. *Fast-forward with speed* ffs: In this case, $step = $ ffs.

3. *Rewind at speed* rws: In this case, $step = -$rws.

4. *Pause*: In this case, $step = 0$.

In the rest of this chapter, we will assume that $data(i, t)$ is a 4-tuple of this sort.

10.4   An Algorithm to Support VCR Functions

In order to design a server architecture that provides access to a set of clustered RAID arrays, we must write a program that takes a user's request for data (which is described by the 4-tuple $data(i, t)$ defined earlier) and that returns an assignment of retrieval tasks to the different disk servers being accessed by the movie-on-demand server.

For example, consider the situation shown in Figure 10.10. Here, our movie-on-demand (MOD) server is providing access to three disks. For the sake of simplicity, these disks contain only one movie, composed of 300 blocks. Disk 1 contains blocks 1–150; disk 2 contains blocks 150–250; and disk 3 contains blocks 200–300.

At time t, suppose user u_1 is watching blocks at the rate of 2 blocks per time unit, and suppose he is watching block 140. His current request is being served by disk 1. Suppose:

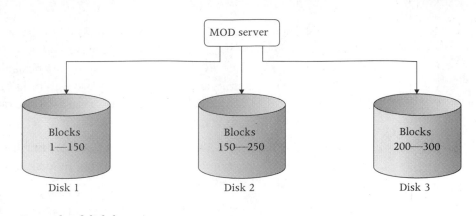

F I G U R E

10.10   Example of disk layout

1. The user continues watching the movie in "ordinary" mode. That is, $data(u_1, t) = (m, 140, 2, 1)$. In this case, the blocks to be retrieved are blocks 140, 141, which can only be served by disk 1. The MOD server therefore ships a request to disk 1's server, requesting these blocks.

2. The user pauses: In this case, $data(u_1, t) = (m, 140, 1, 0)$. In this case, the user is shown no blocks, and the block that was previously on the screen stays on.

3. The user fast-forwards at 6 blocks per second: In this case, $data(u_1, t) = (m, 140, 2, 6)$. That is, the blocks to be retrieved are blocks 146, 152. Block 142 exists only on disk 1, and block 152 exists only on disk 2. Hence, to satisfy this request by the user, the MOD server must dispatch two requests—one each to the servers controlling disks 1 and 2.

4. The user rewinds at 6 blocks per second: In this case, $data(u_1, t) = (m, 140, 2, -6)$. That is, the blocks to be retrieved are blocks 134 and 128, both of which can be retrieved from disk 1 only.

The situation becomes somewhat more complicated if we assume that we have two clients watching movies simultaneously. Continuing the same single-movie example discussed above, let us suppose that we now have a second user, u_2, and this user is watching movie block 199 at the rate of 2 blocks per second.

Now, two transactions can occur at any given time—one each corresponding to users u_1 and u_2. Furthermore, let us suppose that each disk can support only one client at a time (this oversimplified example is used only for purposes of clear exposition, and more complex algorithms will be given later in this section). This constraint may be due to the limited buffer that the disks have, or their low transfer rates (i.e., they read data very slowly).

Suppose users u_1 and u_2 are both accessing movies at the same time, at the rate of 2 blocks per time unit, and users u_1 and u_2 are watching blocks 140 and 199, respectively. Suppose now that user u_1 fast-forwards at the rate of 5 blocks per time unit, while user u_2 continues normal viewing.

1. At time t, user u_1 wants blocks 140 and 145, while user u_2 wants blocks 199 and 200. User u_1's request should be satisfied by disk 1, while user u_2's request is satisfied by disk 2.

2. At time $t + 1$, user u_1, continuing the same transaction as above, wants blocks 150 and 155, while user u_2 wants blocks 201 and 202. Here are some constraints that need to be taken into account when attempting to satisfy this:

   - Block 150 is available on both disks 1 and 2.
   - Block 155 is available only on disk 2.
   - Blocks 201 and 202 are available on both disks 2 and 3.

   Either of the following assignments can be used to handle the requests of the two users:

   - The user u_1's transaction $\mathtt{data}(u_1, t + 1) = (m, 150, 2, 5)$ is *split* into two subtransactions, denoted by the 4-tuples $(m, 150, 1, 5)$, $(m, 155, 1, 5)$. The first subtransaction is served by disk 1, the second by disk 2. In the same way, user u_2's transaction $\mathtt{data}(u_2, t + 1) = (m, 200, 2, 1)$ is split into two subtransactions, denoted by the 4-tuples $(m, 201, 1, 1)$ and $(m, 202, 1, 1)$. The first subtransaction is served by disk 2, the second by disk 3. (Notice that the second subtransactions of both users' requests could be satisfied by disk 2, but in the first user's case, only disk 2 can satisfy it, while in the second user's case, either disk 2 or disk 3 can satisfy it.)
   - An alternative possibility is that we split user u_1's transaction into two as above and have disks 1 and 2 satisfy the subtransactions; however, instead of splitting user u_2's request, we *switch* his entire transaction to disk 3.

Looking at the above example, we notice that we have informally introduced two new operations: *splitting*, which causes a user's transaction to be split into two or more pieces (called *twins*), and *switching*, which causes a user's transaction (or its descendant subtransactions) to be switched from the server that was originally handling the request to another server.

Before proceeding to describe an algorithm for handling VCR-like operations, we introduce a couple of other basic concepts that form important components of the MOD server algorithm.

The first concept we would like to introduce is *priority*. When a set of events (transactions) occur, each of these transactions must have an associated priority because it is entirely possible that a MOD server cannot serve all clients requesting service because of resource limitations. In such cases, it must satisfy clients based on some appropriate notion of priority. In general, events can be assigned a numeric priority—the higher the priority, the more important the client. While the algorithm we will describe below is capable of working with any notion of priority, it is nevertheless important to understand what priorities are in the context of a MOD system.

One such simple notion of priority assigns numbers in the range 1–5 to transactions according to the following table:

Transaction	Priority
exiting client	5
continuing client—normal viewing	4
continuing client—fast-forwarding	4
continuing client—rewind	4
continuing client—pause	4
new (entering) client	2

The above prioritization scheme indicates that continuing clients who are exiting the system have the top priority (because they free up system resources), while other continuing clients have lower priority. New clients have a priority of 2. The idea behind priority 3 is as follows: after satisfying exiting clients, we try to satisfy all clients of priority 4 *without doing any switching or splitting*. Any transaction that must be either switched or split is demoted to priority 3. This ensures that all routine transactions are handled quickly, while more involved transactions are temporarily moved out of the way till the straightforward transactions are all handled. Once they are completed, the splittings and switches involved with transactions of continuing clients are performed, and only then do we handle new clients.

For example, consider the following simple table describing some transactions:

Transaction	Transaction type	Initial priority	Adjusted priority
tr_1	exiting client	5	5
tr_2	continuing client—normal	4	4
tr_3	continuing client—needs switching	4	3
tr_4	continuing client—needs splitting	4	3
tr_5	new client	2	2
tr_6	new client—needs splitting or switching	2	1

"Initial priority" specifies the priority of the transaction when the MOD server first considers it. If the MOD server determines that this transaction requires either splitting or switching, then it demotes the client. For example, a continuing client doing a fast-forward may issue a transaction (e.g., tr_3) that requires switching. In this case, once the MOD server determines that splitting is required, it temporarily demotes that client's priority to 3. The same applies to new clients as well.

Splitting and switching of resources are caused by the fact that servers assigned initially by the MOD server to satisfy a transaction are unable to do so because of inadequate resources. Thus, when the MOD server assigns a client to a disk server, it must ensure that the disk server has the resources required to satisfy the request. This may be done by asking the following three questions:

1. *Data:* Does the disk have the data being requested by the transaction?

2. *Buffer:* Does the disk have enough buffer to serve this new client (in addition to those that it is already serving)? This can be formulated as a simple buffer constraint,

$$\left(\sum_{j \in \mathrm{d\_active}(i,t)} \mathrm{bufreq}(j, i, t) \right) \leq \mathrm{buf}(i)$$

where $\mathrm{bufreq}(j, i, t)$ denotes the buffer space needed at server i to match the consumption rate of client j.

3. *Transfer rate:* Is the disk's transfer rate fast enough to satisfy this client without violating the server's commitment to its existing clients? That is,

$$\left(\sum_{j \in \mathrm{d\_active}(i,t)} \mathrm{cons}(j, t) + \frac{\mathrm{switchtime}(i, t) \times \mathrm{dtr}(i)}{\mathrm{cyctime}(i, t)} \right) \leq \mathrm{dtr}(i)$$

We are now ready to present an algorithm (developed by Candan, Hwang, and Subrahmanian [35]) for handling a set, $EV(t)$, of transactions that are submitted by users at time t (including new users). Thus, $EV(t)$ is a set of quadruples of the form $(m, b, len, step)$. This algorithm, called FindSOL, maintains two tables. One table, called a *state* table, contains fields describing the state of a MOD system at time t. Some of these fields are *Client*, *Server*, *Movie*, *Start*, *Length*, and *Step*. Note that a single client may be serviced by multiple servers at a given point in time, and this may be represented in the state table as multiple tuples involving the same client. Similarly, another table, called the *resource* table, contains fields such as *Server*, *AvBuf*, *AvCycTime*, and *AvBWidth*, which describe the resources available at the servers at time t. Clearly, only one tuple is needed per server in the resource table.

Algorithm 10.1 FindSOL

1. Split $EV(t)$ into 6 sets: new(t), exit(t), cont(t), pause(t), ff(t), and rw(t), depending upon whether the client involved in the event is a new client, exiting client, normal continuing client, continuing client doing a pause, continuing client doing a fast-forward, continuing client doing a rewind, respectively. For each event in new(t), there is a *priority* $(1, \ldots, 5)$.

2. Set the priority of all events in new(t) to 2.

3. For all events e_i set *link*(e_i) to $\emptyset$. (No client has been split yet.) Intuitively, *link*(e_i) denotes the "twin" of e_i in the event e_i was created by splitting another event into two subevents.

4. (Handling Exiting Clients) For each client C_i in exit(t), do the following:

   (a) Let $r_1, \ldots, r_w$ be all rows in the state table corresponding to client C_i.
   (b) For $j = 1, \ldots, w$, do the following:
      - If r_j.Server $= k$, then update the record in the resource table corresponding to server k appropriately.
      - Delete row r_i from the state table.

5. (Handling Continuing-Pausing Clients) For each client C_i in pause(t), do **nothing**.

6. (Handling Continuing Clients) For each event e_i in $\text{cont}(t) \cup \text{ff}(t) \cup \text{rw}(t)$, where e_i is of the form $\text{data}(C_i, t) = (\mathcal{M}_i, s_i, \ell_i, step_i)$, do the following:

   (a) Let $r_1, \ldots, r_w$ be all rows in the state table with $\text{Client} = c_i$.

   (b) If, for all $j = 1, \ldots, w$, $r_j.\text{Server}$ satisfies the constraints, then

        i. Modify each $r_j.Start$, $r_j.Length$, and $r_j.Step$ to match the new $start_i$, $length_i$, and $step_i$.

      else

        i. Move event e_i into $\text{new}(t)$ with the priority set to 4.

        ii. Update the resource table as in Step 4b.

        iii. Delete each r_j from the state table.

7. (Handling New Clients) Let $e_1 \ldots e_m$ be all the events in $\text{new}(t)$, and let $\text{nlist}(t)$ be the list of events in $\text{new}(t)$ sorted in descending order of priority.

   (a) While $\text{nlist}(t) \neq \emptyset$, do the following:

        i. Let e_i be $head(\text{nlist}(t))$, where e_i is of the form $data(C_i, t) = (\mathcal{M}, s, l, step)$. Set $\text{nlist}(t)$ to $tail(\text{nlist}(t))$.

        ii. Let $SRV(e_i) = \{s \mid s$ is a server that satisfies the placement constraint of movie $\mathcal{M}\}$.

        iii. If $SRV(e_i) = \emptyset$, then ($*$ split event e_i into smaller events $*$)

           A. If the length l is smaller than $MINLENGTH$, then mark the event e_i as unsatisfiable, delete all the events in $link(e_i)$ from $\text{new}(t)$, and undo the effects of any events in $link(e_i)$ that have already been processed. Then go to 7a.

           B. If the priority of e_i is 4, then set the priority of e_i to 3 and put it back into $\text{nlist}(t)$ and go to 7a.

           C. If the priority of e_i is 2, then set the priority of e_i to 1 and put it back into $\text{nlist}(t)$ and go to 7a.

           D. If the priority of e_i is neither 2 nor 4, then

              ■ Let e_i' be $data(C_i, t) = (\mathcal{M}, s, \lfloor l/2 \rfloor, step)$, and $link(e_i') = link(e_i) \cup e_i''$.

              ■ Let e_i'' be $data(C_i, t) = (\mathcal{M}, s + \lfloor l/2 \rfloor, \lceil l/2 \rceil, step)$, and $link(e_i'') = link(e_i) \cup e_i'$.

              ■ Place e_i' and e_i'' at the head of nlist, and go to 7a.

        iv. Otherwise ($SRV(e_i) \neq \emptyset$): Let $CONS(e_i) \subseteq SRV(e_i)$ be the set of servers that can satisfy the consumption rate of client C_i.

    v. If $CONS(e_i) = \emptyset$, then (* split event e_i into smaller events *)

        A. If the length l is smaller than $MINLENGTH$, then mark the event e_i as unsatisfiable, delete all the events in $link(e_i)$ from $new(t)$, and undo the effects of any events in $link(e_i)$ that have already been processed. Then go to 7a.

        B. If the priority of e_i is 4, then set the priority of e_i to 3 and put it back into $nlist(t)$ and go to 7a.

        C. If the priority of e_i is 2, then set the priority of e_i to 1 and put it back into $nlist(t)$ and go to 7a.

        D. If the priority of e_i is neither 2 nor 4, then

          ▪ Let e_i' be $data(C_i, t) = (\mathcal{M}, s, \lfloor l/2 \rfloor, step * 2)$, and $link(e_i') = link(e_i) \cup e_i''$.

          ▪ Let e_i'' be $data(C_i, t) = (\mathcal{M}, s + step, \lceil l/2 \rceil, step * 2)$, and $link(e_i'') = link(e_i) \cup e_i'$.

          ▪ Place e_i' and e_i'' at the head of $nlist$, and go to 7a.

    vi. Let $BUF(e_i) \subseteq CONS(e_i)$ be the set of servers that can satisfy the buffer requirement of client C_i.

    vii. If $BUF(e_i) = \emptyset$, then (* split event e_i into smaller events *)

        A. If the length l is smaller than $MINLENGTH$, then mark the event e_i as unsatisfiable, delete all the events in $link(e_i)$ from $new(t)$, and undo the effects of any events in $link(e_i)$ that have already been processed. Then go to 7a.

        B. If the priority of e_i is 4, then set the priority of e_i to 3 and put it back into $nlist(t)$ and go to 7a.

        C. If the priority of e_i is 2, then set the priority of e_i to 1 and put it back into $nlist(t)$ and go to 7a.

        D. If the priority of e_i is neither 2 nor 4, then

          ▪ Let e_i' be $data(C_i, t) = (\mathcal{M}, s, \lfloor l/2 \rfloor, step * 2)$, and $link(e_i') = link(e_i) \cup e_i''$.

          ▪ Let e_i'' be $data(C_i, t) = (\mathcal{M}, s + step, \lceil l/2 \rceil, step * 2)$, and $link(e_i'') = link(e_i) \cup e_i'$.

          ▪ Place e_i' and e_i'' at the head of $nlist$, and go to 7a.

   viii. Otherwise (i.e., $BUF(e_i) \neq \emptyset$), if s_j is the member of $BUF(e_i)$ that returns the maximum evaluation value, and if e_i is of the form $data(C_i, t) = (\mathcal{M}, s, l, step)$, then add $(C_i, s_j, \mathcal{M}, s, l, step)$ to the state table, and update the resource table accordingly.

10.5   Selected Commercial Systems

Selecting an appropriate disk system for corporate or personal use must be done cautiously. Industry vendors quoting transfer rates and storage capacities often do so under different assumptions (e.g., compressed data vs. uncompressed data). As a consequence, all technical materials documenting a system's performance must be carefully examined. In this section, we briefly present some information about existing drive systems. Note that these are certain to change over time.

Storage Dimensions (408-954-0710) provides a range of disk arrays based on the RAID architecture. For instance, according to promotional material, their SuperFlex family of systems has up to seven bays and a capacity of 63.7 GB. The SuperFlex 5200 system is stated to achieve peak transfer rates of 40 MB/second and sustained transfer rates of 30 MB/second.

Seagate's 2-GB SCSI hard disk drive family has a capacity (for a single disk, as opposed to the disk array described above) of about 2.15 GB each and can support five disks. It uses 10 physical heads and has an average seek read time of 10.4 ms, a maximum read time of 20.4 ms, and a rotational speed of 5,411 rpm. Its buffer size is 512 KB, and its transfer rate (buffer to host) is 10 MB/second at burst/peak, and 5.5 MB/second sustained rate.

Seagate's Cheetah system may have a capacity of up to 9.1 GB, accompanied by an external transfer rate of 20–40 MB/second, track-to-track seek time of 0.78 ms for reads and 1.04 ms for writes, and a rotational speed of 10,033 rpm.

Seagate's Hawk family of disk drives has capacities of 1.05 and 2.15 GB, with rotational speeds of 5,400 rpm. External transfer rates vary from 10–20 MB/second. Average seek times are 9 ms for reads and 10.5 ms for writes, while the maximum seek time is 22 ms.

Disk servers for supporting video and audio applications have proliferated in recent years, though superior buffer capabilities and higher transfer rates are still desirable. Here is some elementary information about a few industrial offerings to give you an idea of the kinds of transfer rates of RAID arrays. Again, this information is certain to change over time.

Unison's Metastor DS-10 system is capable of containing up to ten 4-GB drives, transferring information at the rate of 14 MB/second. Further information may be obtained by accessing *http://www.unisoninfo.com/diskarra.htm*.

Ciprico offers several series of RAID arrays, ranging in transfer speeds of anywhere between 30 MB/second to 100 MB/second. Further information may be obtained by accessing *http://www.europe.access.com/pp/Ciprico/CIproducts.htm.*

FWB provides RAID array servers that are suitable for the creation and delivering of both local and networked video presentations. Their Sledgehammer RAID disk arrays may have speeds of up to 32 MB/second. Further information may be obtained by accessing *http://www.infsol.com/FWB.html.*

10.6   Bibliographic Notes

Over the last few years, there has been growing interest in the efficient retrieval of multimedia data from disk. Buddhikot et al. [33] provide an excellent survey of the state of the art techniques used in video storage and retrieval. In this section, we give an overview of the current research on multimedia information retrieval from disk, and we show how the algorithm we provide differs from these approaches.

10.6.1   Work on Placement Mappings

Vin, Rao, and Goyal [215] develop two different ways of placing media data on disk arrays and analyze the performance of media systems based on these placement strategies. Similarly, Berson et al. [21] argue that staggered striping (a particular kind of placement mapping) enhances performance in video-on-demand systems. Ozden, Rastogi, and Silberschatz [153] propose movie-on-demand systems where each movie is stored on a separate disk, which, of course, is a special kind of placement mapping.

10.6.2   VCR Capabilities

Several authors develop disk models that facilitate supporting different kinds of VCR operations such as fast-forward, rewind, pause, and so on. Chen et al. [45] provide ways of scheduling rewind operations. Chen, Kandlur, and Yu [48] develop techniques to support browsing video sequences at variable rates (thus implicitly supporting fast-forward, rewind, etc.). They are interested in sampling segments of video and minimizing the variation on the number of video segments skipped during fast-forward/rewind. Dey-Sircar et al. [54] develop a statistical model of video retrieval that maximizes statistical quality of service under some conditions. The FindSOL algorithm described in this chapter was developed by Candan, Hwang, and Subrahmanian [35]. Hwang, Kilic, and Subrahmanian [97] have developed an extension of FindSOL that accommodates disk crashes and that can interleave updates.

10.6.3   Buffering and Prefetching Issues

Ng and his colleagues have developed efficient buffer management techniques to handle video data and ensure that the clients' consumption rate requirements are met [133, 146]. They show that prefetching techniques enhance performance and that multiple media streams may neatly share buffers. Freedman and Dewitt [66] develop simulation studies showing that certain buffer page replacement and prefetching algorithms perform better than other algorithms, such as the grouped sweeping algorithm of Yu, Chen, and Kandlur [230].

10.7   Exercises and Projects

1. Suppose we have a cluster of four disks, arranged using the RAID-0 architecture. Suppose we have three movies, m_1, m_2, m_3, stored, and these movies have 20, 28, and 21 blocks, respectively. Show pictorially which blocks are stored on which disks, assuming that each is striped over all four disks.

2. Suppose $d_1, \ldots, d_n, d_{n+1}$ are $(n + 1)$ disks that form a cluster in the RAID-5 architecture, and suppose d_{n+1} is a parity disk for the other n disks. Suppose d_i is any disk, $1 \leq i \leq n$, that crashes.
   (a) Prove that using the parity disk, and using disks $d_1, \ldots, d_{i-1}, d_{i+1}, \ldots, d_n$, it is possible to reconstruct the contents of disk d_i.
   (b) Suppose two disks, d_i and d_j, both crash. Is it possible to recover the contents of both these disks? If so, prove it. If not, provide a counterexample.

3. Consider a single disk that reads data at the rate of k MB/second, and that has two clients, c_1 and c_2. c_1 consumes data at the rate of r_1 MB/second, while c_2 consumes data at the rate of r_2 MB/second. The disk has b MB of buffer space. You may assume that the time taken for clients to read from the buffer is 0. Both clients c_1 and c_2 watch the same movie (containing *size* MB of data), and both started watching it at the same time. Under what conditions will we be able to satisfy both clients without ever reading the same block twice from disk?

4. Unless specified otherwise, we use the same notation as in the preceding exercise. Suppose for clients c_i ($i = 1, 2$), we use the notation $rmin_i$ and $rmax_i$

to denote the minimal and maximal consumption rates of client c_i. In other words, suppose that the clients can consume data at varying rates, as long as those rates fall within the specified bounds. Further suppose that both clients watch the same movie, but the first client starts watching the movie at time t_1, while the second starts watching it at a later time, t_2. Derive an expression showing how we can minimize the number of bytes that are read twice from disk.

5. As a project, develop a prototype program that simulates a video server retrieving video data from a single disk for one client at a time. Your program may take the following as input:

   (a) A table having the scheme (Movie, Numblocks), specifying, for each movie stored on the disk, how many blocks that movie has (you may assume these blocks are numbered 1 through Numblocks)

   (b) A specification of the disk's transfer rate and buffer size

   (c) A specification of the user's consumption rate, as well as the user's request (expressed in the form of the quadruple (m,b,len,step) discussed in this chapter)

   Your program must return the block number(s) being retrieved by the video server in response to the user's request as output. In addition, you should create a small multimedia archive of video clips (MPEG) and play the retrieved video clips using suitable utilities (e.g., mpegplay in Unix systems).

11 Retrieving Multimedia Data from CD-ROMs

What new concepts will you learn in this chapter?
You will learn how data is laid out on compact disks, and how CD-ROM drives read such disks. You will learn how a CD-ROM server can serve a number of concurrent read requests.

What new abstractions are needed to realize these concepts?
As in the case of disk servers, CD-ROM servers provide access to compact disks using certain resources (disk bandwidth, buffer availability). We will define formal analytic models of how much buffer is required to provide certain quality of service guarantees.

What new techniques are needed to implement these abstractions?
Scheduling algorithms will be presented that show how multiple client requests can be serviced while keeping in mind the physical parameters of the CD-ROM read hardware.

What technological features support these implementation methods?
You will receive a quick overview of existing CD-ROM devices.

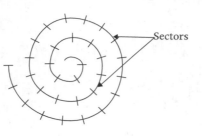

F I G U R E

11.1   Spiral trajectory of CD-ROM head

The compact disc (CD) is fast gaining popularity as a high-fidelity, inexpensive, reliable storage device. In raw form, a compact disc costs under a dollar on the average and can currently store over 1 GB of data. Within the next couple of years, CD-ROMs will be able to store 5 GB of data or more, leading to an inexpensive method of storing massive quantities of data. This has made CD-ROMs a relatively inexpensive medium of storage when compared to disk drives whose cost/storage ratio is much higher. In this chapter, we will study how CD-ROMs work and how we may model them so as to facilitate the continuous retrieval of media data.

11.1   CD-ROM Modeling

Unlike disk drives, a CD-ROM drive typically contains only one platter on which the CD-ROM is placed. The CD-ROM contains a single spiral track that is traversed by the read head, as shown in Figure 11.1. This spiral track is divided up into equal-sized sectors. As a consequence, we may think of this spiral track as a piece of string, with alternating black and white shadings (of equal length), each depicting a sector. The read head traverses this string at a constant velocity. Unlike a disk drive system, where the disk head moves at a constant *angular* velocity, in the case of a CD-ROM-based system, the disk head moves at a constant *linear* velocity. If we think of the "string" as being straightened, the shadings (i.e., location/sizes of the sectors) do not change, of course. Thus, for all practical purposes, we may think of the data on a CD-ROM as being laid out in even-sized sectors on a straight line, as shown in Figure 11.2. Without loss of generality, we will assume that these sectors are labeled consecutively from 1 to N, for some integer N that describes the capacity of the CD-ROM.

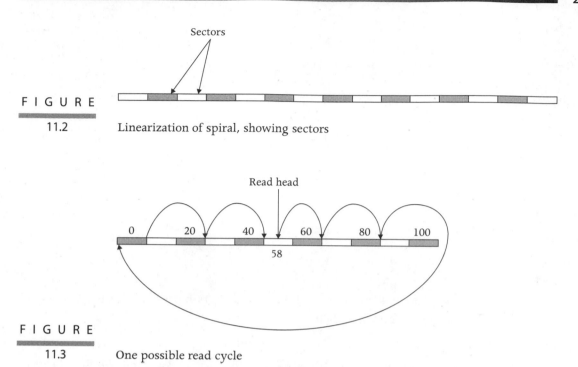

F I G U R E

11.2   Linearization of spiral, showing sectors

F I G U R E

11.3   One possible read cycle

Let's examine exactly what happens when the CD-ROM driver receives a request for sectors $s_1, \ldots, s_n$. Let's further assume that the client process requesting these sectors wishes to consume them in the order listed. It would be desirable if we could read these sectors into a buffer associated with the client, and then let the client consume them in the order it likes. This would then allow the CD-ROM server to fetch the sectors in any order it likes, as long as sector s_i is in the client's buffer *before* the client wishes to consume it.

Figure 11.3 shows a simple example of this phenomenon. For our purposes, this particular CD-ROM contains 100 sectors (in practice, a CD-ROM contains thousands of sectors). The read head is currently at location 58. A client wishes to read the sectors 10, 30, 50, 70, and 90, and this client has enough buffer to accommodate three sectors. In what order should the CD-ROM read the data?

- *Possibility 1:* One possibility is that the CD-ROM reads sector 70 first, then sector 90, then sector 10, then sector 30, and then sector 50. Figure 11.4 shows this phenomenon. In this case, what happens is that sectors 70 and 90 get buffered first. Then sector 10 gets buffered. At the next time instant, sector 10 gets consumed, and sector 30 can be buffered. Subsequently,

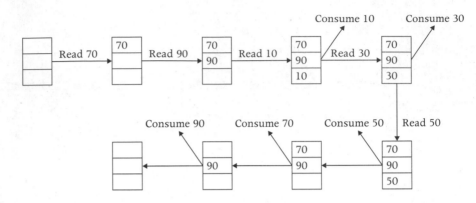

FIGURE

11.4   Status of buffers during read cycle

sector 30 gets consumed, and sector 50 gets buffered. Finally, sectors 50, 70, and 90 get consumed.

- *Possibility 2:* Another possibility is to start by resetting the disk head to point to zero, and then move the head so that sectors 10, 30, and 50 get buffered. We then consume 10 and buffer 70. Next we consume sector 30 and buffer 90. Next, we consume sectors 50, 70, and 90.

Generally speaking, most CD-ROM drivers do not allow possibility 1. Instead, reading is done in *rounds*. Each round starts with the read head at location 1. In any given round, we attempt to read a sorted (in ascending order of sector number) set of sectors.

11.1.1   Buffer Requirements

Let's suppose that reading is done in rounds, as described above, and that we have one client who wishes to read sectors $s_1, \ldots, s_n$ of a CD-ROM. Furthermore, suppose that the hardware architecture of our CD-ROM device is as shown in Figure 11.5. Here, we have a CD-ROM drive containing an internal buffer, used for prefetching. The disk's read head transfers data into this buffer, which is then transferred across a bus to the main memory device. The disk read bandwidth, and the bandwidth of the bus between main memory and the

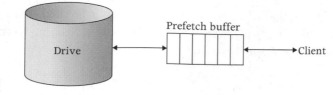

FIGURE

11.5   Architecture of CD-ROM disk subsystem

prefetch buffer, may vary. The table below shows these quantities (note that some of these quantities may vary from one client to another):

Symbol	Description	Units
ss	sector size	bytes
bw_d	bandwidth of disk to prefetch buffer	bytes/second
dcr	decompression rate	bytes/second
cr	compression ratio	integer
$cons$	consumption rate of client	bytes/second
sk	average seek time	seconds
t_{fill}	buffer filling time	seconds

All the above quantities are known—what remains to be determined is an appropriate buffer size. (Here, $cr = 4$ means that 4 blocks of data are compressed into 1 block. Similarly, dcr is the rate at which data is decompressed by the client.) The key question is what buffer size our client needs so as to ensure two properties:

■ *Continuity of playback:* The client should be able to read data from the buffer without any interruption.

■ *Buffer utilization:* At no time should the buffer get overwritten before the client reads the data.

Given the above parameters, we may determine *buf* through the following sequence of steps. To ensure that the buffer does not overflow or underflow, we need to ensure that the client's consumption rate is equal to the retrieval rate of the server; that is, *cons* must equal the rate at which the buffer is filled. Why is this so? There are two possibilities:

■ If *cons* is greater than the rate at which the buffer is filled, then it is possible that at some time, the buffer is empty, but the client is trying to read something. This violates our continuity requirement.

- If *cons* is less than the rate at which the buffer is filled, then it is possible that data is being written into the buffer too fast, leading to the possibility that the buffer is overwritten.

Let's see what happens:

1. In t_{fill} seconds, the server can read $(t_{fill} \times bw_d)$ bytes of compressed data into the buffer.

2. In 1 second, the client can consume *cons* bytes of *uncompressed* data.

3. One byte of compressed data is equivalent to *cr* bytes of uncompressed data.

4. The maximal amount of uncompressed data consumable by the client in t_{fill} seconds is given by the equation

$$t_{fill} = (\delta \times t_{fill}) + \frac{\delta \times t_{fill} \times dcr \times cr}{cons}$$

where δ is a real number between 0 and 1, inclusive, denoting the fraction of time within the cycle of t_{fill} seconds in which the client is decompressing compressed data. The first term in the above equation specifies the time used to decompress (within a cycle of t_{fill} seconds); the second term specifies the amount of time needed to consume the data thus decompressed. The numerator of the second term specifies the quantity (in bytes) of decompressed data, while the denominator specifies the consumption rate of the client.

5. Solving the above equation for the variable δ, we get

$$t_{fill} = (\delta \times t_{fill}) + \frac{\delta \times t_{fill} \times dcr \times cr}{cons}$$

$$1 = \delta \times (1 + \frac{dcr \times cr}{cons})$$

$$\delta = \frac{cons}{cons + dcr \times cr}$$

6. Therefore, in $t_{fill} + sk$ seconds, the server can write $(t_{fill} - sk) \times bw_d$ bytes (of uncompressed data) into the buffer, and the client can consume $\delta \times t_{fill} \times dcr \times cr/cons$ bytes (of uncompressed data). If these two quantities are equal, then it is sufficient to guarantee both continuous playback and

no overwriting of the buffer. Thus, we may set

$$(t_{fill} - sk) \times bw_d = \frac{\delta \times t_{fill} \times dcr \times cr}{cons}$$

$$= \frac{cons}{cons + dcr \times cr} \times \frac{t_{fill} \times dcr \times cr}{cons}$$

$$= \frac{t_{fill} \times dcr \times cr}{cons + dcr \times cr}$$

By a straightforward rewriting of the above equation, we obtain

$$t_{fill} = \frac{(sk - bw_d) \times (cons + dcr \times cr)}{(bw_d \times cons) + (dcr \times cr) \times (bw_d - 1)}$$

7. The minimal buffer size needed is $(bw_d \times t_{fill})$. Hence, the minimal amount of buffer needed is given by

$$bw_d \times \left(\frac{(sk - bw_d) \times (cons + dcr \times cr)}{(bw_d \times cons) + (dcr \times cr) \times (bw_d - 1)} \right)$$

11.2 Scheduling Retrieval of Multiple Sectors from CD-ROMs

Consider a CD-ROM server that receives requests for a set $\{s_1, \ldots, s_k\}$ of sectors. There are many different algorithms that may be used to retrieve these sectors. Each of these algorithms builds upon previous algorithms, designed for similar purposes, for retrieval from disk systems. We now briefly discuss some of these algorithms below. For the sake of brevity, our descriptions provide a sketch of the basic idea underlying each algorithm and thus many details are hidden.

11.2.1 First Come First Serve (FCFS)

Given an interval I of time, this algorithm considers service requests that arrive within that interval, in the order in which they arrived, and processes them. The total seek time taken to serve the entire set of k requests is given by

$$\frac{\sum_{i=1}^{k} abs(s_i - s_{i-1})}{lv}$$

where s_0 is defined to be sector 1, and lv is the linear velocity of the read head, expressed in sectors per second. As usual, abs() denotes absolute value.

Thus, for instance, if we consider an FCFS approach to serving requests for sectors 25, 5, 35, 15, 5, and 10 in a case where the linear velocity is 2 sectors per millisecond, then the total time taken is

$$seek = \frac{\begin{array}{c} abs(25-1) + abs(5-25) + abs(35-5) \\ + abs(15-35) + abs(5-15) + abs(10-5) \end{array}}{2}$$

$$= \frac{24 + 20 + 30 + 20 + 10 + 5}{2}$$

$$= 54.5 \text{ milliseconds}$$

11.2.2   SCAN Algorithm

In this approach, we collect a set of requests, and then sort the sectors in increasing order of seek distance. If the read head is at location 1 initially, then this results in a single, unidirectional sweep that reads the sectors (contrast this with the bidirectional sweep in the case of FCFS). On the other hand, if the read head is initially not at the start location, then this might lead to a bidirectional sweep.

For example, if we reconsider the request for the sectors 25, 5, 35, 15, 5, and 10 when the read head is positioned at sector 1, the SCAN algorithm would first sort these into the order 5, 10, 15, 25, 35. Notice that one advantage of this kind of sorting is that sector 5 is read only once. This leads to the following seek time:

$$seek = \frac{(5-1) + (10-5) + (15-10) + (25-15) + (35-25)}{2}$$

$$= 17 \text{ milliseconds}$$

Obviously, this is a substantial improvement on the FCFS algorithm, though we must keep in mind that the time required to sort the requests has not been counted in the above analysis.

However, if the read head is positioned at sector 10, then the sort order is different. One of the two orderings listed below would result:

Sector	Distance from read head	Sector	Distance from read head
10	0	10	0
5	5	15	5
15	5	5	5
25	15	25	15
35	25	35	25

11.2.3 SCAN-EDF Algorithm

In the preceding algorithms, we have not explicitly described the deadlines involved. The SCAN-EDF algorithm sorts incoming service requests on two keys: first it sorts them in ascending order of deadline; if a set of service requests have the same deadline, it then processes those service requests using the SCAN algorithm.

Let us consider a simple example to see how the SCAN-EDF algorithm works. Suppose the table below shows a set of sectors being requested, as well as the deadline by which those sectors need to be read:

Job_Id	Sector	Deadline
1	15	10
2	20	5
3	10	10
4	35	10
5	50	5

We may group the requests into two groups, G_1 and G_2, where G_1 consists of jobs 2 and 5 (both of which have the same deadline, 5) and G_2 contains jobs 1, 3, and 4 (all of which have the same deadline, 10). G_1 is serviced first because it has the earlier deadline, and G_2 is serviced later. The servicing of G_1 causes sector 20 to be read first and sector 50 next (as the SCAN algorithm is applied within a group). The servicing of G_2 causes sectors 35,15,10 to be read in that order. Thus, the order in which the read head reads data is 20,50,35,15,10.

11.3   Placement Methods

The above algorithms assume that the sectors on a CD-ROM will be laid out in some predetermined manner. Two natural questions that arise are "How are blocks in a movie/audio file laid out on a CD-ROM? And is it possible for the layout strategy to optimize retrieval of such files?" In this section, we will discuss the answers to both these questions. Throughout the discussion in this section, we will assume that the CD-ROM has physical sectors numbered 1 through N. Our task will be to determine how to "place" data into these sectors.

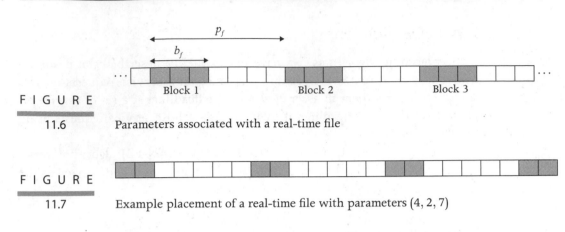

FIGURE 11.6 Parameters associated with a real-time file

FIGURE 11.7 Example placement of a real-time file with parameters $(4, 2, 7)$

11.3.1 Real-Time Files (RTFs)

A real-time file f is a triple (ℓ_f, b_f, p_f) where

- $\ell_f \geq 0$ is an integer called the *length* of the file. Intuitively, file f is broken down into ℓ_f "blocks." Different blocks in an RTF may be stored at dispersed locations on the CD-ROM.

- $b_f \geq 1$ is an integer called the *block size* of the file. Intuitively, b_f is the number of sectors contained within a block. All these sectors are assumed to be contiguous, and, in fact, all sectors of a given block are stored in contiguous sectors of the CD-ROM.

- $p_f \geq 0$ is an integer called the *period* of file f. Intuitively, p_f specifies the distance (in sectors) between the first sector of two consecutive blocks of a real-time file.

Figure 11.6 shows this situation diagrammatically.

For example, consider a real-time file f_1 described by the triple $(4, 2, 7)$. This means that file f_1 has four blocks in it, and that each block contains two sectors of data. Furthermore, the number of sectors between the start sector of two consecutive blocks is seven. Figure 11.7 shows one possible layout of this file onto a CD-ROM. There are obviously several other possible layouts as well.

Suppose f is a real-time file. Once we know the start location of the first block of file f, then the set of all sectors occupied by that file is uniquely determined. Suppose $st(f)$ denotes the start location of file f. Then, the set of sectors occupied by the ith block of file f is given by

$$occ_i(f) = \{j \mid st(f) + (i - 1) \times p_f \leq j \leq st(f) + (i - 1) \times p_f + b_f - 1\}$$

Since there are ℓ_f blocks in file f, it follows that the sectors occupied by file f as a whole are given by the expression

$$occ(f) = \bigcup_{i=1}^{\ell_f} occ_i(f)$$

$$= \bigcup_{i=1}^{\ell_f} \{j \mid st(f) + (i-1) \times p_f \leq j \leq st(f) + (i-1) \times p_f + b_f - 1\}$$

For example, if we return to our example involving the file f_1 described by the triple $(4, 2, 7)$, and if we assume that $st(f_1) = 3$, then we may easily observe that

$$occ_1(f_1) = \{j \mid 3 \leq 3 + 2 - 1\}$$
$$= \{3, 4\}$$
$$occ_2(f_1) = \{j \mid 3 + 7 \leq j \leq 3 + 7 + 2 - 1\}$$
$$= \{10, 11\}$$
$$occ_3(f_1) = \{j \mid 3 + 2 \times 7 \leq j \leq 3 + 2 \times 7 + 2 - 1\}$$
$$= \{17, 18\}$$

$occ_4(f_1)$ may be similarly described.

11.3.2 Start Assignment Problem (SAP)

Suppose we have a CD-ROM containing N sectors, numbered 1 through N, and we have a set $\mathcal{F}$ of real-time files. The start assignment problem is the problem of finding a function $st : \mathcal{F} \rightarrow \{1, \ldots, N\}$ such that the noncollision axiom below holds:

Axiom 11.1 Noncollision Axiom For all $f_i, f_j \in \mathcal{F}$, $f_i \neq f_j \Rightarrow occ(f_i) \cap occ(f_j) = \emptyset$. If such a function st exists, then it is called a *placement function*.

Intuitively, recall that for any real-time file f, once we know f's start location, $st(f)$, then $occ(f)$ is well defined. What the SAP tries to do is to assign a start location to each file in such a way that no sector on the CD-ROM contains data belonging to two or more files.

For example, suppose we consider two simple real-time files, f_1 and f_2, characterized by the triples $(2, 2, 5)$ and $(3, 1, 4)$, respectively, and suppose our CD-ROM has 10 sectors labeled 1 through 10. Then the following is a valid start assignment:

$$st(f_1) = 2$$
$$st(f_2) = 1$$

Note that the function st satisfies the noncollision axiom because

$$occ(f_1) = \{2, 3, 7, 8\}$$
$$occ(f_2) = \{1, 5, 9\}$$

Unfortunately, the problem of finding start assignments for different files is NP-hard—a result that has been proved under slightly different terminology by Korst and Pronk [118].

Below, we present a simple algorithm to place two real-time files f_1 and f_2. This algorithm may easily be extended to handle n files.

Algorithm 11.1 Placement(f_1, f_2)
$(\star\ f_1 : (\ell_1, b_1, p_1).\ f_2 : (\ell_2, b_2, p_2)\ \star)$
```
maxstart1 = N − (b₁ − 1) × p₁ − (b₁ − 1);
maxstart2 = N − (b₂ − 1) × p₂ − (b₂ − 1);
nogo = maxstart1≤ 0 ∨ maxstart2≤ 0;
if nogo then Return ''No Solution''.  Halt.
for i = 1 to maxstart1 do
    {
```
        $st(f_1) = i;$
```
        for j = 1 to maxstart2 do
            {
```
            $st(f_2) = j;$
            `if` $occ(f_1) \cap occ(f_2) = \emptyset$ `then`
            `Return` $st(f_1) = i, st(f_2) = j.$ `Halt.`
```
            }

    }
Return ''No Solution''.  Halt.
end
```

The above solution is rather complicated and, for two files, takes time proportional to `maxstart1` × `maxstart2`. In the worst case, the time is $O(N^2)$.

Note that once $st(f_1)$ and $st(f_2)$ have been picked, the check

$$occ(f_1) \cap occ(f_2) = ?$$

is very easy to make. This is because $occ(f_1) \cap occ(f_2)$ is nonempty iff for some $1 \leq i \leq b_1$ and some $1 \leq j \leq b_2$, it is the case that $occ_i(f_1)$ and $occ_j(f_2)$ intersect. For a fixed i, j, this check is equivalent to checking if the following four linear constraints have an integer solution:

$$x \geq st(f_1) + (i - 1) \times p_1$$
$$x \leq st(f_1) + (i - 1) \times p_1 + (b_1 - 1)$$
$$x \geq st(f_2) + (j - 1) \times p_2$$
$$x \leq st(f_2) + (j - 1) \times p_2 + (b_2 - 1)$$

It is easy to see that these constraints are solvable in constant time. In total, we need to make $(b_1 \times b_2)$ such constant time checks, one for each $1 \leq i \leq b_1$ and $1 \leq j \leq b_2$.

In general, if this procedure is extended to handle k files, then it will take time $O(N^k)$, thus making it exponential in the number of files being placed. This, taken together with the fact that the number of sectors, N, on a CD-ROM is itself very large, makes the algorithm fairly impractical.

In general, finding a solution to the start assignment problem is equivalent to finding a solution to a mixed integer linear programming problem (Hillier and Lieberman [90]). Numerous excellent algorithms for mixed integer programming are known. All of these algorithms are based on first solving a polynomial time linear programming relaxation of the integer programming problem, and then attempting to find an integer programming solution later, if so desired.

11.4   Selected Commercial Systems

Information about ordering a vast variety of CD-ROM drives is available from Baber Information Services (*http://www.baber.com*). For instance, they list (among others) the following CD-ROM drives:

Model	Speed	Seek time (ms)	Transfer rate (KB/second)
Toshiba (internal)	14	99	2,100
NEC Multispin	8	140	1,200
Creative Labs Blaster	12	150	1,800
IBM (internal)	4	200	600

In general, CD-ROM drives that have lower transfer rates are cheaper in price. The above is only a small, representative sample of the transfer rates of selected CD-ROM devices on the market. As always, technology changes rapidly, so check the latest speeds and costs with reliable vendors.

11.5 Bibliographic Notes

Compared to the existing body of work on modeling disk drives, there has been relatively little work on modeling CD-ROM storage. Korst and Pronk [117] provide an excellent overview of CD-ROM devices.

Yu et al. [229] propose methods for the placement of audio data on CD-ROM. This was the first such paper that we are aware of. Later, Korst and Pronk [118] provided a formal theoretical solution to the problem of storing multiple real-time files on a CD-ROM. They also proved that a variant of SAP, called RAP, is NP-complete. They then developed heuristics to compute solutions to SAP. The treatment in Section 11.3 of this book is based on their work.

Shastri et al. [185] provide an excellent framework within which we may model the performance of a CD-ROM server for multimedia applications. They also provide techniques for computing buffer requirements. The treatment in Section 11.1.1 of this book is based on their work.

The techniques described in Section 11.2 are based on existing techniques for accessing data on disks. Detailed descriptions of these algorithms, as well as various extensions and enhancements, may be found in many sources [230, 213, 70, 212, 196].

11.6 Exercises and Projects

1. A minor variant of the SCAN algorithm works as follows: Suppose the disk head is positioned at location h, and we wish to retrieve all sectors in set S. A *minimal h-sorting* of S is a sequentialization of S such that the total distance traveled by S is minimized. Write, in pseudocode, an algorithm that takes h and S as input and returns a minimal h-sorting of S.

2. Write, in pseudocode, an implementation of the SCAN-EDF algorithm. Then show how the SCAN-EDF algorithm may take into account the notion of h-sorting described in the preceding exercise.

3. Write, in pseudocode, an algorithm to solve the following problem referenced in Algorithm 11.1: take $occ_i(f_1)$ and $occ_j(f_2)$ as input and return as output "true" if these sets intersect, and "false" otherwise. Based on this function, write a program that takes f_1's and f_2's specifications as input as well as two integers, x_1 and x_2, reflecting possible start assignments for f_1 and f_2, respectively, and returns as output "true" if $occ(f_1)$, $occ(f_2)$ intersect, and "false" if they do not.

4. Using Algorithm 11.1 as a starting point, develop an algorithm that takes a set $\mathcal{F}$ of real-time files and a positive integer N (denoting the number of sectors on a CD-ROM) as input and returns a possible start assignment as output.

5. As a project, implement the FCFS, SCAN, and SCAN-EDF algorithms (you may assume that the read head is always at location 0). Run experiments to see which of these algorithms performs best according to each of the following two performance measures:

   (a) Total distance traveled by the read head.

   (b) Total time taken for the algorithm to terminate.

12 Retrieving Multimedia Data from Tapes

CHAPTER

What new concepts will you learn in this chapter?
You will learn about two different types of tape recordings—serpentine tapes and helical tape recordings. You will learn how tape readers scan tapes in each of these architectures. Later, you will learn how robotic tape libraries are organized to facilitate maximum system throughput.

What new abstractions are needed to realize these concepts?
A storage management server that mediates access to a set of storage devices must maximize system throughput, subject to the resource constraints and physical constraints existing on the system. We will study optimization techniques for these servers to handle client requests.

What new techniques are needed to implement these abstractions?
As in the case of disks and CD-ROMs, the principles of resource allocation are somewhat independent of the specific storage device considered. However, because of differences in physical constraints and in the layout of data on tapes, new scheduling techniques need to be developed so as to handle requests from multiple clients.

What technological features support these implementation methods?
We will discuss existing tape servers in the commercial market, as well as current research on tape servers.

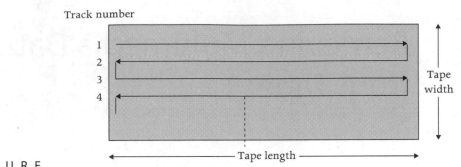

FIGURE

12.1   Serpentine tape recording

Of all computational storage devices, tapes have been around for the longest time. They are relatively inexpensive and can store massive amounts of data. Unfortunately, accessing data on tape is a time-consuming operation. Many of us familiar with the classic audiotape have encountered problems when attempting to search for a given song on the tape. With magnetic tape storage, the situation is somewhat better and depends upon the type of tape being used.

In this chapter, we will briefly describe different kinds of tape recording/storage mechanisms and describe how such tapes can be modeled. Then we will describe what are commonly known as "robotic tape libraries" and show how the performance of these systems may be modeled. Finally, we will discuss hierarchical storage systems, where multiple storage devices are used for storing continuous media data.

12.1   Tape Recording Mechanisms

There are two widely used methods used to store data onto tapes: *serpentine* and *helical* recordings.

12.1.1 Serpentine Tape Recording

In a serpentine tape, the tape contains several *tracks* that are parallel to the length of the tape. Each track has a *track number* and is composed of a linear set of tape *blocks* that are read one at a time. When reading a serpentine tape, we traverse the tape as shown in Figure 12.1. That is, the tape is first "rolled" forward (i.e., in the left-to-right direction), and the read head of the tape drive is positioned over track 1. When we reach the end of track 1, the read head gets repositioned over track 2, and we read the contents of track 2 moving from right to left. When we reach the end of track 2, the read head gets repositioned over track 3, and we read from left to right. The process continues until we reach the end of the tape.

Thus, in general, if we have a tape containing n tracks, labeled 1 through n, then a simple algorithm for traversing these n tracks is the following:

Algorithm 12.1 `Tape_traverse(`n`)`
   $i = 1;\ \ block = 1;$
`while` $i \le n$ `do`
`{`
   `end_of_track = false;`
   `while` ¬`end_of_track do`
     `{`
       `if` i `mod` $2 = 1$ `then block = block + 1`
       `else block = block - 1;`
       `Read block;`
     `}`
   $i = i + 1;$ `(* shift tracks *)`
   `Position read head over track` i`;`
`}`
`end`

In the above algorithm, the step where the check `if i mod 2 = 1` is used to determine whether the tape should be traversed from left to right, or from right to left.

Typical tape widths range from 4 to 125 millimeters. Obviously, the greater the width of the tape, the larger the number of tracks in the tape.

Suppose now that the read head of a tape is positioned at block j of track i, and we wish to read block j' of track i'. Then we must traverse all blocks of the tape that lie in between, and in addition, we must reposition the read head abs$(i - i')$ times, once for each track change. For example, as shown in Figure 12.2, suppose the read head is currently positioned over track 4, and we are reading block 90 (shown as A in the figure) on this track. Suppose we wish to read block 10 of track 1 now. Then the tape must be rewound (as shown by the dotted lines) to the beginning of track 4, then the read head must be switched to track 1 (jumping tracks 2 and 3)—not all tape systems support such jumps—and finally, we move the tape ahead to block B.

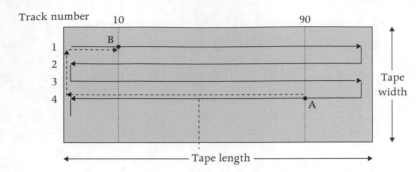

FIGURE

12.2   Switching to a new block on a serpentine tape

Reading from a Serpentine Tape

Suppose we consider a serpentine tape where the read head is currently positioned over block b_1 on track t_1, and suppose we now wish to have the read head positioned over block b_2 of track t_2. Further suppose that multiple tracks may be skipped. This may be accomplished in one of two ways:

- *Alternative 1:*

  1. Rewind tape to the left till the read head is positioned over block 1 of track t_1. This requires traversing $(b_1 - 1)$ blocks.
  2. Then reposition the read head to track t_2, jumping $\mathrm{abs}(t_1 - t_2)$ tracks.
  3. Roll tape forward till the read head is positioned over block b_2. This requires traversing $(b_2 - 1)$ blocks.

- *Alternative 2:*

  1. Fast-forward tape to the right till the read head is positioned over the last block (denoted *nblock*) of the track. This requires traversing $(nblock - b_1)$ blocks.
  2. Then reposition the read head to track t_2, jumping $\mathrm{abs}(t_1 - t_2)$ tracks.
  3. Rewind the tape (moving left) till the read head is positioned over block b_2. This requires traversing $(nblock - b_2)$ blocks.

If *ff* and *rew* denote the fast-forward and rewind speeds (in blocks/second) and if *trkspeed* denotes the number of tracks that can be jumped per second, then the time τ_1 taken for alternative 1 is given by

$$\tau_1 = \frac{(b_1 - 1)}{rew} + \frac{\mathrm{abs}(t_1 - t_2)}{trkspeed} + \frac{(b_2 - 1)}{ff}$$

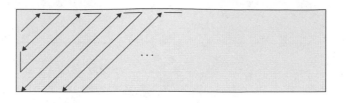

FIGURE

12.3   Traversal of a helical tape recording

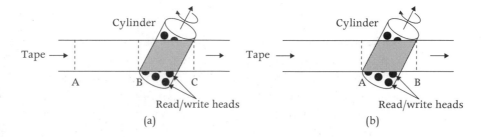

FIGURE

12.4   Relative motion of tape vs. cylinder: (a) reading of tape by read heads before
movement; (b) reading of tape by read heads after tape movement and cylinder
rotation

Likewise, the time τ_2 required for alternative 2 is given by

$$\tau_2 = \frac{(nblock - b_1)}{rew} + \frac{abs(t_1 - t_2)}{trkspeed} + \frac{(nblock - b_2)}{ff}$$

Thus, the minimal time needed to reposition the head to block b_2 of track t_2,
given that the head is currently positioned at block b_1 of track t_1, is

$$\tau = min(\tau_1, \tau_2)$$

*Note that the above calculations change when jumps over multiple tracks are not
allowed.*

12.1.2   Helical Tape Recording

Unlike a serpentine tape recording, in a helical tape recording, the tracks are
"diagonal" tracks, as shown in Figure 12.3, because the tape winds around a
cylinder in a spiral fashion. Read/write heads are embedded in the surface
of the cylinder, as shown in Figure 12.4. The axis across which the cylinder
rotates is somewhat tilted, relative to the tape itself. Thus, as the heads pass the

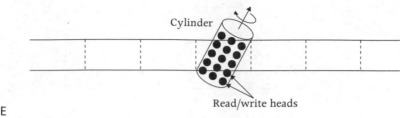

FIGURE

12.5   Linear rendering of tape

linear movement of the tape, different parts of the tape, corresponding to the diagonal tracks shown in Figure 12.4, are read.

Figure 12.4 shows two different snapshots of what happens. In Figure 12.4(a), the shaded region shows which part of the tape (i.e., the shaded part of the sector demarcated by B and C) is being read. Each read head on the surface of the cylinder underneath the shaded region reads the appropriate block of the tape. Notice that the region read looks exactly like a rectangular slice of the tape shown in Figure 12.3.

A few units of time later, two things happen: the tape has rolled to the right somewhat, and the cylinder has rotated somewhat (in a clockwise direction). Figure 12.4(b) shows the new situation. It resembles exactly what we saw before except that the portion of the tape read in Figure 12.4(a) has now moved to the right, and a new portion of the tape (i.e., the shaded part of the sector demarcated by A and B) is being read.

Thus, unlike a serpentine tape drive that, at any given point in time, reads one block, a helical tape drive reads k blocks, where k is the total number of read heads on the surface of the cylinder that may concurrently impinge on the surface of the tape. In effect, helical tapes allow parallel reads through the existence of multiple read heads. We can model this behavior as follows. Suppose we linearly "stretch out" our tape as shown in Figure 12.5. In effect, a helical tape drive "horizontally" moves the rectangular regions of Figure 12.5 from left to right. The speed at which this move occurs depends upon the rotation speed of the cylinder. At any given time, this window concurrently reads all the tape blocks within that window using the read heads on the cylinder surface.

12.1.3   Handling "Bad" Sectors

As anyone who has ever played audiotapes is aware, the quality of recording of a magnetic tape diminishes with prolonged contact. The older the tape, the more blocks on the tape that are damaged.

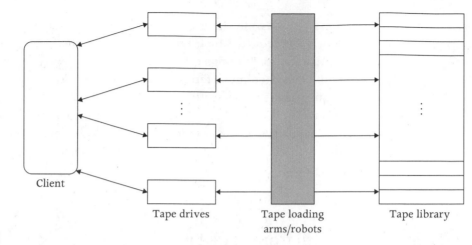

Client

Tape drives

Tape loading
arms/robots

Tape library

FIGURE

12.6   Architecture of a robotic tape library

A two-step procedure is followed when we are writing a block: first we write it, and then we immediately read it back. If the result of reading back is the same as what was written (this test may be efficiently computed with a checksum operation), then the block is okay; otherwise there is a problem. If there is a problem, then we add this block to a list of bad blocks and try to rewrite the information onto the next block. Of course, when reading the tape, the list of bad blocks must be taken into account.

12.2   Robotic Tape Libraries

In large-scale multimedia applications, such as the Sample Multimedia Scenario, most data is likely to be stored on inexpensive storage devices such as tape. For example, police departments around the world may create massive archives of surveillance videos documenting all video surveillance conducted over the years. Such videos may not be frequently used; yet, when needed, they must be readily and easily accessible. Tapes constitute a cheap but reliable method of storing such data.

However, in practice, such a large body of data will be stored not on one tape, but hundreds, or thousands, or perhaps even millions of such tapes. Thus, it is important that we be able to organize these tapes into a well-defined tape *library*.

Figure 12.6 provides a simple architecture for the creation and storage of massive tape libraries. In these libraries, the physical tapes are accessible to a robot arm. Think of the tape library as a huge shelf, and a robot arm as something that can pick things off the shelf. Once a tape is picked up by the robot arm, it is inserted into a tape drive, which may then play the tape, using the techniques described in Sections 12.1.1 and 12.1.2.

Note that the relative cost of obtaining the tape from the "shelf" and loading it into a tape drive is a very expensive, time-consuming operation. Thus, minimizing such accesses is a key requirement of tape-based storage and retrieval algorithms.

12.3   Retrieval from Tape Libraries

Having described tapes and robotic tape libraries briefly, we are now in a position to describe algorithms to schedule the retrieval of tapes and to display continuous media data stored on tapes.

For now, suppose that we have a set $td_1, \ldots, td_r$ of tape drives, but only one robot arm. When a client C requests a tape, the following steps are performed, once the robot arm is available to service the request: First, we must check if there is a free drive into which the robot can insert the desired tape. If not, we must wait till a drive becomes available. Once a drive is available, we rewind the tape currently in the drive, eject it, return it to its correct location in the tape library, pick up the requested tape, insert it into the tape drive, and then let the tape drive access the desired blocks for the client. The following algorithm, adapted from Golubchik, Muntz, and Watson [75], explains this process formally:

Algorithm 12.2
```
   Tape_retrieve(tape_id,Set_of_drives)
indrive = false;
if all drives in Set_of_drives are busy then
   { wait for time δ;
   Call Tape_retrieve(tape_id,Set_of_drives) again
   };
```

```
    else
    {
        { If there is a free tape drive with tape
            tape_id in it, then set TD to this tape drive; and
            set indrive to true; else set TD to any free tape drive
        };
        if (¬ indrive) then
    {
        if there is a tape τ in TD then
        { rewind τ;
          eject τ;
          pick up τ with the robot arm;
          return τ to the tape library;
        };
        Pick up the requested tape, tape_id;
        Insert tape_id into TD;
    };
    };
Fast-forward tape_id to the desired starting block in drive TD;
Play back requested blocks.
end
```

Let's consider a simple example where we have a tape library consisting of 100 tapes, $tape_1, \ldots, tape_{100}$, but only one robot arm, and two tape drives. Now suppose that the following sequence of events occurs:

1. Client C_1 requests tape 50.

2. Client C_2 requests tape 65.

3. Client C_3 requests tape 70.

4. Client C_2 completes viewing tape 65.

5. Client C_1 completes viewing tape 50.

6. Client C_4 requests tape 50.

Let's examine what happens at each stage:

1. *Client C_1 requests tape 50*. Since both tape drives are free, the robot arm obtains tape 50 from the library, inserts it into drive td_1, which then proceeds to deliver the required blocks to the client.

2. *Client C_2 requests tape 65.* Since tape drive td_2 is free, the robot arm obtains tape 65 from the library, inserts it into drive td_2, which then proceeds to deliver the required blocks to the client.

3. *Client C_3 requests tape 70.* Because both tape drives are currently busy, client C_3 must wait until one of the clients releases the resource (tape drive).

4. *Client C_2 completes viewing tape 65.* At this stage, client C_2 releases the tape drive td_2 for use by other clients. Note that tape 65 is still in drive td_2.

   Now the preceding request for tape 70 by client C_3 may be satisfied as follows. Tape drive td_2 is assigned to client C_3. But tape 65 is still in the drive. Hence, tape 65 is rewound first, and then ejected. The robot arm picks it up from tape drive td_2 and returns tape 65 to the tape library. From there, it retrieves tape 70 and inserts it into drive td_2 (note that tape 70 is already rewound).

5. *Client C_1 completes viewing tape 50.* At this stage, client C_1 releases the tape drive td_1 for use by other clients. Note that tape 50 is still in drive td_1.

6. *Client C_4 requests tape 50.* At this stage, tape drive td_1 is available and it contains tape 50, which is the tape being requested by client C_4. Hence, we may immediately assign tape drive td_1 to service the needs of client C_4.

12.4   Striping

We have already examined the concept of striping when we discussed RAID disk arrays. Just as data can be striped across disk arrays, data can also be striped across tapes.

Suppose we consider a media object o (for example, o could be a movie). When we decide to stripe object o across a set of tapes, we must make two other decisions:

- *Granule size:* First, we must divide the object o up into equal-sized granules, which requires that we determine an appropriate granule size. Once a granule size has been determined, the size of the object allows us to deduce the number of granules that the object may be decomposed into. The granule size should not be so large that it is infeasible to read it in one unit of time.

- *Stripe width:* Next, we must determine how many tapes the object o will be striped across. When determining stripe width, we notice that the larger

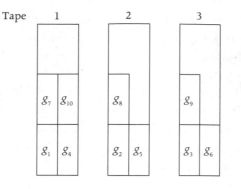

FIGURE

12.7   Granules in striped tape systems

the stripe width, the larger the effective bandwidth available for the retrieval request at hand. However, in multiclient environments, this means that other clients may have fewer resources.

Figure 12.7 shows a simple media object o of 200 MB, with granule size equal to 20 MB, and stripe width equal to 3. This means that object o is split up into 10 granules, each of size 20 MB. Suppose these granules are called $g_1, \ldots, g_{10}$, where g_i represents the block of size 20 MB starting at location $addr(o)+(i-1)\times 20$ where $addr(o)$ represents the start location of object o.

Suppose now that we consider a striped architecture. In this case, we must store a simple table (which we will henceforth refer to as S_Table, for "stripe table") that associates, with each object o, its size, its granule size, its stripe width, and the set of tapes on which it is stored. For example, the table below says that object o_1 has size 200 MB, granule size 40, stripe width 3, and that the data is stored on tapes $t_1, t_2,$ and t_3. This means that megabytes 1–40 and 121–160 are stored on tape t_1, 41–80 and 161–200 are stored on tape t_2, and 81–120 are stored on tape t_3.

Object	Size	Granule size	Stripe width	List of tapes
o_1	200	40	3	t_1, t_2, t_3
o_1	200	40	3	t_4, t_5, t_6
o_2	100	25	3	t_1, t_2, t_3
o_2	100	20	3	t_4, t_5, t_6
$\vdots$	$\vdots$	$\vdots$	$\vdots$	$\vdots$

Note that two different records can have the same object associated with them (indicating replication of the object). For the sake of simplicity, in this case, we require that the set of tapes associated with the two records be disjoint. This assumption can easily be removed.

Let us now examine how our retrieval algorithm (which applies to the case where we have one robot arm) must be modified when we have a striped layout of data, and a client requests that we fetch a given media object. The following algorithm is an extension (to handle replication) of an algorithm developed originally by Golubchik, Muntz, and Watson [75].

Algorithm 12.3

```
    Striped_tape_retrieve(obj)
SW = S_Table.Stripe_width(obj);
Tapes_avail = {tape | t is not currently being used};
Tape_sets_needed= {S_Table.List | S_Table.Object = obj};
while (∀ℓ ∈ Tape_sets_needed) ℓ ⊄ Tapes_avail do wait;
Sel_list = ℓ for some ℓ ∈Tape_sets_needed such that
        ℓ ⊆ Tapes_avail;
while SW drives are not available do wait;
Let FTD = the set of all free tape drives;
    while FTD ≠ ∅ do
    {
        while ℓ ≠ ∅ do
            { select tapeᵢ ∈ ℓ; ℓ = ℓ − {tapeᵢ};
            if there is a tape drive in FTD with tape
            ℓᵢ in it, then set tdᵢ to this tape drive,
            set indrive to true, and set FTD = FTD − {tdᵢ};
            };
    if (¬ indrive) then
    {
        select any tape drive tdᵢ ∈ FTD;
        if there is a tape τ in tdᵢ then
        { rewind τ;
            eject τ;
            pick up τ with the robot arm;
            return τ to the tape library;
        };
```

```
        Pick up the requested tape, t_i:
    Insert t_i into td_i;
    FTD = FTD - {td_i};
};
Fast forward tape_id to the desired starting block;
Play back requested blocks.
    }
end
```

Note that, in this algorithm, the variable ℓ is instantiated to *sets* of tapes, not individual tapes.

To see how this algorithm works, let's consider a simple example where we have one robotic arm; a library of 100 tapes, $t_1, \ldots, t_{100}$; and a collection of objects partially described by the following incomplete table:

Object	Size	Granule size	Stripe width	List of tapes
o_1	200	40	3	t_1, t_2, t_3
o_1	200	40	3	t_4, t_5, t_6
o_2	100	25	3	t_1, t_2, t_3
o_2	100	20	3	t_4, t_5, t_6
o_3	125	25	2	t_5, t_6
$\vdots$	$\vdots$	$\vdots$	$\vdots$	$\vdots$

Suppose we have six tape drives, td_1, td_2, td_3, td_4, td_5, and td_6, and the following events occur in the order listed below:

1. Client C_1 requests object o_1.

2. Client C_2 requests object o_2.

3. Client C_3 requests object o_3.

4. Client C_2 completes processing and releases resources.

The above events are handled in the following way:

1. *Client C_1 requests object o_1.* At this stage, all tape drives are free. Client C_1 needs three drives, so these are assigned to the client. The robot arm fetches tapes t_1, t_2, and t_3 and inserts them into the tape drives. The desired data is then read from these tapes.

2. *Client C_2 requests object o_2.* Client C_2 needs three tape drives. Thus, client C_2 is assigned tape drives td_4, td_5, and td_6, and his service needs are met in the same manner as above by loading tapes t_4, t_5, and t_6 into the above drives.

3. *Client C_3 requests object o_3.* Client C_3 needs two tape drives. Since two tape drives are unavailable, client C_3 is placed in a queue.

4. *Client C_2 completes processing and releases resources.* At this stage, tape drive td_4 contains tape t_4, tape drive td_5 contains tape t_5, and tape drive td_6 contains t_6. These tapes continue to stay in these drives when client C_2 relinquishes control of tape drives td_4, td_5, and td_6.

   Client C_3 is currently in the queue and needs two tape drives. In this case, tape drives td_5 and td_6 already contain the tapes t_5 and t_6 needed by client C_3. Hence, these two drives may be assigned to client C_3 and tape drive td_4 is free.

Note that the above algorithm can be optimized and improved in many possible ways:

1. The algorithm can be generalized to allow for the availability of N robotic arms, instead of just one.

2. The current algorithm allows for nondeterministic choice in assigning drives to clients. Any available drive can be assigned to a client. However, if we know that a drive contains a tape that the client needs, then the algorithm can (and should) be easily modified to take advantage of this extra knowledge.

3. Multiple queueing strategies can be used. Above, we have assumed a simple FIFO queue. However, this could lead to a situation where client A wants three drives, but only two are available. Later, client B joins the queue, but only needs two drives. In some applications, it may make sense to assign the two available drives to client B even though this means that client B has jumped ahead in the queue. However, this must be done with caution to ensure that no client is starved.

4. It is possible that robotic arm movement can be minimized by allowing it to bring back up to K tapes at a time (for some fixed K). In this case, methods to schedule such accesses are vitally needed.

5. In the above algorithm, some waiting needs to be done until we find an ℓ such that $\ell \subseteq$ *Tapes_avail*. However, it may be possible, using our knowledge of stripe width and granule sizes, to mix and match across multiple records in the *S_Table*. For example, consider the following very simple table:

Object	Size	Granule size	Stripe width	List of tapes
o_1	100	25	4	t_1, t_2, t_3, t_4
o_1	100	25	4	t_5, t_6, t_7, t_8

If tape t_1 and t_6 are busy, then the above algorithm will not consider the possibility of loading tapes t_5, t_2, t_3, and t_4, all of which contain the required data. It is easy to extend the algorithm to handle this case.

12.5   Selected Commercial Systems

To give you a quick idea of the state of commercially available tape systems, we will present systems specifications of some selected systems.

Storage Dimensions provides a whole range of tape systems; in particular, their SuperFlex tape array system can have a seven-bay, 168-GB capacity. Likewise, their MegaFlex four-bay system can have a capacity of up to 192 GB. This tape array, when appropriately configured, can have transfer rates of as much as 20 MB/second. We were not able to determine whether this assumed striping across drives or not.

Transitional Technology's tape systems all provide up to 40 GB of storage capacity. Their single-drive systems have capacities ranging from 7–14 GB to 20–40 GB, with transfer rates of anywhere from 0.5–1 MB/second to 3–6 MB/second. These drives may also be configured as dual-drive systems. IBM's MAGSTAR tape systems also have capacities ranging as high as 40 GB.

Information about commercially available tape drives may be obtained from a variety of sources. Detailed specifications on tape drives offered by Qualstar may be obtained from *http://www.qualstar.com*. For useful information on a variety of storage devices (not just tapes) offered by Sony, see *http://www.sony.com/products/storage*. Detailed information on a wide variety of tape storage devices offered by Exabyte is available at *http://www.exabyte.com*. Excellent information on storage solutions offered by StorageTek is available at *http://www.storagetek.com*. Other vendors of tape storage devices, such as IBM's (*http://www.storage.ibm.com/storage/hardsoft/ menu.htm*) and Quantum's DLT range of tape storage devices (*http://www.quantum.com/products/dlt/*), have easily accessible Web pages.

Other interesting Web sites that contain information relevant to tape-based storage include *http://alumni.caltech.edu/~rdv/comp-arch-storage/ FAQ-1.10.html* and *http://www.minet.uni-jena.de/~stoerl/storage.html*.

12.6   Bibliographic Notes

There has been a good deal of research in the area of tape-based storage systems. Carey, Haas, and Livny [42] have shown how relational databases may be stored on tapes. This approach does not, however, apply to continuous media data, though it provides a valuable first step.

Hillyer and Silberschatz have developed a comprehensive model of the performance of serpentine tape drives [91] as well as scheduling techniques for tertiary storage access [92]. They have also compiled a survey of storage systems [93]. The Strata project at Lucent Technologies, based on their work, concentrates exclusively on tertiary storage systems (further information on it may be obtained from *http://www.bell-labs.com/project/strata/*).

Drapeau and Katz [55, 56] were the first to develop the concept of a striped tape array, carrying over the previous work of Katz and his colleagues on disk arrays [158]. They provide comprehensive overviews of commercial hardware products and provide elegant characterizations of their performance.

Golubchik, Muntz, and Watson [75] have taken this one step further by providing a formal, queueing theoretic model of striped tape arrays. The algorithms `Tape_retrieve` and `Striped_tape_retrieve` given in this chapter build upon their approach in a fairly straightforward way.

12.7   Exercises and Projects

1. In Section 12.1.1, we derived an expression specifying the time taken for a read head to be repositioned over block b_2 of track t_2, given that it is currently positioned over block b_1 of track t_1. The derivation in Section 12.1.1 assumes multiple tracks may be jumped. However, many tape systems do not allow this. Using the same notation as in Section 12.1.1, obtain a formula for the situation where no jumps are allowed; i.e., where every track between tracks t_1 and t_2 must be traversed as well.

2. Write, in pseudocode, an algorithm that retrieves a contiguous segment of good (i.e., noncorrupted) blocks from a serpentine tape drive. Your algorithm should extend the `Tape_retrieve` algorithm described in this chapter.

3. Consider the discussion of helical tape drives in Section 12.1.2, and suppose the "shaded window" of Figures 12.4(a) and 12.4(b) contains k read heads, and this window is "moving" to the right at w mm/second. Let ℓ be the length of this window. In one unit of time, how many blocks will be read altogether?

4. The algorithm `Striped_tape_retrieve` assumes that only one robot arm is available for the retrieval of tapes from the tape archive and for loading/removing tapes from the drives. Write, in pseudocode, an algorithm called `N_Arm_Striped_tape_retrieve` that performs the same task, but instead of just one arm, we have N arms available for retrieval.

5. Consider a situation where k tapes, $t_1, \ldots, t_k$, are to be retrieved from the tape library, and we have r robotic arms, each of which can carry up to w tapes at a time. A plan for accomplishing this task is a mapping σ from $(\mathbf{N} \times \{1, \ldots, r\})$ to $\{t_1, \ldots, t_k\}$ such that
   - for all $i \geq 1$ and all $1 \leq h \leq r$, $\sigma(i, h)$ has at most w elements in it,
   - $\bigcup_{i \geq 1} \bigcup_{h=1}^{r} \sigma(i, h) = \{t_1, \ldots, t_k\}$,
   - $(\forall h) 1 \leq h \leq r \;\&\; i \neq j \Rightarrow \sigma(i, h) \cap \sigma(j, h) = \emptyset$,
   - $(\forall i \geq 1)(\forall 1 \leq h, h' \leq r) h \neq h' \Rightarrow \sigma(i, h) \cap \sigma(i, h') = \emptyset$, and
   - for all $i \geq 1$ and all $1 \leq h \leq r$, $\sigma(i, h)$ is a linearly ordered set, $t_{\alpha(1)}, \ldots, t_{\alpha(s)}$ ($s \leq w$).

   The cost of this sequence, denoted $\chi_{i,h}$, is defined to be

$$\sum_{z=1}^{s-1} \text{abs}(\alpha(z) - \alpha(z + 1))$$

The cost of a plan, σ, is defined to be

$$\text{cost}(\sigma) = \sum_{i \geq 1} \sum_{j=1}^{r} \chi_{i,j}$$

Write, in pseudocode, an algorithm that will compute a least-cost plan for this situation.

6. As a project, write, in pseudocode, two functions that model the read/write behavior of a serpentine tape with bad blocks:

(a) `write_tape(t,b)`: This operation writes block b of track t and either returns "yes" (write succeeded) or "no" (the block is bad). This procedure is also responsible for updating a bad block list.

(b) `read_next_block(t,b)`: This function reads the next good block after block b on track t.

You may use a random number generator to generate bad blocks, but the generator should be biased to ensure that over 90% of the blocks are good.

IV

CREATING AND DELIVERING NETWORKED MULTIMEDIA PRESENTATIONS

Creating Distributed Multimedia Presentations

What new concepts will you learn in this chapter?
You will learn that a multimedia presentation consists of a set of media objects, and a set of spatial and temporal constraints that govern the presentation of these objects. You will learn what form these constraints take, and how they can be solved efficiently to create something called a *presentation plan*.

What new abstractions are needed to realize these concepts?
The new abstraction we will introduce in this chapter is a form of arithmetic linear constraints called *difference constraints*. It will turn out that for the purposes of multimedia presentations, difference constraints are more than enough to express everything we are likely to encounter.

What new techniques are needed to implement these abstractions?
You will learn about a classic algorithm (by Bellman and Ford) for solving sets of difference constraints. This will, in particular, show how presentation plans may be efficiently generated.

What technological features support these implementation methods?
You will receive a quick overview of existing multimedia authoring and presentation environments available on the commercial market.

When creating a multimedia presentation, three basic questions must be answered:

- *What* objects should be included in the presentation?

- *When* should these objects be presented to the user?

- *Where* should the objects appear on the screen?

These three questions can only be answered by the individual who creates the presentation (called the *author* of the presentation). Once the above questions have been answered by the author, a *presentation schedule* can be created that will specify when and where someone viewing the presentation will actually see the objects constituting the presentation.

Informally speaking, the answers to the *when* and *where* questions are most naturally expressed through the use of constraints. Different solutions to the *when* constraints yield different presentation schedules.

Clearly, the choice of a constraint language within which such constraints are expressed plays a central role in the *types* of temporal/spatial relationships that can be expressed, and the *efficiency* with which such constraints can be solved.

Initial efforts in the multimedia presentation community largely assumed that most constraints were "hard" equality constraints. Such constraints included, for instance, statements of the form "The presentation of objects 1 and 2 must start at the same time, and the termination of objects 2 and 3 must occur at the same time. Object 3 must start at the time object 1 ends." Such constraints are relatively easy to solve. However, in practice, though these constraints are often easy to solve, they offer very little flexibility in actually scheduling the retrieval of the media objects from local/remote servers. Such flexibility is very helpful because in distributed multimedia applications, a constant interaction with remote servers and the network service provider is critically needed, and the resources that these servers offer vary with time and are usually rather unpredictable.

As a consequence, later efforts, building on the initial work on hard constraints, focused on widening the class of constraints to handle more flexible inequality constraints. Such constraints allow presentation authors to express broader temporal relationships, such as "The presentation of objects 1 and 2 must start at the same time, and the termination of object 2 must occur at least 5 time units before the termination of object 1." It is apparent that, because the pair of inequalities $a \leq b$ and $b \leq a$ are jointly equivalent to the equality

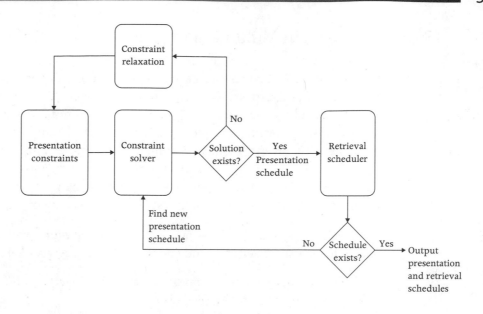

FIGURE

13.1   Interaction between presentation and retrieval schedules

$a = b$, such flexible constraints strictly extend the expressive power of the hard constraint language. This is what we will study in this chapter.

Once a presentation schedule has been created, we need to create a *retrieval schedule* that ensures that the resources needed to deliver the presentation to the client are in fact available. Such resources may include availability (load and buffer) of remote data servers, availability of bandwidth from the network, and availability of buffer space at the client. We will study this problem in detail in Chapter 14.

Figure 13.1 shows the cycle of how presentation schedules and retrieval schedules interact. The presentation author specifies constraints that are fed to a constraint solver, which solves the constraints (if possible) or explains why the constraints are unsolvable and suggests ways of relaxing the constraints. A solution is a presentation schedule. Any solution may be picked nondeterministically with a view to creating a retrieval schedule for it. If this is possible, then we need go no further. If no retrieval schedule can be created for a specified presentation schedule, then we must pick another presentation schedule. This cycle is continued till a presentation schedule is found that has a corresponding retrieval schedule.

13.1 Objects in Multimedia Presentations

Whenever we create a multimedia presentation, we must specify a set of objects that will constitute the "data" to be presented. For example, consider the Sample Multimedia Scenario. Suppose a police officer wishes to come into his office every morning and receive a multimedia presentation reflecting the status of certain investigations in which he has an interest. Such a status report might, for example, include surveillance photos taken during the last 24 hours, as well as recent bank transactions and, perhaps, some video imagery.

Figure 13.2 shows a very small presentation consisting of four objects:

- Objects o_1 (a photo) and o_2 (a bank transaction summary) are displayed simultaneously. They start and end together and are visible for 10 seconds.

- Object o_3 (another photo) appears as soon as objects o_1 and o_2 disappear, and stays on screen for 10 seconds as well.

- Object o_4 (a video) appears 5 seconds after object o_2 disappears, and it must disappear within 2–4 seconds after object o_3 disappears.

Note, however, that in the above example, the identity of the objects involved may change with time. For example, object o_2's identity will, in all likelihood, change with time, as new bank transactions occur and get flagged as being suspicious.

Suppose $\mathcal{O}$ is a set whose elements are objects. Without loss of generality, we will assume that each object in $\mathcal{O}$ can be rendered on a computational output device. For example, the contents of $\mathcal{O}$ may include all images, files, and documents on the World Wide Web. Notice that the set $\mathcal{O}$ may not be physically constructed! However, at any given point in time, this set certainly exists and is well defined! In addition, $\mathcal{O}$ could include a user's local file system.

Definition 13.1 A *virtual object*, vo, is a *set of triples* $(O_1, Q_1, C_1), \ldots,$ (O_k, Q_k, C_k) where

1. $C_1, \ldots, C_k$ are conditions that are mutually exclusive;

2. $Q_1, \ldots, Q_k$ are queries, and

3. $O_1, \ldots, O_k$ are objects.

Generally speaking, the conditions C_i may, in theory, be in any logical language, and the queries Q_i may, in theory, be in any query language. However,

o_1

Name	Type	Other party	Amount
o_2 John Smith	deposit	Denis Dopeman	15000.00
Denis Dopeman	deposit	Jane Shady	14000.00
Bill Bosco	deposit	John Smith	19000.00

o_3

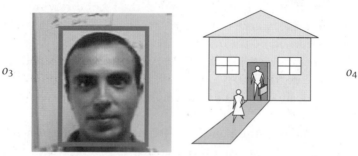

o_4

FIGURE

13.2   An example presentation

to fix intuitions, we will generally assume that queries are in SQL syntax, and conditions are expressed in standard predicate logic. Let's see how this definition can be used to specify different kinds of virtual objects.

Consider a virtual object vo_1 that we are yet to specify. We would like vo_1 to be the latest weather map of Bosnia if the user making the request has clearance level "secret." Otherwise, we want it to show a day-old map. This can be expressed by the set of two triples, $vo_1 = \{(O_1, Q_1, C_1), (O_2, Q_2, C_2)\}$, where the notation $\succeq$ denotes a partial ordering on clearance levels.

Object	Query	Condition
any O_1	SELECT map FROM map_db WHERE place=bosnia AND date = today	clearance $\succeq$ secret
all O_2	SELECT map FROM map_db WHERE place=bosnia AND date = today $-$ 1	clearance $\not\succeq$ secret

The intuitive reading of the first row in the above table is the following: "If the user's clearance is greater than or equal to *secret*, then return some object O_1 in the result of the query." Likewise, the second row in the above table says: "If the user's clearance is not greater than or equal to the secret level, return all objects returned by the query."

In general, the triple (O_i, Q_i, C_i) is interpreted as the following: If the condition C_i is true, then O_i is any (or all) object(s) in the result of evaluating query Q_i. If Q_i's evaluation leads to an empty table, then O_i is a special object denoted null.

Now consider the police investigator and the multimedia presentation he wishes to see. It may well turn out that for every *new* person who meets with Denis Dopeman, he wishes to see the bank records of this person (if they are available). Of course, if they are not available, then this object cannot be shown (since no such bank records are known to exist). The situation may be modeled by declaring the object to be shown as a virtual object and by setting it to a null object in case no such object exists. This can be expressed by the set consisting of just one triple, $\{(O_1, Q_1, C_1)\}$, where

Object	Query	Condition
all O_1	SELECT B.bankrecord FROM bank B, surveillance S WHERE S.person1 = Denis Dopeman AND B.name=S.person2 AND S.date=today AND NOT EXISTS (SELECT S'.date FROM surveillance S' WHERE S'.name = S.person2 AND S'.date < today.)	true

Note that if the result of the query is empty, then O_1 is automatically set to `null` by the semantics specified above.

Finally, notice that the definition of a virtual object allows users, if they so desire, to set their objects to be "instantiated." This can be accomplished by merely declaring a virtual object to be the triple $\{(O, Q, C)\}$, where

Object	Query	Condition
O	$O =$ `file1.gif`	true

Good authoring environments, such as Macromedia Director and Asymetrix Toolbook, allow access to external databases that are ODBC compatible. ODBC (Open Database Connectivity) is a standard interface through which different databases may be uniformly queried. However, the concept of a virtual object was proposed for the first time by Candan and Subrahmanian [38] and implemented cleanly within their CHIMP system [36]. CHIMP, in addition to allowing multiple heterogeneous databases to be accessed through its associated query language, also allows World Wide Web data to be accessed.

13.2 Specifying Multimedia Documents with Temporal Constraints

In this section, we will assume that the presentation author has selected a set, $VO = \{vo_1, \ldots, vo_k\}$, of virtual objects that are to be included in the presentation.

After the objects to be included in a presentation are determined, the author must specify *when* these objects are to be presented. This is best expressed through a set of *presentation constraints* that are expressed in a *constraint language*. In the rest of this section, we will quickly explain what this constraint language is.

Constraint language associated with $VO = \{vo_1, \ldots, vo_k\}$:

1. *Constants:* Every integer (positive and negative) is a constant.

2. *Variables:* Associated with each vo_i are two integer variables, s_i (denoting the "start" of virtual object vo_i) and e_i (denoting the "end" of virtual object vo_i).

3. *Elementary terms:* Elementary terms are defined inductively as follows:

    (a) Every constant is an elementary term.

    (b) Every variable is an elementary term.

4. *Difference constraint:* If t_1 and t_2 are elementary terms, and c is a constant, then

$$t_1 - t_2 \leq c$$

is a difference constraint.

Using the above definition, it is easy to see that $(-3)e_2$ is not an elementary term. Likewise, $(e - 1)$ is not an elementary term either.

The following are all examples of difference constraints:

1. $e_1 - s_1 \leq 10$.
   This constraint says that object vo_1 must end within 10 time units after the time its presentation starts.

2. $s_2 - e_1 \leq 0; e_1 - s_2 \leq 0$.
   These two constraints jointly state that virtual object vo_2's presentation starts as soon as virtual object vo_1's presentation ends.

3. $s_2 - e_1 \leq 3$.
   This constraint says that virtual object vo_2's presentation starts within 3 time units of the end of the presentation of virtual object vo_1.

As usual, we will use the shorthand $t_1 - t_2 = c$ to denote the pair of difference constraints:

$$t_1 - t_2 \leq c$$
$$t_2 - t_1 \leq -c$$

Returning to the example presentation in Figure 13.2, we may encode the temporal requirements that we had previously stated in English, as difference constraints, as follows:

- Objects o_1 (a photo) and o_2 (a bank transaction summary) are displayed simultaneously. This can be expressed by the difference constraints:

$$s_1 - s_2 = 0$$
$$e_1 - e_2 = 0$$

- Object o_3 (another photo) appears as soon as objects o_1 and o_2 disappear, and stays on screen for 10 seconds as well. This can be encoded as three constraints:

$$s_3 - e_1 = 0$$
$$s_3 - e_2 = 0$$
$$e_3 - s_3 = 10$$

- Object o_4 (a video) appears 5 seconds after object o_2 disappears, and it must disappear within 2–4 seconds after object o_3 disappears. This can be expressed by the following set of difference constraints:

$$s_4 - e_2 = 5$$
$$e_4 - e_3 \leq 4$$
$$e_3 - s_4 \leq -2$$

Definition 13.2 A *temporal presentation* is a pair $TP = (VO, DC)$ where VO is a finite set of virtual objects, and DC is a finite set of difference constraints in the constraint language generated by VO.

Thus, in our example multimedia presentation, our temporal presentation is the pair $TP_{law} = (VO_{law}, DC_{law})$ where $VO_{law} = \{o_1, \ldots, o_4\}$ and DC_{law} is the following set of constraints:

$$s_1 - s_2 = 0$$
$$e_1 - e_2 = 0$$
$$s_3 - e_1 = 0$$
$$s_3 - e_2 = 0$$
$$e_3 - s_3 = 10$$
$$s_4 - e_2 = 5$$
$$e_4 - e_3 \leq 4$$
$$e_3 - e_4 \leq -2$$

Figure 13.3 shows a diagrammatic representation of these constraints.

Definition 13.3 Suppose DC is a set of difference constraints over $VO = \{vo_1, \ldots, vo_n\}$ of virtual objects. A *solution* of DC is an assignment of integers to each of the variables, $s_1, \ldots, s_n, e_1, \ldots, e_n$, which makes all the constraints true.

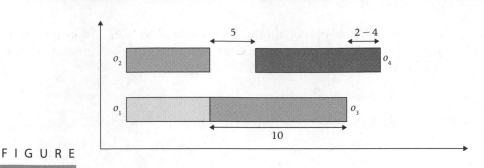

13.3   Constraints associated with TP_{law} example

Note that this definition of solution forces us to only assign integer values to all variables. For example, the set DC_{law} of constraints has infinitely many solutions, some of which are described by the following table:

Solution	s_1	e_1	s_2	e_2	s_3	e_3	s_4	e_4
σ_1	0	10	0	10	10	20	15	22
σ_2	0	10	0	10	10	20	15	23
σ_3	0	10	0	10	10	20	15	24
σ_4	3	10	3	10	10	20	15	22
σ_5	3	10	3	10	10	20	15	23
σ_6	3	10	3	10	10	20	15	24

Definition 13.4 A *temporal presentation* $TP = (VO, DC)$ is *feasible* iff the set, DC, of difference constraints has a solution σ. In this case, σ is said to be a *schedule* for TP.

Definition 13.5 Suppose σ is a schedule for temporal presentation $TP = (VO, DC)$, where $VO = \{vo_1, \ldots, vo_n\}$. The *start* and *end* of σ, denoted $start(\sigma)$ and $end(\sigma)$, are defined to be

$$start(\sigma) = min\{\sigma(s_i) \mid 1 \leq i \leq n\}$$
$$end(\sigma) = max\{\sigma(e_i) \mid 1 \leq i \leq n\}$$

Note that in the above formulation, we are assuming that the constraints $\{s_i - e_i \leq 0 \mid 1 \leq i \leq n\}$ are included in DC.

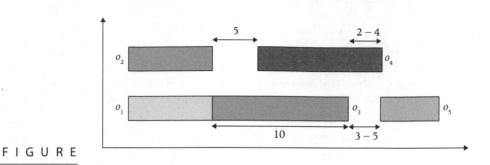

FIGURE

13.4   Constraints associated with TP_{ext} example

In the context of our running TP_{law} example, the start/end times of our six possible presentations are given by the following table:

Solution	Start	End
σ_1	0	22
σ_2	0	23
σ_3	0	24
σ_4	3	22
σ_5	3	23
σ_6	3	24

Suppose now that we were to extend our TP_{law} example to include a new object, o_5, such that the presentation of o_5 starts between 3 and 5 seconds from the time at which o_3 is completed. This causes the following two extra constraints to be added to DC_{law}. Let's use $TP_{ext} = (VO_{ext}, DC_{ext})$ to denote this extended problem, as shown in Figure 13.4. DC_{ext} consists of all difference constraints in DC_{law}, together with two extra constraints:

$$s_5 - e_3 \leq 5$$
$$e_3 - s_5 \leq -3$$

It is easy to see that, like TP_{law}, there are infinitely many schedules for TP_{ext}, three of which we show below:

Solution	s_1	e_1	s_2	e_2	s_3	e_3	s_4	e_4	s_5	e_5
σ_7	0	10	0	10	10	20	15	22	23	30
σ_8	0	10	0	10	10	20	15	22	24	30
σ_9	0	10	0	10	10	20	15	22	23	30

Should a user view a presentation that uses the (correct) schedule σ_8, he would encounter a "gap" because at time instant 23, no object is being presented, according to schedule σ_8. In fact, he would also encounter a gap if σ_7 was used for the presentation. The reason is that the actual passage of time is continuous (while our model of it is discrete) and hence, at any real time instant r such that $22 < r < 23$, no object would be presented to the user. In contrast, this does not occur in the presentation delivered according to schedule σ_9, which is obviously more suitable for presentation to a user. The following definition specifies, formally, what it means for a schedule to be gap-free.

Definition 13.6 Suppose σ is a schedule for temporal presentation $TP = (VO, DC)$, where $VO = \{vo_1, \dots, vo_n\}$. σ is said to be *gap-free* iff for every real number r such that $start(\sigma) \leq r \leq end(\sigma)$, it is the case that there exists a virtual object vo_i such that

$$\sigma(s_i) \leq r \leq \sigma(e_i)$$

As we have already seen, different temporal schedules can start at different times. The person watching a presentation would certainly be happy if the presentation starts as soon as possible from the time he made a request to view the presentation. Thus, some schedules (e.g., σ_1) are better than others (e.g., σ_4) in the sense that they start earlier. The following definitions explain this concept, both for ordinary and for gap-free schedules.

Definition 13.7 Suppose $TP = (VO, DC)$ is feasible. A schedule, σ, for TP is said to be *earliest* iff there is no other schedule σ' for TP such that $start(\sigma') < start(\sigma)$.

Definition 13.8 Suppose $TP = (VO, DC)$ is feasible. A gap-free schedule, σ, for TP is said to be an *earliest gap-free schedule* for TP iff there is no other gap-free schedule σ' for TP such that $start(\sigma') < start(\sigma)$.

In the next section, we will describe detailed algorithms for the generation of earliest schedules, both ordinary and gap-free.

13.3   Efficient Solution of Temporal Presentation Constraints

It is easy to see, by definition, that schedules are just solutions of sets of linear constraints. Techniques to solve systems of linear constraints have been known for over 50 years, through extensive work in the operations research community. Algorithms such as the simplex algorithm [90], Khachian's polynomial time linear programming algorithm [106], as well as Karmarkar's interior point algorithm [104] all form valuable starting points.

However, linear programming attempts to find solutions of linear equations that assign real numbers to the variables occurring in those equations. In other words, the solutions of linear programming may not be schedules because schedules require integers to be assigned to the variables. This problem may be easily handled by using the well-known class of "mixed-integer" programming algorithms—these algorithms build on top of methods for linear programming, such as simplex, interior point methods, and so on, by augmenting them through techniques such as branch and bound and the Gomory cut algorithm [90].

In the context of multimedia systems, Buchanan and Zellweger [31] were the first to examine the use of operations research–based techniques to create presentation schedules. They used the simplex algorithm as the basis of their multimedia presentation system. However, later, Candan, Prabhakaran, and Subrahmanian [36, 37] showed that much more efficient solutions are possible using classical algorithms, such as the Bellman-Ford algorithm [49] instead of simplex. In the rest of this section, we will describe how to use the Bellman-Ford algorithm for solving sets of difference constraints.

13.3.1   The Bellman-Ford Algorithm

The basic idea behind the Bellman-Ford algorithm is that we can take a set, DC, of difference constraints, and convert it, in linear time, to a weighted graph, $\mathcal{G}_{DC}$. The nodes in this graph correspond to the variables s_i and e_i associated with the virtual objects in our presentation. A schedule is obtained very simply as follows:

- For each $1 \leq i \leq n$ do:

    - Find the shortest path in $\mathcal{G}_{DC}$ from a designated start node to node s_i. Let c_i be the sum of the edges on this path. If no such path exists, then DC is unsolvable. Halt with failure.
    - Find the shortest path in $\mathcal{G}_{DC}$ from a designated start node to node e_i. Let d_i be the sum of the edges on this path. If no such path exists, then DC is unsolvable. Halt with failure.

■ Return the set of equations

$$\{s_i = c_i \mid 1 \le i \le n\} \cup \{e_i = d_i \mid 1 \le i \le n\}$$

This is a schedule.

The above pseudoalgorithm provides a very general, high-level description of the working of the Bellman-Ford algorithm. However, in order to explain its workings, we need to specify three things:

■ What is the definition of $\mathcal{G}_{DC}$?

■ What is the definition of a shortest path from a designated start node to node N?

■ How can we efficiently compute the above?

In the rest of this section, we will discuss these three issues.

Converting DC to $\mathcal{G}_{DC}$

Suppose DC has variables $\{s_1, \ldots, s_n, e_1, \ldots, e_n\}$. Then $\mathcal{G}_{DC} = (V, E, \omega)$ has, as its set V of vertices, each variable $\{s_1, \ldots, s_n, e_1, \ldots, e_n\}$, together with one distinguished additional vertex called *start*.

The set E of edges of $\mathcal{G}_{DC}$ is defined as follows:

■ If the constraint $(x - y) \le c$ is in DC, then there is an edge from y to x with weight c. In this case, $\omega(y, x) = c$.

■ There is an edge from the start node, *start*, to each s_i and each e_i. This edge has weight 0; that is, $\omega(start, s_i) = 0 = \omega(start, e_i)$.

For example, consider a very simple presentation with two objects, vo_1 and vo_2, having the following set, DC, of presentation constraints:

$$s_1 - e_1 \le -3$$
$$e_1 - s_1 \le 5$$
$$s_2 - e_2 \le -4$$
$$e_2 - s_2 \le 6$$
$$e_1 - s_2 \le 0$$
$$s_2 - e_1 \le 2$$

Figure 13.5 shows the weighted graph, $\mathcal{G}_{DC}$, associated with this set of differ-

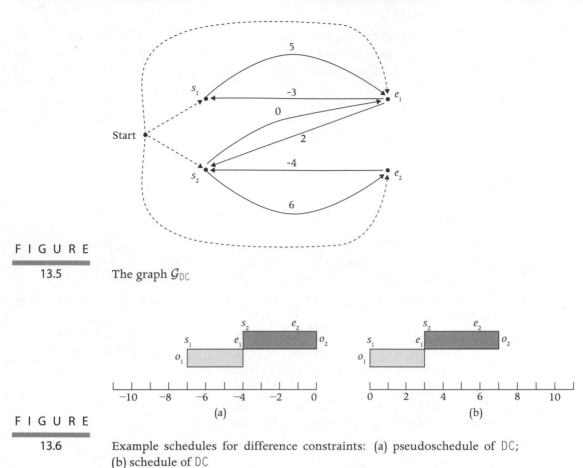

FIGURE

13.5

The graph $\mathcal{G}_{DC}$

FIGURE

13.6

Example schedules for difference constraints: (a) pseudoschedule of DC; (b) schedule of DC

ence constraints.

The following table summarizes the cost of the shortest path from the start node to each node:

Node N	Shortest path from *start* to N	Cost of shortest path
s_1	$start \xrightarrow{0} e_2 \xrightarrow{-4} s_2 \xrightarrow{0} e_1 \xrightarrow{-3} s_1$	-7
e_1	$start \xrightarrow{0} e_2 \xrightarrow{-4} s_2 \xrightarrow{0} e_1$	-4
s_2	$start \xrightarrow{0} e_2 \xrightarrow{-4} s_2$	-4
e_2	$start \xrightarrow{0} e_2$	0

Using the above table, we note that the presentation shown in Figure 13.6(a) satisfies all the constraints in DC. However, it is not a schedule because all variables have been assigned a negative integer. This is easily fixed by a "translation" operation—moving the entire schedule 7 units to the right. Now we obtain a schedule, as shown in Figure 13.6(b). This yields the schedule

Variable	Value
s_1	0
e_1	3
s_2	3
e_2	7

What Is a Shortest Path?

It is easy to see that given any node $N \in \{s_1, \dots, s_n, e_1, \dots, e_n\}$, there is always at least one path between the start node and N—the path of length 0 consisting of the single edge $(start, N)$. Thus, the set of all paths, denoted $\texttt{paths}(N)$, from the start node to N is always nonempty. Let $\texttt{costs}(N) = \{c \mid c$ is the cost of some path from $start$ to $N\}$.

It is also easy to see that there is no "shortest path" from the start node to N iff the set $\texttt{costs}(N)$ is not well founded [87]; that is, it has an infinitely descending chain in it. To see how such chains can arise, consider the following example.

Suppose we consider a simple presentation with two virtual objects, $\texttt{vo}_1$ and $\texttt{vo}_2$, having the following constraints:

$$3 \le e_1 - s_1 \le 7$$
$$4 \le e_2 - s_2 \le 6$$
$$s_1 = s_2$$
$$e_2 - e_1 \ge 5$$

The first constraint says that object $\texttt{vo}_1$ should be presented for 3 to 7 seconds. The second constraint says that object $\texttt{vo}_2$ should be presented for 4 to 6 seconds. The third constraint says that objects $\texttt{vo}_1$ and $\texttt{vo}_2$ should start together, while the fourth constraint says that object o_2 should end at least 5 seconds after object o_1 ends. Of course, this set of constraints has no solution.

The above set of constraints is captured by the following set of difference constraints:

$$e_1 - s_1 \le 7$$
$$s_1 - e_1 \le -3$$
$$e_2 - s_2 \le 6$$

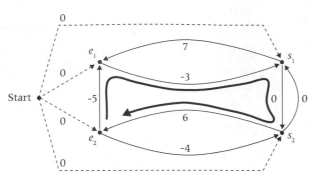

FIGURE

13.7

Example graph with negative cycle

$$s_2 - e_2 \leq -4$$
$$s_1 - s_2 \leq 0$$
$$s_2 - s_1 \leq 0$$
$$e_1 - e_2 \leq -5$$

Figure 13.7 shows the graph associated with this set of difference constraints. Consider now the shortest path from node e_2 to itself. We might be tempted to think that the cost of this path is 0 by considering the empty path (of length 0) from e_2 to itself.

However, this would be incorrect. Consider instead the loop shown in boldface in Figure 13.7. It is apparent that the cost of executing the whole loop is -2. Were we to traverse this loop twice, the cost would be -4. The more we traverse this loop, the smaller is the cost of the path, leading to $\texttt{costs}(e_2)$ being a set whose elements have an infinitely descending sequence.

There are two facts about this graph that are not coincidental. The first is that this graph contains a loop whose edges sum up to a negative integer. The second is that the set of difference constraints that caused this graph to be generated is unsolvable.

As we shall see shortly, these two facts are not accidental! Before proceeding to this, we provide some definitions.

Definition 13.9 Suppose $\mathcal{G} = (V, E, \wp)$ is any weighted graph. A *cycle* in $\mathcal{G}$ is a sequence of nodes $v_1, \ldots, v_k$ such that $v_k = v_1$. For all $1 \leq j < k$, (v_j, v_{j+1}) is an edge in the graph. $v_1, \ldots, v_k$ is said to be a *negative cycle* in graph $\mathcal{G}$ iff $\sum_{j=1}^{k-1} \wp(v_j, v_{j+1})$ is a negative number.

Bellman and Ford established the following beautiful result [49]:

Theorem 13.1 A set DC of difference constraints has no solution iff $\mathcal{G}_{DC}$ has a negative cycle.

Therefore, if we can establish that $\mathcal{G}_{DC}$ has no negative cycles, then we could be certain that DC is solvable.

How Do We Compute Shortest Paths?

The following algorithm shows how we may compute schedules associated with a temporal presentation *TP* by using the Bellman-Ford algorithm. The Bellman-Ford algorithm associates, with each node *N* in $\mathcal{G}_{DC}$, the following two fields:

- Bestval: This specifies the cheapest path from the start node to the node *N* that has been discovered thus far.

- Bestpar: Bestpar(*N*) specifies the immediate predecessor of node *N* along the best path from the start node to node *N* that we have found thus far. In particular, Bestpar(*N*) is a pointer field.

The algorithm we show below uses the notation card(*S*) to denote the cardinality of set *S*.

1. *Initialization:* First, all nodes *N* are initialized so that Bestval(*N*) = ∞ and Bestpar(*N*) = NIL. This step can be encoded through the following subroutine:

Algorithm 13.1
```
    Initialize(V, E);
n = card(V); m = card(E);
for i = 1 to n do
{
    Bestval(vᵢ) = ∞;
    Bestpar(vᵢ) = NIL
}
Bestval(start) = 0;
end
```

---

2. *Refinement:* This step takes two nodes v_i and v_j as input and determines if the shortest path from the start node to v_j is made cheaper by going through v_i.

Intuitively, suppose that at time t the shortest path from $start$ to v_j has cost $\mathtt{Bestval}(v_j)$ and $\mathtt{Bestpar}(v_j)$. Suppose also that there is an edge in the graph from v_i to v_j. Then the following path

$$start \overset{\mathtt{Bestval}(v_i)}{\rightarrow} v_i \overset{\omega(v_i, v_j)}{\rightarrow} v_j$$

is a valid path from $start$ to v_j. In the event that

$$\mathtt{Bestval}(v_i) + \omega(v_i, v_j) < \mathtt{Bestval}(v_j)$$

then this "new" path is better than the best-known existing path to v_j. This step can be encoded through the following subroutine:

Algorithm 13.2

```
    Refine(vᵢ, vⱼ);
new = Bestval(vᵢ) + ω(vᵢ, vⱼ);
if new < Bestval(vⱼ) then
{
    Bestval(vⱼ)=new;
    Bestpar(vⱼ)=vᵢ
}
end
```

---

3. The Bellman-Ford algorithm must traverse all possible paths and vertices to ensure that no edges that could possibly lead to a better path have been omitted from consideration. This main algorithm can now be encoded as follows.

Algorithm 13.3

```
    Bellman_Ford(V, E, ω);
n = card(V); m = card(E);
(* we assume V = {v₁, ..., vₙ} *);
(* we assume E = {(v₁¹, v₁²), ..., (vₘ¹, vₘ²)} *);
Initialize(V, E);
for i = 1 to (n − 1) do
    for j = 1 to m do
        Refine(vⱼ¹, vⱼ²);
    end (* inner for *);
end (* outer for *);
```

```
for j = 1 to m do
    if Bestval(v²ⱼ) > Bestval(v¹ⱼ) + ω(v¹ⱼ, v²ⱼ) then
        Return error and Halt;
end (* for *);
for i = 1 to n do
    Return vᵢ.Name = vᵢ.Bestval.
end (* for *);
end (* algo *)
```

The Bellman-Ford algorithm listed above intuitively works in the following way: first, we make $(n - 1)$ passes over the graph, and in each pass, we consider each edge in the graph and refine the best estimated values for each node. This is what is captured by the first set of nested `for` loops. This takes time $O(V \times E)$. Once we are done with this, we make one final pass to ensure that no negative loops are present. This is done by considering each edge, and making sure that this is indeed the case. This is what the `for` loop toward the end of the algorithm does.

To see how the Bellman-Ford algorithm works, consider the set of constraints associated with the constraint graph in Figure 13.5. The constraint graph contains five vertices, including the start vertex. The total number of edges in this graph is 10. The algorithm has three phases—initialization, execution of the initial nested `for` loops, and finally, execution of the closing `for` loop. We will use tables to depict the values assigned to the `Bestpar` and `Bestval` fields.

- *Initialization:* After initialization, the `Bestpar` and `Bestval` fields of the vertices look as follows:

Vertex	Bestval	Bestpar
s_1	∞	null
e_1	∞	null
s_2	∞	null
e_2	∞	null

- *Execution of nested `for` loops:* The outer `for` loop toward the beginning of the Bellman-Ford algorithm is executed four times. Each execution invokes the inner `for` loop ten times. Below, we show the state of the table after the execution of each of the four outer `for` loop invocations. When constructing these tables, we assume that the order in which the edges of the graph are enumerated is

$$(start, s_1), (e_1, s_1), (start, s_2), (e_2, s_2), (e_1, s_2)$$

$$(start, e_1), (s_1, e_1), (s_2, e_1), (start, e_2), (s_2, e_2)$$

Note that the first two pairs reflect edges incident upon s_1, the next three reflect edges incident upon s_2, the next three represent edges incident upon e_1, and the last two reflect edges incident on e_2.

1. After the first execution of the outer `for` loop is completed, the `Bestpar` and `Bestval` fields of the vertices look as follows:

Vertex	Bestval	Bestpar
s_1	0	start
e_1	0	start
s_2	0	start
e_2	0	start

Figure 13.8(a) depicts this situation. The numbers inside the nodes depict the `Bestval` of the node. Each node has a single bold-faced arrow emanating from it—this depicts the `Bestpar` field of that node.

2. After the second execution of the outer `for` loop is completed, the `Bestpar` and `Bestval` fields of the vertices look as follows:

Vertex	Bestval	Bestpar
s_1	-3	e_1
e_1	-4	s_2
s_2	-4	e_2
e_2	0	start

Figure 13.8(b) depicts this situation.

3. After the third execution of the outer `for` loop is completed, the `Bestpar` and `Bestval` fields of the vertices look as follows:

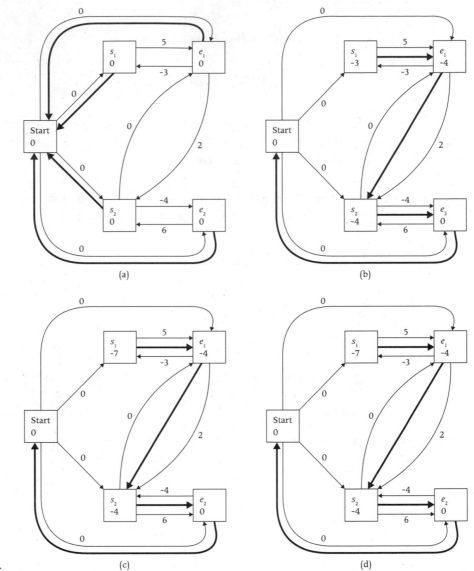

Intermediate steps during execution of Bellman-Ford algorithm: (a) after first iteration of outer for loop; (b) after second iteration of outer for loop; (c) after third iteration of outer for loop; (d) after fourth iteration of outer for loop

Vertex	Bestval	Bestpar
s_1	-7	e_1
e_1	-4	s_2
s_2	-4	e_2
e_2	0	start

Figure 13.8(c) depicts this situation.

4. After the fourth (and final) execution of the outer for loop is completed, the Bestpar and Bestval fields of the vertices remain unchanged.

Vertex	Bestval	Bestpar
s_1	-7	e_1
e_1	-4	s_2
s_2	-4	e_2
e_2	0	start

Figure 13.8(d) depicts this situation.

■ *Closing* for *loop execution:* In this step, we merely check to ensure that there are no negative loops. We do this by examining each node's Bestval field and making sure that there are no cheaper paths than the ones found (if so, it means there is a negative loop). We may do this either by looking at Figure 13.8(d) or the table associated with it.

1. s_1's final Bestval field is -7. Its predecessors in the graph are *start* and e_1. The path from e_1 to s_1 has value $(-4 + -3) = -7$ (adding the path cost, plus the Bestval field of e_1). As $-7 \not< -7$, this is okay.
2. e_1's final Bestval field is -4. e_1's predecessors in the graph are *start*, s_2, and s_1. The value of the path from s_2 to e_1 is $(-4 + 0) = 2 \not< -4$. The same reasoning applies to s_1.
3. s_2's final Bestval field is -4. The path from e_1 to s_2 yields a value of -2, which is not strictly smaller than the Bestval field of s_2. Similarly, the path from e_2 to s_2 yields a value of $(0 + -4 = -4)$, which is not strictly smaller than the Bestval field of s_2. Hence, this is okay.
4. e_2's final Bestval field is 0. Its predecessors in the graph are *start* and s_2. The path from s_2 to e_2 has value $(-4 + 6) = 2$, which is not strictly smaller than the Bestval field of e_2. Hence, this is okay.

- *Answer returned:*

$$s_1 = -7; e_1 = -4; s_2 = -4; e_2 = 0$$

- *Answer returned after normalization/translation:* Add 7 to everything (as -7 is the smallest negative value in the above assignment).

$$s_1 = 0; e_1 = 3; s_2 = 3; e_2 = 7$$

Before concluding this section, we note that the Bellman-Ford algorithm for multimedia presentations runs in time $O(Num\_ob \times C)$, where Num_ob is the number of objects and C is the number of difference constraints.

13.4   Spatial Constraints

In the preceding sections of this chapter, we have shown how the author of a multimedia presentation may specify *when* they wish objects to be shown. However, in practice, when multimedia presentations are delivered using a computer or TV monitor, it is also important to specify *where* on the screen these objects should be laid out. It will turn out that such constraints can also be easily specified using the language of difference constraints (with one change).

Given a set $\{vo_1, \ldots, vo_n\}$ of virtual objects, we associate, with each object vo_i, the following variables:

- W_i: width of the window in which object vo_i is shown

- H_i: height of the window in which object vo_i is shown

- X_i: x-coordinate of the lower-left corner of the window in which object vo_i is shown

- Y_i: y-coordinate of the lower-left corner of the window in which object vo_i is shown

- R_i: equal to $(W_i + X_i)$, denoting the right vertical edge of the window containing vo_i

- U_i: equal to $(H_i + Y_i)$, denoting the upper horizontal edge of the window containing vo_i.

Most intuitive spatial relationships can be expressed using these constraints. The following table shows how this might be done:

Relationship	Constraint
vo_i is to the left of vo_j	$-R_i - X_j \leq 0$
vo_i is to the right of vo_j	$-R_j - X_i \leq 0$
vo_i is above vo_j	$U_j - Y_i \leq 0$
vo_i is below vo_j	$U_i - Y_j \leq 0$

Thus, the only difference between the constraint language for expressing temporal presentation conditions and the constraint language for expressing spatial presentation conditions is that the sets of variables that the two use are different. However, as all the constraints are difference constraints, spatial constraints may also be solved using the Bellman-Ford algorithm.

For example, suppose we consider a simple multimedia presentation with three objects, vo_1, vo_2, and vo_3, that are to be displayed together. We want the left edges of vo_1 and vo_2 to be aligned, with vo_1 on top. In addition, we want vo_3 to be to the right of both vo_1 and vo_2. This can be expressed by the following set of difference constraints. As usual, we will use equality constraints as shorthand for two $\leq$ constraints.

$X_1 - X_2 = 0$ align left edges of vo_1 and vo_2
$U_2 - Y_1 \leq 0$ vo_1 is above vo_2
$R_1 - X_3 \leq 0$ vo_3 is to the right of vo_1
$R_2 - X_3 \leq 0$ vo_3 is to the right of vo_2

13.5 Selected Commercial Systems

There are numerous examples of excellent multimedia authoring tools, both from industry, as well as state-of-the art authoring software being developed in academia.

The best-known multimedia authoring system is perhaps Microsoft's PowerPoint package, which allows users to include images, video, and animation in their presentations. Though PowerPoint may be viewed as a multimedia authoring and presentation system in the sense of this chapter, future generations of presentations will allow flexible presentations where constraints are not hard (e.g., the scheduler should have the ability to solve not only hard constraints, such as "Show A first, then show B, then show C . . . ," but also flexible constraints that may not nail down the order in which objects are to be shown).

Astound from Gold Disk is a very easy-to-use multimedia presentation package that allows timeline-based editing of a multimedia document. Creating a presentation in Astound is much like in PowerPoint, but a nice feature is the ability to use buttons for different types of transitions. Asymetrix's Compel is a similar product. Information about Astound and Compel are available from *http://www.compuserve.com/Forums/GOLDDISK/Abstract.htm* and *http://www.asymetrix.com/products/compel/*.

An interesting multimedia authoring package is ToolBook from Asymetrix. ToolBook uses a specialized scripting language that is fairly easy to learn. Tools are also available that eliminate the need for programming. A presentation is viewed as a "book" with pages, sections, and so on. Each page may have various objects that can be "dragged and dropped" with a simple point-and-click approach. Interactive objects must have scripts attached to them. Relevant information on the latest family of ToolBook products is available from *http://www.asymetrix.com/products/toolbook2*.

Macromedia's Director software, which is well described at *http://www.macromedia.com/software/director/*, is one of the most popular multimedia authoring systems that allows multimedia objects to be synchronously presented as well as animated through scripts. Such objects include not just 2-d modeling, but also 3-d modeling and rendering. Unlike ToolBook, which uses a "book" analogy, Director uses a "movie" analogy—thus, you can describe *scenes* replete with a cast of actors, and then create a Director presentation ("movie") by weaving the scenes together. However, learning the Lingo language used for creating sophisticated Director applications does require some effort. Using a specialized product called Shockwave, Director can access the Web, as well as export presentations to users across the Web.

Macromedia's Authorware (*http://www.macromedia.com/software/authorware/*) is an icon-based tool that provides flexibility by having a time flow line that allows the creation of multimedia presentations that involve movies, as well as Web pages. It is closely tied to the Internet, making it suitable for many applications that require Web access. It also provides access to databases through the use of ODBC drivers. Another nice feature of Authorware is that it allows cross-platform authoring.

Another icon-based authoring tool is AimTech's IconAuthor, which is well described at *http://www.aimtech.com/*. IconAuthor allows users to create presentations using an iconic interface where each icon is an object. Building presentations on IconAuthor is very easy, which is a big advantage for many.

In addition, IconAuthor allows for the creation of multimedia presentations that can be delivered across the Web (through Java applet technology).

AimTech's Jamba product is advertised (on *http://www.jamba.com:80/*) as being a form of "Java Without Tears..." It contains facilities for capturing images and video, editing them, as well as creating Java applets that may be delivered across the Web.

Another elegant multimedia authoring tool is Allen Communication's Quest package. Information is available from *http://www.allencomm.com/*. You can even download an evaluation copy of Quest. Like Director and IconAuthor, by using Quest, multimedia presentation authors can create multimedia presentations that can be deployed across the Internet.

Candan and Cutler [34] provide an excellent description of various multimedia authoring systems on the market.

13.6   Bibliographic Notes

Multimedia authoring has been studied extensively in the literature [31, 36, 111, 126, 130, 131, 161]. Initial efforts included work involving hard constraints. Steinmetz and his colleagues [195, 197] used an approach based on communicating sequential processes (CSP). Petri net approaches were used by several others [163, 166, 164, 165]. In addition, the Petri net approach was used to provide browsing semantics in hypertext applications [200, 161, 201]. Little and Ghafoor [129] have proposed a model, called the *object composition Petri nets* (OCPN), based on timed Petri nets, which enables the formal specification and modeling of multimedia composition with intermedia timing.

The time-flow graph model of Li, Karmouch, and Georganas [126] is based on intervals and represents fuzzy presentation scenarios. In their framework, fuzziness can be due to unknown object presentation durations or unknown relative timing of the events.

Buchanan and Zellweger's FireFly system was perhaps one of the first to develop methods for creating multimedia presentations, using constraints [31]. Like Little and Ghafoor [129], they used *arbitrary* constraints (not just difference constraints) to specify presentations, and then used the simplex algorithm for solving such constraints. Buchanan and Zellweger allow the user to specify an optimal duration for a multimedia object along with costs for shrinking and stretching it.

Marcus and Subrahmanian [136] proposed the use of a fragment of Datalog queries and showed that extending this fragment with arbitrary linear constraints could be used to specify spatial and temporal characteristics.

The CHIMP (Collaborative Heterogeneous Interactive Multimedia Platform) project at the University of Maryland provides a difference-constraint-based approach to specifying temporal constraints. Figure 13.9 shows a CHIMP authoring window, through which the author creates a presentation with drag-and-drop options. CHIMP allows the user to import objects from the Web, as well as access multiple, heterogeneous databases through a program called WebHERMES [202]. A window that allows declarations of objects and facilitates such accesses is shown in Figure 13.10. CHIMP solves constraints using the Bellman-Ford algorithm, extended for incremental constraint solving, as well as to relax constraints when a given set of constraints specifying a presentation is unsolvable. Figure 13.11 shows a snapshot during the middle of a CHIMP presentation. Kim's group at the IBM Watson Research Center has also studied the problem of scheduling multimedia documents using difference constraints [111, 191].

Hakkoymaz and Ozsoyoglu [86] use constraints to specify a multimedia presentation, and then try to deduce a presentation graph from it, which specifies the playout order of the objects included in the presentation.

13.7   Exercises and Projects

1. Suppose you are creating a multimedia presentation and you wish to present three objects, vo_1, vo_2, and vo_3, to different users. The identity of each object depends on the user u_i who is viewing the object and is determined through a query Q_i. Furthermore, suppose that each object can be viewed in one of three resolutions: low, medium, and high. A user can specify his preferences about the objects; for example, user u_1 may state that he wants to see object vo_1 at high resolution, but he is happy to see the other objects at low resolution. Show how you can succinctly solve the above problem by defining vo_1, vo_2, and vo_3 as virtual objects.

2. Suppose you have a set DC of difference constraints over virtual objects $\{vo_1, \ldots, vo_n\}$, and a schedule σ that satisfies the above difference constraints. You now want to insert a new virtual object vo_{n+1} and a new set DC' of difference constraints involving the new virtual object; that is, if $(x - y) \leq c$ is a new constraint in DC', then either $x \in \{s_{n+1}, e_{n+1}\}$ or $y \in \{s_{n+1}, e_{n+1}\}$. Develop

CHIMP object creation/search windows (see also color plate Figure 13.9)

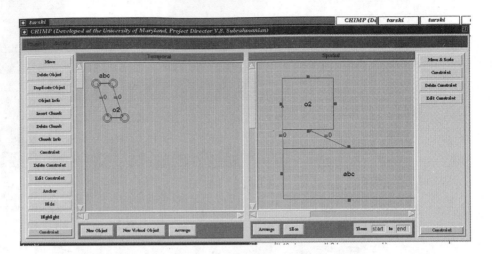

FIGURE

13.10

CHIMP spatial/temporal specification window (see also color plate Figure 13.10)

FIGURE

13.11

CHIMP presentation playout snapshot (see also color plate Figure 13.11)

an *incremental* algorithm, perhaps one that extends/modifies the Bellman-Ford algorithm, that achieves this task.

3. Suppose you have a set DC of difference constraints over virtual objects $\{vo_1, \ldots, vo_n\}$. A set DC' is said to be a $\subseteq$-relaxation of DC iff
   - DC' is solvable and
   - there is no solvable set DC* such that $DC' \subset DC^* \subseteq DC$.

   Write, in pseudocode, an algorithm that takes DC as input and returns a solution of some $\subseteq$-relaxation DC' of DC as output.

4. Suppose you have a set DC of difference constraints over virtual objects $\{vo_1, \ldots, vo_n\}$. A set DC' is said to be a *card*-relaxation of DC iff
   - DC' is solvable and
   - there is no solvable set DC* such that $DC^* \subseteq DC$ and $card(DC^*) > card(DC')$.

   Write, in pseudocode, an algorithm that takes DC as input and returns a solution of some *card*-relaxation DC' of DC as output.

5. Suppose you have a set DC of difference constraints over virtual objects $\{vo_1, \ldots, vo_n\}$, and further suppose that each constraint c in DC has an associated positive integer, denoted $pr(c)$, called its *priority*. A set DC' is said to be a priority relaxation of DC iff
   - DC' is solvable and
   - there is no solvable set DC* such that $DC^* \subseteq DC$ and
   $$\sum_{c \in DC^*} pr(c) \geq \sum_{c \in DC'} pr(c)$$

   Write, in pseudocode, an algorithm that takes DC as input and returns as output, a solution of some priority-relaxation DC' of DC.

6. As a project, implement your algorithms for computing solutions of $\subseteq$-relaxations, *card*-relaxations, and priority relaxations of sets of constraints. Run experiments to determine, if possible, which one is the "best."

14 Distributed Media Servers

CHAPTER

What new concepts will you learn in this chapter?
Presentation plans, described in the preceding chapter, specify when the author of a multimedia presentation wants to see an object. You will now learn how such objects can be retrieved (perhaps from across the Net). Retrievals are complicated by the fact that different servers on the network may all have different capabilities, some or all of which may not exactly match the client's resources, or the requesting server's requirements, or both. You will learn how such difficulties may be overcome.

What new abstractions are needed to realize these concepts?
You will learn about the concept of a retrieval plan. Informally, a retrieval plan specifies how a server trying to deliver a multimedia presentation to a client can download the data from local/remote sources in a manner that is consistent with available resources.

What new techniques are needed to implement these abstractions?
You will learn how optimal retrieval plans can be generated. A retrieval plan is optimal if it minimizes some specified cost function. The algorithm you will study in this chapter takes the cost function as an input and is guaranteed to create optimal retrieval plans with respect to that cost function, as long as the cost function satisfies two sensible properties.

What technological features support these implementation methods?
You will learn about current trends in the creation of such retrieval plans.

14.1   Introduction

In the preceding section, we studied techniques to create presentation schedules. Intuitively, once the presentation author has specified his presentation constraints, a presentation schedule is a solution of those presentation constraints. A presentation schedule specifies *when* the display of media objects should start and *when* they should end. However, in general, there may be zero, one, or more presentation schedules that satisfy a presentation author's presentation constraints.

Presentation schedules specify one possible display schedule that satisfies the presentation author's constraints. However, not all presentation schedules are *deliverable*. The reason for this is that in order to show an object o at time t, the server retrieving o must obtain commitments of resources from several sources. For example, if the object o resides on a remote machine, then bandwidth must be allocated by the network service provider, and furthermore, the remote server must agree to deliver the required object at the required time. A retrieval plan/schedule, as outlined in the previous chapter, is a plan for retrieving objects in a timely manner, keeping in mind the available resources (bandwidth, load, buffer, etc.) and, at the same time, obtaining commitments from third-party servers to deliver in an on-time manner. In this chapter, we will describe techniques and algorithms for the creation of retrieval schedules.

Before proceeding any further, we remark on a simple analogy between scheduling inventories at a factory warehouse and the problem of creating retrieval schedules. Figure 14.1(a) shows a simple railroad system consisting of factories/warehouses connected by rail. Suppose you are the inventory manager at warehouse W, and you want to obtain a steady supply of a given item (say, 100 units per day). Your loading dock has a capacity of at most 10 items; that is, you can hold at most 10 units at a time. Figure 14.1(b) shows this situation.

In order to obtain this steady stream of units flowing into your warehouse, you must do the following:

- You must identify factories/depots that are capable of supplying the item you want.

- Then you must obtain a commitment from one or more of these factories to deliver the supplies you want. This may not always be possible because one or more of these factories may be functioning below its production capacity.

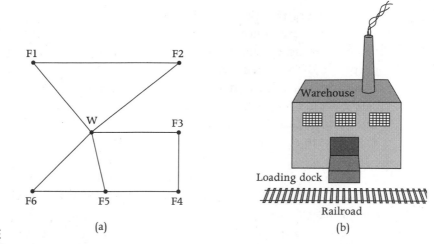

F I G U R E

14.1

Railroad analogy: (a) warehouse/factory network; (b) detail of warehouse

- Finally, you must be able to obtain a commitment from the railroad company to provide freight cars to carry the shipment from the factory (or factories) to your warehouse.

The similarities between our problem of creating retrieval schedules and the railroad scheduling problem are the following:

- Think of the item being requested as a piece of media data.

- Think of the warehouse requesting the supplies as a client requesting a movie.

- Think of the warehouse's loading dock as being a clientside buffer.

- Think of the factory supplying the movie as a media server.

- Think of the railroad company as being a network service provider (shipping bytes instead of production items).

Before proceeding to the technical sections of this chapter, we must note that the above analogy is a simplification of the retrieval scheduling problem. The retrieval scheduling problem is somewhat more complex because it involves the additional requirement that media blocks arrive "just in time" so that once block i of the movie is consumed (i.e., watched by the user), block $(i + 1)$ is ready to be consumed (i.e., is in the client's buffer). In the railroad scenario, this additional (important!) requirement is not present.

In the rest of this chapter, we will proceed as follows. First, we will formally introduce the concept of a distributed multimedia server system (DMSS). Video-on-demand systems may be viewed as a special case of the more general concept of a DMSS. Then we will define a concept called a *distributed retrieval plan*. Intuitively, a distributed retrieval plan involves a detailed plan created to satisfy a given client request, keeping in mind the temporal requirements and display capabilities of the client. Later, we will show that not all distributed retrieval plans that achieve a given objective are necessarily desirable. Some plans are better than others. In particular, we will introduce two objective functions associated with retrieval plans and define a notion of optimality based on these objectives. Finally, we will present an efficient algorithm to compute optimal retrieval plans.

14.2   Distributed Multimedia Server Architecture

In this section, we introduce the concept of a *distributed multimedia server system* (DMSS). The DMSS architecture consists of a network of multimedia data servers located at potentially geographically dispersed locations on the Internet. Each server provides access to a body of media data on its local disk. For the sake of simplicity, we will assume that all media data being retrieved is video; other forms of media data are typically much easier to handle than video because they have no continuous playback requirements (except for audio). Audio data has the same continuity requirements as video, but is typically easier to handle because it requires less bandwidth. A network service provider handles requests for future allocation of network bandwidth. Figure 14.2 shows the simple architecture of such a system.

A *customer* interested in retrieving data at or by a given time contacts his local server. For example, the customer may be someone interested in watching a video. The customer contacts his local server (called the *originating server*) and requests that a given body of media data be delivered to him. This local originating server is then charged with the responsibility of creating a retrieval schedule by interacting with other servers on the network. Each server on the network has an associated body of media objects stored on its local disk.

Suppose $\mathcal{MOVIE}$ is the set of all movies available in the DMSS system, and each movie m has an associated number of *blocks*, denoted bnum(m). Without loss of generality, we will assume that movie m's blocks are labeled 1

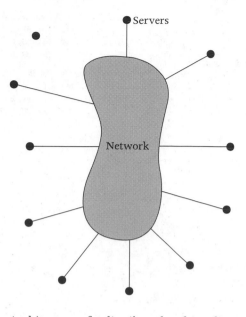

FIGURE

14.2   Architecture of a distributed multimedia server system

through bnum(m). For example, the following table shows the number of blocks associated with three movies:

Movie M	bnum(M)
M1	25
M2	25
M3	25

Definition 14.1 A *placement mapping* is a mapping, $\wp$, that takes the following as input:

1. a movie $m_i \in \mathcal{MOVIE}$ and

2. a block number, $1 \leq b \leq$ bnum(m_i), and returns a subset of V as output. Here, V is the set of all servers available in the DMSS system.

For example, Figure 14.3 shows a simple placement mapping. This particular situation has six servers, labeled $s_1, \ldots, s_6$. The system as a whole has only the three movies, M1, M2, and M3 referred to earlier. In the situation depicted

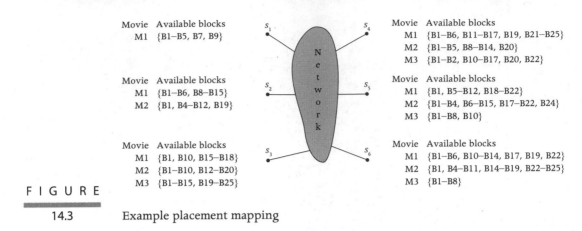

Movie   Available blocks
  M1   {B1–B5, B7, B9}

Movie   Available blocks
  M1   {B1–B6, B11–B17, B19, B21–B25}
  M2   {B1–B5, B8–B14, B20}
  M3   {B1–B2, B10–B17, B20, B22}

Movie   Available blocks
  M1   {B1–B6, B8–B15}
  M2   {B1, B4–B12, B19}

Movie   Available blocks
  M1   {B1, B5–B12, B18–B22}
  M2   {B1–B4, B6–B15, B17–B22, B24}
  M3   {B1–B8, B10}

Movie   Available blocks
  M1   {B1, B10, B15–B18}
  M2   {B1–B10, B12–B20}
  M3   {B1–B15, B19–B25}

Movie   Available blocks
  M1   {B1–B6, B10–B14, B17, B19, B22}
  M2   {B1, B4–B11, B14–B19, B22–B25}
  M3   {B1–B8}

FIGURE

14.3   Example placement mapping

in Figure 14.3, it is easy to see that

$$\wp(M1,B1) = \{s_1, s_2, s_3, s_4, s_5, s_6\}$$
$$\wp(M1,B2\text{–}B4) = \{s_1, s_2, s_4, s_6\}$$
$$\wp(M1,B5) = \{s_1, s_2, s_4, s_5, s_6\}$$

The rest of the function $\wp$ may be easily specified in a similar way.

In order to describe a detailed model of such an architecture, we need to describe the following components:

- characteristics of the servers

- characteristics of the customers

- characteristics of the networks as well as the customer-originating server links

We now treat these one by one:

1. *Server parameters:*

   (a) *Server buffer size:* We use the notation $\mathrm{buf}(v)$ to denote the amount of buffer space that server v has.

2. *Customer parameters:* In general, different customers may view a video on different machines. Machines may differ in terms of buffer availability and display/consumption rates. These parameters may be summed up as follows:

(a) *Customer consumption rate:* The value, $\mathrm{ccr}(C)$, specifies the rate at which customer C consumes media data. We will assume this quantity to be specified in MB/second.

(b) *Customer buffer size:* The value, $\mathrm{buf}(C)$, specifies the total amount of buffer space available at the customer's end.

3. *Network parameters:* The parameters associated with the network are server-server bandwidth and customer-server bandwidth.

(a) *Server-server bandwidth:* The quantity $\mathrm{bw}(v_1, v_2)$ specifies the total, physically feasible bandwidth available between servers v_1 and v_2. Note that the actual amount of bandwidth available to a given job at a given time depends upon how much of the total quantity, $\mathrm{bw}(v_1, v_2)$, has been allocated to other jobs.

(b) *Customer-server bandwidth:* This value, denoted $\mathrm{bw}(C, v) = \mathrm{bw}(v, C)$, specifies the bandwidth of the link between the customer C and server v assigned to them.

14.3 Distributed Retrieval Plans

Given the DMSS architecture, as well as the various parameters associated with servers, customers, and the network, we are now ready to discuss what a distributed retrieval plan is. Intuitively, when a customer contacts an originating server with a request for part or all of a movie, the originating server must create a plan to satisfy the request. This plan must take the following criteria into account:

- *Who has the requested data (i.e., which servers)?* This query may involve not one server, but possibly a "team" of servers who possess the desired data. Thus, for instance, if we consider the placement mapping of Figure 14.3, and we consider a request for blocks B1–B7 of movie M1, then it is clear that servers s_1 and s_2 are capable of *jointly* satisfying this request.

- *When (or at what times) can these servers provide the data?* For example, continuing the above-mentioned example, it may turn out that server s_2 can provide block B6 right away, but it is 100% committed over the next 100 time units.

- *Does the customer's consumption rate match the delivery rate? If not, at what rate should data be delivered to the customer to ensure that the available buffer at the customer side can be utilized?* For example, it is pointless if the originating server delivers data to the customer at 100 MB/second, if the customer can only consume data at 1 MB/second and only has 2 MB of buffer available. The flood of data coming into the customer's communications port will overwrite the buffer, causing the customer to, for all practical purposes, lose data.

14.3.1 Commitment Record List

In order to create a retrieval plan that takes factors such as the above into account, each server must know what commitments it has made. A simple data structure that can be used for this purpose is a *commitment record list*. Each server maintains a commitment record list, specifying what commitments it has made. When a request for services is received by the server, the commitment record list is consulted to determine if the service request can be satisfied. If so (i.e., when a new commitment is made), the commitment record list is updated to reflect the new commitment. Figure 14.4 shows a flowchart of what a server does when it receives a request.

The following table summarizes the commitment record structure. A commitment record list is merely a set of such commitment records. A server s maintains one such commitment record for every request that it honors. Thus, for instance, if at time t a server has made three commitments, then the commitment record list will contain three commitment records, one for each commitment.

BegCom	This specifies the start time of a commitment.
FinCom	This specifies the finish time of a commitment.
Client	This could either be a customer or another server to whom a commitment is being made.
Movie	This specifies what movie forms part of the commitment.
BlockSt	This specifies the starting block of the movie.
BlockEnd	This specifies the ending block of the movie associated with this commitment.
BWCom	This specifies the amount of bandwidth committed to this commitment.

For example, the table below shows a simple commitment record list. Let us say that this is the commitment list associated with some server S. There are three commitment records shown in this table.

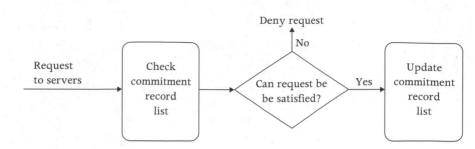

FIGURE

14.4 What a server does upon receiving a request

BegCom	FinCom	Client	Movie	BlockSt	BlockEnd	BWCom
5	15	John	*The Rope*	B5	B35	0.5 MB/second
5	10	s_4	*The Abyss*	B25	B45	0.25 MB/second
15	25	s_5	*Dracula*	B50	B70	0.5 MB/second
...	...	...	...	...	...	...

The first commitment record states that server S has made a commitment to a customer, John, to deliver blocks B5–B35 of the movie *The Rope* to him at a bandwidth of 0.5 MB/second. This commitment applies between time 5 and 15, which means that these blocks start getting streamed to John at time 5, and the stream ends at time 15. Note that, in this case, the client is a human customer.

The second commitment record states that server S has made a commitment to another server, s_4, to deliver blocks B25–B45 of the movie *The Abyss* at a bandwidth of 0.25 MB/second. This commitment applies between time 5 and 10, which means that these blocks start getting streamed to server s_4 at time 5, and the stream ends at time 10. Note that, in this case, the client is another server, not a human.

The third commitment record states that server S has made a commitment to another server, s_5, to deliver blocks B50–B70 of the movie *Dracula* at a bandwidth of 0.5 MB/second. This commitment applies between time 15 and 25, which means that these blocks start getting streamed to server s_5 at time 15, and the stream ends at time 25.

Note that the commitment record list above indicates a bandwidth commitment. In general, a data server cannot make a bandwidth commitment—rather, that is the task of the network service provider. It is important to realize that creating a retrieval plan involves a tripartite agreement between two data servers and the network service provider. Once such an agreement has been reached, the data servers can record the guarantee provided by the network service provider and store that guarantee as the BWCom field of the commitment records. This is what we are doing above.

14.3.2   Retrieval Plans

While a commitment record list specifies the commitments that a server has made at some given point in time, the originating server that is processing a customer's request must attempt to create a retrieval plan to satisfy the client. In this section, we define a data structure called a *retrieval record*. Given any customer request r, the originating server for that customer creates a retrieval record $RR(r)$. A retrieval record consists of a total of 14 fields. However, for the sake of simplicity, it is useful to split these 14 fields into two parts—those intended for server-server interaction, and those intended for server-customer interaction.

The fields associated with server-server interactions are listed in the table below. These fields describe the identities of the originating and target servers, as well as the movie being requested and the blocks of the movie being requested. In addition, we specify when the first block will be requested. The ConOK field specifies when the connection is successfully made (because there will usually be a delay between the time the connection is requested and the time the connection is actually made). As in the case of commitment records, the BWAssign field is jointly determined by the target server and the network service provider. The DelivSt field specifies when the delivery of blocks starts.

1	Orig	Specifies the server that originated the request.
2	Target	Specifies the server that will satisfy the request.
3	Movie	Specifies the movie-id associated with the request.
4	Start	Specifies the first movie block being requested.
5	End	Specifies the last block being requested.
6	Reqtime	This is the time at which block request is initiated.
7	ConOK	This is the time at which the connection is successfully made.
8	BWAssign	This is the bandwidth assigned to the request by the target server.
9	DelivSt	This is the time at which delivery starts.

Note that fields 1–9 specify only the parameters relevant to "downloading" blocks from the remote server to the originating server. The originating server must afterward transmit these blocks to the actual customer. This is what the last five fields, numbered 10–14, do. These fields are somewhat more complicated than the previous nine fields, and hence we will discuss them in some detail. They are shown below.

10	DelivEnd	For each block b_w, where $r.\text{Start} \leq w \leq r.\text{End}$, $r.\text{DelivEnd}[w] = r.\text{DelivSt} + \frac{(w-r.\text{Start}+1)\times \text{bsize}}{r.\text{BWAssign}}$
11	CustShipSt	For each block b_w, where $r.\text{Start} \leq w \leq r.\text{End}$, $r.\text{CustShipSt}[w] \geq r.\text{DelivEnd}[w]$
12	CustShipEnd	For each block b_w, where $r.\text{Start} \leq w \leq r.\text{End}$, $r.\text{CustShipEnd}[w] = r.\text{CustShipSt}[w] + \frac{\text{bsize}}{\text{bw}(r.\text{Orig},C)}$
13	CustConsStart	For each block b_w, where $r.\text{Start} \leq w \leq r.\text{End}$, $r.\text{CustConsStart}[w] \geq r.\text{CustShipEnd}[w]$
14	CustConsEnd	For each block b_w, where $r.\text{Start} \leq w \leq r.\text{End}$, $r.\text{CustConsEnd}[w] = r.\text{CustConsStart}[w] + \frac{\text{bsize}}{\text{ccr}(C)}$

The DelivEnd field is an array. The wth element of this array specifies when the wth block being downloaded from the remote server actually arrives at the originating server. The reason we want to keep this information on a block-by-block level is that as soon as block b_w is in the originating server's buffer, it can be immediately shipped to the customer.

The CustShipSt field, like the DelivEnd field, is also an array field. The wth element of the array specifies when the wth block downloaded from the remote server can get shipped off to the actual customer. Obviously, the earliest time that the originating server can ship data to the customer is *after* it has downloaded the data from the remote server.

The CustShipEnd is also an array field, whose wth element specifies when shipment of the wth block to the customer is completed. Obviously, the shipment ends δ time units after shipment starts, where δ is the time taken for the transmission. This time is obviously the size of the data block, divided by the bandwidth of the channel between the customer and the originating server.

The CustConsStart and CustConsEnd fields are also array fields, whose wth entry specifies when the customer will start/finish consuming the wth data block.

Definition 14.2 A *retrieval request* issued by customer C is a triple, $Req(C) = (m, b_1, b_2)$. Intuitively, $Req(C) = (m, b_1, b_2)$ denotes the request by user C for all blocks b of movie m such that $b_1 \leq b \leq b_2$.

Definition 14.3 A *retrieval plan* is a finite sequence $r_1, \ldots, r_n$ of retrieval records such that for all $1 \leq i < n$, $r_i.\text{End} + 1 = r_{i+1}.\text{Start}$.

Rather than formally define what it means for a retrieval plan RP to satisfy a retrieval request $Req(C) = (m, b_1, b_2)$, we will explain informally what this means (for a formal definition, refer to the detailed mathematical exposition contained in Hwang, Prabhakaran, and Subrahmanian [98]). The constraints to be satisfied are the following:

- *Continuity of playback constraint:* At all times t such that r_1.CustConsStart $\leq t \leq r_n$.CustConsEnd, there must exist exactly one block b_i of the movie such that b_i is being viewed by the customer.

- *Server-server bandwidth constraint:* At all times t such that r_1.DelivSt $\leq t \leq r_n$.DelivEnd, and for all network connections between two servers (s_1, s_2), the total assignment of bandwidth to jobs using the channel (s_1, s_2) should be less than or equal to the total physical bandwidth of the channel.

- *Server-customer bandwidth constraint:* At all times t such that r_1.CustShipSt $\leq t \leq r_n$.CustConsEnd, the total assignment of bandwidth to jobs using the channel between the customer and the originating server should be less than or equal to the total physical bandwidth of the channel.

- *Customer buffer constraint:* At all times t such that r_1.CustShipSt $\leq t \leq r_n$.CustConsEnd, the total number of blocks that have been shipped by the originating server to the customer, but that have not yet been consumed by the customer, should occupy space less than or equal to the total buffer space available at the customer's machine.

- *Originating server buffer constraint:* At all times t such that r_1.DelivEnd $\leq t \leq r_n$.CustShipEnd, the total number of blocks that have been shipped by a remote server to the originating server, but that have not yet been shipped to the customer, should occupy space less than or equal to the total buffer space available at the originating server.

In the rest of this chapter, when we use the term "retrieval plan" with respect to a specific retrieval request, we will mean a retrieval plan that satisfies the above constraints.

14.3.3   An Example

Let us consider a situation where we have the six servers $s_1, \ldots, s_6$ and placement mapping shown in Figure 14.3. Suppose, for now, that all servers are completely free (i.e., they all have empty commitment record lists). Suppose a customer, Jane, requests movie M1 from server s_2. We may now proceed to satisfy this request as follows.

1. *Identifying remote servers with blocks required:* Server s_2 only has blocks B1–B6 and B8–B15 of the movie. Hence, the missing blocks, B7, B16–B25, need to be obtained from remote servers. The following table shows which servers have these blocks:

Block	Servers having block
B7	s_1, s_5
B16	s_3, s_4
B17	s_3, s_4, s_6
B18	s_3, s_5
B19	s_4, s_5, s_6
B20	s_5
B21	s_4, s_5
B22	s_4, s_5, s_6
B23	s_4
B24	s_4
B25	s_4

2. *A retrieval plan:* Figure 14.5 presents the server-server interaction records for a retrieval plan. Server-customer interaction records may be similarly created. We are using connection times of 1 in the following, and all bandwidths are assumed to be 1 block/second for the sake of simplicity.

   Note that it is just one of several possible retrieval plans. Other plans may differ based on which servers are used to request data.

3. *Relevant commitment records:* The relevant commitment records associated with the retrieval plan given above are as follows:

   - Server s_1: Empty commitment record list
   - Server s_2:

BegCom	FinCom	Client	Movie	BlockSt	BlockEnd	BWCom
2	7	Jane	M1	B1	B6	1 block/second

   - Server s_3: Empty commitment record list

1	Orig	s_2
2	Target	s_2
3	Movie	M1
4	Start	B1
5	End	B6
6	Reqtime	1
7	ConOK	2
8	BWAssign	1 block/second
9	DelivSt	2

1	Orig	s_2
2	Target	s_5
3	Movie	M1
4	Start	B7
5	End	B12
6	Reqtime	7
7	ConOK	8
8	BWAssign	1 block/second
9	DelivSt	8

1	Orig	s_2
2	Target	s_4
3	Movie	M1
4	Start	B13
5	End	B17
6	Reqtime	13
7	ConOK	14
8	BWAssign	1 block/second
9	DelivSt	14

1	Orig	s_2
2	Target	s_5
3	Movie	M1
4	Start	B18
5	End	B22
6	Reqtime	18
7	ConOK	19
8	BWAssign	1 block/second
9	DelivSt	19

1	Orig	s_2
2	Target	s_4
3	Movie	M1
4	Start	B23
5	End	B25
6	Reqtime	23
7	ConOK	24
8	BWAssign	1 block/second
9	DelivSt	24

F I G U R E

14.5

Sample retrieval plan: server-server interaction

■ Server s_4:

BegCom	FinCom	Client	Movie	BlockSt	BlockEnd	BWCom
14	18	s_2	M1	B13	B17	1 block/second
24	26	s_2	M1	B23	B25	1 block/second

- Server s_5:

BegCom	FinCom	Client	Movie	BlockSt	BlockEnd	BWCom
8	13	s_2	M1	B7	B12	1 block/second
19	23	s_2	M1	B18	B22	1 block/second

- Server s_6: Empty commitment record list

14.4   Optimal Distributed Retrieval Plans

As we can easily see from the preceding example, there may be many retrieval plans that can be used to satisfy a given user request. Some of these
might be "better" than others, from one point of view or another. As is common in mathematics and operations research, optimality of a plan means that
the plan minimizes some objective function (note that maximization problems
are expressible as minimization problems, and hence there is no loss of generality in restricting interest to minimization problems). In the case of retrieval
plans, different optimality criteria may be used:

- *Minimizing customer wait time:* Consider the wait time for the user—the
  value of the quantity r_1.CustConsStart—associated with a given retrieval
  plan *RP*. *RP* is said to be *wait-minimal* iff there is no other retrieval plan
  RP' that can satisfy the request such that RP' has a strictly smaller wait
  time than *RP*.

- *Minimizing the access bandwidth:* *RP* is said to be *access bandwidth minimal* iff the sum of the number of disk accesses and the number of network
  accesses is minimal; that is, there is no other retrieval plan RP' such that
  the sum of the number of disk accesses and the number of network accesses
  made by RP' is strictly less than the sum of the number of disk accesses and
  the number of network accesses made by *RP*. Here, the plan is generated
  in such a way that the accesses (local disk or network) required for buffer-
  ing the movie blocks in the VoD server are minimized. (We minimize the
  amount of bandwidth used, both at the disk level and the network level,
  rather than minimize the total number of accesses.)

Each of the above objectives has advantages and disadvantages. For instance, if a customer *C* makes a request, and we try to minimize his wait time,
then we may jeopardize the responses for future customers. To see how this can
happen, suppose we have several retrieval plans to satisfy *C*'s request, but RP_1

is wait-optimal (with wait time 2 units of time). We may have another nonoptimal (with respect to wait time) retrieval plan RP_2 with wait time 2.002 units. The plan RP_2 may not minimize wait time for customer C, but it may in fact be obtained by merging some data streams together, thus allowing certain existing system resources to be used to serve two or more customers together. Is RP_2 a "better" plan than RP_1? We may be tempted to argue that the answer is "yes." However, according to the objective of minimizing wait times, it is not.

The objective of minimizing access bandwidth, on the other hand, goes to another extreme. It says that when satisfying a customer request, we would like to see how many disk accesses and how many network accesses are required to satisfy the job. Accesses that the system is committed to making prior to the arrival of client C's request are not counted again. This system obviously minimizes the use of system resources. Minimizing disk accesses allows each server to potentially make better use of the limited disk bandwidth, thus allowing it to serve more clients. Likewise, minimizing network bandwidth usage allows other future clients to use the network. In general, however, minimizing network/disk accesses may force the customer to wait somewhat longer than in the case of the "minimize customer wait time" objective function discussion above.

When designing algorithms to compute optimal retrieval plans, we will assume that the originating server OS has access to the movie placement function and knowledge about the physical network bandwidth, bw, between servers.

For example, in order to minimize the access bandwidth, the originating server OS may group together multiple requests for the same movie that arrive within a small temporal window. In such cases, the originating server OS can minimize the access bandwidth by utilizing available buffer as follows.

The originating server OS fixes a time τ called the *buffer latency time*. When the OS downloads data from a remote server, it reserves the option of keeping that data in buffer even after it has been shipped to a customer. This way, if a future customer C_{new} needs the same data at or about the same time as the original customer C_{old}, it will be able to satisfy the request using the buffered data without having to reread it from disk (or having to reship it across the network). This obviously decreases the access bandwidth.

14.5 An Algorithm to Compute Optimal Retrieval Plans

In this section, we present an algorithm to compute optimal retrieval plans. The algorithm we present, called *optimal split search* (OSS), computes optimal retrieval plans *given any cost function whatsoever*. In other words, as long as a cost function, cf, is specified, our algorithm will compute retrieval plans that are optimal with respect to cf. Thus, this algorithm is completely general and may be used to generate optimal retrieval plans for a variety of performance criteria, not just one or two.

Before defining our algorithm, we define an *implicit retrieval tree*. Suppose we are given a client request $Req(C) = (m, b_1, b_2)$ and a cost function cf that describes how retrieval plans are evaluated. Our goal is to minimize cost. Without loss of generality, we will assume that the cost function is monotonic; that is, if RP_1 is a subplan of RP_2, then $cf(RP_1) \leq cf(RP_2)$. This makes intuitive sense anyway—if we have a plan with cost c and we do some things over and above what is in the old plan, then the new plan cannot have a lower cost than the old.

14.5.1   Implicit Retrieval Trees

In this section, we will describe an abstract mathematical tree, $IRT(m, b_1, b_2, cf)$. Anytime a user makes a request for blocks $[b_1, b_2]$ of movie m, part of the tree $IRT(m, b_1, b_2, cf)$ is constructed by the originating server in its attempt to create a retrieval plan satisfying the user's request. Figure 14.6 provides a picture of part of an implicit retrieval tree. Intuitively, the nodes in $IRT(m, b_1, b_2, cf)$ are labeled with jobs that are yet to be accomplished. For instance, in the above case, the root of $IRT(m, b_1, b_2, cf)$ is labeled with the entire sequence $[b_1, b_2]$ because a retrieval plan to retrieve this entire segment of movie m has to be constructed. If a server s can guarantee delivery of an *initial* segment $[b_1, b_3]$, then we would need to only construct a retrieval plan for $[b_3, b_2]$ that is synchronized with server s's temporal guarantees. In our tree, $IRT(m, b_1, b_2, cf)$, this situation would be represented by the root having a child, labeled with the interval $[b_3, b_2]$, for which a schedule is to be constructed. This process is now repeated.

The above intuitive description is obviously incomplete and requires further elucidation, which we will provide below. However, even at this stage, it is apparent that $IRT(m, b_1, b_2, cf)$ is very large and clearly is not something we want to construct. However, it is worth noting what this tree is, because the process of finding an optimal retrieval plan with respect to the objective function cf is equivalent to an incremental construction of *part* of the implicit tree $IRT(m, b_1, b_2, cf)$.

$IRT(m, b_1, b_2, cf)$ may now be described as follows:

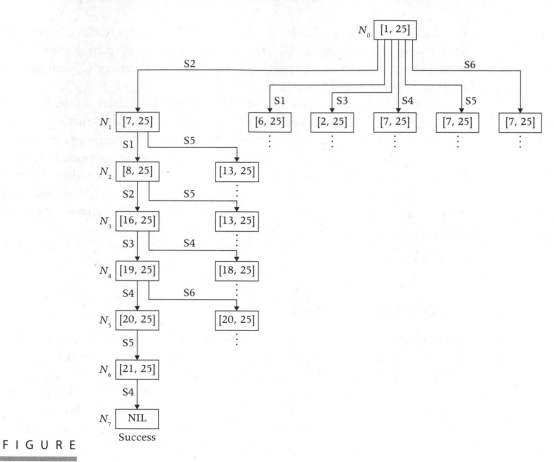

F I G U R E

14.6   A partial implicit retrieval tree

1. Each node in $IRT(m, b_1, b_2, cf)$ has five fields—$(LB, UB, cost, Serv, Tset)$—
   where $b_1 \le LB \le UB \le b_2$. The field $Serv$ ranges over the server-ids of
   servers in the system. $Tset$ is a table containing two fields: a *time* field and
   a *bandwidth* field. Usually, each row in the time column will be a constraint
   whose solution is a set of time points. Thus, for example, the constraint
   $20 \le t \le 30$ indicates that the row in question talks about the time interval 20–30. If the bandwidth associated with this row is 10, then this
   means that between times 20–30, a bandwidth of 10 MB/second is guaranteed jointly by the remote server associated with the node and the network
   service provider.

2. The root R of $IRT(m, b_1, b_2, cf)$ has $R.LB = b_1$, $R.UB = b_2$, and $R.Serv =$ NIL. In addition, $R.Tset$'s field has all possible numbers in it (instead of explicitly listing these, a constraint such as $t \geq 0$ can be used to specify this infinite set).

3. If N is a node with children $N_1, \ldots, N_k$, then it must satisfy the following constraints:

$$N.cost = min\{N_i.cost \mid 1 \leq i \leq k\}$$

$$\{b \mid N.LB \leq b \leq N.UB\} = \bigcup_{i=1}^{k}\{b' \mid N_i.LB \leq b' \leq N_i.UB\}$$

$$i \neq j \Rightarrow \{b^* \mid N_i.LB \leq b^* \leq N_i.UB\}$$
$$\cap \{b^\circ \mid N_j.LB \leq b^\circ \leq N_j.UB\} = \emptyset$$

(Note that constraints can be satisfied by adjusting the cost field of the parent.)

4. Suppose N is a node in $IRT(m, b_1, b_2, cf)$. Suppose s is a server such that

   (a) there exists a block b, $N.LB \leq b \leq N.UB$, of movie m such that server s can supply blocks $[N.LB, b]$ of movie m, and
   (b) $\{t \mid t = r.time$ for some record r in $N.Tset$ and server s can start supplying blocks $[N.LB, b]$ at time t and bandwidth $r.bw$ to the originating server OS without overloading s or overwriting the buffer of $OS\} \neq \emptyset$.

   Then N has a child N' such that

   (a) $N'.LB = min(b + 1, bnum(m))$,
   (b) $N'.UB = N.UB$,
   (c) $N'.cost = N.cost + cf(trans)$, where $trans$ is the cost of shipping blocks $[N.LB, b]$ from server s to the originating server OS,
   (d) $N'.Serv = s$, and
   (e) $N'.Tset = \{(t + \delta, bw') \mid (t, bw) \in N.Tset$, and δ is the time taken to ship data from s to OS at the bandwidth bw and $bw' > 0\}$.[1]

Intuitively, a node represents a goal to be achieved. For example, the label of the root, which has $R.LB = b_1, R.UB = b_2$, specifies that we are trying to plan for the retrieval of all blocks between b_1 and b_2 of movie m. Likewise, an interior node N labeled with $N.LB = 400$ and $N.UB = 450$ is trying to determine

---

[1]We abuse notation here. $(t + \delta)$ denotes the set of all time points $\{t' + \delta \mid t'$ is a solution of the constraint represented by $t\}$.

from which servers and at what times and at what bandwidths we may obtain blocks 400–500 of movie m.

When constructing (part of) $IRT(m, b_1, b_2, cf)$, the cost field of nodes might keep changing. The reason is that the cost field specifies the "least cost" schedule found so far.

The Serv field tells us which server was selected so as to lead to a particular node. Thus, for instance, if node N has node N' as a child, then N' is obtained from N by selecting a server that can provide an initial segment of the blocks required by N at a time convenient to N. The fact that node N' was obtained in this way from node N is recorded in the Serv field of node N'.

Figure 14.6 provides a partial example of how we may construct *part* of the tree $IRT(m, b_1, b_2, cf)$ associated with the retrieval plan discussed in Section 14.3.3. In this case, we are interested in constructing $IRT(M1, 1, 25, cf)$. For now, let's say that cf is the total amount of network bandwidth consumed. Thus, any local data is preferred to downloading data from remote sources. The cost function here is being intentionally kept simple for pedagogical purposes to show what $IRT(m, b_1, b_2, cf)$ looks like.

Each node N in Figure 14.6 is labeled with its appropriate interval of blocks that are yet to be retrieved. For example, the fact that the root is labeled with $[1, 25]$ indicates that all 25 blocks of the movie M1 are yet to be retrieved. The server field of a node is shown as the label of the incoming edge incident upon that node. For example, consider the leftmost child (we will call this node N_1 for now) of the root. The server field of this node is S2, since the edge coming into the node from the root is labeled S2. Intuitively, this edge indicates that server S2 has the ability to provide blocks B1–B6 of the movie, leaving blocks B7–B25 yet to be delivered. This is why the leftmost child of the root is labeled with blocks $[7, 25]$, indicating that a retrieval schedule to download these blocks must be created. All other child-subchild relationships in Figure 14.6 are similarly obtained.

Let's now consider what the Tset field of N_1 contains. Intuitively, this is a specification of when, and at what bandwidth, server S2 can provide blocks B1–B6 of movie M1. For example, the Tset field may look like the following table:

Time	Bandwidth
$0 \leq t \leq 5$	9
$100 \leq t \leq 120$	12
$400 \leq t \leq 415$	20

Intuitively, this Tset field says the following: Server S2 can deliver the required blocks at 9 units per second (e.g., megabytes per second) *starting* at any time between 0 and 5, at 12 units per second starting any time between 100 and 120, and at 20 units per second anytime between times 400 and 415. From the above table, we may infer that server S2 cannot commit to start delivery of blocks B1–B6 of movie M1 starting at a time between 6 and 99.

We say a path $\wp = N_0 N_1, N_2, \ldots, N_k$ in $\mathrm{IRT}(m, b_1, b_2, \mathrm{cf})$ is *successful* iff the following conditions hold:

1. N_0 is the root of $\mathrm{IRT}(m, b_1, b_2, \mathrm{cf})$.

2. The interval labeling N_k is NIL.

3. There exists a function $\mu : \{1, \ldots, k\}$ to the natural numbers such that

   (a) $\mu(i)$ is a time point obtained as a solution of the constraint in some row, $r_i.time$ of $N_i.\mathrm{Tset}$ (intuitively, $\mu(i)$ should specify when the blocks associated with the edge incoming into node N_i should start getting downloaded) and

   (b) for all $1 \leq i \leq k$, $\mu(i)$ should equal the sum of $\mu(i-1)$ and the time required to download the blocks at bandwidth $r_i.\mathrm{bw}$.

It is important to note that a μ that satisfies the conditions listed above is actually a schedule! For example, consider $\mu(N_2)$, where N_2 is the node shown in Figure 14.6. Suppose this value is 5. Then this means that we may start downloading block 7 from server S1 at time 5. Likewise, consider N_7, and suppose $\mu(N_7) = 13$. Then this means that at time 13, we can start downloading blocks B21–B25 from server S4.

For example, consider the one successful path shown in Figure 14.6, and further suppose that Figure 14.7 shows the Tset field of all nodes along this path. The single successful path in this tree leads to several possible successful schedules, μ. Two such μs are shown below.

Node N	$\mu_1(N)$	$\mu_2(N)$
N_0	0	0
N_1	0	1
N_2	3	4
N_3	4	5
N_4	8	9
N_5	11	12
N_6	12	13
N_7	13	14

N_0:			N_1:	
$t \geq 0$	—		$0 \leq t \leq 5$	2 blks/sec
N_2:			N_3:	
$2 \leq t \leq 5$	1 blk/sec		$3 \leq t \leq 10$	2 blks/sec
N_4:			N_5:	
$5 \leq t \leq 12$	1 blk/sec		$5 \leq t \leq 12$	1 blk/sec
N_6:			N_7:	
$5 \leq t \leq 15$	1 blk/sec		$5 \leq t \leq 20$	2 blks/sec

FIGURE

14.7   Example of the Tset field of different nodes

Finally, consider the cost of the path shown in Figure 14.6. If we assume that the cost function merely counts the total number of blocks downloaded from remote sites, then it is easy to see that the cost of the successful path shown in Figure 14.6 is 11.

14.5.2   Computing Optimal Plans

You may have noticed that an implicit retrieval tree is nothing more than a massive (infinite) search tree. A good deal of efficient technology for searching such trees, generated in the artificial intelligence literature, finds a ready application here.

In general, an implicit retrieval tree, $IRT(m, b_1, b_2, cf)$, has the following properties:

- Each node is either a *failure* node, a *success* node or an *interim* node.

- Every failure/success node is a leaf, and every leaf is either a failure or a success node.

- A success node corresponds to a path in the tree $IRT(m, b_1, b_2, cf)$.

- A single success node may lead to multiple schedules, each with different costs.

Thus, computing an optimal retrieval plan involves two steps: (1) finding success nodes and (2) finding the best plan associated with a success node by solving the affiliated constraints. Both these goals may be easily achieved through the use of the well-known $A^\star$ algorithm, described very well in Nilsson [148]. For those unfamiliar with $A^\star$, we provide a brief description below.

$A^\star$ works by maintaining two lists—an *Open* list and a *Closed* list. Initially, the *Open* list contains one node, the root of $\mathrm{IRT}(m, b_1, b_2, \mathtt{cf})$, while the *Closed* list is empty. Each node N in the *Open/Closed* lists has a cost derived from the cost function, $\mathtt{cf}$, in the obvious way. For example, the cost associated with the node N_2 of Figure 14.6, using the measure of only counting the number of blocks downloaded from remote servers, is 1; the cost of N_3 according to the same measure is 1 too, but N_4 has a cost of 4.

$A^\star$ picks any node N in the *Open* list that has the least cost and computes its children $C_1, \ldots, C_r$. Initially, it has a variable called *bestval*, which is initialized to ∞. At this point, the following steps are executed:

- N is placed in the *Closed* list. It maintains an array of CHILD pointers, one to each of its children.

- Each child C_i has its parent field set to N.

- Forall $i = 1$ to r do:
   1. If the child is a success node, then output the path from the root to C_i—this is a valid schedule. Let p_i be the cost of the path from the root to C_i. If $p_i < \mathtt{bestval}$, then set $\mathtt{bestval}$ to this cost, and set $\mathtt{BestSol}$ to this path. If $p_i = \mathtt{bestval}$, then add this path to $\mathtt{BestSol}$; otherwise, do nothing.
   2. If $\mathrm{cost}(C_i) > \mathtt{bestval}$, then go to Step 4 below.
   3. Check if there is a node N' in the *Open* list with the same LB, UB, and Tset fields as a node in *Closed*. If yes, then replace N' by C_i if $\mathrm{cost}(C_i) < \mathrm{cost}(N')$; otherwise, do nothing.
   4. If the previous case is inapplicable, check if there is a node N^* in the *Closed* list with the same LB, UB, and Tset fields as C_i. If no such N^* exists, then insert C_i in the *Open* list. Otherwise, do the following:
      (a) Check if $\mathrm{cost}(N^*) \leq \mathrm{cost}(C_i)$. If so, do nothing.
      (b) Otherwise, replace all fields (except the CHILD fields) of node N^* by C_i's corresponding fields. Let $\delta = \mathrm{cost}(N^*) - \mathrm{cost}(C_i)$. Now examine the subtree rooted at N^*. For each node N° in this subtree, check if N°'s parent field is set to the node in this subtree having N° as its child. If so, then decrease N°'s cost field by δ and continue.

It is well known that the $A^\star$ algorithm as described above is guaranteed to find the optimal solution for any search tree and any cost function of the sort we have described. Note that the above algorithm can be easily modified to find not just the best schedule with respect to the specified cost function, but also many other schedules.

A word of caution is in order here. In general, computing an optimal retrieval plan is a time-consuming task, and in many cases there is a need to rapidly compute a retrieval plan to accomplish a given request, even if that plan is suboptimal. Hwang, Prabhakaran, and Subrahmanian [98] provide efficient ways of computing retrieval plans that may not always be optimal.

14.5.3   Making Reservations

A final important step in the above algorithm is to determine when the originating server makes reservations of its potential remote sites that have the desired data. The reason for this is that each remote server may receive requests for availability of data and bandwidth and resources from not one, but many different servers.

One simple approach is that the originating server only makes a reservation when it has found a schedule. For example, suppose our originating server spends some time executing the $A^\star$ algorithm alluded to above and, at the end, finds a schedule σ. The danger is that during the time OS received information from a remote server RS about resource availability, the remote server may have made commitments to other clients, thus invalidating the information it had provided earlier. In this case, the schedule found by OS became invalid *during* the computation of this schedule.

If this occurs, one simple possibility is that OS merely continues its search through the implicit search space and finds an alternative solution.

Another possibility is that as the search for a retrieval plan is conducted, OS stops after every k steps of node expansion (i.e., generation of children of a node) and makes a *tentative* reservation for servers along the best partial schedule found thus far. This tentative reservation automatically times out within a given time interval, unless reconfirmed by OS. The advantage of this approach is that as OS comes closer to finding a complete retrieval plan, its reservations get guaranteed by the servers. This situation is analogous to that of an airline that requires passengers to guarantee their reservations by buying tickets within a specified time, after which any unticketed reservations are no longer held for them.

14.6   Bibliographic Notes

There has been a great deal of work on the development of multimedia-on-demand servers. However, most of this work has focused on theoretical advances, and the practical realization of multimedia-on-demand systems is still some way off.

For example, several authors [141, 128, 32, 102] present algorithms through which multimedia servers may retrieve objects from remote locations on the network. These algorithms exploit knowledge of data access patterns to improve system throughput. Experimental results are provided by these authors to establish performance aspects of their systems.

The network requirements for multimedia-on-demand are discussed in several places [149, 143, 166]. Zhang et al. [234] present resource reservation schemes for guaranteeing network throughput. Candan, Prabhakaran, and Subrahmanian [37] describe how retrieval schedules can be determined by a client based on flexible temporal specifications of multimedia document presentation.

Caching of movie blocks has been described by Dan and Sitaram [50]. They also provide valuable data on user access patterns of movies derived from an actual video rental store.

14.7   Exercises and Projects

1. Using the example in Section 14.3.3, suppose that at time 3, server s_3 receives a request from a customer who wants to also watch movie M1. Assuming that no server can read more than two blocks/second from its local disk, create a schedule that can accommodate this request. Also assume that no network link can handle more than 2 blocks/second. Show the commitment records at the end of this task.

2. Suppose now that a new customer makes a request for blocks 10–25 of movie M1 at time 8, and further suppose that this customer's primary host (originating server) is s_3. Find a schedule that minimizes the total network bandwidth used.

3. Given any implicit retrieval tree, $IRT(m, b_1, b_2, cf)$, show that if there is a path in the tree from the root to a node N, and this path is a subpath of the path from the root to node N', then the cost of the first path must be no greater than the cost of the second.

4. Modify the $A^\star$ algorithm so that it returns the top K retrieval plans for any positive integer K provided as an additional input to this algorithm.

5. As a project, implement an algorithm that maintains commitment records. This algorithm involves the following parts:

   ■ Select an appropriate tabular data structure for commitment records.

   ■ Develop an algorithm that takes a time point as input and returns the amount of bandwidth that the server can provide at that time as output. You may assume the existence of constants specifying network bandwidth and maximal load per server.

   ■ Develop an algorithm that, given two blocks b_1, b_2 for $b_1 \leq b_2$ and a movie m, specifies all starting times at which that server can start shipping blocks $[b_1, b_2]$, together with the bandwidth available.

   ■ Develop an algorithm that, given two blocks b_1, b_2 for $b_1 \leq b_2$ and a movie m, both finds a maximal initial segment $[b_1, b_3]$ and specifies all starting times at which that server can start shipping blocks $[b_1, b_3]$, together with the bandwidth available.

15 Future Directions

Multimedia database systems is an exciting new area, with a wealth of new, emerging trends. Covering all of these is not feasible. Hence, this chapter gives a small selection to whet your appetite.

15.1 Querying the Web

Though database systems have traditionally been tightly characterized syntactic entities, there is now a growing trend to consider "unstructured" bodies of data (such as the documents available on the World Wide Web) as a database. Though it may be appropriate to call the set of all documents WebDoc(t) available on the Web at time t a database, it is also important to recognize that few of the features that make a relational DBMS or an object DBMS or a spatial DBMS useful are available on the Web. In particular, there is very little support for indexing and querying on the Web. Querying the Web is more or less synonymous with using a Web search engine (e.g., Alta Vista, Lycos, Infoseek, Yahoo, etc.).

Recently, there has been a concerted effort to build query languages to query the Web. Most of these languages use a mix of *path* queries and *content* queries. Path queries allow the user to zero in on specific parts of the Web; content queries allow the user to specify the types of pages that he wants to obtain as an answer to a query. Path queries were initially proposed by Shneiderman and Thomas [189, 188]. One of the first query languages to query the Web, called WebLog, was the work of Lakshmanan and his group [122]. WebLog was a language based on logic programming that allowed users to write logical queries with a mix of browsing and querying.

Building on the important contributions made to WebLog are more recent efforts [140, 139, 4]. We will focus in this section on the work on WebSQL, developed at the University of Toronto by Mendelzon and his group [140, 139].

Their approach (which is similar to what Lakshmanan and his colleagues suggested earlier) is to think of the whole Web as consisting of two relations: a document relation and an anchor relation. Note that these two relations are not actually constructed—they are merely relational abstractions of the Web. Such an abstraction enables us to query the Web using the relational abstraction as a declarative paradigm, with a nonrelational underlying implementation.

When considering the document relation, we must first choose a scheme. This is done as follows: first, we include an attribute, called url, that specifies the URL of the Web page being described. In addition, we identify a set $\{p_1, \ldots, p_n\}$ of properties that we care about as far as that Web page is concerned. This set of properties may include fields such as TITLE (the title field of the Web page), LENGTH, and TYPE (image, text, MPEG, etc.).

The anchor relation models the connectivity of the Web. This relation has the scheme

(Base,Label,HREF)

Thus, for instance, the tuple

(http://www.place1.com, BigDogs,http://www.bigdog.com)

tells us that the web page at *http://www.place1.com* has a link labeled Big Dogs to the web page at *http://www.bigdog.com*.

Querying the web is now a fairly straightforward task by using a few special constructs. Suppose we wish to find all sites that mention "Denis Dopeman." To do this, we can construct the following query:

```
SELECT   d.url
FROM     document d
WHERE    d MENTIONS "Denis Dopeman"
```

Note that this query assumes the existence of a special Boolean predicate called MENTIONS, which has the intuitive meaning. It is easy to implement this query on top of existing commercial search engines on the Web.

Now suppose we wish to extend the previous query to find all Web pages maintained by the company FrontOperation that mention Denis Dopeman. Assuming this company's main Web page is located at *http://www.frontop.com*, we may express this query as follows:

```
SELECT   d.url
FROM     document d SUCH THAT http://www.frontop.com→D
WHERE    d MENTIONS "Denis Dopeman"
```

This query makes use of a SUCH THAT construct that restricts our attention to Web pages that have *http://www.frontop.com* as a prefix.

Finally, suppose we wish to find all documents on the Web that contain a link to Denis Dopeman's home page, which is located at *http://www.dopeman.com*. This may be done as follows:

```
SELECT  d.url
FROM    anchor d
WHERE   d.HREF = http://www.dopeman.com
```

The above three examples present a very brief overview of WebSQL. At this point, WebSQL has made a small but important start toward the development of techniques to query the Web (for more useful information, see *http://www.cs.toronto.edu/websql*). In the future, building WebSQL on top of a collection of search engines such as that provided by the ISee project at Rensselaer Polytechnic Institute may be a worthwhile effort. More information on this project is at *www.cs.rpi.edu/sibel/research/isee*.

15.2 Mobile Multimedia Systems

As information technology becomes increasingly sophisticated, users will demand access to data from anywhere and at any time. A user may be in his office, on his private yacht, or in his car, yet he might want instantaneous global access to data irrespective of his physical location. Wireless mobile systems support this kind of access.

In a wireless mobile environment, the entire world is divided up into a number of cells. Each cell represents a region on the ground. Every user u who wishes to access data from mobile locations across wireless channels must have a "home" cell $home(u)$. Typically, this home cell would correspond to the cell in which the user's house or office is located. Notice that the home cell of a user is fixed, but the actual location of the user may change over time as the user moves from one place to another. Each cell has a server that can access clients (i.e., users) within that cell. Obviously, the precise set of clients within a given cell may change over time.

There are two modes in which data transfer can now take place—*push* and *pull*. In today's everyday world, pagers and paging services are very primitive push devices, while a cellular laptop is an example of a pull device.

15.2.1 Pull Accesses

A pull access is user initiated and is typically a query or a request posed by the user. For now, let us assume that the pull request is a request to access some database (multimedia or otherwise) via a query Q. The bandwidth required to specify query Q itself is usually negligible. When the user makes a pull request, the first task of the server associated with the cell c in which the user is currently located is to identify and authenticate the user. This is typically done through an encryption mechanism. Second, if the user u's home is not in the current cell (i.e., the user is "traveling"), then the current cell, c, must update a visitor log to indicate that the user is currently a visitor to its cell. The third task is for the system to identify the sources from which data is being requested. This requires that load balancing be done, as the server may be attempting to process multiple simultaneous requests. The fourth task is to ship the user's query to the data server that provides the service requested (this would usually be done on a wired channel). The fifth and final task is to ship the answer to the user's query back to the user across the same wireless channel. This requires identifying where the user is currently (he could have moved out of the cell he was in when posing the query), and allocating bandwidth/load to deliver the answer to the user. Approaches to the first problem are briefly sketched in the next section.

15.2.2 Push Accesses

In contrast to pull accesses that are user initiated, a push action is one where a server is contacted by the user, and data and/or instructions are pushed to him. When a mobile server performs a push operation, the server must solve the following problems:

- *To whom* to push: In some cases, this will be apparent because the intended recipient of data is explicitly specified.

- *What* to push: This is particularly important in the case of multimedia data because multimedia data is very large and resources for mobile communications are limited. When pushing media objects to users, care must be taken to ensure that the users really do want it. For example, when pushing the answer to a query to a user, if the answer contains lots of images, then sending a single image composed of thumbnail sketches of the images may be appropriate. Even if the answer consists of just one image, degrading the quality to match the available resources may sometimes be an option.

> Very preliminary techniques for diminishing quality in logical networks have been developed, though those techniques apply to wired, rather than to wireless networks [40].

- *How* to push: Answering this question is complicated. The first step is for the server to determine the current location of the client to whom we wish to push data. Typically, the host associated with the client would associate a set of *partitions* with the client specifying the "regions" where the client may usually be found. Each partition represents a set of cells. For example, clients may have associated partitions consisting of cells near their home and cells near their office (and perhaps a third partition consisting of cells in the route usually taken by the client between the two).

> Searching for the client involves first checking which partitions are associated with that client by his host. If the client is in none of those cells, then various protocols have been developed to determine where he is. This is done by accessing visitor logs and checking for recent visits.

For further research on wireless multimedia systems, see [5, 9, 57, 59]. The following sites provide excellent bibliographies and pointers on the topic of wireless mobile computing:

- *http://www.vtt.fi/tte/staff/ojp/mobile.html*

- *http://www.seas.smu.edu/jfyao/others_mc.html*

- *http://rtlab.kaist.ac.kr/sikang/mobile.html*

15.3 Watermarking and Steganography

The growing use of the Internet has led to some unexpected uses:

1. There is now a vast array of image and video data on the Internet.

2. If Mr. X puts up a Web site, almost anyone can read it, unless Mr. X provides only partial access to his site.

These two observations, both of which, on the face of it, appear simple and innocuous, lead to substantial possibilities for both good and evil. To see why, consider the two scenarios described below. One of them involves a benevolent use of multimedia data, while the other reflects malevolent usage.

In our first example, a provider of multimedia content across the Web (e.g., an electronic publishing enterprise) may wish to insert hidden "digital watermarks" into their media data. The situation is analogous to a homeowner who places small identification marks on his electronic gadgets so as to ensure that he can identify his property if it is stolen. An electronic watermark is a digital mark on documents or objects that can be demonstrated to establish authorship and/or ownership of documents. For success, watermarking technology must guarantee that (1) ordinary users of the document are not affected by the watermark, and (2) the watermark can be made clearly visible (or audible) by the creator when needed.

Unfortunately, the same technical features that make an electronic watermark useful to companies interested in protecting intellectual property and proprietary information also make it useful to criminal organizations. For our next example, consider a criminal who puts up a Web site containing an innocuous picture (e.g., the Mona Lisa). However, the picture may contain a "mark" hidden in the picture using watermarking technology. This mark may then provide a channel for communication between the criminal and his disreputable associates, and furthermore, this communication channel may prove unbreakable.

As the study of sociological issues involved in the use of media data is beyond the scope of this book, we will restrict ourselves to a brief technical sketch of techniques used to hide information within image data. The same principles apply to hiding data within audio and document data.

An image is nothing more than a two-dimensional array of pixels, each having various properties. In general, if we consider an $(m \times n)$ pixel array, and each array element has a vector of associated properties (e.g., RGB values, texture, etc.) and this vector can assume a total of k possible values, then we have a total of $(m \times n \times k)$ images. Possible values for m and n are $m = n = 1,024$. In the case of k, take 8 values for each of R, G, and B, and another 8 for texture; that is, $k = 8^4 = 4,096$.

Suppose we wanted to superimpose a hidden image H on top of a regular image I. We could accomplish this through a superimposition function s that takes H and I as input, and returns a new image $s(H, I) = I'$ as output. Clearly, s must be invertible, in the sense that given I' and I, we should be able to retrieve the hidden image H. It is easy to verify that there is a total of $factorial(mnk)$ such functions. This is a truly large number, and hence easy techniques for both image hiding and public key–based image decoding (to extract hidden images) are needed.

The field of information hiding is called *steganography* [113, 138, 8]. The following sites contain exhaustive bibliographies on this topic and also provide pointers to other locations:

- *http://patriot.net/johnson/html/neil/sec/sbib00.htm*

- *http://www-nt.e-technik.uni-erlangen.de/hartung/watermarkinglinks.html*

- *http://cosimo.die.unifi.it/piva/Watermar/watermar.html*

15.4   Other Directions

In this section, we briefly outline some other directions in multimedia database systems that seem to hold promise.

15.4.1 Dynamic Queries

Shneiderman has proposed a paradigm called *dynamic queries* [204, 187, 120]. Informally speaking, dynamic queries are a visual interface to multidimensional data that provides continuous feedback to the user posing a query. The reason that this is useful is that users usually do not precisely express what they want when they first specify a query. There is evidence to believe that dynamic query interfaces are less error prone, faster, and easier to use than other interfaces. The dynamic query interface paradigm has been used to build elegant applications for real estate finding. It includes some incremental query algorithms that update the answer to a query when the user changes it.

15.4.2 Maintenance of Multimedia Views

A view over a database is a query expressed in the query language associated with the database. A view over a multimedia database therefore is a query expressed using any of the multimedia query languages described in this book. Unlike a query though, a view definition is persistent—the query is stored after the user is done with it. If V is a view, then $Mat(V)$, called the *materialization of V*, is the answer to the query V. Materialized view maintenance is the problem of incrementally updating the answer to view V; that is, updating $Mat(V)$ when the data upon which V is defined changes. While there is a vast literature on the maintenance of materialized views (Gupta and Mumick's [83] forthcoming book contains the classic works in the area) for a variety of databases, the only work that explicitly includes multimedia data that we are aware of is Lu et al. [132]. Maintaining materialized multimedia views is currently an important open problem.

15.4.3 Optimizing Multimedia Queries

In preceding chapters, we have defined what a multimedia database query is. However, there has been almost no research done to date on the problem of optimizing queries to multimedia databases. For instance, consider a multimedia query of the form "Find all pictures of John Smith and the spouse of someone whose taxes have been reported in the *Wall Street Journal*." This query involves a join operation across three data sources:

- An *image* database containing photographs

- A *relational* database containing a relation called spouse

- A *text* database that indexes the content of the *Wall Street Journal*

There are numerous ways to execute this query; yet, to date, there are few cost models to evaluate query plans against which such queries can be executed. A fruitful open research area is to develop such cost models, and to develop techniques for query planning based on them.

A start has been made on a specific aspect of querying multimedia databases by Chaudhuri and Gravano [44]. Adali et al. [7] provide a very general framework for optimizing queries over heterogeneous data sources that could include multimedia data, and they report on experiments involving video data.

A   Term Projects

Each of the term projects described in this appendix should be assigned at the beginning of the semester. Each project has associated interim deadlines (e.g., week 5 indicates that a given component must be handed in at the beginning of the fifth week of the semester). In addition, each project may be implemented under a variety of platforms and/or programming languages. Thus, in our description, each project has two components—a project description and an implementation hints section, which discusses how to implement each part of the project on a different platform.

The implementation hints in this appendix have been written by Robert Ross, whose assistance is gratefully acknowledged. They assume that you are familiar with C (or C++) and its constructs, like structures (or classes), but that you are not familiar with the X windows toolkit named Tcl/Tk. Thus, these hints will cover some basics about Tk needed to complete the exercises.

A.1   Individual Project: Image Databases

You are required to write, in a standard programming language such as C, C++, or Java, a complete image database system that allows users to insert/delete image objects, update image objects, and query the image database. You may assume, for the sake of simplicity, that images are matched in entirety (i.e., objects are not identified in images). The project consists of the following tasks:

1. *Week 2:* Read Chapter 5.

2. *Week 6:* Write a function called dct_ize that takes the following as input: an image I (of type file), two integers xsize and ysize that specify the size of the image, and two other integers out_xsize and out_ysize spec-

ifying an output size. The program must create, using the discrete cosine transform, a new image, called *I.out*, of size out_xsize × out_ysize.

For instance, the call *dct_ize(file1, 25, 26, 16, 16)* converts the (256 × 256) image file1 and produces an (8 × 8) image, called file1.out, as output.

3. *Week 7:* Obtain a set of 100 or more images from the World Wide Web, and create a directory called raw_images containing the images. Run your algorithm dct_ize on each image in the raw_images directory, placing the resulting files in a directory called dct_Images.

4. *Week 10:* Write a function called CreateIndex that creates an index from this set of 100 DCT-compressed images. Your CreateIndex should closely mimic the IndexCreation algorithm in Section 5.4.1.

5. *Week 13:* Write an algorithm called GetBestMatch that takes an image (not necessarily one in your set of 100 images above) and a positive integer $n \geq 1$ as input and that searches your DCT-compressed archive to find the best n matches. This algorithm should use an algorithm that generalizes the FindMostSimilarObject algorithm described in Section 5.4.1.

Implementation Hints

The dct_size() function needs to read in a GIF image. This can be accomplished by using some predefined Tk functions. A detailed description of these support routines can be found in the FindPhoto man page. Below is a sample program that reads the red attribute of pixel (0, 0), the green attribute of pixel (0, 1), and the blue attribute of pixel (1, 1). It also shows how to transfer values between Tk and C by manipulating a dummy variable z.

```c
// 'sample1.c'
#include <stdio.h>
#include <stdlib.h>
#include <tcl.h>
#include <tk.h>

#define BUF_LEN 80
typedef char *STR;
STR FileName;

void retErr(STR errMsg) {
    printf("%s : %s.\a\n", "Error", errMsg);
    exit(1);
} // retErr()
```

```
int readGif(ClientData clientData, Tcl_Interp *interp, int argc, STR *argv) {
    Tk_PhotoHandle       ph = Tk_FindPhoto(argv[1]);   // Photo handle
    int                  w, h, xSize, ySize;           // Block attribs
    int                  *rgbOffset;                   // Block attrib ptr
    int                  r, g, b;                      // Output values
    Tk_PhotoImageBlock   block;                        // Block for ph
    unsigned char        *p;                           // Traverses block

    if (ph == NULL) retErr("GIF file not found");
    Tk_PhotoGetImage(ph, &block);
    w = block.width; h = block.height; p = block.pixelPtr;
    xSize = block.pixelSize; ySize = block.pitch; rgbOffset = block.offset;
    // X (Y) coordinates should go from 0 to w-1 (h-1)
    r = p[0 * ySize + 0 * xSize + rgbOffset[0]];
    g = p[0 * ySize + 1 * xSize + rgbOffset[1]];
    b = p[1 * ySize + 0 * xSize + rgbOffset[2]];
    printf("Red %d, Green %d, Blue %d\n", r, g, b);
    printf("z1 %s\n", Tcl_GetVar(interp, "z", 0));
    Tcl_SetVar(interp, "z", "z-value-2", 0);
    printf("z2 %s\n", Tcl_GetVar(interp, "z", 0));
    return TCL_OK;
} // readGif()

int Tcl_AppInit(Tcl_Interp *interp) {
    char s[BUF_LEN];  // String buffer

    if (Tcl_Init(interp) == TCL_ERROR || Tk_Init(interp) == TCL_ERROR)
        retErr(interp->result);
    Tcl_CreateCommand(interp, "callReadGif", readGif, NULL, NULL);
    // Tcl_Eval evaluates a Tk command
    Tcl_Eval(interp, "wm geometry . 0x0+0+0");

    Tcl_Eval(interp, "set z \"z-value-1\"");
    // We must first create a Tk photo widget for our picture
    sprintf(s, "image create photo m -file %s", FileName);
    Tcl_Eval(interp, s);
    // To call function f(a, b, c) in Tk, use "f a b c"
    Tcl_Eval(interp, "callReadGif m");
    // To leave the Tk window open, call Tk_MainLoop();
    exit(0);
} // Tcl_AppInit()

int main(int argc, STR *argv) {
    if (argc != 2) retErr("Use sample1 <picture.gif>");
```

```
    FileName = argv[1];
    Tk_Main(argc, argv, Tcl_AppInit);
} // main()
```

To compile sample1.c, try the following command:

g++272 -Wall -o sample1 sample1.c -I/usr/imports/include
-L/usr/imports/lib/X11 -ltk41 -ltcl75 -lX11 -lm

Note that the compilation command is system dependent. If there are errors, try replacing g++272 with g++, or try replacing all instances of /usr/imports with /usr/local.

A.2   Individual Project: Video Databases

This project requires that you implement a video database using the concept of a frame segment tree. Your implementation must consist of several modules, some of which are listed below.

1. *Week 2:* Read Chapter 7 on video databases.

2. *Week 6:* Develop a function called CreateIndex that takes a movie name, a solid set of frame sequences from that movie, and a pointer to the root of a frame segment tree as input, and that inserts these frame sequences into a frame segment tree. The algorithm must also concurrently update OBJECTARRAY and ACTIVITYARRAY.

3. *Week 7:* Write and implement a function called FindObjects that takes the name of a movie, a sequence $[s_1, s_2]$ of frames, and either the word exists or forall as input. Your algorithm should return as output the set of all objects that appear in every frame in the interval $[s_1, s_2]$ (when the third argument is forall) and the set of all objects that appear in some frame in the interval $[s_1, s_2]$ (when the third argument is exists).

4. *Week 10:* For this week, you must do three things:
   - Write and implement a function called FindActivities that takes the name of a movie, a sequence $[s_1, s_2]$ of frames, and either the word exists or forall as input. Your algorithm should return as output the set of all activities that occur in every frame in the interval $[s_1, s_2]$ (when the third argument is forall) and the set of all activities that appear in some frame in the interval $[s_1, s_2]$ (when the third argument is exists).

> ■ Expand the function FindActivities listed above to also return roles, not just activities.
> ■ Develop a graphical user interface through which the user can specify *conjunctive* queries. Your interface must contain one button for each function listed thus far in this project. When the user clicks on one of these buttons, a menu should pop up, asking him to fill in the parameters of the call. The user should be able to click on multiple buttons, or even the same button more than once (with different parameters being filled in).

5. *Week 13:* Connect up your graphical user interface to the functions to create a working video database system.

Implementation Hints

After reading Chapter 7, you should be able to finish every exercise except the GUI. A sample GUI, written entirely in Tk, is given below. It demonstrates how to create buttons, entries, windows, and so on. Notice that it gets user input (for function parameters) and puts the results into a text widget ($txt). As a bonus, the program also shows how to call arbitrary Unix commands (via the exec command). This is especially useful when you wish to call a C executable from a Tk script.

```
#!/usr/imports/bin/wish4.1
# 'sample2.tk'
# First line should contain your path to 'wish' (the Tk executable)

set WinCount 0

proc showEntry { frame entry text } {
    set f [frame $frame.$entry]
    label $f.name -text "$text : "
    entry $f.entry -width 40
    pack $f.name $f.entry -side left
    pack $f -padx 10 -pady 10
    return $f.entry
}; # showEntry

proc addToText { txt fName e1 e2 e3 } {
    set t1 [$e1 get]; set t2 [$e2 get]; set t3 [$e3 get]
    if { $t1 == "" || $t2 == "" || $t3 == "" } {
        bell; return }
    if [string length [$txt get 1.0 1.end]] {
```

```
        set s " & \n" }
      append s "$fName\($t1, $t2"
      if { $e2 != $e3 } {
          append s ", $t3" }
      $txt insert insert "$s\)"
      $txt see end
      return 1
}; # addToText

proc showF1 { txt } {
    global WinCount
    incr WinCount
    set f1 [toplevel ".f1-$WinCount" -bd 3 -relief groove]
    wm title $f1 "Function 1"
    set e1 [showEntry $f1 e1 "Param 1"]
    set e2 [showEntry $f1 e2 "Param 2"]
    set fb [frame $f1.buttons]
    set add [button $fb.add -text "Add" -width 4 \
        -command "addToText $txt f1 $e1 $e2 $e2"]
    set close [button $fb.close -text "Close" -width 4 \
        -command "destroy $f1"]
    pack $add $close -side left -padx 20
    pack $fb -pady 10
}; # showF1

proc showF2 { txt } {
    global WinCount
    incr WinCount
    set f2 [toplevel ".f2-$WinCount" -bd 3 -relief groove]
    wm title $f2 "Function 2"
    set e1 [showEntry $f2 e1 "Param 1"]
    set e2 [showEntry $f2 e2 "Param 2"]
    set e3 [showEntry $f2 e3 "Param 3"]
    set fb [frame $f2.buttons]
    set add [button $fb.add -text "Add" -width 4 \
        -command "addToText $txt f2 $e1 $e2 $e3"]
    set close [button $fb.close -text "Close" -width 4 \
        -command "destroy $f2"]
    pack $add $close -side left -padx 20
    pack $fb -pady 10
}; # showF2

proc main { } {
    wm title . "Sample Tk Application (Conjunctive Queries)"
    wm geometry . +250+250
```

```
# Put widgets into frames
set main [frame .main -bd 4 -relief groove]
set result [frame $main.result -bd 2 -relief raised]
set txt [text $result.txt -yscrollcommand "$result.sb set" \
    -width 50 -height 10]
set sb [scrollbar $result.sb -orient vert -command "$result.txt yview"]
pack $txt $sb -side left -fill y

set f1 [button $main.f1 -text "Function 1" -width 12 -
command "showF1 $txt"]
set f2 [button $main.f2 -text "Function 2" -width 12 -
command "showF2 $txt"]
    # This button prints the result of executing the UNIX "cal" program
set unix [button $main.unix -text "Unix command" -width 12 \
    -command { puts [exec cal 7 1997] } ]
set exit [button $main.exit -text "Exit" -width 12 -command "exit 0"]
pack $f1 $f2 $unix $exit -pady 10
pack $result $main -padx 10 -pady 10
}; # main


main
```

Remember to type chmod u+x sample2.tk before typing sample2.tk to run the program. Notice that Tk is interpreted, not compiled.

A.3 Individual Project: Multimedia Database with Uniform Representation

In this project, you will implement a multimedia database system using the uniform representation described in Chapter 9. This will require that you implement part of the concept of a media abstraction described there.

1. *Week 2:* Read Chapter 9.

2. *Week 6:* Write a program called CreateIndex that takes a file name F as input. Each line in file F has the scheme (File,Feature) specifying that a given feature appears in the stated file. Note that there may be several rows in the file F with the same File field. Your program must create an enhanced inverted index structure from the input file F.

3. *Week 7:* Write a function called FindFeaturesinObj that, given an index *I* of the sort created above and a feature name, finds all objects (i.e., files) in the index that contain that feature.

4. *Week 10:* You are required to perform the following three tasks:

   ▪ Write a function called `FindObjsWithFeatures(L)` that takes a linked list of feature names as input and finds an object that contains all features in `L`.

   ▪ Write a function called `Check` that takes a feature name and an object (file) as input, and returns true/false if the specified feature appears in the object.

   ▪ Develop a graphical user interface through which the user can specify conjunctive queries. Your interface must contain one button for each function listed thus far in this project. When the user clicks on one of these buttons, a menu should pop up, asking him to fill in the parameters of the call. The user should be able to click on multiple buttons, or even the same button more than once (with different parameters being filled in).

5. *Week 13:* Connect up your graphical user interface to the functions to create a working video database system.

Implementation Hints

The GUI to be created here is very similar to the one needed for Section A.2. Please refer to the hints for that section.

A.4   Group Project: Heterogeneous Multimedia Content Project

This project can be assigned to a group of three to five students. An optimal number is four. The aim of this project is to implement a heterogeneous multimedia database system that uses the hybrid multimedia architecture described in Chapter 9.

▪ Have one student implement the image database system described in Section A.1. The student does not need to implement the graphical user interface.

▪ Have one student implement the video database system described in Section A.2. The student does not need to implement the graphical user interface.

- Have one student implement the simple uniform representation database system described in Section A.3. The student does not need to implement the graphical user interface.

- Have one student implement a single graphical user interface through which all the above three programs' functions may be accessed and that may be used to create and successfully execute conjunctive queries.

Group projects are usually plagued by wayward group members who occasionally contribute to the downfall of their hard-working colleagues. The design of this project attempts to minimize this phenomenon by breaking up the project into individual pieces. An alternative way to break this project into pieces is to assign each of the projects in Sections A.1 through A.3 to the entire group. This leads to 12 programming projects (excluding the graphical interfaces) that may be split up among the students, with the integration and unified conjunctive query interface coming toward the end.

Implementation Hints

Here, we are simply combining work from the previous projects. Try to keep everything modular so errors can more readily be isolated.

A.5   Individual Project: A Disk Server Simulator

You are required to write a program that simulates the behavior of a disk server that satisfies multiple clients, each of whom has a retrieval request (i.e., who makes a request for a certain segment of blocks $[b_1, b_2]$ of a specified movie m).

1. *Week 2:* Read Chapter 10.

2. *Week 6:* Write a function called CreateSchedule that takes a client request for blocks $[b_1, b_2]$ of a specified movie m as input. The function CreateSchedule consults a table of commitments. This table has the following scheme:

    (Starttime,ClientId,Blocks,Movie,Bandwidth)

    Intuitively, if this table contains a tuple such as $(10, C_5, [20, 30], m_3, 2)$, then this means that the server has an existing commitment to provide blocks

[20, 30] of movie m_3 to client C_5 starting at time 10 at a bandwidth of 2 blocks/second. Server parameters, such as disk bandwidth (transfer rate) and buffer, may be defined using constants. Your function CreateSchedule must be able to consult this commitment table, and construct a schedule from it that services the new client as soon as possible (i.e., by minimizing the wait time for the new client).

3. *Week 7:* Modify your CreateSchedule algorithm (and call the result New-CreateSched) to handle a somewhat more sophisticated request from a client. Instead of requesting one contiguous sequence $[b_1, b_2]$ of blocks, the customer instead specifies a quadruple (*movie, startblock, len, step*) as specified in Chapter 10. This is a request from the client for a set of possibly noncontiguous blocks.

4. *Week 10:* During this week, you must do two things:

   - Implement an algorithm called HandleEvents that takes two sets of clients—clients that request a contiguous sequence of blocks as in CreateSchedule and clients that request possibly noncontiguous blocks, as in algorithm NewCreateSched above. Create and implement the algorithm HandleEvents that takes any pairs of sets of client requests of this form and creates a schedule to satisfy their requirements.
   - Create a graphical user interface through which a system manager (simulating multiple clients) may specify which videos a set of clients want to see. This graphical user interface should contain a browsable menu of options, and the user should be able to select many of these.

5. *Week 13:* Connect up the graphical user interface and the functions defined elsewhere in this project so that each client's request is displayed in a separate window.

Implementation Hints

The Tk script below should help in creating the GUI. Here, the system manager selects multiple file and client assignments (use the <Ctrl> key or drag the mouse to select more than one listbox option). Each client has his own window that shows the results of these selections. The files for the sample script are all files in the current directory; replacing this with a list of available videos should be straightforward.

```
#!/usr/imports/bin/wish4.1
# 'sample3.tk'
```

```
set NumClients 3

proc addAssigns { lb } {
    global NumClients Client
    if { [$lb curselection] == "" } {
        bell; return }
    set count 0
    for { set i 1 } { $i <= $NumClients } { incr i } {
        if !$Client($i) {
            incr count; continue }
        set txt ".top-$i.reqs.txt"
        foreach elt [$lb curselection] {
            $txt insert insert "[$lb get $elt]\n"
            $txt see end } }
    if { $count == $NumClients } bell
}; # addAssigns

proc clrAssigns { lb } {
    global NumClients Client
    $lb selection clear 0 end
    for { set i 1 } { $i <= $NumClients } { incr i } {
        set Client($i) 0 }
}; # clrAssigns

proc showClient { clientNum } {
    set f [toplevel ".top-$clientNum" -bd 3 -relief groove]
    wm title $f "Client $clientNum Requests"
    wm geometry $f +0+[expr ($clientNum - 1) * 250]
    set reqs [frame $f.reqs -bd 2 -relief raised]
    set txt [text $reqs.txt -yscrollcommand "$reqs.sb set" -width 30 -
height 10]
    set sb [scrollbar $reqs.sb -orient vert -command "$reqs.txt yview"]
    pack $txt $sb -side left -fill y
    pack $reqs -padx 5 -pady 5
}; # showClient

proc main { } {
    global NumClients Client
    wm title . "Sample Tk Application (System Manager)"
    wm geometry . +450+150
    set main [frame .main -bd 4 -relief groove]

    pack [label $main.l1 -text "Files" -height 2 -anchor s]
    set f1 [frame $main.f1 -bd 2 -relief raised]
```

```
set lb [listbox $f1.list -width 43 -selectmode extended \
        -yscrollcommand [list $f1.sb set]]
set sb [scrollbar $f1.sb -command [list $lb yview]]
# Generate the file list
foreach item [lsort [glob -nocomplain *]] {
   $lb insert end $item }
pack $lb $sb -side left -fill y
pack $f1 -padx 10 -pady 10

pack [label $main.l2 -text "Clients" -height 2 -anchor s]
set f2 [frame $main.f2 -bd 2 -relief raised -bg grey]
pack [frame $f2.topFill -height 2 -bg grey]
for { set i 1 } { $i <= $NumClients } { incr i } {
    set cb [checkbutton $f2.$i -variable Client($i) \
            -text "Send to client $i" -anchor w -padx 5 -pady 4]
    pack $cb -fill x -pady 2 -padx 4 }
pack [frame $f2.bottomFill -height 2 -bg grey]
pack $f2 -padx 10 -pady 10 -fill x

set fb [frame $main.buttons]
set add [button $fb.add -text "Add" -width 4 -command "addAssigns $lb"]
set clr [button $fb.clr -text "Clear" -width 4 -command "clrAssigns $lb"]
set exit [button $fb.exit -text "Exit" -width 4 -command "exit 0"]
pack $add $clr $exit -side left -padx 20
pack $fb -pady 20

pack $main -padx 10 -pady 10
for { set i 1 } { $i <= $NumClients } { incr i } {
    showClient $i }
}; # main

main
```

A.6   Individual Project: A CD-ROM Server for VCR Functions Simulator

In this project, you will build software that simulates the behavior of a CD-ROM based video server.

1. *Week 2:* Read Chapter 11.

2. *Week 6:* Implement an algorithm called Layout that takes a set S of real-time files and an integer N reflecting the number of sectors on a CD as

input. You may assume that the set S is represented in a file whose rows are quadruples containing the file name f and the triple (ℓ_f, b_f, p_f) as specified in Chapter 11. Your algorithm must lay out all the files on the CD-ROM (if possible) or declare that it is impossible. In the latter case, it must lay out a maximal subset $S' \subseteq S$ of files on the CD. S' is maximal iff there is no other subset S^*, such that $S' \subset S^* \subseteq S$, that can be laid out on the CD-ROM.

3. *Week 7:* Implement an algorithm called `ReadSectors` that takes a movie m and a set of blocks from that movie as input and creates a read schedule for reading these sectors. You may assume the existence of a commitment table, as in the previous individual project, that is consulted and updated/maintained by your program.

4. *Week 10:* Implement an algorithm called `ScanEDF` that takes a set of read requests, each with a deadline, as input and uses the Scan-EDF algorithm described in Chapter 11 to schedule reads from the CD-ROM.

5. *Week 13:* Create a graphical user interface through which a system manager (simulating multiple clients) may specify which blocks of which movies a set of clients wants to see. This graphical user interface should contain a browsable menu of options, and the user should be able to select many of these. Connect up the graphical user interface and the functions defined elsewhere in this project so that each client's request is displayed in a separate window.

Implementation Hints

The GUI here is similar to the one discussed in Section A.5 except the system manager must also specify movie blocks. Adding this extension should be straightforward. For instance, an easy way to do this is to add an "entry" widget and modify `addAssigns`.

A.7 Individual Project: A Tape Server for VCR Functions Simulator

This project deals with the implementation of a simple simulated system for the retrieval of data from *serpentine* tapes. Thus, in the following, you may assume that the word "tape" refers to a serpentine tape.

1. *Week 2:* Read Chapter 12.

2. *Week 6:* Using an array, implement a simulated version of a serpentine tape. The rows in the array denote tracks. The *i*th entry in a row may be viewed as the *i*th element of the track. Write an algorithm called `GetTapeData` that takes the current position of the read head, a track number, and a block number as input. Your algorithm must specify how the tape head gets repositioned over the desired location, using alternative 2, specified in Chapter 12.

3. *Week 7:* Implement a function called `GetTape` that takes the name of a tape (`tape_id`) as input and retrieves the tape from a tape library. If no tape drive is available, then your function must return an error. If a tape drive is available, but it has a tape in it, then that tape must be returned to the library. This function implements the algorithm `Tape_retrieve` of Chapter 12.

4. *Week 10:* Implement a function `ScheduleTapeRetrievals` that takes as input a *set* of requests to view a movie. Each request has a given priority. Your algorithm must attempt to schedule retrievals from the tape library so that the following quantity (called *prioritized wait time*) is minimized:

$$\sum_{i=1}^{n} wait_i \times priority_i$$

where $wait_i$ is the time taken before client i's requested tape is loaded into the drive, and $priority_i$ denotes the priority of client i.

5. *Week 13:* Implement a graphical user interface through which a system manager (simulating multiple clients) may specify which tapes a set of such clients wants to see. This graphical user interface should contain a browsable menu of options, and the user should be able to select many of these. Connect up the graphical user interface and the functions defined elsewhere in this project so that each client's request is displayed in a separate window.

Implementation Hints

The GUI here is similar to the one discussed in Section A.5 except the listbox should contain the names of tapes instead of videos.

A.8   Group Project: A Heterogeneous Storage Manager Project

The aim of this project is to implement a very simple (and naive) storage manager that, given a set of client requests, must determine whether the request is to be retrieved from disk, from CD-ROM, or from tape.

1. One student must implement the disk retrieval project described in Section A.5 (without the graphical user interface).

2. One student must implement the CD-ROM retrieval project described in Section A.6 (without the graphical user interface).

3. One student must implement the tape retrieval project described in Section A.7 (without the graphical user interface).

4. One student must implement a program that takes a set of client requests (with priorities) as input and decides which of these requests will be satisfied by retrieval from disk, which from tape, and which from CD-ROM. There exist constants specifying the total number of CD-ROM drives and tape drives available, as well as the disk bandwidth and buffer resources. This algorithm must minimize the prioritized wait time of the clients.

Implementation Hints

Here, from the GUI standpoint, we are simply combining work from the previous projects.

A.9   Individual Project: A Multimedia Presentation Engine

You are required to implement a simple multimedia presentation engine using the difference constraints paradigm described in Chapter 13.

1. *Week 2:* Read Chapter 13.

2. *Week 6:* Download from the World Wide Web an archive of at least 50 images in standard format (GIF or TIFF), 20 video clips (MPEG-1), and some ASCII text files. Create a simple graphical interface through which the multimedia presentation author can browse the above collection by type (image, video, or text), and select one or more objects to include in the presentation.

3. *Week 7:* Extend the above graphical interface so that the user can associate a set of temporal difference constraints with each object selected.

4. *Week 10:* You should do three things for this part of the project:
   - Extend the above graphical interface so that the user can specify spatial layout constraints using the spatial layout relations specified in Section 5.8.
   - Convert the above spatial relationships into sets of difference constraints.
   - Implement the Bellman-Ford algorithm to solve this system of difference constraints, thus creating a presentation schedule for the objects involved.

5. *Week 13:* Using commercially available/shareware viewers, show how you can render a multimedia presentation that obeys the user-specified spatial and temporal constraints, and implement your solution.

Implementation Hints

Modifying the GUI from Section A.5 to browse collections by type should be straightforward (as an extra hint, use `$lb delete 0 end` to remove all items from listbox `$lb`). Specifying temporal/spatial constraints can easily be accomplished by using the entry and/or text widgets demonstrated above. Those who are more ambitious may wish to create a direct manipulation interface where constraints are specified through box diagrams (for a good example, see the CHIMP program). This type of interface can be created by using the line, rectangle, and text items of Tk's canvas widget. Type `man canvas` for a full description.

There are many available viewers. Consider, for instance, the Unix domain. Here, we can use `mpeg_play` to play MPEG movies, `play` to play audio files, `xanim` to play animations (FLCs, DLs, AVIs, etc.), `xv` to display still pictures (GIFs, JPEGs, BMPs, etc.), Netscape plugins to run specified programs in Web browsers, and so on.

Bibliography

[1] S. Abiteboul, S. Cluet, and T. Milo. 1993. "Querying and Updating the File." *Proc. Intl. Conf. on Very Large Data Bases (VLDB)*, pp. 73–84.

[2] S. Abiteboul, R. Hull, and V. Vianu. 1995. *Foundations of Databases*. Reading, MA: Addison-Wesley.

[3] S. Abiteboul and P. Kanellakis. 1992. "Object-Identity as a Query Language Primitive." In F. Bancilhon, C. Delobel, and P. Kanellakis, *Building an Object-Oriented Database System: The Story of O_2*. San Francisco: Morgan Kaufmann, pp. 98–127.

[4] S. Abiteboul and V. Vianu. 1997. "Queries and Computation on the Web." *Proc. 1997 Intl. Conf. on Database Theory*, Athens, Greece, January.

[5] A. Acharya and B. R. Badrinath. 1995. "Framework for Delivering Multicast Messages in Networks with Mobile Hosts." *ACM/Baltzer Journal of Wireless Networks*, Special Issue on Routing in Mobile Communication Networks.

[6] S. Adali, K. S. Candan, S.-S. Chen, K. Erol, and V. S. Subrahmanian. 1996. "Advanced Video Information Systems." *ACM Multimedia Systems Journal* 4, pp. 172–186.

[7] S. Adali, K. S. Candan, Y. Papakonstantinou, and V. S. Subrahmanian. 1996. "Query Caching and Optimizing in Distributed Mediator Systems." *Proc. 1996 ACM SIGMOD Conf. on Management of Data*, pp. 137–148.

[8] A. Anderson, ed. 1996. *Proc. of the First International Workshop on Information Hiding*, Lecture Notes in Computer Science, Vol. 1174.

[9] J. B. Anderson, T. S. Rappaport, and S. Yoshida. 1995. "Propagation Measurements and Models for Wireless Communications Channels." *IEEE Communication Magazine* 33(1):42–49.

[10] E. Ardizzone and M. La Cascia. 1996. "Video Indexing Using Optical Flow Field." *Proc. Intl. Conf. on Image Processing, ICIP-96,* Lausanne, Switzerland, September 16–19.

[11] E. Ardizzone, M. La Cascia, and D. Molinelli. 1996. "Motion and Color Based Video Indexing and Retrieval." *Intl. Conf. on Pattern Recognition, ICPR,* Wien, Austria, August.

[12] F. Arman, A. Hsu, and M. Chiu. 1993. "Image Processing on Compressed Data for Large Video Databases." *First ACM Intl. Conf. on Multimedia,* pp. 267–272.

[13] M. Arya, W. Cody, C. Faloutsos, J. Richardson, and A. Toga. 1995. "Design and Implementation of QBISM, a 3D Medical Image Database System." In V. S. Subrahmanian and S. Jajodia, eds., *Multimedia Database Systems: Issues and Research Directions.* New York: Springer-Verlag.

[14] S. Arya, D. M. Mount, N. S. Netanyahu, R. Silverman, and A. Y. Wu. 1994. "An optimal algorithm for approximate nearest neighbor searching," *Proc. 5th Ann. ACM-SIAM Symposium on Discrete Algorithms,* pp. 573-582.

[15] M. Atkinson, F. Bancilhon, D. DeWitt, K. Dittrich, D. Maier, and S. Zdonik. 1992. "The Object-Oriented Database System Manifesto." In F. Bancilhon, C. Delobel, and P. Kanellakis, *Building an Object-Oriented Database System: The Story of O_2.* San Francisco: Morgan Kaufmann, pp. 3–20.

[16] P. Atzeni and V. De Antonellis. 1993. *Relational Database Theory.* Redwood City, CA: Benjamin/Cummings.

[17] F. Bancilhon, C. Delobel, and P. Kanellakis. 1992. *Building an Object-Oriented Database System: The Story of O_2.* San Francisco: Morgan Kaufmann.

[18] N. Beckmann, H. P. Kriegel, R. Schneider, and B. Seeger. 1990. "The $R^\star$-tree: An Efficient and Robust Access Method for Points and Rectangles." *Proc. 1990 ACM SIGMOD Intl. Conf. on Management of Data,* Atlantic City, NJ, pp. 322-331.

[19] S. Berchtold, D. A. Keim, and H.-P. Kriegel. 1996. "The X-tree: An Index Structure for High-Dimensional Data." *Proc. 1996 Intl. Conf. on Very Large Databases,* Bombay, India, pp. 28–39.

[20] M. W. Berry, S. T. Dumais, and G. W. O'Brien. 1995. "Using Linear Algebra for Intelligent Information Retrieval." *SIAM Review* 37:573–595.

[21] S. Berson, S. Ghandeharizadeh, R. Muntz, and X. Ju. 1994. "Staggered Striping in Multimedia Information Systems." *Proc. 1994 ACM SIGMOD Conf. on Management of Data,* pp. 79–90.

[22] S. Berson, L. Golubchik, and R. Muntz. 1995. "Fault Tolerant Design of Multimedia Servers." *Proc. 1995 ACM SIGMOD Conf. on Management of Data*, San Jose, CA, pp. 364–375.

[23] E. Bertino and L. Martino. 1993. *Object Oriented Database Systems, Concepts and Architecture*. Reading, MA: Addison-Wesley.

[24] P. J. Besl and R. Jain. 1988. "Segmentation through Variable Order Surface Fitting." *IEEE Transactions on Pattern Analysis and Machine Intelligence* 10(2):167–192.

[25] T. Blum, D. Keislar, J. Wheaton, and E. Wold. 1995. "Audio Databases with Content-based Retrieval." *Proc. 1995 IJCAI Workshop on Intelligent Multimedia Information Retrieval,* Montreal, Canada.

[26] G. Boole. 1964. *The Laws of Thought*. London: Macmillan.

[27] A. Brink. 1996. *An Optimized Storage Structure for Multimedia Database Systems*. M. S. Thesis, George Mason Univ., May.

[28] A. Brink, S. Marcus, and V. S. Subrahmanian. 1995. "Heterogeneous Multimedia Reasoning." *IEEE Computer* 28(9):33–39.

[29] T. Brinkhoff, H. P. Kriegel, R. Schneider, and B. Seeger. 1994. "Multi-Step Processing of Spatial Joins." *Proc. ACM SIGMOD International Conf. on Management of Data.*

[30] E. W. Brown, J. P. Callan, and W. B. Crof. 1994. "Fast Incremental Indexing for Full-Text Information Retrieval." *Proc. 1994 Intl. Conf. on Very Large Databases,* Santiago, Chile, pp. 192–202.

[31] M. C. Buchanan and P. T. Zellweger. 1993. "Automatic Temporal Layout Mechanisms." *ACM Multimedia* 93:341–350.

[32] M. Budhikot, G. Parulkar, and J. R. Cox, Jr. 1994. "Design of a Large Scale Video Server." *Journal of Computer Networks and ISDN Systems* 27:504–517.

[33] M. M. Buddhikot, S. S. Kumar, G. M. Parulkar, and P. Venkat Rangan. 1997. "Storage Hierarchies and Video Servers." In W. Grosky, R. Jain, and R. Mehrotra, eds. *Handbook of Multimedia Information Management*. Englewood Cliffs, NJ: Prentice Hall, pp. 279–333.

[34] K. S. Candan and R. Cutler. 1995. "Multimedia Authoring Systems." In V. S. Subrahmanian and S. Jajodia, eds., *Multimedia Database Systems: Issues and Research Directions*. New York: Springer-Verlag, pp. 279–296.

[35] K. S. Candan, E. Hwang, and V. S. Subrahmanian. "An Event-Based Model for Continuous Media Data on Heterogeneous Disk Servers." *ACM Multimedia Systems Journal* (accepted).

[36] K. S. Candan, B. Prabhakaran, and V. S. Subrahmanian. 1996. "CHIMP: A Framework for Supporting Multimedia Document Authoring and Presentation." *Proc. ACM Multimedia Conference,* Boston, MA, November.

[37] K. S. Candan, B. Prabhakaran, and V. S. Subrahmanian. "Retrieval Schedules Based on Resource Availability and Flexible Presentation Specifications." *ACM Multimedia Systems Journal* (accepted).

[38] K. S. Candan and V. S. Subrahmanian. "Towards an Implemented Theory of Interactive Multimedia Presentations." Draft manuscript.

[39] K. S. Candan, V. S. Subrahmanian, and P. Venkat Rangan. 1996. "Towards a Theory of Collaborative Multimedia." *Proc. 1996 IEEE Multimedia Systems Conference,* Hiroshima, Japan, June, pp. 279–283.

[40] K. S. Candan, V. S. Subrahmanian, and P. Venkat Rangan. "Collaborative Multimedia Systems: Synthesis of Media Objects." *IEEE Trans. on Knowledge and Data Engineering* (under review).

[41] A. F. Cardenas, I. T. Ieong, R. Barket, R. K. Taira, and C. M. Breant. 1993. "The Knowledge-Based Object-Oriented PICQUERY+ Language." *IEEE Trans. on Knowledge and Data Engineering* 5(4):644–657.

[42] M. Carey, L. Haas, and M. Livny. 1993. "Tapes Hold Data Too: Challenges of Tuples on Tertiary Storage." *Proc. ACM SIGMOD Conf. on Management of Data,* Washington, DC, pp. 413–417.

[43] R. G. G. Cattell, ed. 1993. *The Object Database Standard: ODMG-93.* San Francisco: Morgan Kaufmann.

[44] S. Chaudhuri and L. Gravano. 1996. "Optimizing Queries over Multi-media Repositories." *Proc. 1996 ACM SIGMOD Conf. on Management of Data,* pp. 91–102.

[45] H. J. Chen, A. Krishnamurthy, T. D. C. Little, and D. Venkatesh. 1995. "A Scalable Video-on-Demand Service for the Provision of VCR-like Functions." *Proc. 1995 IEEE Intl. Conf. on Multimedia Computing Systems,* pp. 65–72.

[46] H. J. Chen and T. Little. 1993. "Physical Storage Organizations for Time-Dependent Multimedia Data." *Proc. of the Foundations of Data Organization and Algorithms (FODO) Conf.,* October.

[47] H. J. Chen and T. Little. 1995. "A Storage and Retrieval Technique for Scalable Delivery of MPEG Video." *Journal of Parallel and Distributed Computing* 30:180–189.

[48] M.-S. Chen, D. D. Kandlur, and P. S. Yu. 1994. "Support for Fully Interactive Playout in a Disk-Array-Based Video Server." *Proc. ACM Multimedia Conference,* pp. 391–398.

[49] T. Cormen, C. Leiserson, and R. Rivest. 1990. *Introduction to Algorithms.* Cambridge, MA: MIT Press and McGraw-Hill.

[50] A. Dan and D. Sitaram. 1996. "A Generalized Interval Caching Policy for Mixed Interactive and Long Video Workloads." *Multimedia Computing and Networking,* San Jose, CA, January.

[51] I. Daubechies. 1992. *Ten Lectures on Wavelets.* Philadelphia: SIAM.

[52] G. Davenport, T. A. Smith, and N. Pincever. 1991. "Cinematic Primitives for Multimedia." *IEEE Comp. Graphics and Applications,* July.

[53] S. Deerwester, S. T. Dumais, G. W. Furnas, T. K. Landauer, and R. Harshman. 1990. "Indexing by Latent Semantic Analysis." *Journal of the American Society for Information Science* 41:391–407.

[54] J. K. Dey-Sircar, J. D. Salehi, J. F. Kurose, and D. Towsley. 1994. "Providing VCR Capabilities in Large-scale Video Servers." *Proc. ACM Multimedia Conference,* pp. 25–32.

[55] A. L. Drapeau and R. Katz. 1993. "Striped Tape Arrays." *Proc. 12th IEEE Symp. on Mass Storage Systems,* Monterey, CA, pp. 257–265.

[56] A. L. Drapeau and R. Katz. 1993. "Striping in Large Tape Libraries." *Proc. Supercomputing 1993*, Portland, OR, pp. 378–387.

[57] D. Duchamp, S. K. Feiner, and G. Q. Maguire. 1991. "Software Technology for Wireless Mobile Computing." *IEEE Network Magazine* 5(6):12–18.

[58] S. T. Dumais. 1991. "Improving the Retrieval of Information from External Sources." *Behavior Research Methods, Instruments and Computers* 23:229–236.

[59] W. W. Erdman. 1993. "Wireless Communication: A Decade of Progress." *IEEE Communications*, pp. 48–51.

[60] C. Faloutsos. 1996. *Searching Multimedia Databases by Content*. Norwell, MA: Kluwer Academic Publishers.

[61] C. Faloutsos and H. V. Jagadish. 1992. "Hybrid Index Organizations for Text Databases." *Proc. EDBT-92*, pp. 310–327.

[62] C. Federighi and L. Rowe. 1994. "A Distributed Hierarchical Storage Manager for a Video-on-Demand System." *Proc. of the 2nd SPIE Symp. on Storage and Retrieval of Video Databases*, pp. 185–197.

[63] B. Feiter and S. Gunzel. 1994. "Automatic Indexing of a Sound Database Using Self-Organizing Neural Nets." *Computer Music Journal* 18(3):53–65.

[64] D. Ferrari. 1990. "Client Requirements for Real-Time Communication Services." *IEEE Communication Magazine* 28(11):65–72.

[65] H. T. Flint. 1967. *Wave Mechanics*. London: Methuen.

[66] C. Freedman and D. J. Dewitt. 1995. "The SPIFFI Scalable Video-on-Demand System." *Proc. 1995 ACM SIGMOD Conf. on Management of Data*, San Jose, CA, pp. 352–363.

[67] K. Fukunaga and P. Narendra. 1975. "A Branch and Bound Algorithm for Computing k-nearest Neighbors." *IEEE Transactions on Computers* 24(7):750–753.

[68] H. Gajewska. 1994. "Argo: A System for Distributed Collaboration." *ACM Multimedia 94*, pp. 433–440.

[69] D. J. Gemmell. 1993. "Multimedia Network File Servers: Multi-Channel Delay Sensitive Data Retrieval." *Proc. ACM Multimedia Conference*, pp. 243–250.

[70] D. J. Gemmell, H. Vin, D. D. Kandlur, P. V. Rangan, and L. Rowe. 1995. "Multimedia Storage Servers—A Tutorial." *IEEE Computer* 28(5):40–49.

[71] S. Gibbs. 1991. "Composite Multimedia and Active Objects." *Proc. OOPSLA '91*, pp. 97–112.

[72] S. Gibbs, C. Breiteneder, and D. Tsichritzis. 1994. "Data Modeling of Time-Based Media." *Proc. 1994 ACM SIGMOD Conf. on Management of Data*, pp. 91–102.

[73] A. Ginsberg and S. Ahuja. 1995. "Automating Envisionment of Virtual Meeting Room Histories." *ACM Multimedia 95*, pp. 65–76.

[74] G. Golub and C. Van Loan. 1989. *Matrix Computations*. Baltimore, MD: Johns Hopkins Press.

[75] L. Golubchik, R. Muntz, and R. W. Watson. 1995. "Analysis of Striping Techniques in Robotic Storage Libraries." *Proc. 1995 IEEE Conf. on Mass Storage Systems*.

[76] F. Gong. 1994. "Multipoint Audio and Video Control for Packet-Based Multimedia Conferencing." *ACM Multimedia 94*, pp. 425–432.

[77] Y. Gong, H. Zhang, H. C. Chuan, and M. Sakauchi. 1994. "An Image Database System with Content Capturing and Fast Image Indexing Abilities." *Proc. 1994 Intl. Conf. on Multimedia Computing and Systems*, pp. 121–130.

[78] W. Grosky. 1984. "Toward a Data Model for Integrated Pictorial Databases." *Comp. Vision, Graphics, and Image Proc.* 25:371–382.

[79] W. Grosky. 1994. "Multimedia Information Systems." *IEEE Multimedia* 1(1):12–24.

[80] W. Grosky, A. Jain, and R. Mehrotra, eds. 1997. *Handbook of Multimedia Information Management*. Englewood Cliffs, NJ: Prentice Hall.

[81] V. N. Gudivada and V. V. Raghavan. 1993. "Design and Evaluation of Algorithms for Image Retrieval by Spatial Similarity." *ACM Transactions on Information Systems* 13(1):115–144.

[82] V. N. Gudivada, V. V. Raghavan, and K. Vanapipat. 1995. "A Unified Approach to Data Modeling and Retrieval for a Class of Image Database Applications." In S. Jajodia and V. S. Subrahmanian, eds., *Multimedia Database Systems*. New York: Springer-Verlag.

[83] A. Gupta and I. S. Mumick, eds. *Materialized Views*. Cambridge, MA: MIT Press (to appear).

[84] A. Gupta, I. S. Mumick, and V. S. Subrahmanian. "Maintaining Views Incrementally." *Proc. 1993 ACM SIGMOD Conf. on Management of Data*, Washington, DC, pp. 157–165.

[85] A. Gupta, T. Weymouth, and R. Jain. 1991. "Semantic Queries with Pictures: The VIMSYS Model." *Proc. 1991 Intl. Conf. on Very Large Databases*, Barcelona, Spain, pp. 69–79.

[86] V. Hakkoymaz and G. Ozsoyoglu. 1997. "A Constraint-driven Approach to Automate the Organization and Playout of Presentations in Multimedia Databases." *Multimedia Tools and Applications* 4:171–197.

[87] P. R. Halmos. 1974. *Naive Set Theory*. New York: Springer-Verlag.

[88] A. Hampapur, R. Jain, and T. Weymouth. 1995. "Production Model Based Digital Video Segmentation." *Journal of Multimedia Tools and Applications* 1(1):9–46.

[89] R. M. Haralick and L. G. Shapiro. 1986. "Image Segmentation Techniques." *Computer Vision, Graphics, and Image Processing* 29:100–132.

[90] F. Hillier and G. Lieberman. 1974. *Operations Research*. Holden-Day.

[91] B. K. Hillyer and A. Silberschatz. 1996. "On the Modeling and Performance Characteristics of a Serpentine Tape Drive." *Proceedings of the 1996 ACM Sigmetrics Conference on Measurement and Modeling of Computer Systems*, Philadelphia, PA, May 23–26, pp. 170–179.

[92] B. K. Hillyer and A. Silberschatz. 1996. "Random I/O Scheduling in On-line Tertiary Storage Systems." *Proceedings of the 1996 ACM SIGMOD International Conference on Management of Data*, Montreal, Canada, June 3–6, pp. 195–204.

[93] B. K. Hillyer and A. Silberschatz. "Storage Technology: Status, Issues, and Opportunities." Draft manuscript available from *http://www.bell-labs.com/user/hillyer/papers/*.

[94] G. Hjaltason and H. Samet. 1995. "Ranking in spatial databases," In M. J. Egenhofer and J. R. Herring, eds., *Advances in Spatial Databases - 4th Symposium*, Lecture Notes in Computer Science 951. Berlin: Springer-Verlag, pp. 83-95.

[95] R. Hjelsvold and R. Midtstraum. 1994. "Modeling and Querying Video Data." *Proc. 1994 Intl. Conf. on Very Large Databases,* Santiago, Chile, pp. 686–694.

[96] S. L. Horowitz and T. Pavlidis. 1976. "Picture Segmentation by a Tree Traversal Algorithm." *Journal of the ACM* 23(2):368–388.

[97] E. Hwang, K. Kilic, and V. S. Subrahmanian. "Handling Updates and Crashes in VoD Systems." To appear in *Multimedia Tools and Applications Journal,* Kluwer, 1998.

[98] E. Hwang, B. Prabhakaran, and V. S. Subrahmanian. 1996. "Presentation Planning for Distributed Video Systems." Univ. of Maryland Technical Report CS-TR-3723, December.

[99] E. Hwang and V. S. Subrahmanian. 1996. "Querying Video Libraries." *Journal of Visual Communication and Image Representation* 7(1):44–60.

[100] M. Iino, Y. F. Day, and A. Ghafoor. 1994. "An Object-Oriented Model for Spatio-Temporal Synchronization of Multimedia Information." *Proc. 1994 Intl. Conf. on Multimedia Computing and Systems,* pp. 110–120.

[101] T. Imai, K. Yamaguchi, and T. Muranaga. 1994. "Hypermedia Conversation Recording to Preserve Informal Artifacts in Realtime." *ACM Multimedia 94,* pp. 417–424.

[102] D. Jaday, C. Srinilta, A. Choudhary, P. B. Berra. "Design and Evaluation of Data Access Strategies in a High Performance Multimedia-on-Demand Server," *Proceedings of IEEE Multimedia,* 1995.

[103] P. Kanellakis, C. Lecluse, and P. Richard. 1992. "Introduction to the Data Model." In F. Bancilhon, C. Delobel, and P. Kanellakis, *Building an Object-Oriented Database System: The Story of O_2.* San Francisco: Morgan Kaufmann, pp. 61–76.

[104] N. Karmarkar. 1988. "Methods and Apparatus for Efficient Resource Allocation." Patent Number 4744028, U.S. Patent Office.

[105] A. Katkere, S. Moezzi, D. Kuramura, P. Kelly, and R. Jain. 1996. "Towards Video-Based Immersive Environments." *ACM-Springer Multimedia Systems Journal,* Special Issue on Multimedia and Multisensory Virtual Worlds.

[106] L. G. Khachian. 1979. "A Polynomial Algorithm for Linear Programming." *Doklady Akad. Nauk USSR* 224:1093–1096. Translated in *Soviet Math Doklady* 20:191–194.

[107] S. Khoshafian and A. Baker. 1996. *Multimedia and Imaging Databases.* San Francisco: Morgan Kaufmann.

[108] M. Kifer, W. Kim, and Y. Sagiv. 1992. "Querying Object-Oriented Databases." *Proc. ACM SIGMOD Intl. Conf. on Management of Data,* pp. 393–402.

[109] M. Kifer and G. Lausen. 1989. "F-Logic: A Higher Order Language for Reasoning about Object, Inheritance and Scheme." *Proc. ACM SIGMOD Intl. Conf. on Management of Data,* pp. 134–146.

[110] M. Kifer, G. Lausen, and J. Wu. 1995. "Logical Foundations of Object-Oriented and Frame-Based Languages." *Journal of the ACM* 42:741–843.

[111] M. Y. Kim and J. Song. 1995. "Multimedia Documents with Elastic Time." *ACM Multimedia 95.*

[112] W. Kim. 1990. *Introduction to Object-Oriented Databases.* Cambridge, MA: MIT Press.

[113] E. Koch and J. Zhao. 1995. "Towards Robust and Hidden Image Copyright Labeling." *Proceedings 1995 IEEE Workshop on Nonlinear Signal and Image Processing,* Neos Marmaras, Halkidiki, Greece, June 20–22.

[114] T. G. Kolda and D. P. O'Leary. 1996. "Latent Semantic Indexing via a Semi-Discrete Matrix Decomposition." Univ. of Maryland Tech. Report Number CS-TR-3713.

[115] T. G. Kolda and D. P. O'Leary. 1996. "A Semi-Discrete Matrix Decomposition for Latent Semantic Indexing in Information Retrieval." Univ. of Maryland Tech. Report Number CS-TR-3724.

[116] D. Konopnicki and O. Shmueli. 1995. "W3QS: A Query System for the World Wide Web." *Proc. 1995 Intl. Conf. on Very Large Databases,* pp. 54–65.

[117] J. Korst and V. Pronk. 1994. "Compact Disc Standards: An Introductory Overview." *ACM Springer Multimedia Systems Journal* 2:157–171.

[118] J. Korst and V. Pronk. 1996. "Storing Continuous Media Data on a Compact Disc." *ACM Springer Multimedia Systems Journal* 4:187–196.

[119] H. Korth and A. Silberschatz. 1986. *Database System Concepts*. New York: McGraw-Hill.

[120] H. P. Kumar, C. Plaisant, and B. Shneiderman. 1995. "Browsing Hierarchical Data with Multi-Level Queries and Pruning." Univ. of Maryland Tech. Report CS-TR-772, March. To appear in *International Journal of Human-Computer Studies*.

[121] V. S. Lakshmanan, N. Leone, R. Ross, and V. S. Subrahmanian. "ProbView: A Flexible Probabilistic Database System." *ACM Transactions on Database Systems* (accepted).

[122] V. S. Lakshmanan, F. Sadri, and I. N. Subramanian. 1997. "A Declarative Language for Querying and Restructuring the Web." *Proc. 6th Intl. Workshop on Research Issues in Data Engineering*, New Orleans, February.

[123] C. Lecluse, P. Richard, and F. Velez. 1992. "O_2: An Object Oriented Data Model." In F. Bancilhon, C. Delobel, and P. Kanellakis, *Building an Object-Oriented Database System: The Story of O_2*. San Francisco: Morgan Kaufmann, pp. 77–97.

[124] D. Le Gall. 1991. "Mpeg: A Video Compression Standard for Multimedia Applications." *Communications of the ACM* 34(4):46–58.

[125] J. Z. Li, M. T. Ozsu, and D. Szafron. 1996. "Spatial Reasoning Rules in Multimedia Management Systems." Dept. of Computing Science Tech. Report TR-96-05, March.

[126] L. Li, A. Karmouch, and N. D. Georganas. 1994. "Multimedia Teleorchestra with Independent Sources: Part 1 and Part 2." *ACM/Springer-Verlag Journal of Multimedia Systems* 1(4):143–165.

[127] K.-I. Lin, H. V. Jagadish, and C. Faloutsos. 1994. "The TV-Tree: An Index Structure for High-dimensional Data." *VLDB Journal* 3:517–542.

[128] T. D. C. Little, G. Ahanger, R. J. Folz, J. F. Gibbon, F. W. Reeve, D. H. Schelleng, and D. Venkatesh. 1993. "A Digital On-Demand Video Service Supporting Content-Based Queries." *Proceedings of ACM Multimedia*, Anaheim, CA, August, pp. 427–436.

[129] T. D. C. Little and A. Ghafoor. 1990. "Synchronization and Storage Models for Multimedia Objects." *IEEE J. on Selected Areas of Communication* 8(3):413–427.

[130] T. D. C. Little and A. Ghafoor. 1991. "Multimedia Synchronization Protocols for Broadband Integrated Services." *IEEE J. on Selected Areas of Communications* 9(9):1368–1382.

[131] T. D. C. Little and A. Ghafoor. 1993. "Interval-Based Conceptual Models for Time-Dependent Multimedia Data." *Transactions on Knowledge and Data Engineering* 5(4):551–563.

[132] J. Lu, G. Moerkotte, J. Schue, and V. S. Subrahmanian. 1995. "Efficient Maintenance of Materialized Mediated Views." *Proc. 1995 ACM SIGMOD Conf. on Management of Data,* San Jose, CA, May.

[133] D. Makaroff and R. T. Ng. 1994. "Schemes for Implementing Buffer Sharing in Continuous Media Systems." *Information Systems* 19(4):33–54.

[134] N. R. Manohar and A. Prakash. "Dealing with Synchronization and Timing Variability in the Playback of Interactive Session Recordings." *ACM Multimedia* 95:45–56.

[135] S. Marcus. 1996. "Querying Multimedia Databases in SQL." In V. S. Subrahmanian and S. Jajodia, eds., *Multimedia Database Systems: Issues and Research Directions*. New York: Springer-Verlag, pp. 263–277.

[136] S. Marcus and V. S. Subrahmanian. 1996. "Foundations of Multimedia Database Systems." *Journal of the ACM* 43(3):474–523.

[137] S. Marcus and V. S. Subrahmanian. 1996. "Towards a Theory of Multimedia Database Systems." In V. S. Subrahmanian and S. Jajodia, eds., *Multimedia Database Systems: Issues and Research Directions*. New York: Springer-Verlag, pp. 1–35.

[138] K. Matsui and K. Tanaka. 1994. "Video-Steganography: How to Secretly Embed a Signature in a Picture." *Journal of the Interactive Multimedia Association Intellectual Property Project* 1(1):187–205.

[139] A. Mendelzon, G. A. Mihaila, and T. Milo. 1996. "Querying the World Wide Web." *Proc. Intl. Conf. on Parallel and Distributed Information Systems,* pp. 80–91.

[140] A. Mendelzon and T. Milo. 1997. "Formal Models of Web Queries." *Proc. 1997 ACM Symp. on Principles of Database Systems,* Tucson, AZ, pp. 134–143.

[141] G. Miller, G. Baber, and M. Gillilana. 1993. "News-on-Demand for Multi-media Networks." *Proc. ACM Multimedia Conference,* pp. 383–392.

[142] A. N. Mourad. 1996. "Issues in the Design of a Storage Server for Video-on-Demand." *ACM/Springer-Verlag Multimedia Systems* 4:70–86.

[143] K. Nahrstedt and Ralf Steinmetz. 1995. "Resource Management in Net-worked Multimedia Systems." *IEEE Computer* 28(4):52–63.

[144] V. Nalwa. 1993. *A Guided Tour of Computer Vision.* Reading, MA: Addison-Wesley.

[145] R. Ng and V. S. Subrahmanian. "Probabilistic Logic Programming." *Information and Computation* 101(2):150–201.

[146] R. T. Ng and J. Yang. "An Analysis of Buffer Sharing and Prefetch-ing Techniques for Multimedia Systems." *ACM Multimedia Journal* (accepted).

[147] W. Niblack, R. Barber, W. Equitz, M. Flickner, E. Glassman, D. Petkovic, P. Yanker, C. Faloutsos, and G. Tobin. 1993. *The QBIC Project: Querying Images by Content Using Color, Texture and Shape.* IBM Research Report, February.

[148] N. J. Nilsson. 1980. *Principles of Artificial Intelligence.* San Francisco: Morgan Kaufmann.

[149] J. Nussbaumer, B. Patel, F. Schaffa, and J. P. G. Sterbenz. 1995. "Net-working Requirements for Interactive Video on Demand." *IEEE Journal on Selected Areas in Communication* 13, January.

[150] K. C. Nwosu, B. M. Thuraisingham, and P. B. Berra. 1996. *Multimedia Database Systems: Design and Implementation Strategies.* Norwell, MA: Kluwer Academic Publishers.

[151] V. E. Ogle and M. Stonebraker. 1995. "Chabot: Retrieval from a Relational Database of Images." *IEEE Computer* 28, September.

[152] E. Oomoto and K. Tanaka. 1993. "OVID: Design and Implementation of a Video-Object Database System." *IEEE Trans. on Knowledge and Data Engineering* 5(4):629–643.

[153] B. Ozden, R. Rastogi, and A. Silberschatz. 1994. "A Low-Cost Storage Server for Movie-on-Demand Databases." *Proc. 20th Conf. on Very Large Databases,* Santiago, Chile, pp. 594–605.

[154] B. Ozden, R. Rastogi, and A. Silberschatz. 1995. "Research Issues in Multimedia Storage Servers." *CM Computing Surveys* 27(4):617–620.

[155] B. Ozden, R. Rastogi, and A. Silberschatz. 1996. "On the Design of a Low-Cost Video-on-Demand Storage System." *ACM Springer Multimedia Systems Journal*, February.

[156] M. T. Ozsu, U. Dayal, and P. Valduriez. 1994. *Distributed Object Management*. San Francisco: Morgan Kaufmann.

[157] N. Pahuja, B. N. Jain, and G. M. Shroff. 1996. "Multimedia Information Objects: A Conceptual Model for Representing Synchronization." *Proceedings of International Conference on Computer Networks, Networks '96,* Bombay, India, January.

[158] D. Patterson, G. Gibson, and R. Katz. 1988. "A Case for Redundant Arrays of Inexpensive Disks." *Proc. ACM SIGMOD Conf. on Management of Data.*

[159] M. J. Perez-Luque and T. D. C. Little. 1995. "A Temporal Reference Framework for Multimedia Synchronization." *IEEE Workshop on Multimedia Synchronization,* May.

[160] B. Prabhakaran. 1996. *Multimedia Database Management Systems*. Norwell, MA: Kluwer Academic Publishers.

[161] B. Prabhakaran and S. V. Raghavan. 1994. "Synchronization Models for Multimedia Presentation with User Participation." *ACM/Springer-Verlag Journal of Multimedia Systems* 2(2):53–62. Also in *Proceedings of the First ACM Conference on MultiMedia Systems,* Anaheim, CA, August 1993, pp. 157–166.

[162] W. H. Press, S. A. Teukolsky, W. T. Vettering, and B. R. Flannery. 1992. *Numerical Recipes in C*. New York: Cambridge University Press.

[163] N. U. Qazi, M. Woo, and A. Ghafoor. 1993. "A Synchronization and Communication Model for Distributed Multimedia Objects." *Proceedings of the First ACM Conference on MultiMedia Systems,* Anaheim, CA, August, pp. 147–155.

[164] S. V. Raghavan, B. Prabhakaran, and S. K. Tripathi. 1994. "Quality of Service Considerations for Distributed, Orchestrated Multimedia Presentation." *Proceedings of High Performance Networking 94 (HPN'94),* Paris, France, July, pp. 217–238. Also available as technical report: CS-TR-3167,

UMIACS-TR-93-113, University of Maryland, College Park, Computer Science Technical Report Series, October 1993.

[165] S. V. Raghavan, B. Prabhakaran, and S. K. Tripathi. 1996. "Handling QoS Negotiations in Orchestrated Multimedia Presentations." *Journal of High Speed Networking* 5(3):277–292.

[166] S. V. Raghavan, B. Prabhakaran, and S. K. Tripathi. 1996. "Synchronization Representation and Traffic Source Modeling in Orchestrated Presentation." *IEEE Journal on Selected Areas in Communication*, Special Issue on Multimedia Synchronization, 14(1):104–113.

[167] S. Rajan, P. V. Rangan, and H. M. Vin. 1995. "A Formal Basis for Structured Multimedia Collaborations." *IEEE Intl. Conf. on Multimedia Computing and Systems.*

[168] T. V. Raman. 1994. "Audio System for Technical Readings." Doctoral Dissertation, Cornell University.

[169] V. Ramasubramanian and K. K. Paliwal. 1991. "Fast *k*-dimensional Tree Algorithms for Nearest Neighbor Search with Application to Vector Quantization Encoding." *IEEE Trans. on Signal Processing* 40(3):518–531.

[170] E. Rosh. 1975. "Cognitive Reference Points." *Cognitive Psychology* 7:532–547.

[171] D. Rotem and J. L. Zhao. 1995. "Buffer Management for Video Database Systems." *Proc. 1995 IEEE Intl. Conf. on Data Engineering,* pp. 439–448.

[172] N. Roussopoulos, C. Faloutsos, and T. Sellis. 1988. "An Efficient Pictorial Database System for PSQL." *IEEE Transactions on Software Engineering* 14(5):639–650.

[173] N. Roussopoulos, S. Kelley, and F. Vincent. 1995. "Nearest Neighbor Queries." *Proc. ACM SIGMOD Intl. Conf. on Management of Data*, pp. 71–79.

[174] L. Rowe and B. C. Smith. 1992. "A Continuous Media Player." *Proc. 3rd Intl. Workshop on Network and Operating Systems Support for Digital Audio and Video,* pp. 237–249, November.

[175] C. Ruemmler and J. Wilke. 1994. "An Introduction to Disk Drive Modeling." *IEEE Computer* 27:17–28.

[176] R. Sacks-Davis and K. Ramamohanrao. 1987. "Multikey Access Methods Based on Super-imposed Coding Techniques." *ACM Transactions on Database Systems* 12(4):655–696.

[177] K. Salem and H. Garcia-Molina. 1986. "Disk Striping." *Proc. 1986 IEEE Conf. on Data Engineering.*

[178] G. Salton and M. McGill. 1983. *Introduction to Modern Information Retrieval.* New York: McGraw-Hill.

[179] H. Samet. 1989. *Applications of Spatial Data Structures: Computer Graphics, Image Processing, and GIS.* Reading, MA: Addison-Wesley.

[180] H. Samet. 1989. *The Design and Analysis of Spatial Data Structures.* Reading, MA: Addison-Wesley.

[181] H. Samet and A. Soffer. 1996. "MARCO: MAp Retrieval by COntent," *IEEE Transactions on Pattern Analysis and Machine Intelligence,* August, 18(8):783–798.

[182] S. Santini and R. Jain. 1996. "Similarity Matching." *IEEE Transactions on Pattern Analysis and Machine Intelligence.*

[183] T. Sellis, N. Roussopoulos, and C. Faloutsos. 1987. "The R^+-Tree: A Dynamic Index for Multi-Dimensional Objects." *Proc. 13th Intl. VLDB Conference,* pp. 507–518.

[184] M. Seltzer, P. Chen, and J. Ousterhout. 1990. "Disk Scheduling Revisited." *Proc. Winter 1990 Usenix Conf.,* Sunset Beach, CA, pp. 313–323.

[185] V. Shastri, V. Rajaraman, H. S. Jamadagni, P. Venkat Rangan, and S. Sampath Kumar. 1996. "Design Issues and Caching Strategies for CD-ROM-based Interactive Multimedia Applications." *Proceedings of IS&T/SPIE Multimedia Computing and Networking 1996,* San Jose, CA, January 29–31.

[186] B. G. Sherlock and D. M. Monro. 1995. "Algorithm 749: Fast Discrete Cosine Transform." *ACM Transactions on Mathematical Software* 21(4):372–378.

[187] B. Shneiderman. 1994. "Dynamic Queries for Visual Information Seeking." *IEEE Software* 11(6):70–77.

[188] B. Shneiderman and G. Thomas. 1980. "An Architecture for Automatic Relational Database System Conversion." *ACM Trans. on Database Systems* 7(2):235–257.

[189] B. Shneiderman and G. Thomas. 1980. "Path Expressions for Complex Queries and Automatic Database Program Conversion." *Proc. 6th Intl. Conf. on Very Large Databases,* Montreal, Canada, pp. 33–44.

[190] A. P. Sistla, C. T. Yu, and R. Haddad. 1994. "Reasoning about Spatial Relationships in Picture Retrieval Systems." *Proc. 1994 Intl. Conf. on Very Large Databases,* Santiago, Chile, August.

[191] J. Song, Y. N. Doganata, M. Y. Kim, and A. N. Tantawi. "Modeling Timed User Interactions in Multimedia Documents." *Proc. IEEE Conf. on Multimedia Computing and Systems* (to appear).

[192] R. F. Sproull. 1991. "Refinements to Nearest-Neighbor Searching in k-Dimensional Trees." *Algorithmica* 6(4):579–589.

[193] R. Srihari. 1995. "Automatic Indexing and Content Based Retrieval of Captioned Images." *IEEE Computer* 28, September.

[194] J. Stefani, L. Hazard, and F. Horn. 1992. "Computational Model for Distributed Multimedia Applications Based on a Synchronous Programming Language." *Computer Communications* 15(2):114–128.

[195] R. Steinmetz. 1990. "Synchronization Properties in Multimedia Systems." *IEEE J. on Selected Areas of Communication* 8(3):401–412.

[196] R. Steinmetz. 1995. "Multimedia File Systems: Approaches for Continuous Media Disk Scheduling." *Computer Communications* (March), pp. 133–144.

[197] R. Steinmetz and T. Meyer. 1992. "Modeling Distributed Multimedia Applications." *Proc. Intl. Workshop on Adv. Comm. and Applications for High Speed Networks*, Munich, March.

[198] G. W. Stewart. 1996. *Afternotes on Numerical Analysis*. Philadelphia: SIAM.

[199] M. Stonebraker with D. Moore. 1996. *Object-Relational DBMSs: The Next Great Wave*. San Francisco: Morgan Kaufmann.

[200] P. D. Stotts and R. Furuta. 1989. "Petri-Net-Based Hypertext: Document Structure with Browsing Semantics." *ACM Trans. on Office Information Systems* 7(1):3–29.

[201] P. D. Stotts and R. Furuta. 1990. "Temporal Hyperprogramming." *Journal of Visual Languages and Computing,* September, pp. 237–253.

[202] V. S. Subrahmanian, S. Adali, A. Brink, R. Emery, J. J. Lu, A. Rajput, T. Rogers, R. Ross, and C. Ward. 1995. "HERMES: A Heterogeneous Reasoning and Mediator System." Univ. of Maryland Tech. Report.

[203] V. S. Subrahmanian and S. Jajodia, eds. 1996. *Multimedia Database Systems: Research Issues and Directions.* New York: Springer-Verlag.

[204] E. Tanin, R. Beigel, and B. Shneiderman. 1996. "Incremental Data Structures and Algorithms for Dynamic Query Interfaces." Univ. of Maryland Tech. Report CS-TR-3730. Also in *Proc. Workshop on New Paradigms in Information Visualization and Manipulation,* November.

[205] H. Thimm and W. Klas. 1996. "δ-Sets for Optimal Reactive Adaptive Playout Management in Distributed Multimedia Database Systems." *12th International Conference on Data Engineering* (February), pp. 584–592.

[206] A. Tomasic, H. Garcia-Molina, and K. Shoens. 1994. "Incremental Updates of Inverted Lists for Text Retrieval." *Proc. 1994 ACM SIGMOD Conf. on Management of Data*, Minneapolis, pp. 289–300.

[207] T. Tonomura, A. Akutsu, Y. Taniguchi, and G. Suzuki. 1994. "Structure Video Computing." *IEEE Multimedia* 1(3):34–43.

[208] D. Tsichritzis and S. Christodoulakis. 1983. "Message Files." *ACM Trans. on Office Information Systems* 1(1):88–98.

[209] A. Tversky. 1977. "Features of Similarity." *Psychological Review* 84(4):327–352.

[210] A. Tversky and I. Gati. 1982. "Similarity, Separability and the Triangle Equality." *Psychological Review* 89:123–154.

[211] J. D. Ullman. 1989. *Principles of Database and Knowledge-Base Systems.* Washington, DC: Computer Society Press.

[212] P. Venkat Rangan and H. Vin. 1991. "Designing File Systems for Digital Audio and Video." *Proc. 13th ACM Symp. on Operation Systems Principles,* pp. 69–79.

[213] P. Venkat Rangan, H. Vin, and S. Ramanathan. 1992. "Designing an On-Demand Multimedia Service." *IEEE Communications Magazine* (July), pp. 56–64.

[214] H. M. Vin and P. Venkat Rangan. 1993. "Design of a Multi-user HDTV Storage Server." *IEEE Journal on Selected Areas in Communication,* Special Issue on High Definition Television and Digital Video Communication 11(1).

[215] H. Vin, S. S. Rao, and P. Goyal. 1995. "Optimizing the Placement of Multimedia Objects on Disk Arrays." *Proc. 1995 IEEE Intl. Conf. on Multimedia Computing Systems,* pp. 158–165.

[216] R. Weiss, A. Duda, and D. K. Gifford. 1994. "Content-Based Access to Algebraic Video." *Proc. 1994 Intl. Conf. on Multimedia Computing and Systems,* pp. 140–151.

[217] D. White and R. Jain. "Similarity Indexing: Algorithms and Performance." Draft manuscript.

[218] D. White and R. Jain. 1996. "Similarity Indexing with the SS-tree." *Proc. 1996 IEEE Intl. Conf. on Data Engineering,* New Orleans, LA.

[219] G. Wiederhold. 1992. "Mediators in the Architecture of Future Information Systems." *IEEE Computer* 25:38–49.

[220] G. Wiederhold. 1993. "Intelligent Integration of Information." *Proc. 1993 ACM SIGMOD Conf. on Management of Data,* pp. 434–437.

[221] I. H. Witten, A. Moffat, and T. C. Bell. 1994. *Managing Gigabytes: Compressing and Indexing Documents and Images.* New York: Van Nostrand Reinhold.

[222] T. M. Wittenburg and T. D. C. Little. 1994. "An Adaptive Document Management System for Shared Multimedia Data." *IEEE Intl. Conf. on Multimedia Computing and Systems,* pp. 245–254.

[223] D. Woelk and W. Kim. 1987. "Multimedia Information Management in an Object-Oriented Database System." *Proc. 13th Conf. on Very Large Databases,* pp. 319–329.

[224] E. Wold, T. Blum, D. Keislar, and J. Wheaton. 1996. "Content-based Classification, Search, and Retrieval of Audio." *IEEE Multimedia Magazine* 3(3):27–36.

[225] K. H. Wolf, K. Froitzheim, and P. Schulthess. 1995. "Multimedia Application Sharing in a Heterogeneous Environment." *ACM Multimedia 95*, pp. 57–64.

[226] L. C. Wolf, L. Delgossi, R. Steinmetz, S. Schaller, and H. Wittig. 1995. "Issues of Reserving Resources in Advance." *Fifth International Workshop on Network and Operating System Support for Digital Audio and Video*, Durham, NC, April.

[227] B. Worthington, G. Granger, and Y. Patt. 1994. "Scheduling Algorithms for Modern Disk Drives." *Proc. 1994 ACM SIGMETRICS Conference*.

[228] S. Wray, T. Glauert, and A. Hopper. 1994. "The Medusa Applications Environment." *IEEE Intl. Conf. on Multimedia Computing and Systems*, pp. 265–274.

[229] C. Yu, W. Sun, D. Bitton, Q. Yang, R. Bruno, and J. Tullis. 1989. "Efficient Placement of Audio Data on Optical Disks for Real-time Applications." *Communications of the ACM* 32(7):862–871.

[230] P. S. Yu, M. Chen, and D. Kandlur. 1993. "Grouped Sweeping Scheduling for DASD-based Multimedia Storage Management." *ACM Springer Multimedia Systems Journal* 1(1):99–109.

[231] C. Zaniolo, S. Ceri, C. Faloutsos, R. Snodgrass, V. S. Subrahmanian, and R. Zicari. 1997. *Advanced Database Systems*. San Francisco: Morgan Kaufmann.

[232] S. Zdonik and D. Maier. 1990. *Readings in Object-Oriented Database Systems*. San Francisco: Morgan Kaufmann.

[233] H. J. Zhang, A. Kankanhalli, and S. W. Smoliar. 1993. "Automatic Partitioning of Video." *ACM/Springer Multimedia Systems Journal* 1(1):10–28.

[234] L. Zhang, S. Deering, D. Estrin, S. Shenker, and D. Zappala. 1993. "RSVP: A New Resource ReSerVation Protocol." *IEEE Network* (September), pp. 8–18.

Index